Police Response to Riots

Garth den Heyer

Police Response to Riots

Case Studies from France, London, Ferguson, and Baltimore

Garth den Heyer
Arizona State University
Phoenix, AZ, USA

ISBN 978-3-030-31812-3 ISBN 978-3-030-31810-9 (eBook)
https://doi.org/10.1007/978-3-030-31810-9

This Springer imprint is published by the registered company Springer Nature Switzerland AG
The registered company address is: Gewerbestrasse 11, 6330 Cham, Switzerland

Introduction to Case Studies

This second section presents four case studies of riots: one from France, one from the United Kingdom and two from the United States of America. All four case studies are based on controversial violent public disorder events that occurred over a number of days, involved a large number of violent individuals, an extensive amount of vandalism and the looting of businesses. They were also triggered by one flashpoint event: the actions of the police.

The French and the United Kingdom case studies each include a section on the background and the context of the rioting in their respective countries, and this forms the foundation for the discussion of the riot and the police response. The background and context for the two riots in the United States of America are described subsequently to this introduction.

The case study section presents a study of the 2005 riots that took place in France, followed by an examination of the riots that took place in London in 2011. The two riots that took place in the United States of America are then presented starting with the 2014 Ferguson, Missouri, riots followed by the 2015 Baltimore riots.

The Background and Context of Rioting in the United States of America

The United States of America has suffered innumerable riots in its short history, with the first riot—known as Shays' Rebellion—involving more than 4,000 rebels in an insurrection against perceived economic and civil rights injustices, which took place in Springfield, Massachusetts, from 31 August 1786 to June 1787 (Richards, 2003). This rebellion was the first in a number of riots and violent confrontations that took place owing to injustices, slavery, civil rights, food shortages and local body corruption.

According to Waddington (2007), the United States of America has experienced two contrasting forms of riots and urban violence. The first form of riot is based on the conflict between the two main ethnic groups (African Americans and Caucasians) involving contested geographical areas (Janowitz, 1969). The second form of riot also involved the two main ethnic groups but usually involved attacks by African Americans "on white-owned properties and symbols of public authority, notably the police" (Waddington, 2007, p. 61). Waddington (2007), claimed that the occurrence of riots in the United States of America and the police response "is inseparable from wider class and ethnic conflicts" (p. 195).

The response taken by the police to the riots that occurred in the United States of America was often severe and brutal (Stark, 1972; Fernandez, 2009), but by the 1970s, following community pressure and the recommendations of the National Advisory Commission on Civil Disorders (known as the Kerner Report), the police changed their response to a more tolerant approach (Fernandez, 2009). The National Advisory Commission had been established following large, urban riots that took place in a number of cities across the country. The function of the Commission was to answer three questions: what happened, why did it happen and what can be done to prevent it from happening again (The National Advisory Commission on Civil Disorders, 1968, p. 1).

The element of ethnicity in rioting in the United States of America was clearly a factor in the riots in the 1960s and was a factor again in the riots in Miami in 1980[1], in Los Angeles in 1992[2], and more recently in Oakland, California, in 2010, Ferguson in 2014 and Baltimore in 2015.

This section presents case studies that have examined the riots that occurred in Ferguson and Baltimore. The Baltimore riots, in particular, were the worst violent protests that the United States of America had experienced in decades and, according to Minteh (2016), are the result of underlying grievances that are rooted in the decades-long, strained relationship between the police and African American communities, such as those in Ferguson and Baltimore.

More than 50 riots took place in the United States of America between 1980 and 2015. Table 1 presents 38 of these riots, which have been identified as being either ethnicity based, triggered by a police incident, involving large numbers of rioters or people arrested, or resulted in extensive damage to property. As can be seen from the table, riots have occurred in various cities across the country, but only a few cities have experienced riots more than once during this 35-year period.

[1] These riots followed the acquittal of four police officers who were involved in the arrest of an African American man after a high-speed car pursuit. The man died from injuries sustained during the arrest.

[2] These riots also followed the acquittal of police officers. The four police officers had been filmed beating an African American man following a car chase.

Table 1 Riots in the United States of America from 1980 to 2015

	Year	Location	Number of days	Number of rioters	Number arrested	Number of death/ injured	Damage cost (US dollars)	Race based	Police incident
1	1980	Miami, Florida	3	5,000	600	18/400	100 million	Yes	Yes
2	1984	Lawrence, Massachusetts	2	300	N/K	N/K	N/K	Yes	No
3	1988	Perth Amboy, New Jersey	2	200	19	0/5	N/K	Yes	Yes
4	1988	Tompkins Square, New York	1	200	13	0/44	N/K	No	Yes
5	1988	Shreveport, Louisiana	2	1,000	4	N/K	N/K	Yes	No
6	1989	Vineland, New Jersey	1	200	30	0/1	100,000	Yes	Yes
7	1990	Miami, Florida	1	200+	15	Nil	2.5 million	Yes	Yes
8	1991	Washington, DC	2	600	33+	N/K	N/K	Yes	Yes
9	1991	Brooklyn, New York	3	N/K	129	2/180	1 million	Yes	No
10	1992	Los Angeles, California	6	N/K	11,000+	55/ 2,000+	1 billion	Yes	Yes
11	1992	Manhattan, New York	4	N/K	11	3/15	N/K	Yes	Yes
12	1993	Portland, Oregon	1	N/K	31	0/0	N/K	No	No
13	1994	Lexington, Kentucky	1	500	N/K	0/1	N/K	Yes	Yes
14	1996	St. Petersburg, Florida	2	200	20+	0/11	N/K	Yes	Yes
15	1999	Seattle, Washington	2	40,000+	500+	N/K	20 million	No	No
16	1999	East Lansing, Michigan	1	5,000+	132	N/K	250,000+	No	No
17	2000	Miami, Florida	1	N/K	180	N/K	N/K	No	Yes
18	2001	Cincinnati, Ohio	5	200+	958	N/K	5.1 million	Yes	Yes
19	2002	Worcester, Massachusetts	N/K	N/K	404	N/K	N/K	Yes	No
20	2002	Minneapolis, Minnesota	1	N/K	N/K	N/K	N/K	Yes	Yes
21	2003	Benton Harbor, Michigan	2	N/K	N/K	N/K	N/K	Yes	Yes

	Year	Location	Number of days	Number of rioters	Number arrested	Number of death/ injured	Damage cost (US dollars)	Race based	Police incident
22	2003	Miami, Florida	3	N/K	250	0/100+	N/K	No	No
23	2004	Boston, Massachusetts	1	N/K	39	N/K	N/K	No	Yes
24	2005	Toledo, Ohio	1	500+	20+	0/12	N/K	Yes	No
25	2006	San Bernardino, California	1	1,500	12+	0/6	N/K	Yes	No
26	2007	Los Angeles, California	1	N/K	5	0/36	N/K	Yes	Yes
27	2009	Oakland, California	1	N/K	105	N/K	N/K	Yes	Yes
28	2009	Pittsburgh, Pennsylvania	2	4,500	190	N/K	50,000	No	No
29	2010	Harrisonburg, Virginia	1	8,000	30+	0/30+	N/K	No	Yes
30	2010	Santa Cruz, California	1	250	2	N/K	100,000	No	No
31	2010	Oakland, California	1	N/K	78	N/K	N/K	Yes	Yes
32	2010	Los Angeles, California	1	30+	0	0	N/A	Yes	Yes
33	2011	State College, Pennsylvania	1	2,000	45	N/K	190,000	No	Yes
34	2011	Brooklyn Bridge, New York	1	N/K	700	N/K	N/K	N/K	No
35	2012	Anaheim, California	2	N/K	N/K	0/6	N/K	Yes	Yes
36	2013	Brooklyn, New York	2	N/K	46	0/1	N/K	Yes	Yes
37	2014	Ferguson, Missouri	26	1,000+	321	1/10	N/K	Yes	Yes
38	2015	Baltimore, Maryland	15	N/K	486	0/2	N/K	Yes	Yes

Source: Author

References

Fernandez, L. (2009). *Policing dissent*. Piscataway, NJ. Rutgers University Press.

Janowitz, M. (1969). Patterns of collective racial violence. In H. Graham and T. Gurr (Eds.), *Violence in America: Historical and comparative perspectives* (pp. 412–444). New York: Bantam Books.

Minteh, B. (2016). *Policing and violence in the United States: A comparative analysis of protest against police violence in Ferguson, Missouri, Baltimore, Maryland, and Cleveland, Ohio (2012–2015)*. Paper presented at the Midwest Political Science Association 74th Annual Conference, 7–10 April, 2016, Palmer House Hilton: Chicago, IL.

National Advisory Commission on Civil Disorders. (1968). *Report of the National advisory commission on civil disorders*. Washington, DC: National Institute of Justice.

Richards, L. (2003). *Shays's rebellion: The American revolution's final battle*. Philadelphia, PA: The University of Pennsylvania Press.

Stark, R. (1972). *Police Riots*. Belmont, CA: Wadsworth Publishing Company.

Waddington, D. (2007). *Policing public disorder: Theory and practice*. Devon, United Kingdom: Willan Publishing.

Contents

Chapter 1
Introduction

1.1 Introduction

There has been an increase in the number, size, and frequency of violent protest activity across the USA, the UK and across most western democracies in recent years. This follows a period of relative quiet between the mid-1980s and the late 1990s. However, since the late 1990s, there has been a rise in the proclivity to demonstrate or riot. An estimated 40,000 people demonstrated their opposition to the World Trade Organization in Seattle, Washington in 1999, and more than 3000 people were arrested during the August 2011 riots in London and other parts of the UK. Causes such as animal rights and climate change have featured regularly in the international public disorder or violent protest calendar.

In addition to an increase in the inclination to protest, protesters have displayed an increase in their willingness to assault innocent bystanders and to perform deliberate violent acts of vandalism. Technology and other modes of social media have also had an impact on the intentions of demonstrators and demonstrations. In the 2011 UK riots, for example, Twitter was used in a "no-notice" protest to direct the actions of protesters to specific locations.[1] According to the Commissioner of the London Metropolitan Police, technological developments used in protests such as these, indicate that "the game has changed" (Her Majesty's Inspectorate of Constabulary, 2011b).

The social and economic changes that have occurred in western societies since the early 1990s have given rise to a multitude of political and community issues, many of which have been the catalyst for an increasing number of violent protests and riots and calls into question the current strategies and tactics used by the police to manage such events (King & Brearley, 1996). The response to violent protest and riots currently used by the police is similar across the western world and usually

[1] Protests directed at retail outlets such as Topshop during the UK Uncut protests in London. See www.ukuncut.org.uk.

G. den Heyer, *Police Response to Riots*,
https://doi.org/10.1007/978-3-030-31810-9_1

involves authorities moving quickly to control the violence and restoring order. This is a new period for the policing of violent protest and riots, as protests and riots are now often unpredictable, short, or even no-notice events and can include changing dynamics and intentional disruption to the public (Her Majesty's Inspectorate of Constabulary, 2011b). Furthermore, it appears that many protests now comprise a minority of people who demonstrate a willingness to instigate extreme acts of vandalism and test the reaction of the police.

This chapter comprises a number of sections that sets the scene in understanding what a riot is, how the police respond to violent disorder and what influences the police in their decision-making during the occurrence of a riot. This chapter also introduces the case studies documents the reasons for choosing the specific riots in the case studies.

1.2 The Policing of Public Disorder and Riots

The occurrence of violent protest and riots poses a number of challenges on an unparalleled scale, the effective response to which, often requires the deployment of a large number of officers, some of which may be deployed from other jurisdictions (Baker, Bronitt, & Stenning, 2017). As public order policing has become more complex (Her Majesty's Inspectorate of Constabulary, 2009), an effective response is needed and accordingly the police must develop appropriate deployment plans and establish a command structure to manage and control the resources deployed. In addition to planning for such events as riots, they must also be able to manage their day-to-day local policing commitments.

The response taken to violent protests and riots is one of the most difficult functions that the police undertake and is often viewed by protesters or rioters as not a response taken by the police, per se, but as a response taken by the state. The difficulty in responding to violent protests and riots originates from the need for the police to balance the security of individuals and the community with the protesters' civil rights. Some researchers claim that the form of the response taken by the police can be a measure of the relationship that the police have with the community (Baker, 2011; della Porta, 1998). The type of response implemented may bring the legitimacy and impartiality of the police to the forefront and call the effectiveness of their response into question (Jefferson, 1990; Waddington, 2007).

The policing of public disorder, a function performed universally, is not a well understood aspect of policing and is usually set apart from "normal" policing. Throughout the history of modern nation-states, the police have been tasked with managing violent protest and riots (Mbadlanyana, 2014), and this has been inextricably linked with the establishment of the London Metropolitan Police and the Office of Constable since 1829 (Critchley, 1967; Her Majesty's Inspectorate of Constabulary, 1999).

Violent public disorder challenges the impartiality and the accountability of the police. In routine encounters with members of the public, police officers face few genuine obstacles to their impartiality. However, the policing of violent disorder and riots is different from routine policing as the police are duty-bound to be partisan (Waddington, 2007). The response by the police to such events challenges the capacity and the will of the state to secure its own homeland (Dahrendorf, 1985). The policing of such events, according to Waddington (2007), places the police "in the position of defending the state that it is ultimately their duty to serve" (p. 376), but for some sections of the community, the actions that the police take during such events is the only contact they have with the police (Jaime-Jimenez & Reinares, 1998). As such, policing violent and civil disorder may conflict with the principles of Community Oriented Policing and the philosophy of being accountable to the community.

The discussion of the police approach to civil disorder has been supported by a significant body of scientific evidence and theory within the realm of social science since the late 1980s and intimates that there is a very close relationship between the dynamics of crowd violence and public order policing (della Porta & Reiter, 1998; Hall & de Lint, 2003; Jefferson, 1990; King & Waddington, 2004, 2005; Sheptycki, 2002; Waddington, 1987, 1991, 1993, 1994, 2007a; Waddington & King, 2005). The policies and practices that have been developed by the police to manage violent protests and riots have not been developed in a vacuum but are a result of historical, political, social and economic factors (de Lint & Hall, 2009). These factors, together with the experience gained from the urban violence that took place in the 1980s and early 1990s, have contributed to the strategies and tactics that make up the police response (Her Majesty's Inspectorate of Constabulary, 1999).

The strategies and tactics used by the police to respond to riots tend to concentrate on past responses to large-sized events that have the potential to become violent and disruptive rather than to all forms of protest. Being able to adapt to the type of protest or riot, or being able to respond to any violence in a protest, highlights the paradox that the police face in facilitating peaceful protest and maintaining order (Baker, 2011). Moreover, the policing of protests, whether peaceful or violent, according to della Porta and Reiter (1998), is a key factor in the professionalization of the police. The factors that comprise how the police learn from their response to a violent protest and the relationship between these factors are presented in Fig. 1.1.

Developing a response and deploying their limited resources is a primary problem for the police as their response will be based on historical events, is risk based and does not usually take into consideration that the majority of protests are peaceful and are policed by what McPhail, Schweingruber, and McCarthy (1998) described as "negotiated management." della Porta and Reiter (1998) supported this observation and claimed that the development of the police response to violent protests and riots resulted from two levels of influence. The first level of influence being:

1. The culture and the organizational structure of the police;
2. The political environment and democratic institutions;
3. Public opinion and support; and
4. Any interaction with the protesters (adapted from della Porta & Reiter, 1998; Waddington, 1998).

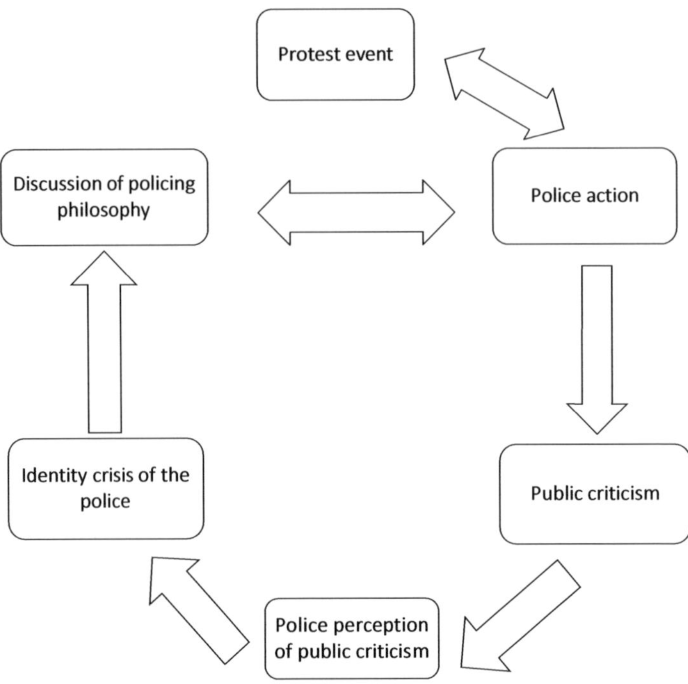

Fig. 1.1 The learning factors and their relationship to the response to riots (Adapted from Winter (1998))

These influences are filtered at a second level using police knowledge and experience (della Porta & Reiter, 1998). Jaime-Jimenez and Reinares (1998) claimed that the police perception of the environment is conditioned by the functions that they carry out and their experience. While the overarching influence is political, it is the police who decide how they will respond to a riot and what strategies and tactics they will use (Eggert, Wouters, Ketelaars, & Walgrave, 2018). The form that the response strategies and tactics take, however, is usually shaped by the characteristics of the riot (Davenport 2000; Earl, McCarthy, & Soule, 2003).

The primary objective of the police when they respond to a violent protest or riot is to control or limit the violence and then to suppress it (Earl & Soule, 2006; Waddington, 1994, 1998). Eggert et al. (2018) asserted that the response actions that the police formulate and the decisions made during a response are predictable and patterned and are based on three factors:

1. Knowledge of any individuals or organization involved in the protest or riot;
2. The political threat exerted by the occurrence of the protest or riot; and
3. The situational threat exerted by the specific protest or riot event.

The framework for understanding how the police develop their response to a violent protest or riot was formed by della Porta and Reiter (1998) and is similar to the research completed by Eggert et al. (2018), in that the police learn from their experience with specific protests or with riot groups and use this experience or knowledge as a basis for developing their response to an event that involves the same protesters or rioters (Eggert et al., 2018). The response developed and implemented by the police therefore, is not only based on a specific event or the behavior of protesters, as most of the previous studies have concluded, but is instead, based on a structured and analytical approach (Eggert et al., 2018).

1.3 A Word in Relation to Previous Research

The first major study of riots in the USA was undertaken by the United States Commission of Civil Disorders (also known as the Kerner Commission) in 1968. This was also the first research to observe that "almost invariably the incident that ignites disorder arises from police action" (quoted in Schneider, 2014, p. 9). Although there is extensive literature available that examines the environment leading up to a riot and models that analyze the occurrence of riots, there is very little literature available as to how the police respond to a riot. Furthermore, the literature that does exist in relation to the police response is limited, in that it is not current, especially since the emergence of transnational protests and the establishment of cross-border police collaboration and intelligence sharing.

With a few exceptions (see for example Brass, 1997; Horowitz, 2001; Rudé, 1981), social scientists have not researched the importance of the police response to a riot nor have they examined the reaction of the police to an initial threat of a riot. There have however, been a few researchers who have attempted to quantitatively model the police response to the occurrence of a riot (see for example DiPasquale & Glaeser, 1998). As Sheptycki (2005) asserted, much work remains to be undertaken in relation to the study of the policing of violent protests and riots. Furthermore, any research that has been undertaken has not been complete and nor has it been effectively conducted (Earl et al., 2003).

One of the principal weaknesses in existing research that concentrates on violent protests and riots is that the research examines the reasons why a riot occurs or examines the factors that cause peaceful demonstrations or protesting crowds to become violent. Furthermore, there has been very little research that has examined the occurrence of riots, although there has been some research undertaken in the UK following the 2011 London riots. Nor is there any research available that has specifically examined how the police have responded to the occurrence of a violent protest or why they responded in a specific way. There is also a lack of international comparative research available that analyzes the response actions taken by the police to violent protest and riots.

A second weakness of the available research that examines the policing of protests is that the researchers draw extensively and sometimes exclusively, on well-publicized historical protest events, where it was alleged that the police had used excessive force or that the tactics they had used to respond to the event failed to bring the crowd under control (Earl et al., 2003). Moreover, a number of researchers have argued that the failure of the police to manage or control a violent protest or riot is fairly typical (Ericson & Doyle, 1999; Hodgson, 2001; Jefferson, 1990;

Waddington, 1998), and they argue that the police are not capable of responding appropriately to violent protests or riots. As a result, using extant research, three primary weaknesses in the study of the policing of protests can be identified. The first weakness that researchers have focused mainly on is examples of protests where the actions of the police have been identified as being repressive. However, researchers have not taken into consideration that in the majority of protests, the police have responded appropriately. Earl et al. (2003), observed that the research that examined the actions of the police was skewed and provided a limited illustration of the responses used by the police. He elaborated on his observation by claiming that previous research did not provide a balanced observation of the tactics that the police use.

The second weakness found in the existing research, owing to the narrow view adopted by researchers when examining protest policing, is that there is little research that has investigated why the police have responded aggressively to a specific protest while similar types of protests did not draw an aggressive response from the police (Earl et al., 2003). The lack of comparative research between the two forms of police response to protests that have similar characteristics leaves a gap in our understanding as to what features of a protest give rise to the different levels of response that the police take (Earl et al., 2003). The third weakness is that when researchers have presented their research on the police response to protests, very few have offered alternative explanations or reasons as to why there were differences in the police response to similar types of protests (Earl et al., 2003). These researchers have instead, only offered one or two explanations in their conclusions.

As a result of these weaknesses, an international comparative study of the policing of protests needs to be documented so that it can contribute to remedying the gap in the available literature. This is the intention of this book. Undertaking comparative research in the policing of protests would increase our understanding as to how specific police protest response strategies and tactics affect protesters and the impact that protester reaction to the police response has on the police (della Porta, 2016; Moran & Waddington, 2016). According to della Porta (2016), to understand how the response to protests by the police varies, three questions need to be answered:

1. Which are the actual styles, strategies and tactics adopted when the police respond to a violent protest or riot?
2. Are there any differences in the styles, strategies and tactics adopted nationally and internationally?
3. Have these styles, strategies and tactics evolved over time? (adapted from della Porta, 2016, p. 104).

1.4 What Constitutes a Riot?

This book is primarily about the response taken by the police to violent protests or riots rather than about the response that the police take to protests that are peaceful or those that have been negotiated. This means that the question must be asked "what is a riot"? According to Moran and Waddington (2016),

> *Riots are complex phenomena and their outbreak is inevitably symptomatic of deeper societal problems. These events may often appear to be 'issueless', or at least lacking a clearly discernible cause that would bring a welcome analytical coherence to the series of events in question* (p. 6).

Riots are also characteristically "chaotic social phenomena and each occurrence represents the violent manifestation of a unique configuration of driving forces and influencing events" (Moran & Waddington, 2016, p. 171). Each occurrence of a riot may have some common features, such as a triggering event, but by its form and composition, each is unique (Moran & Waddington, 2016). This uniqueness occurs because of the different outcomes which arise from a mixture of distinct underlying and background factors that can vary considerably from protest to protest (Moran & Waddington, 2016). The irony of a riot is that the logic of its occurrence is a contradiction as they do not occur in a vacuum but "hold considerable social, cultural, and political significance, and are, fundamentally, symptomatic of a broader societal malaise" (Moran & Waddington, 2016).

1.4.1 The Influence of the "Battle in Seattle"

In the USA, between 1991 and 2001, rioting occurred in a number of large cities, including Washington, DC, Los Angeles, New York and Cincinnati (Waddington, 2007b). The riots resulted primarily from the deteriorating relationship between the police and minority ethnic communities (Gilje, 1996). The USA has also experienced a number of violent anti-globalization and anti-war protests (Waddington, 2007b), the most infamous being the 1999 protests against the World Trade Organisation (WTO) Ministerial Conference in Seattle. The Seattle WTO protests became known as "the Battle in Seattle" and set a benchmark for subsequent WTO protests in other major cities around the world (Noakes and Gillham (2006) for both protesters and the police.

The protest and the protesters' actions, which included the use of disruptive tactics, such as, not cooperating with the police, vandalism and the blocking of intersections were proclaimed as a success by many activists (Wood, 2014). The protests were code-named "N30" and were similar to other demonstrations but included anarchist individuals and groups (such as the Black Bloc) and comprised between 35,000 and 40,000 protesters (Burton, 2014). In response to the tactics and the violence used by the protesters, the police adopted a more high-end strategy that included the use of pepper spray, tear gas, and stun grenades (Reynolds, 1999), to reestablish order and reduce the disruption caused by the protesters.

The form of tactics and the violence used by the protesters during the WTO demonstrations and the responding actions taken by the police have been identified as transformative or a watershed event in the policing of protests and have been used by the police to justify the use of more high-end strategies at similar types of international events or protests (Wood, 2014). According to Wood (2014), the strategies and tactics adopted by the police have led to the militarization of the policing of protests in Europe, Australia, New Zealand, and the USA. The adoption of high-end protest response strategies and tactics that are based primarily on paramilitary policing and the use of riot technology has been described as a "new police order" by Baker (2002).

1.4.2 The Influence of Protests in the UK

Following the major industrial disputes and riots held in the UK during the 1980s, the UK did not experience any violent protests until the 2009, G20 meeting which was held in London. There had, however, been several large-sized protests that related to animal rights and climate change between the 1980s and 2009, and these did contain some form of disorder (Her Majesty's Inspectorate of Constabulary, 2011a). As a result of the violence that occurred during the G20 protests and the November 2010 student protests that were held in London, the then Metropolitan Police Commissioner Sir Paul Stephenson noted that "the game has changed" (quoted in Her Majesty's Inspectorate of Constabulary, 2011a, p. 3). According to the Her Majesty's Inspectorate of Constabulary (2011a), protests had become fast moving and unpredictable and a change had occurred in the character of protesting. The report outlined six factors that described how the character of protests had changed:

1. The numbers of protesters taking part in each protest;
2. The spread of protesting across the country;
3. Associated sporadic violence;
4. The disruption caused to the public and the economy;
5. The number of short notice or no-notice events, and
6. The swift changes in protester tactics and actions (adapted from Her Majesty's Inspectorate of Constabulary, 2011a).

Her Majesty's Inspectorate of Constabulary (2011a) also claimed that what had become evident in these recent protests was the use of social media and mobile phones to organize protesters and the willingness of the protesters to test the police. This meant that the violent protest and riot response strategies that the police adopted needed to be flexible if the dynamic tactics used by the protesters were to be countered (Her Majesty's Inspectorate of Constabulary, 2011a).

1.5 Changes in the Policing of Violent Protests and Riots

A number of studies (see for example: della Porta, 1998; della Porta & Reiter, 1998; Fillieule & Jobard, 1998; Hall & de Lint, 2003; McPhail et al., 1998; Waddington, 1994; Winter, 1998) that were completed prior to the 1999 Battle of Seattle riots claimed that the response taken by the police to violent protests and riots had changed in a number of western countries since the 1980s; from one based on the escalated use of force to one of being more tolerant of the protesters (Kienscherf, 2014; Saari, 2009). The more tolerant approach was characterized by Baker (2011) and della Porta (2016), as comprising the under-enforcement of the law, negotiation with protesters and the collection of intelligence by the police. These tactics enabled the police to contain violent protest through co-operation rather than the use of physical, confrontational tactics (Baker, 2011). della Porta and Reiter (1998) summarized the change in response as being part of the professionalization of the police.

Specialized riot response capabilities and squads were established to respond to violent protest and riots at the same time that the more tolerant approaches were being adopted by the police (Jefferson, 1990). According to Waddington (1994) and Baker (2002), the capability included paramilitary-style squads or units that were specifically trained and equipped to suppress violent protests and riots and enabled the police to remain dominant during their response.

The changes as to how the police respond to violent protests and riots has been disputed since the Battle of Seattle, with a number of researchers (della Porta, Peterson, & Reiter, 2006; Noakes & Gillham, 2006; Noakes, Klocke, & Gillham, 2005; Vitale, 2005), claiming that the police strategy of tolerance should not apply to transnational protests, such as those held against the WTO. These studies have also maintained that the return to a less tolerant form of protest response in relation to transnational protest events has influenced how the police respond to protests more generally (Saari, 2009), with some researchers, such as Kienscherf (2014) and Wood (2014), asserting that the response strategies used by the police have changed further as a result of the 9/11 terrorist attacks and the wars in Afghanistan and Iraq in the early 2000s. This argument is balanced, however, by Baker (2016), who claimed that the increasing sophistication of the response by the police to violent protests and riots is because police leaders are now better-educated, have been trained in management and have an understanding of the media's role in society.

1.6 The Case Studies

In 1964, New York City experienced the first in a number of violent, race-related riots. The riots began in Harlem, New York following the shooting of a 15-year-old African American youth by a white police officer (Shapiro & Sullivan, 1964). An estimated 8000 Harlem residents were involved in the rioting, which spread to nearby neighborhoods and continued for six days. As a result, one resident died, over 100 people were injured and more than 450 arrests were made (Shapiro & Sullivan, 1964). Thirty-nine years later, in Paris, France, a riot occurred following the deaths of two teenagers of North African and Malian descent. They were attempting to escape a police identity-check. The riot quickly spread to 300 cities and towns across the country (Katz, 2008). Seven years after this riot, extensive rioting occurred in London that spread to a number of boroughs and then on to several major towns and cities in England. More than 3000 people were arrested.

These three events, that occurred over a 46-year period, in three different countries on opposite sides of the Atlantic displayed several similarities. The first similarity is that each of the riots occurred because of the actions taken by the police and the second is that the riots began where the incident occurred, spreading rapidly to neighboring communities and then on to towns and cities across the nations. The similarities between these riots raises three questions:

1. Why did the police in different countries interact with members of the minority community in similar ways?
2. Why did the interactions with the minority community lead to riots in one location and then spread to numerous cities and towns across the respective countries?
3. Why didn't racially based riots occur on such a large-scale in these countries in the late 1960s to the early 2000s?

Riots are not a new occurrence in the USA, the UK, or France and to assist in the understanding of the relationship of the police with the riots and to answer the three questions above, four case studies, based on the occurrence of riots, have been developed and have been presented and analyzed in this book. The riots described in the case studies and the reasons why they were included in the analysis have been presented in Table 1.1.

The methodological approach taken in the case studies is comparative and includes an interactive framework that incorporates a number of key variables. These variables examine how each riot began, how they developed, the response strategies and tactics used by the police, and how the riots eventually ended. The use of these variables ensures that the analysis concentrates primarily on the actions of the police, as they are the centerpiece of the case studies, not the reason why the riots occurred, although this has been discussed in the case studies.

Table 1.1 Reasons for including specific riot as a case study

	Riot event	Reasons for inclusion
1	France 2005	Size of riot Geographical spread Number arrested Length of riots
2	London 2011	Speed of geographical spread Participants travelled to attend Level of damage Number arrested Use of social media
3	Ferguson 2014	Use of social media Alleged militarization of police response Development of social movement
4	Baltimore 2015	Deficiency in police response Gaps in the occurrence of riots

1.6.1 A Note on the Development of the Case Studies

There is very little existing literature, especially peer-reviewed literature available that examines operational areas of policing. This has probably occurred because the topic has not struck the interest of researchers or the police have not encouraged or enabled independent research into the matter to take place. Although there are a few articles written in relation to the 2011 riots in the UK, there is nothing available that has examined the police response to these riots. Because the availability of academic literature is limited, the only information available to develop the case studies was from newspaper articles, government or independent research institution reports and non-government organization briefings and reports. There were very few peer-reviewed articles available. However, where these were available, extracts of the articles have been included in the development and analysis of the case studies.

While it may be argued that such articles and reports are biased, each article and report that was referenced was analyzed, cross-referenced and collaborated. Furthermore, the articles and reports underwent a thematic analysis (Braun & Clarke, 2006) to analyze the qualitative data before it was included in the case studies. This analysis followed six-phase process:

1. Familiarization with the data;
2. Coding;
3. Searching for themes;
4. Reviewing themes;
5. Defining and naming themes; and
6. Documenting the themes.

1.7 Conclusion

Historically, relevant events become turning points. Turning points are based on learning from past mistakes and are those which led to the development of new understanding and strategies. If the reasons for the response adopted by the police to a specific violent protest or riot are to be understood, the perception that the police hold of the event as it unfolds needs to be studied. della Porta (2016) recommended that extant police knowledge be examined so that the responses adopted by the police can be understood. As with other areas of policing, the policing of riots is principally influenced by the culture of the organization and the external environment.

Although individual occurrences of violent protest and riots have been studied in some detail, few have been studied in an international comparative context (Body-Gendrot, Hornqvist, & Newburn, 2016), and none have examined specifically the response taken by the police. It is vital that international comparative studies be taken into account as they have the capability to provide new or alternative perspectives (Tonry, 2015).

The approach adopted in this book has been to structure the considerations into three distinct but overlapping strands. Firstly, an analysis has been undertaken to identify what constitutes a riot, why they occur and the involvement of the police. Secondly, a "snapshot" of the current response taken by the police to a riot has been documented. Four case studies have then been developed and are discussed. Finally, in the concluding section, the main themes of the analysis are drawn together and discussed with the aim of improving how the police respond to the occurrence of violent protest and riots.

References

Baker, D. (2002). The changing Australian prototype of policing, pickets, and public order. *International Journal of Comparative and Applied Criminal Justice, 26*(1), 1–28.

Baker, D. (2011). A case study of policing responses to camps for climate action: Variations, perplexities, and challenges for policing. *International Journal of Comparative and Applied Criminal Justice, 35*(2), 141–165.

Baker, D. (2016). Paradoxes of policing and protest. *Journal of Policing, Intelligence and Counter Terrorism, 3*(2), 8–22.

Baker, D., Bronitt, S., & Stenning, P. (2017). Policing protest, security and freedom: The 2014 G20 experience. *Police Practice and Research: An International Journal*. https://doi.org/10.1080/15614263.2017.1280674

Body-Gendrot, S., Hornqvist, M., & Newburn, T. (2016). Introduction to special issue. *European Journal of Criminology, 13*(5), 537–539.

Brass, P. (1997). *Theft of an idol: Text and context in the representation of collective violence in India*. Princeton, NJ: Princeton University Press.

Braun, V., & Clarke, V. (2006). Using thematic analysis in psychology. *Qualitative Research in Psychology, 3*(2), 77–101.

Burton, L. (2014, November 29). *WTO riots in Seattle: 15 years ago*. Seattle PI. Retrieved from https://www.seattlepi.com/local/article/WTO-riots-in-Seattle-15-years-ago-5915088.php.

Critchley, T. (1967). *A history of police in England and Wales 900–1966*. London: Constable and Company Limited.

Dahrendorf, R. (1985). *Law and order, The Hamlyn Lectures 37th Series*. London: Stevens & Sons.

Davenport, C. (2000). Introduction. In C. Davenport (Ed.), *Paths to state repression* (pp. 1–24). Lanham, Maryland: Rowman and Littlefield.

de Lint, W., & Hall, A. (2009). *Intelligent control: Developments in public order policing in Canada*. Toronto, ON: University of Toronto Press.

della Porta, D. (1998). Policing knowledge and protest policing: Some reflections on the Italian case. In D. della Porta & H. Reiter (Eds.), *Policing protest: The control of mass demonstrations in Western democracies* (pp. 228–252). Minneapolis, USA: University of Minnesota Press.

della Porta, D. (2016). The policing of protest repression, bargaining, and the fate of social movements. *African Studies, 56*(1), 97–127.

della Porta, D., & Reiter, H. (1998). Introduction: The policing of protests in western democracies. In D. della Porta & H. Reiter (Eds.), *Policing protest: The control of mass demonstrations in Western democracies* (pp. 1–34). Minneapolis, USA: University of Minnesota Press.

della Porta, D., Peterson, A., & Reiter, H. (2006). Policing transnational protest: An introduction. In D. della Porta, A. Peterson, & H. Reiter (Eds.), *The policing of transnational protest* (pp. 1–13). Aldershot, UK: Ashgate Publishing Limited.

DiPasquale, D., & Glaeser, E. (1998). The los Angeles riot and the economics of urban unrest. *Journal of Urban Economics, 43*(1), 52–78.

Earl, J., & Soule, S. (2006). Seeing blue: A police centred explanation of protest policing. *Mobilization, 11*(2), 145–164.

Earl, J., McCarthy, J., & Soule, S. (2003). Protest under fire? Explaining the policing of protest. *American Sociological Review, 68*(4), 581–606.

Eggert, N., Wouters, R., Ketelaars, P., & Walgrave, S. (2018). Preparing for action: police deployment decisions for demonstrations. *Police and Society: An International Journal of Research and Policy, 28*(2), 137–148.

Ericson, R., & Doyle, A. (1999). Globalization and the policing of protest: The case of APEC 1997. *British Journal of Sociology, 50*(4), 589–608.

Fillieule, O., & Jobard, F. (1998). The policing of protest in France: Toward a model of protest policing. In D. della Porta & H. Reiter (Eds.), *Policing protest: The control of mass demonstrations in Western Democracies* (pp. 70–90). Minneapolis, USA: University of Minnesota Press.

Gilje, P. (1996). *Rioting in America*. Bloomingdale and Indianapolis: Indiana University Press.

Hall, A., & de Lint, W. (2003). Policing Labour in Canada. *Policing and Society, 13*(3), 219–234.

Her Majesty's Inspectorate of Constabulary. (1999). *Keeping the peace policing disorder*. London: Her Majesty's Inspectorate of Constabulary.

Her Majesty's Chief Inspectorate of Constabulary. (2009). *Adapting to protest: Nurturing the British model of policing*. London: Her Majesty's Chief Inspectorate of Constabulary.

Her Majesty's Inspectorate of Constabulary. (2011a). *Policing public order—An overview and review of progress against the recommendations of Adapting to Protest and Nurturing the British Model of Policing*. London: Her Majesty's Stationery Office.

Her Majesty's Inspectorate of Constabulary. (2011b). *The rules of engagement: A review of the August 2011 disorders*. London: Her Majesty's Chief Inspectorate of Constabulary.

Hodgson, J. (2001). Police violence in Canada and the USA: Analysis and management. *Policing: An International Journal, 24*(4), 520–551.

Horowitz, D. (2001). *The deadly ethnic riot*. Berkeley, California: University of California Press.

Jaime-Jimenez, O., & Reinares, F. (1998). The policing of social protest in Spain: From dictatorship to democracy. In D. della Porta & H. Reiter (Eds.), *Policing protest: The control of mass demonstrations in Western democracies* (pp. 166–187). Minneapolis: University of Minnesota Press.

Jefferson, T. (1990). *The case against paramilitary policing*. Milton Keynes: Open University Press.

Katz, M. (2008). Why don't American cities burn very often? *Journal of Urban History, 34*(2), 185–208.

Kienscherf, M. (2014). Beyond militarization and repression: Liberal social control as pacification. *Critical Sociology, 42*(7–8), 1–16.

King, M., & Brearley, N. (1996). *Public order policing: Contemporary perspectives on strategy and tactics*. Leicester: Perpetuity Press.

King, M., & Waddington, D. (2004). Coping with disorder? The Changing relationship between police public order strategy and practice–a critical analysis of the Burnley Riot. *Policing & Society: An International Journal of Policy and Research, 14*(2), 118–137.

King, M., & Waddington, D. (2005). Flashpoints revisited: A critical application to the policing of anti-globalization protest. *Policing and Society, 15*(3), 255–282.

Mbadlanyana, M. (2014). *Analysis of the public order policing units*. Research Unit, Parliament of the Republic of South Africa.

McPhail, C., Schweingruber, D., & McCarthy, J. (1998). Policing protest in the United States: 1960–1995. In D. della Porta & H. Reiter (Eds.), *Policing protest: The control of mass demonstrations in Western democracies* (pp. 49–69). Minneapolis: University of Minnesota Press.

Moran, M., & Waddington, D. (2016). *Riots: An International comparison*. London: Macmillan Publishers Ltd.

Noakes, J., & Gillham, P. (2006). Aspects of the 'new penology' in the police response to major political protests in the United States, 1999–2000. In D. della Porta, A. Peterson, & H. Reiter (Eds.), *The policing of transnational protest* (pp. 97–115). Ashgate: Burlington, Vermont.

Noakes, J., Klocke, B., & Gillham, P. (2005). Whose streets? Police and protester struggles over space in Washington, DC, 29–30 September 2001. *Policing and Society: An International Journal of Policy and Research, 15*(3), 235–254.

Reynolds, P. (1999). *Eyewitness: The battle of Seattle*. BBC News, 2 December. Retrieved from: http://news.bbc.co.uk/2/hi/547581.stm.

Rudé, G. (1981). *The crowd in history: A study of popular disturbances in France and England, 1730–1848*. London: Serif.

Saari, K. (2009). Crowd situations and their policing from the perspective of Finnish police officers - a case study of Finnish police knowledge. *Journal of Scandinavian Studies in Criminology and Crime Prevention, 10*(2), 102–119.

Schneider, C. (2014). *Police power and race riots: Urban unrest in Paris and New York*. Philadelphia: University of Pennsylvania Press.

Shapiro, F., & Sullivan, J. (1964). *Race riots: New York, 1964*. New York: Crowell.

Sheptycki, J. (2002). Accountability across the policing field: Towards a general cartography of accountability for post-modern policing. *Policing and Society: An International Journal of Policy and Research, 12*(4), 323–338.

Sheptycki, J. (2005). Policing political protest when politics go global: Comparing public order policing in Canada and Bolivia. *Policing and Society: An International Journal of Policy and Research, 15*(3), 327–352.

Tonry, M. (2015). Is cross-national and comparative research on the criminal justice system useful? *European Journal of Criminology, 12*(4), 505–516.

Vitale, A. (2005). From negotiated management to command and control: How the New York Police Department polices protests. *Policing and Society: An International Journal of Research and Policy, 15*(3), 283–304.

Waddington, D. (2007a). *Policing public disorder: Theory and practice*. Devon: Willan Publishing.

Waddington, D. (2007b). Seattle and its aftershock: Some implications for theory and practice. *Policing, 1*(4), 380–389.

Waddington, D., & King, M. (2005). The disorderly crowd: From classical psychological reductionism to socio-contextual theory—The impact on public order policing strategies. *The Howard Journal of Criminal Justice, 44*, 490–503.

Waddington, P. (1987). Towards paramilitarism: Dilemmas in policing public disorder. *British Journal of Criminology, 27*, 37–46.

Waddington, P. (1991). *The strong arm of the law: Armed and public order policing*. Oxford, United Kingom: Clarendon Press.

Waddington, P. (1993). Dying in a ditch: The use of police powers in public order. *International Journal of the Sociology of Law, 21*(4), 335–353.

Waddington, P. (1994). *Liberty and order: Public order policing in a capital city*. London: University College London Press.

Waddington, P. (1998). Controlling protest in contemporary historical and comparative perspective. In D. della Porta & H. Reiter (Eds.), *Policing protest: The control of mass demonstrations in Western democracies* (pp. 117–140). Minneapolis: University of Minnesota Press.

Waddington, P. (2007). Editorial – Policing of public order. *Policing: A Journal of Policy and Practice, 1*(4), 375–379.

Winter, M. (1998). Police philosophy and protest policing in the Federal Republic of Germany, 1960–1990. In D. della Porta & H. Reiter (Eds.), *Policing protest: The control of mass demonstrations in Western democracies* (pp. 188–212). Minneapolis: University of Minnesota Press.

Wood, L. (2014). *Crisis and control: The militarization of protest policing*. Toronto, ON: Pluto Press.

Chapter 2
What Constitutes a Riot?

2.1 Introduction

This book is a study of the responses that the police take to modern, urban riots. Some researchers and sections of the media have used terms such as ghetto riots, urban uprising or urban disorders (Schneider, 2014), to describe riots, while others use terms such as demonstrations, marches or permitted protest to describe the same form of event. This book does not examine the cause of riots, but examines the response that is taken by the police to those in crowds who engage in confrontations, throw missiles, such as stones, bottles, bricks, or petrol bombs, loot stores and burn and/or vandalize cars, public and private buildings and other symbols of the state. This is the type of rioting that has been experienced in France (Paris), the UK (London) and the USA (Ferguson and Baltimore).

Riots are difficult to study despite the frequency and the number of riots that have taken place around the world (Stott, Drury, & Reicher, 2017). The difficulty arises because of their scale, their unpredictability and because they evolve so quickly (Stott et al., 2017). It is also difficult to study the reasons why people participate in riots (Akram, 2014), as the reasons are too numerous.

Many researchers have attempted to describe riots (see for example Stott, 2009; Stott & Drury, 1999, 2000; D. Waddington, 1992, 1996, 2007a). Tilly (2003) described rioting as "broken negotiations," "scattered attack," and "opportunism" (p. 148) and stated that riots occur when "actors on at least one side respond by engaging in co-ordinated attacks on sites across the boundary while those on the other side engage in defense against those attacks" (p. 227). Schneider (2014), on the other hand, claimed that riots occur because those who are participating seek to improve their material standing or are seeking revenge.

The term "riot" has been used in this book to describe the violent criminal activity that has occurred in the various locations mentioned in the case studies, primarily for simplicity, but also for the reasons identified and discussed in Chap. 1. The term has also been used to describe the civil disorder that has been depicted in each

G. den Heyer, *Police Response to Riots*,
https://doi.org/10.1007/978-3-030-31810-9_2

of the case studies, of which, politicians and academics have labelled riots (Newburn, 2016).

This chapter comprises five sections. The first section discusses the difficulties in defining a riot. An abundance of definitions of a riot can be found in literature, which makes examining riots and the response taken by the police problematic. The second section attempts to understand why riots occur and examines critical consensus, such as whether the police cause riots and the perspective of the police as to the causes of riots. The third section considers the relationship that the police have with the community within a riot context and the fourth section discusses the factors that influence the behavior of a crowd and the relationship of the police with a crowd. The final section offers an analysis of the response tactics adopted by the police.

2.2 The Problem with the Definition of a Riot

It is difficult to define a riot because of the number of different terms that researchers use to describe riots and because of the number of different explanations there are for the violent actions that some members of the public take when they are in a crowd. It is also difficult to establish whether a specific incident of violence committed by individuals or a group in a crowd constitutes a riot. Bateman (2012), claimed that riots, in some respects, are exceptional as they comprise individuals or groups of people and may be short-lived unless organized forms of resistance step in to maintain the momentum.

Early literature that discussed rioting has drawn on social psychology and has used explanations that refer to crowd psychology (Drury & Stott, 2011; Le Bon, 1895; Reicher, 2001; Tarde, 1903), but most of the research that has been conducted about the behavior of crowds has been based on Gustave Le Bon's (1895) book "The crowd: A study of the popular mind." Le Bon described the characteristics of crowd psychology as: "impulsiveness, irritability, incapacity to reason, the absence of judgment of the critical spirit, the exaggeration of sentiments, and others …" (cited in van Ginneken, 1992, p. 130). Akram (2014) supported Le Bon's theory of crowds and suggested that a crowd does not have a unique characteristic of its own but comprises a number of different characteristics and stated that when a crowd forms, individuals take on the characteristics of the crowd. D. Waddington (2007b) advocated that an individual's conscious personality disappears when they are in a crowd and becomes replaced by the mind of the group, which is essentially evil and menacing. In the past, large crowds were viewed as being irrational and animalistic and were often associated with communist attempts to overthrow governments (Winter, 1998)

Le Bon's approach to understanding riots has been criticized by a number of researchers (Bagguley & Hussain, 2008; Keith, 1993), and was not supported in the report released by the United States National Advisory Commission on Civil Disorders (1968). This report is commonly referred to as the Kerner Commission Report. The Commission found that rioting is a complicated, social phenomenon and is not undertaken by criminals or social deviants but by participants who are well-educated and are politically active members of society (National Institute of Justice, 1968; D. Waddington, 2007b). This view was supported by later research, which was undertaken by Reicher (1984), who claimed that crowd behavior is not irrational and that individuals form crowds for specific and justified reasons.

It is generally perceived that there are two types of people who participate in modern riots. The first type are criminals or youths who engage in opportunistic crime and violence (Clarke, 2011), and the second type are individuals who come from deprived neighborhoods, have low educational achievement and are unemployed or under-employed (Akram, 2014). D. Waddington (2007a) and Kawalerowicz and Biggs (2014) both expand on this perspective and claim that civil or urban disorder results from a number of underlying, usually social, community conditions, such as deprivation, substandard housing, unemployment or underemployment, and frustration with the political system. This view adopts the assumption that individuals who experience these difficulties do not see social institutions as legitimate and as a result, have more to gain by rioting and looting than from being arrested (Kawalerowicz & Biggs, 2014). P. Waddington (2007), added that these conditions could include any grievances that the community have with the police, which is often based on the perception of the type of policing undertaken in their neighborhood, any alleged harassment, or any negative incidents that involve local members of the community and the police. Smelser (1962) considered the form of policing undertaken in a neighborhood to be an important factor and perceived that the tactics used by the police could trigger further disorder.

There are three terms used in literature that describe violence that has been perpetuated by crowds or large groups: disorder, protest-demonstration, and riots. The term disorder is preferred by a number of researchers who agree with Tilly's (2003, p. 18), suggestion that the term riot, expresses a political judgment rather than reflecting an analytical distinction. Whereas Body-Gendrot (2013) determined that the actions undertaken during a riot have a political meaning, while the actions taken during a disorder do not. From these perspectives, rioting can be seen as a form of political protest in response to structural or social inequality (Akram, 2014).

According to Her Majesty's Inspectorate of Constabulary (2009a), protest "is a broad term, referring to various activities undertaken by those who wish to express their opposition to, or support for, amongst other things, an idea, policy, campaign or event" (p. 20) and does not necessarily include violence. Public protest is usually organized and can take many forms, such as demonstrations, assemblies and rallies, marches, parades, processions (Her Majesty's Inspectorate of Constabulary, 2009a), and in the majority of developed countries, is a legitimate form of political action and is usually undertaken within a framework determined by a city council or a police permitting system. This means that protests will usually come under one of the following categories: non-declared but planned, non-declared but spontaneous, long-term (such as occupations) or violent disorderly activity (Her Majesty's Inspectorate of Constabulary, 2009a).

Riots have been defined as an event in which a large number of people deliberately damage or vandalize property, loot retail outlets or private residences and attack others (Kawalerowicz & Biggs, 2014). Bateman (2012) concluded that riots can, however, take many forms and are not just mindless acts of violence or criminality, whereas Bohstedt (1994) proposed that riots are complex exhibitions of "social/political behavior set in historical contexts comprising distinctive social networks, conflicts, and ideologies that create and equip the opposing collective actors and thus shape both the incidence and dynamics of riots" (p. 257).

According to Bateman (2012), all riots share common foundations and factors and must include violence and damage to public or private property to warrant the term and that any confrontation between the rioters and the police is a consequence of the incident. Wilkinson (2009), however, proposed that the legal definitions of "riot" and "rioter" were developed by nations to allow them to prosecute any individual involved in the violence. The 1716 British Riot Act, for example, defined a riot as 12 or more people disturbing the public peace for a common purpose, while at the same time, English common law defined a riot as an unlawful assembly of three or more people (Bohstedt, 1988).

In a modern context, most people view riots as involving groups of 30–50 or more people (Rudé, 1981), while Bohstedt (1983) proposed that riots should be understood as "an incident in which a crowd of 50 or more people damaged or seized property, assaulted someone or forced a victim to perform some action" (p. 5). However, it is generally accepted that riots are primarily political and can be interpreted through a left or right-wing lens and may be initiated by the actions of demonstrators or the police (Marx, 1970). Tilly (2003) claims that the term riot is problematic, because it involves a normative and a political judgment.

The disparity between understanding what a riot is and the legal definition of a riot should make researchers cautious when describing the cause of a riot and the response taken by the police. While the police and rioters will hold incompatible definitions of an incident, there is usually a general agreement that an incident was a riot, even though it may have occurred over several days and in a number of distinct locations (Wilkinson, 2009).

2.3 An Attempt to Understand Riots

How or why do riots happen? Or should we be seeking the answer to the question posed by Newburn (2016), how do we analyze why riots do not happen? David Waddington and colleagues developed the flashpoints model in an attempt to understand riots. This approach, according to D. Waddington, Jones, and Critcher (1989), attempted "to theorize the factors found … to be crucial determinants of order and disorder" (p. 157), through six levels of analysis: structural, political/ideological, cultural, contextual, situational, and interactional. This approach may give the appearance of order in the process of understanding the determinants of a riot and this section of the chapter describes a framework that will give some understanding as to why the riots examined in this book may have happened. It does not add to the theory of what causes a riot. The possible causes and triggers for each of the riots that have been discussed in this book provide a context for evaluating the police response and for examining the occurrence of the riot. The cause or the trigger for each of the riots discussed has not been examined as the topic has been examined on many other occasions by numerous researchers and is outside the scope of this book.

This section attempts to understand the occurrence of modern riots and is based on a synthesis of social science literature. The discussion presented does not support any perspective that has been included in the narrative but offers a non-judgmental presentation as to the reasons why riots may occur. This approach has been taken because it creates a framework for analysing the actions taken by the police and because the information contained in the literature is open to interpretation. The other reason that this approach has been taken is because there are no reasons for the trigger of the riots described in the case studies in this book. As Taylor (1984) observed, the claim that there is a single factor or univariate explanation for the occurrence of a riot does not do justice to such a multifaceted social phenomenon (p. 171). The contents of this section generally endorse this view but also support the other observation that Taylor (1984), made, which is, that there are two primary, distinct causes of riots; preconditions and precipitants.

Riots are far from being random occurrences and the social or political events that lead to a riot are often interpreted as being symbolic and meaningful to the perpetrators (Reicher, Stott, Cronin, & Adang, 2004). However, riots only seem random when the event is examined from an outsider's perspective and not from the perspective of the person involved in the riot (Reicher et al., 2004). Politicians and the media usually look for a reason as to why a riot has occurred. A renowned explanation as to why the 2011 London riots occurred was given by the prime minister of the UK, who maintained that the cause was "criminality, pure and simple" (cited in Muddle, 2016).

Although a riot is clearly different from a protest, describing a riot as being a result of a social problem or a political event makes certain claims about rioters and their actions, which differentiates them from being criminals or looters (Akram, 2014). Treadwell, Briggs, Winlow, and Hall (2012) pose the question, "At what stage does a protest, which is based on a political event, become a riot? A political movement, for example, was present during the protests after the shooting of Mark Duggan in 2011 in London, the shooting of Michael Brown and the death of Freddie Gray in Baltimore, but the protests quickly escalated into rioting and looting. The problem with arguing that riots are a result of political motivation is that this argument does not add up when a riot occurs spontaneously (Akram, 2014).

A number of factors have been proposed to help to understand why riots occur. Factors such as the actions of youth (Jahoda, 1982); the uprising of a community (Gilroy, 1991); deprivation; minority ethnicity, political grievances (D. Briggs, 2012d; Kawalerowicz & Biggs, 2014); and the power that comes with being part of a crowd (Cantle, 2001; National Advisory Commission on Civil Disorders, 1968; Scarman, 1981) have been proposed as being some of the reasons why rioting occurs. P. Waddington (2007) agreed that there are factors that help us to understand why a riot occurs and he described them as determinants. P. Waddington, also claimed that there are six determinants; structural conduciveness, structural strain, the growth and spread of a generalized hostile belief, precipitating factors, the mobilization of participants for action, and social control (p. 40). Kawalerowicz and Biggs (2014) proposed that the occurrence of a riot can be explained in various ways but concluded that there are only two explanations for the occurrence of a riot; as a result of the participants of a riot living in economically deprived neighborhoods and because in these neighborhoods, the police have less legitimacy than in others. Briggs (2012d), held the view that racism and poverty were the two primary reasons for the occurrence of riots.

Early research in the USA, which was based on the interviews of the residents of three unspecified cities in which rioting occurred, found that the riots occurred in the presence of a "pre-existing hostile belief system" (Spiegel, 1969). The research identified that there were four stages to a riot: a precipitating incident, a street confrontation, a Roman[1] holiday and a siege (Spiegel, 1969). The research emphasized that the majority of riots do not go beyond the end of the Roman holiday stage. P. Waddington (2007) observed that these findings are of significance as they highlight the role of the police in the life cycle of riots and that the police are capable of either suppressing or inflaming riots.

Similar research was undertaken in four cities across the USA that had experienced rioting in the early 1970s. This research proposed that there were three aspects to a riot: general preceding conditions; immediate or proximate conditions; and internal dynamics (Hundley, 1975, cited in D. Waddington, 2007b). The research also described five background conditions that were necessary for a riot to occur:

- Potential participants must perceive that a crisis exists (they must subjectively experience some form of inequality, discrimination or deprivation);
- They must believe that legitimate channels for expressing grievances are closed off to them;
- They must share the view that rioting is likely to produce beneficial change(s);
- They must be in close enough proximity to each other for communication to occur; and
- There must have been a substantial breakdown in police–community relations (with the police being perceived as brutal, impolite or disrespectful) (adapted from Hundley, 1975, cited in D. Waddington, 2007b, p. 42).

Hundley (1975) claimed that five background conditions created four immediate or "proximate" conditions that are considered to be fundamental for an outbreak of rioting:

- the generation of rumor proposing rioting as a possible solution to salient ghetto problems, such as slum landlords or police brutality;
- the occurrence of an event that typifies enduring or historical grievances;
- the gathering together of large numbers of people around the event; and

[1] Roman holiday is an occasion on which enjoyment or profit is derived from others' suffering or discomfort.

- communication of particular grievances among the crowd, leading to an agreed course of action (adapted from D. Waddington, 2007b, pp. 42–43).

It is important to remember that there is a difference between a trigger event that starts a riot and the background conditions that created the environment for a riot to occur (Benyon, 1987). The part that rumor plays in a riot occurring was researched by Allport and Postman (1947), who claimed that "no riot ever occurs without rumours to incite, accompany, and intensify the violence" (p. 193, cited in Wilkinson, 2009, p. 333). This research proposed a theory, comprising four stages, in which rumor played a part in the occurrence of riots:

1. generalized rumor spreading,
2. the spreading of rumors about specific threats,
3. a specific trigger, e.g., a rumor of an assault, and
4. the intense spreading of often false rumors during riots (Allport & Postman, 1947, pp. 193–96, cited in Wilkinson, 2009, p. 333).

The claim that rioting occurs as a result of various social factors and a history of poor relationships between the police and the community has been supported by research conducted in the USA (Hundley, 1975; Smelser, 1962; Spiegel, 1969) and the UK (Akram, 2014; Briggs, 2012d; D. Waddington, 2007b). Recent research completed by academics in the UK found that rumor and media sensationalism influenced the occurrence of riots and extended the duration of a riot (D. Waddington, 2007b). This recognizes the impact that wider social structural factors have on a riot occurring and that riots can be "a form of political protest in response to structural inequality" (Akram, 2014, p. 376). From a review of these research findings, four general premises in relation to riots and to those who participate in them can be drawn. Those who participate in riots commonly come from areas or neighborhoods that are:

1. economically and socially deprived;
2. socially disorganized;
3. suffer from poor relations with the police; and
4. have a large number of ethnic minority communities (Kawalerowicz & Biggs, 2014).

The problem with accepting that riots occur because of social problems means that the dynamic aspect of a riot has been forgotten (Kawalerowicz & Biggs, 2014); that riots evolve or change in form as they occur. Gilroy (1991) suggested that rioting can be seen as "a long-term strategic war of position," meaning that there is a need to understand what a riot is attempting to achieve. This point has been expanded on by Keith (1993), who proposed that rioting is not a form of a "self-conscious deliberate strategy" and unless the spontaneous nature of rioting is understood, what occurs during a riot cannot be comprehended (p. 185).

As discussed above, a riot usually lacks the organized, political motivation of a protest and as a result, a number of different social, personal and environmental factors contribute to an individual's decision to riot (Baudains, Braithwaite, &

Johnson, 2013). A crowd that has gathered to protest has done so for a reason (Borch, 2013). As McPhail and Miller (1973) observed, when protesters assemble, they do so with a purposeful intent. However, while a crowd may have an intent, the fact that people assemble is not, in itself, evidence of a common grievance (D. Waddington, 1996).

The classical view taken of crowds is that they are irrational and prone to manipulation (Borch, 2013; Moran & Waddington, 2016; Reicher et al., 2004; D. Waddington, 2007a), which according to P. Waddington (2007), is the view that is held by the majority of police officers in the UK. The view that crowds are irrational is now out of step with academic understanding of crowd behavior (King & Brearley, 1996; Moran & Waddington, 2016), with researchers since the mid-1970s (see for instance Giner, 1976; McPhail, 1991; Reicher, 1982, 1987, 2001; Turner & Killian, 1987; D. Waddington et al., 1989, 1996), challenging the idea of crowd irrationality. As early as 1964, Rudé claimed that crowds were not irrational or spontaneous but had a clear political purpose and that any violence was highly patterned, with care being taken in the selection of targets (Rudé, 1981).

According to Reicher et al. (2004), individuals do not lose their identity in a crowd but their identity changes from being a personal identity to a social identity. This means that individuals do not lose their values and standards but will act in terms of the values and standards of the crowd (Reicher et al., 2004). P. Waddington (1991) claimed that some crowds can mistakenly edge toward the "mindless mob" end of the spectrum rather than the "politically motivated" end and this could explain crowd violence.

Further research conducted into crowd behavior was undertaken by Reicher et al. (2004), who found that individual members interpret the actions of others based on their own stereotypes. As a result, crowds, in a public order context, can react negatively to the actions of the police, even if those actions assist the crowd (Reicher et al., 2004). Furthermore, crowds are capable of a collective memory, which can go beyond the lives of the current members of a crowd and in a protest or demonstration can "remember" previous mistreatment carried out by the police (Reicher et al., 2004). As a result of the memory of a crowd, the police need to recognize that the individuals that make up a crowd are fundamentally rational and that their actions may affect the dynamic processes of a crowd (King & Brearley, 1996).

2.3.1 Critical Consensus

"Critical consensus" was proposed by P. Waddington (1991), as an explanation as to why riots occur. Critical consensus refers to the consensual, core view that riots occur because of grievances arising from deprivation, discrimination and police harassment. This view is in direct opposition to the "establishment-conservative" view that describes rioters as irrational and riots as a "criminal outburst" (P. Waddington, 1991, p. 221). P. Waddington (1991) explained that the critical consensus perspective is "fatally flawed" and gives the appearance of being more of a model for advocacy rather than an analysis of riots. Taylor (1984), took a similar view as P. Waddington (1991), and proposed that there are three lenses that are useful in identifying the reasons as to why riots occur. The lens used depends upon the individual's political view; irrational and criminal for conservatives, deprivation and injustice for liberals and revolutionary for radicals (pp. 244–245).

P. Waddington (1991) described critical consensus as giving no more of a conclusive explanation as to the reasons why riots occur than the explanation that the establishment-conservation offers, but critical consensus has now become widely accepted by academics and politicians. This means that because the background conditions are accepted as fact, the post-examination of the occurrence of a riot concentrates principally on the alleged triggers of a riot, which is usually the actions taken by, or the attitudes held by the police. As a result, this may mean that any media or political examination of a riot will not identify the reasons for the riot but will concentrate more on the event that allegedly triggered the riot. A number of post-investigations into the causes of riots have claimed, for example, that the increase in the use of stop and search of minority youth by the police has been the event that has triggered a riot and that any investigation into a riot has failed to look at the social issues that led to the need for the police to implement the strategies that were necessary to minimize the occurrence of criminal offending.

2.3.2 *Police Cause Riots*

There are two opposing views as to whether the police contribute to the occurrence of riots; researchers who agree that the police contribute to the occurrence of riots and researchers who do not. Those who take the view that the police contribute to the occurrence of a riot (Bergesen & Herman, 1997; Kawalerowicz & Biggs, 2014; Myers, 1997; Olzak & Shanahan, 1996; Olzak, Shanahan, & McEneaney, 1996; Perez, Berg, & Myers, 2003; Schneider, 2014) base their view on the form of policing adopted within a geographical area, especially on the tactics used, for example, the stopping and searching of minority youths or the use of stop and search in a neighborhood. Tensions between the police and the local community, or grievances about the form of policing used, according to Kawalerowicz and Biggs (2014), are the major reasons why riots occur and these researchers believe that riots are usually triggered by an incident in which the police have been seen to over-react or act unjustly.

The view that the police contribute to the occurrence of riots is not supported by P. Waddington (1991), who claimed that the methods used by the police did not "explain why riots erupt where and when they do" (p. 229). Despite the findings of the Kerner Commission and Lord Scarman's report that the police were primarily responsible for creating the conditions that could cause disorder, American research does not endorse the view that the actions of the police are the major contributing factor for rioting to occur (see Horowitz, 1983; Marx, 1970).

Examining the literature to determine whether the actions of the police can cause a riot to occur raises two points. The first point is the use of terminology. The actions taken by the police may be a trigger for a riot but do not cause a riot. The cause of a riot can usually be traced to historical, underlying social, racial or exclusion factors. This, however, is not to say that the form of policing is not a variable in the aggregate of factors that cause dissent (see the flashpoints model discussed below). The second point is that it is generally easier for politicians and the media to blame the police for causing a riot and by doing so, demand police reform. This is much easier to do than having to face the social problems that created the environment in which the riot occurred.

2.3.3 The Police Perspective as to the Causes of Riots

As a result of the number of riots that have occurred since the 1960s, a significant body of research has been conducted into their cause; the dynamics of crowds and civil disorder (Drury & Stott, 2001; Reicher et al., 2004; Stott & Adang, 2004; Stott & Reicher, 1998a; D. Waddington, 2007b), but little research has been undertaken from the perspective of the police as to why riots occur (Davis & Dawson, 2015).

There are studies from the 1970s that have concentrated predominantly on the interaction between the police and protesters and on obtaining an organizational perspective on civil disorder (Kreps, 1973; Quarantelli, Ponting, & Fitzpatrick, 1974). By the 1990s, research relating to the police and their interaction with crowds was, however, "based almost entirely on the social-psychological perspective" (Davis & Dawson, 2015, p. 134). To examine the relationship and the interaction of the police with a crowd, the Social Identity Model (SIM) and the Elaborated Social Identity Model (ESIM) (Stott & Adang, 2004) were developed.

Davis and Dawson (2015) determined that a milestone in the development of understanding the police perspective in the context of their relationship with crowds was the research undertaken by Stott and Reicher (1998a). This research was based on an interview study of 26 police officers, who were trained in public order and who were deployed during the English Poll Tax Riot on March 31, 1990. Stott and Reicher's research revealed that the police denied any responsibility for the disorder and tended to blame the crowd for the violence. Their research revealed that there were three themes that formed the police perception of a crowd:

1. Crowds, which are typically heterogeneous and representative of society in general, are divided into a majority and a minority during events involving an incident of disorder;
2. Crowds pose a homogeneous threat; and
3. Public order policing is largely driven by the fear and danger experienced by the police during crowd events (Stott & Reicher, 1998a).

2.4 Crowds

The principle factor that influences the behavior of a crowd is whether the crowd perceives the approach that the police have adopted for managing the protest and whether the tactics that they use to control violent members in a crowd is legitimate (Jefferson, 1990; P. Waddington, 1999). Research has shown that incidents caused by crowds "cannot be reduced to a generic set of behaviours" (Reicher, 1996, p. 115), and that these phenomena exist whether a crowd is violent or not, whether acts of vandalism have been committed (King, 1963; Moore, 1978), or whenever selective or patterned violence has occurred (Feagin & Hahn, 1973; Fogelson, 1971; Stephenson, 1979).

The problem for the police is that crowds usually do not have a "formal authority structure" (Reicher et al., 2007). This implies that it would be difficult for the police to negotiate with a crowd or gain information in order to be able to plan a response and this often results in the police treating all of the members of a crowd in the same manner (Reicher et al., 2007). This can in turn, result in individual members of a crowd cohering or joining together depending on the common experience of the police response (Reicher et al., 2007). Furthermore, if this group perceives the police as being illegitimate, or any action that the police take as being illegitimate, then the crowd will become violent toward the police (Reicher et al., 2007). Reicher et al. (2007) claimed that a proviso to this scenario is that the shared experience does not lead to all members of a crowd confronting the police, nor is there a dichotomy of violence or non-violence, but rather, there is a spectrum of individual behavior. At one end of the spectrum is violence and at the other end, non-violence, with the police having the ability to impact any of the points on the spectrum (Reicher et al., 2007).

The fact that the police have an influence on how a crowd will behave is the main reason that the police need to adopt response strategies and tactics that have been developed on this understanding rather than on classic crowd psychology (Reicher et al., 2007). Classic crowd psychology encourages the police to view all members of a crowd as dangerous and causes them to respond accordingly, which in turn, could have an impact on some members of the crowd, causing them to react violently (Reicher et al., 2007). If individuals or small groups within a crowd become violent, how then do the police design and implement differentiated crowd control strategies and tactics (Drury, Stott, & Farsides, 2003)?

The question may be answered in a theoretical sense but not in a practical sense and a theoretical answer will not assist the police to develop appropriate response strategies and tactics. There are two other points that need to be considered in relation to the management of crowds. The first is that despite the academic discourse regarding the practical strategies for governing crowds there is no guarantee that the understanding of crowds and their actions will result in a suitable control strategy (Borch, 2013). Secondly, the national disorder training framework that is used by the police in England and Wales (and no doubt elsewhere) does not include modern crowd dynamics and according to Hoggett and Stott (2010a) and White (2006), this limits the police to thinking about the means rather than the ends.

Table 2.1 Five principles of crowd policing

	Principle	Summary
1	Education	Crowds comprise a number of different groups, there is a need for the police to understand the social identities of the various groups in a crowd; their values and standards, aims and goals, their sense of what is right, their stereotypes and expectations of other groups, their history of interaction with these groups and anything that may have a particular symbolic significance. The police should be aware of the cultural norms of particular crowds and the legitimate forms of conduct that flow from this.
2	Communication	The police should be capable of communicating their intentions. If the police seek to avoid a conflictual relationship then it is important that they communicate with crowd members. How they communicate and with whom needs to be considered.
3	Facilitation	The police should facilitate legitimate forms of conduct. This involves a change from crowd control or crowd management to an emphasis on facilitation. The police need to understand the legitimate aims of members of a crowd in order to consider how to best organize policing so that the aims may be met.
4	Differentiation (Definition)	The biggest danger for police is to treat all members of a crowd the same and at the least, as potentially dangerous. The actions of the police should be subtle enough to differentiate between groups and individuals in the crowd.
5	Use of force	The police should avoid indiscriminate use of force.

Adapted from Reicher et al. (2004, pp. 566–569, 2007)

Reicher et al. (2004), developed four principles for policing crowds. They are education, communication, facilitation, and definition, and these have been adapted to summarize the discussion in this section. The adaptation of the four principles has been presented in Table 2.1. An additional principle has been included to assist with the design of disorder response plans.

2.5 Police–Crowd Relationship

As a result of the police holding the view that crowds are inherently irrational and dangerous, Hoggett and Stott (2010b) suggested that the police are missing the opportunity "to develop more efficient, effective and less confrontational approaches to the management of public order events" (p. 226). Using less confrontational approaches to the management of public order events, according to Hoggett and Stott (2010b), can form the basis for the development of police crowd management tactics, such as containment and dispersal (Drury & Reicher, 2000; Reicher, 1996; Stott, Adang, Livingstone, & Schreiber, 2008; Stott & Reicher, 1998b). The problem with the claims of Hoggett and Stott (2010b) is that they are more applicable to an organized public protest or a demonstration rather than to a riot, such as those experienced in London in 2011 and in Ferguson, Missouri in 2014. Disorder can and does occur during protests and demonstrations (Drury & Reicher, 2000; Reicher, 1996; Stott et al., 2008; Stott & Reicher, 1998b), and to ensure that the public has confidence in the police, the police need to adopt tactics and manage crowds in a manner that is appropriate for the event and does not lead to an incident that will trigger violence. The danger in the police believing that crowds are irrational and failing to adopt more of a community-focused management of civil disorder means that any such event could become a self-fulfilling prophecy (D. Waddington, 2013).

Using the word "criminal" as a frame of reference when developing crowd control tactics can lead to the police believing that crowds are irrational and any crowd control tactics that have been designed on this assumption will not succeed. For crowd control tactics to be successful they need to have the support and the involvement of the community (King & Waddington, 2004). Realizing that there was a need for community support during civil disorder incidents led "to a sea-change in the policing of disorder" in the late 1980s (Brewer, Guekle, Hume, Moxon-Browne, & Wilford, 1988, p. 32), and by the end "of the twentieth century, [the] police [had] developed a new, softer and seemingly more tolerant style of policing protest [which was] dubbed "negotiated management" by social scientists" which included the police sharing the "partial control of public spaces to demonstrators" (Noakes, Klocke, & Gillham, 2005, p. 239). This stoic approach by the police enabled the actions of a crowd to be predicted, resulting in the fringe element committing less acts of violence in the majority of protests (Noakes et al., 2005).

There are, however, three weaknesses in the new style of disorder management and these limit the effectiveness of the use of negotiated management to only small-sized protests and demonstrations and to those that have been issued a permit by the police or municipality. The first weakness is that negotiated management was only adopted by the police when protests were held within a contained or cordoned area or when demonstrations and demonstrators were limited and controlled by the police (Tilly, 2000). The second weakness arose as a result of the emergence of more confrontational protest groups in the late 1980s. These groups were more professional in planning and organizing their activities, with some group members adopting anarchist-type principles (Kaufman, 2002; Rootes, 1999; Wall, 1999), and would not negotiate with the police. The last weakness is that the new style of disorder management focuses on the protest event per se and not on the actions of the protesters. As a result, the police perceive that models such as the flashpoints model are not appropriate for use when responding to violent protests or riots (Gorringe & Rosie, 2008).

2.5.1 *Elaborated Social Identity Model*

According to Hoggett and Stott (2010a), the early theoretical models for analysing crowd behavior, based on Le Bon's classical research, have been replaced by theories that have been based on the rational and normative character of crowd action (see for example McPhail, 1991; Turner & Killian, 1987), and on the theory of the Elaborated Social Identity Model of crowd behavior (Drury & Reicher, 2000; Reicher, 1996; Stott & Reicher, 1998a, 1998b). The Elaborated Social Identity Model is based on the perceived actions of the police, especially when the actions are viewed as being unjustified or illegitimate. It is the effect of perceived illegitimate actions taken by the police that produces crowd solidarity, with opposition to the police being based on the crowd having a shared social identity (D. Waddington, 2007a).

The basis for the model is the police use of force and legitimacy (Stott, Hoggett, & Pearson, 2012), which is similar to the model of "process-based regulation" proposed by "procedural justice theory"[2] (PJT; Tyler, 1990, 2003, 2007; Tyler & Huo, 2002). The theory proposes that as a result of people perceiving the police as being legitimate they are more likely to have trust in the police and comply with their directions (Stott et al., 2012). As a result, an individual's compliance is understood to be "mediated psychologically by social identity and self-categorization processes" (Stott et al., 2012, p. 382). This means that an individual's compliance is assumed to emanate from their judgment "concerning the legitimacy [of the police] in the intergroup context," which is similar to the Elaborated Social Identity Model (Stott et al., 2012, p. 382).

The Elaborated Social Identity Model is founded on the theories of social identity (Tajfel & Turner, 1979) and self-categorization (D. Briggs, 2012d; Turner, Hogg, Oakes, Reicher, & Wetherell, 1987), because individuals in a crowd have "a common and socially determined identity" (Reicher, 1982, 1984, 1987). However, this identity is proximity and context dependent and can therefore change during an event (Hoggett & Stott, 2010a; D. Waddington, 2007b). The model supports the perspective that individuals act in terms of a shared social identity (Drury, 2000), and Hoggett and Stott (2010a) observed that the riot tactics used by the police are based on the belief that crowds are irrational and can cause a cycle of escalating violence. As a result of the model focusing on the interactional elements that increase the occurrence of violence, Reicher et al. (2004, 2007) suggested that there are five principles that underpin the successful policing of disorder. These are presented and discussed in Table 2.1.

The model also addresses the dynamics between individuals and groups within a crowd (D. Briggs, 2012d). A supposition of the model, as noted by D. Waddington (2013), is that any force used by the police during a disorder that is perceived by the crowd as being indiscriminate or illegitimate, can lead to the crowd unifying and challenging the police (Drury & Reicher, 2000; Reicher, 1996; Stott et al., 2012, 2017; Stott & Reicher, 1998a; D. Waddington, 2013). Any opposition to the police can escalate if a crowd perceives the police as being "numerically or tactically vulnerable" (D. Waddington, 2007b).

---

[2] PJT is based upon the idea of "normative compliance," which is where individuals conform to the law, which they perceive that they have a moral, ethical and ideological obligation to do so (Tyler, 1990; Hough 2007; Stott et al., 2012).

As a result of Stott's (2009) review of the police response to civil disorder and the practical implications that the model has for the police, the work has become the basis for the management of peaceful crowds, protests and demonstrations (D. Waddington, 2013). There are, however, other models such as the "flashpoints" model, which focuses more on the broader contextual factors of crowd behavior (Stott, 2009), and this model will be discussed below.

2.5.2 *The Flashpoints Model*

The second model used for examining the reasons for the occurrence of riots is the flashpoints model, which was developed by D. Waddington et al. (1989). The model originated from the examination of the inner-city riots that occurred in England and Wales during the 1980s (King & Waddington, 2005), and evolved from the frustration that D. Waddington et al. (1989) felt with the reasons given for the occurrence of a riot being "sparked off" (Gorringe & Rosie, 2008). The model emphasized that a disorder should be examined within a wider context and that two elements need to be present for disorder to occur; precursor or prerequisite conditions (the "tinder") mixed with interpersonal interaction (the "spark") (Gorringe & Rosie, 2008). According to D. Waddington (2013), the objective of the model was to incorporate the factors that were identified in the literature as having a causal role in the reason for any disorder.

The model comprises seven interrelated "levels of structuration" which are presented in a series of concentric circles and provide a method for explaining specific disorder events:

1. structural—comprises the political and economic issues that relate to the underlying structural social problems;
2. political/ideological—the relationship of the protesters to established institutions;
3. institutional/organizational—the police agency;
4. cultural—how the protesters understand or interpret the world;
5. contextual—the long term and existing relations between those involved;
6. situational—the spatial determinant of a specific event; and
7. interactional—the dynamic between the protesters and the police at the time of the protest or event (King & Waddington, 2005; Sheptycki, 2005; D. Waddington et al., 1989).

The levels of structuration provide a means for identifying the flashpoints (the combination of the tinder and the spark) of a disorder depending on the "localized interaction" but the form that the specific disorder will take will be influenced by six other levels of structuration (Gorringe & Rosie, 2008, p. 189). In other words, "what is reacted to violently in one setting, with particular structural, political/ideological, cultural, contextual and situational features, may evoke a less dramatic response in another" (D. Waddington et al., 1989, p. 166).

A second group of researchers examined the reasons why riots occur. This research was led by della Porta (1995, 1998) and her colleagues (della Porta & Fillieule, 2004; della Porta & Reiter, 1998). They identified a number of variables that could determine or influence the occurrence of a disorder. Although these variables are similar to those classified in the flashpoints model, della Porta claimed that they operate at two different levels:

Level 1—includes factors such as political power, the institutional characteristics and culture of the police and public opinion.

Level 2—The filtering of the level 1 variables through "police knowledge"[3] (1995, 1998).

What is different with the della Porta (1995, 1998) approach to examining riots is that it takes into account the fact that police knowledge is dynamic and evolving and as a result, the police are likely to change their riot response tactics based on their experience (King & Waddington, 2005). Another difference between the flashpoints model and the della Porta approach is the measure in which they regard specific policing tactics as being "responsible for the instigation and escalation of conflict" (D. Waddington, 2007a, p. 193).

2.5.3 *Features of the Flashpoints Model*

The major strength of the flashpoints model is that it focuses on the "broader contextual determinants" which assists in the understanding of the "police-protester interaction before and during organized protest, and the extent to which it is conducive to disorder" (D. Waddington, 2013, p. 49). The model uses the information from the analysis of this interaction to identify the factors that explain the reasons for specific events "igniting" a riot, while other factors do not (Gorringe & Rosie, 2008). This means that the model moves any debate away from the factors that shape and constrain a riot (Tilly, 1986), such as violent police actions, to the factors that trigger riots (Gorringe & Rosie, 2008). According to King and Waddington (2005), the model is capable of more than "simply pointing to the immediate cause" of a riot and places the cause within a wider contextual structure, which enables a more in-depth analysis of the triggers (p. 257).

Although the flashpoints model may be an improvement on previous riot analytical frameworks, the model does have a number of weaknesses. Both P. Waddington (1991, 1994, 2000, 2003) and della Porta (1995, 1998) drew attention to the fact that the model did not explain the spatial and temporal aspects of the context of a riot or the police relationship with a crowd in a riot. P. Waddington (1991) also questioned

[3] Police knowledge is defined as "the police's perception of external reality, which shapes the concrete policing on the ground" and is "the main intervening variables between structure and action" (della Porta & Reiter, 1998, p. 2, 9). Police knowledge is not static (King & Waddington, 2005), but is "probably shifting and possibly contradictory, different for different levels of police hierarchy and for different police branches" (della Porta & Reiter, 1998, p. 27).

the utility of the model and argued that the model is "neither analytically useful nor empirically testable" (p. 159), as it cannot account for all of the incidents that lead to a riot as there is a time-lag between an incident occurring and a riot occurring (King & Waddington, 2005). The model also places some significance on an incubation period, which is usually founded on a social problem and a rise in tension between the police and the community (D. Waddington, 2007a). Gorringe and Rosie (2008) claimed that these weaknesses suggest that the model does not take into account the factors for a riot occurring and is therefore, not suitable for analysing global protests.

The model has also been criticized for its lack of analysis of the mobilization and the organization of a crowd and the police (Otten, Boin, & van der Torre, 2001). To improve the model, Otten et al. (2001) adapted its structure to take into account the way that events unfold and proposed that there are six separate stages to a disorder; Incubation, Tension, Precipitating, Onset, Adjustment and Learning (p. 16). Criticism of the model, which P. Waddington (1994) supported, emphasized that the police response is an important factor in the occurrence of riots. P. Waddington (1994) explained that the manner in which the police respond to a riot is not just based on preplanning but on a number of strategic options. Which option is implemented depends upon the geographical space and the actions of the crowd (P. Waddington, 1994).

The weaknesses in the flashpoints model that have been discussed above indicates that the model needs some improvement if it is to be useful in interpreting contemporary riots (Gorringe & Rosie, 2008; King & Waddington, 2005).

2.6 Research and Police Response Tactics

Prior to the 1960s, the police in the UK based their crowd control strategies on the belief that crowds were irrational. The perception that the police held of crowds and the violence that they caused gradually changed to one that was seen as a rational response to "particular socioeconomic problems" (Borch, 2013). Research since the 1980s has, however, indicated that there is a relationship between crowd violence and the response tactics taken by the police (see for example, della Porta & Reiter, 1998; Hall & de Lint, 2003; Jefferson, 1990; King & Waddington, 2004, 2005; Sheptycki, 2000; D. Waddington, 2007a; P. Waddington, 1987, 1991, 1993a, 1994; Waddington & King, 2005). According to the literature, the policing of civil disorder has moved from a reactive approach to one that is more proactive, relying more on consensual policing (Hall & de Lint, 2003; McCarthy & McPhail, 1998; McPhail, Schweingruber, & McCarthy, 1998), or as Wright (2002) described, has moved from "simply coping" to one of "managing" it.

According to P. Waddington (2007), there has been a major transformation over the past 30 years in both the USA and Europe in the methods that the police use to manage public order events. The changes in the USA were first identified by

McPhail et al. (1998), who noted that the police were no longer using an "escalated force" approach to public order and that they had moved to a "negotiated management" approach. The reason for the change in managing such events was attributed to the recommendations made by a number of different government commissions that had been established to examine urban unrest in a number of American cities during the 1960s and early 1970s (P. Waddington, 2007). The police were also concerned with the escalating levels of violence from disorder and were receptive to adopting less confrontational crowd management techniques (P. Waddington, 2007).

Similar changes to the way that the police managed disorder also took place in Europe. P. Waddington (2007) described the change in the management of protests during the 1950s and 1960s as being "based on a more liberal understanding of demonstration rights" (della Porta & Fillieule, 2004, p. 220). However, the change was slower in the UK because of the adoption of a more paramilitaristic style of policing in the UK from the 1970s to the 1990s (King & Brearley, 1996) and because of the number of violent industrial and tax reform protests (P. Waddington, 1998).

The reasons for the change in the policing of crowd disorders may be different in the USA and the UK, but researchers from both sides of the Atlantic agree that the changes are likely to be linked to restoring and maintaining the legitimacy of the police (P. Waddington, 2007). While there is an agreement in the literature that there has been a change in the police approach to the management of disorder there is some debate as to how negotiated management can be better delivered at a tactical level (Hoggett & Stott, 2010b). The debate centers on the use and the definition of the word "paramilitarization", with P. Waddington (1987, 1991, 1993a, 1994) claiming that the negotiated management approach to managing disorder is best realized through paramilitarization. Whereas Jefferson (1990) claimed that paramilitarization, because of its definition in an operational policing sense, infers the capability of a force via "a massive and highly oppressive police presence" (Jefferson, 1990, p. 85), it is the best form for managing disorder.

Whether police knowledge governs the use of tactics in the management of disorder (Hoggett & Stott, 2010b) is also debated in literature. The debate, however, is inconclusive as there has only been a limited amount of research undertaken that has examined the relationship between the police knowledge of crowds and their response to disorder (Hoggett & Stott, 2010b). The debates have assumed that the actions and the tactics used by the police "can and do have the capacity to negatively impact upon crowd dynamics" (Hoggett & Stott, 2010b). The problem with trying to understand the effect that the actions of the police have on a crowd is that different police strategic and tactical approaches can be applied simultaneously by different units within the same police force or by different forces within the same country and even within the same event (de Lint, 2005; della Porta & Reiter, 1998; Sheptycki, 2000). The strategy and the tactics that are selected result in different outcomes.

The most comprehensive theoretical model for examining the effect that the actions that the police take have on a crowd is that developed by della Porta and Reiter (1998). Their model comprises the legal framework, the culture of the police, the political context and the pattern of interaction between the police and the crowd, all of which converge to produce "police knowledge" (Hoggett & Stott, 2010b).

The production of "police knowledge" in turn, then determines the form of policing or response that is adopted (Hoggett & Stott, 2010b).

There is, however, a weakness in the della Porta and Reiter (1998) model. Their research examined the role that theoretical understanding of crowd psychology plays in "police knowledge" and how it influences the strategic and tactical decisions made by the police during such events, but their analysis of how the police make decisions is limited (Hoggett & Stott, 2010b, p. 224). Other research that has been conducted has highlighted that the police base their knowledge or understanding of crowds on Le Bon's theories, which according to Stott and Reicher (1998a) interacts with the practical constraints of the police response to disorder, thereby increasing the possibility that the police will use indiscriminate force. As a result of the gaps in the research, it is not known with confidence whether there is a relationship between "police knowledge" and the decisions made by the police (Hoggett & Stott, 2010b).

Although researchers cannot agree on the influence of "police knowledge," they concur that police legitimacy during the police response and the perception of the use of specific tactics within the response influences the occurrence of violence (Jefferson, 1990; P. Waddington, 1999). According to a number of researchers (see for example Chen & Bargh, 1997; Snyder, Tanke, & Berscheid, 1977), there is a relationship between the police perspective of a crowd and their response during demonstrations and protests, "and that this relationship can be understood as a self-fulfilling prophesy" (Stott, 2003, p. 642). What Stott (2003) is meaning by this statement is that if the police perceive the crowd as being dangerous, their response tactics will include "particular forms of practice which in turn functions to unite the crowd in hostility against the police" (p. 643).

2.6.1 The Theory of the Police Response

P. Waddington (2007) surmised that an examination of the theoretical approaches to public order policing and disorder would provide a foundation for understanding the form and the effect that the actions taken by the police would have. The policing of public disorder and public violence is not only reactive (Brearley & King, 1996; King, 1997, 1998; King & Brearley, 1996; D. Waddington, 1996) but also comprises police response strategies and tactics. Crowd violence and the police reaction to the violence combine at both the individual and aggregate level to either "pre-empt or de-escalate potential disorder or lead to a mutual spiral of conflict" (King & Waddington, 2004, p. 119).

To assist with constructing a theory as to the effect of and the range of strategic and tactical public order response options that are available at the different stages of a disorder and the "return to normality" after a disorder, the police in the UK developed a "riot-curve" (Association of Chief Police Officers, 1992, cited in King & Waddington, 2004, p. 121). The riot curve that was developed for command-level officers included eight different pre-, during, and post-rioting stages (Association

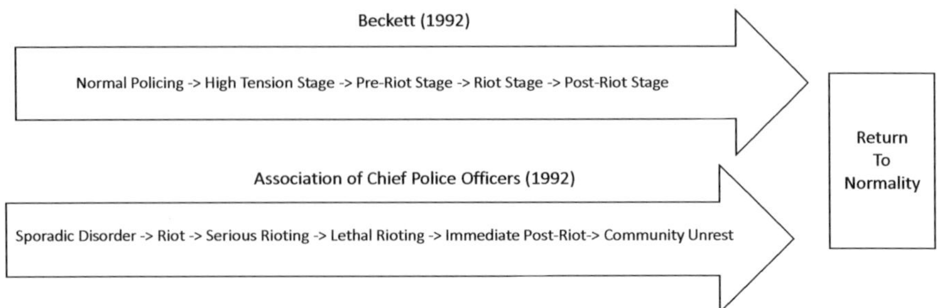

Fig. 2.1 The UK police riot curve (*Adapted from:* Association of Chief Police Officers, 1992, *cited in* King & Waddington, 2004; Beckett, 1992)

of Chief Police Officers, 1992: Appendix B, paragraph 2.2, cited in King & Waddington, 2004, p. 121). However, a second riot curve, which was presented by Beckett (1992), only comprised six stages. The two forms of riot curve have been presented in Fig. 2.1. As can be seen, that while the stages of the two curves are similar, the curve of the Association of Chief Police Officers (1992) concentrates more on the type of rioting than the one developed by Beckett (1992).

As a result of the riot curve concentrating more on the form of rioting, per se, researchers claim that the riot curve may not be an appropriate model for examining the life cycle of riots. King and Brearley (1996) cautioned that there was a weakness in the curve, which arises from it assuming that there is "a 'natural' escalation of violence on the part of the crowd, regardless of the environment and police action and the response to it" (p. 7). A second weakness in the curve is that it is based on the police version of the riot events (Waddington, 2007), and this forms a circular argument by reinforcing the way that the police view riots. In other words, the police version of the events of a riot follows the format of the curve: "Normality, High Tension Disorder, De-escalation, Normality" (D. Waddington, 2007a, p. 103).

2.6.2 *The Actions Taken by the Police*

Since the early 1970s, research that has examined the cause of riots has accepted that the actions of the crowd are not the only factor that influences the occurrence of violence and that the actions taken by the police can also influence the behavior of a crowd (Benyon, 1984; della Porta & Reiter, 1998; Earl, McCarthy, & Soule, 2003; Feagin & Hahn, 1973; Keith, 1993; McPhail et al., 1998; Reicher et al., 2004). Reicher et al. (2004) suggested that there are advantages in the police adopting a more interactive strategy with a crowd. The use of such an approach establishes "contact and trust," but also differentiates between groups within a crowd, such as non-violent and violent protesters and it enables the police to separate violent protesters from the rest of the crowd (Reicher et al., 2004). The danger for the police when violence occurs, is to view the crowd as homogeneous and to respond with forceful tactics to the entire crowd rather than only responding to the violent group within the crowd (Drury et al., 2003; Drury & Reicher, 1999, 2000; Reicher, 1996; Stott & Drury, 1999, 2000; Stott, Hutchison, & Drury, 2001; Stott & Reicher, 1998a).

Two outcomes may result from the actions taken by the police both of which depend on the strength of the contact between the crowd and the police. The first outcome is that the crowd will group together "in order to gain collective strength" and the second is that the crowd isolates the violent group and the violence does not spread across the crowd (Reicher et al., 2004, pp. 563–564).

To minimize any misunderstanding perceived by the crowd, the police should remove any "targets of derision" (D. Waddington, 2013). What D. Waddington (2013) refers to in this statement, is the removal of "particularly detested members of a rival faction" (p. 50); the rival faction in this sense, is the police and the detested members are officers fitted out in protective riot equipment. The deployment and presence of officers fitted out with protective riot equipment is provocative and can present the "unintended message that the police have no intention of accommodating the protesters' goals and interests" (D. Waddington, 2013, p. 50).

The risk of the actions of the police being misinterpreted is one of the main reasons why the police prefer to negotiate with protest organizers prior to an event (D. Waddington, 2007a). D. Waddington (2007a) emphasizes that during the negotiations the police will assert control and will use a number of ploys to ensure that the organizers of the event comply. One ploy is to ensure that the protesters have a chance to peacefully make their point (Her Majesty's Inspectorate of Constabulary, 2009).

2.6.3 The Police Response

The modern approach to managing crowds may be accepted by researchers and academics but in practice, the managed approach is only practical in managing non-violent crowds and is of no value when policing violent public disorder (King & Waddington, 2005). The practicality of the modern approach raises two questions. The first is the level to which the modern approach has been accepted by the police and the second is whether the modern approach works in reality.

In the 1980s, the view that the police took was that if a crowd was perceived to be a threat, then the crowd, as a whole, should be treated as a threat (Drury et al., 2003). Stott and Reicher (1998a) supported this view and argued that there was an ideological rationale and tactical reason for treating a crowd as a single body and that the rationale was grounded in the classic crowd theory that had been proposed by Gustave Le Bon (1895) (Drury et al., 2003). Le Bon determined that the occurrence of violence was simply a characteristic of crowds (Reicher & Potter, 1985).

The police acknowledge that they will not have any success in gaining control of a protest if they view the crowd from a criminal perspective. The police also acknowledge that they need the support and the involvement of the local community and for a crowd to accept the role of the police as legitimate if they are to be able to manage protests (King & Waddington, 2005). The police also accept that if they approach a crowd from the perspective that the crowd is irrational and that if they implement any strategy on this premise it could increase tensions in the crowd causing violence rather than reducing it (Borch, 2013; Gorringe & Rosie, 2011; Hoggett & Stott, 2010b; Reicher et al., 2007).

Other researchers contend that the policing of a protest is not just about understanding the crowd (Hoggett & Stott, 2010a) and that there are a number of other factors that influence the successful management of a crowd, such as deploying a sufficient number of officers, for as King and Waddington (2005) cautioned, the police cannot be successful in gaining control of a protest "where initial police numbers, reinforcements, equipment and tactical coordination are deficient" (p. 135). The expectations placed on the police by "those who scrutinise them" (Cronin & Reicher, 2006; P. Waddington, 1993a, 1994) are also a factor that influences the successful management of a crowd. According to Hoggett and Stott (2010a), the accountability of the police to internal and external stakeholders produces a dimension to managing disorder that needs to be understood and catered for in the response that the police take.

There are weaknesses in the preparations made to respond to protests and they are in the planning, training and equipment areas (King & Waddington, 2004). This was recognized in a 1999 Her Majesty's Inspectorate of Constabulary report, which highlighted that the majority of police forces in the UK had been developing public disorder "strategies, tactics, training and equipment" based on the lessons learned from the inner-city riots of the 1980s and early 1990s (Her Majesty's Inspectorate of Constabulary, 1999, p. 5). Cerrah (1998) maintained that the public order training that was provided in police organizations in the UK and in a number of other western countries was based on the Le Bonian (Le Bon, 1895) model of crowd control. The weakness of the Le Bon theory, as noted above, is that police officers will see the crowd as irrational and vulnerable to the influence of powerful individuals and as a result, to disorder (Drury et al., 2003). This means that any crowd control tactics used by the police will result in the production of, or the escalation of disorder (Drury et al., 2003). The view that the tactics used by the police causes or escalates violence, however, has been questioned by the Elaborated Social Identity Model, as the development of crowd conflict with the police "is characteristically a dynamic intergroup process" (Drury et al., 2003, p. 1496).

The failure to base the development of a police response on the lessons learned from the riots that occurred during the 1980s and 1990s resulted in more confrontational, rather than facilitative responses, which meant that the police perpetuated the view that crowds were dangerous. This was the view that was taken by Her Majesty's Inspectorate of Constabulary in a 1999 report. The report stated that the threat of a potential disorder was increasing and that as a result, the police needed to adopt a more "measured response" to the occurrence of a riot (Her Majesty's Inspectorate of Constabulary, 1999, p. 5, 9).

In the 1960s, the police in the USA relied primarily on an escalated force model to respond to public disorder (McPhail et al., 1998), but toward the end of the

1970s, a more tolerant, negotiated, management approach had been adopted (D. Waddington, 2007a). The changes in the police response to public disorder were attributed to findings made by several government commissions that had been established to examine urban unrest. The findings of the commissions concluded that the police had used excessive violence to manage this type of unrest in the 1960s and early 1970s (D. Waddington, 2007a). D. Waddington (2007a) explained that some of the reasons that the police changed their approach to public disorder in the late 1990s was a respect for the rights of protesters and better communication practices with the crowd. The manner in which the police in the USA responded to riots during this period was similar to that which the police in the UK took.

Researchers in the USA and Europe have agreed that since the 1980s, there has been a major change in the way that the police manage crowds and public order (D. Waddington, 2007a). Up until the 1980s, the majority of police agencies in the USA believed that the most effective response to a riot was the use of firm, but targeted intervention tactics that were designed to divide the crowd into smaller, more manageable groups. Dividing a crowd into smaller groups helps to prevent any kind of leadership from developing within the crowd and would assist to disrupt communication between the members of the crowd (Hundley, 1968; Smelser, 1962; Spiegel, 1969). Both Hundley (1968) and Spiegel (1969) advocated that the most effective method of dividing a crowd into more manageable groups was for the police to charge into a crowd, but noted that this could provoke the crowd and they warned that any sign that the police were not going to disperse the crowd would display a lack of conviction. Smelser (1962) also considered riots to be handled more effectively if the police did not negotiate with the crowd.

The reason for the change in the approach taken to respond to disorder in the UK was different from that taken in the USA. King and Brearley (1996) claimed that the police in the UK were more paramilitaristic in the 1970s and 1980s and that the changes in the police response could be traced to a number of "watershed" events. These events, according to D. Waddington (2007a), were the lessons that were learnt during the violent confrontations experienced during the miners' strikes and the poll tax riots in the 1980s (D. Waddington, 2007a). The police and the government of the UK realized that violence and disorder was a result of the "uncompromising police tactics that not only endangered human lives, but was also uneconomical in terms of police resources and damaging to police legitimacy" (D. Waddington, 2007a, p. 11).

However, by the mid-1990s, the police in both the UK and the USA had become aware of the human and the organizational cost of responding to riots with a large number of officers and from using proactive crowd management and dispersal tactics. Their awareness was also being influenced by a number of European academics who had conducted research into the management of crowds and it was their research that found that if the police negotiated with the crowd there was less likelihood of violence occurring (Reicher, 1982, 1984, 1996; D. Waddington, 1992, 1996). The experience of the police in dealing with crowds and protests in the 1990s continues to influence the police response to these types of events.

The response and the management of disorder is different in Canada. According to Torrance (1986), Canada has historically had "a low tolerance of public disorder and strong public support" for vigorous policing of public disorder (p. 205). The policing of public disorder in this manner is, however, changing. Two distinct approaches have been taken, one of which is conciliatory and consultative and the other concerns capability and is one of militarization (de Lint, 2005). The militarized approach is supported by the adoption of police intelligence methods, which use disorder-countering strategies and tactics that are more "proactive and pre-emptive" (de Lint, 2005, p. 180).

In the mid- to late 1990s, the police in the USA and the UK did not take a confrontational stance during protests, which the police hoped, would encourage trust and cooperation. However, if there were any factors present in the crowd, such as a predisposition toward violence, then violence was likely to occur (D. Waddington, 2013). The acts of violence committed by individuals in crowds usually arose from a single incident or a series of incidents (either initiated by the crowd or by the police who had responded to a perceived overreaction to a specific incident) or if the incident(s) involved "intensifiers," such as children, or other vulnerable people (D. Waddington, 2013). By the early 2000s, however, the police acknowledged that acts of violence were more likely to occur if liaison with the crowd had not taken place or if the crowd had not been informed of any action that the police would take (King & Waddington, 2004).

A weakness of the negotiated approach is that a number of protest movements are now decentralized and often do not have any formal leadership with whom the police can communicate with and this means that the police need to rely on intelligence gathering (King & Waddington, 2005; Mawby, 2002).

Because of an increase in the interest taken in the research and the development of the Elaborated Social Identity Model and the flashpoints model, as well as the improvement in the police understanding of crowds, it has become apparent that any excessive use of force by the police will not control or manage an unruly crowd (Perez et al., 2003), and that there is no "one size fits all" approach (Reicher et al., 2007). Although the police may have a range of crowd management and protest response strategies, tactics and techniques available, these need to be designed and used to suit the specific circumstances (Reicher et al., 2007).

There are two documents that form a backdrop for the development of more modern theories and policies and can be used for the training of police officers in crowd management techniques in the UK. The first is Her Majesty's Inspectorate of Constabulary's Adapting to Protest (2009). This report underpins the recognition of the Human Rights Act and the need for the act to be considered when making command decisions (Drury et al., 2003). The report also focused on the adoption of the use of non-coercive methods in all public order events.

The second document is the Association of Chief Police Officers (ACPO) Public Order Manual. This manual recognizes that crowd facilitation is a key principle in protest management and notes that the "policing of crowds is a dynamic and interactive process." Violence can be initiated by crowd participants and as a result of the dynamics of the interaction between the crowd and the police (Hoggett & Stott, 2010b,

p. 229). The research undertaken by Reicher and colleagues in 2007 provided the theoretical foundation for the development of the manual (Association of Chief Police Officers, 2010). The Reicher research emphasized that the police needed to change their perception that crowds were irrational and that they needed to use more rational crowd management techniques, such as communicating with the crowd and by having officers being more visual within a crowd (Borch, 2013).

According to Borch (2013), current police crowd management strategies alternate between viewing crowds as irrational or viewing crowds as ignorant and this is one of the reasons why the police response to the 2011 London riots failed. How crowds are perceived by the police is a complex matter and the research that has been completed to date only applies to permitted protests, football crowds and civic protests, and does not apply to violent situations, such as those experienced in London in 2011.

Gorringe and Rosie (2011) noted that the communication techniques that the police used in an attempt to manage the crowd during the London riots did not appear to be very successful but what did appear to work in controlling the violence was "the deployment of very large numbers of officers" (Gorringe & Rosie, 2011, p. 5).

The Gorringe and Rosie (2011) findings, according to Borch (2013), relate to three intertwining points, which weaken the argument for the police to base their crowd control strategies on the Rationalist Crowd theory.[4] The first weakness is that police documentation, such as riot guidelines and manuals are not linked to the training of the police to manage and respond to riots and nor are they linked to the behavior of police officers (Borch, 2013). The second weakness is that the Rationalist Crowd theory does not take into account the different types of groups within a protest or rioting crowd. Gorringe and Rosie (2011) suggested that the negotiation and communication strategies proposed by the Rationalist Crowd theory may only be successful when dealing with particular protest groups, such as those who have political demands, those who are looting (Borch, 2013), or those who wish to confront the police. The third weakness, which is linked to the second weakness, is that the theory does not provide for emotional crowd arousal, which has been defined by Borch (2013), as the collective action that is triggered by the dynamics of a crowd.

The final method that will be discussed is that which has been suggested by Stott and Reicher (1998a), and Drury et al. (2003). These researchers proposed that the police in England and Wales have an "agitator" perception of crowds and that such a view leads to an increased chance that the police will use more forceful tactics when responding to any violence perpetrated by the crowd, which according to Hoggett and Stott (2010a, 2010b), could be a "self-fulfilling prophesy" if the police implement crowd management tactics with this mindset. A vulnerability for the police that has been identified is that the agitator mindset will be reinforced by a crowd management strategy—a strategy that focuses on the control and disruption

[4] Rationalist crowd theory is that aggregate social behavior results from the behavior of individual actors, each of whom is making their individual decisions (Hedstrom & Stern, 2008).

of potential or suspected instigators of violence (Hoggett & Stott, 2010a, 2010b). The problem with this strategy lies in its implementation. The police often cannot identify potential troublemakers and separate them from a crowd (Stott et al., 2008), or when they can identify such persons, they have to use tactics which enables them to physically apprehend the person, such as snatch and grab.[5] The Le Bon and the agitator view of public disorder, according to D. Waddington (2007a), have been discredited in favor of models such as the Elaborated Social Identity Model.

This section has discussed the literature relating to crowd control strategies and tactics used by the police and the theoretical origins of these strategies and tactics. Although the literature examining riots has not directly concentrated on policing or the police use of force (see for example, Bergesen & Herman, 1997; Myers, 1997; Olzak et al., 1996; Olzak & Shanahan, 1996), the findings of the majority of these studies indicate that police use of force is a critical factor for gaining an understanding of why riots occur and what triggers them (Perez et al., 2003). The application of repressive crowd management tactics, according to Perez et al. (2003), is ineffective in controlling or subduing violence and riots, and can actually increase the occurrence of violence, looting, and vandalism. An increase in violence from the use of repressive tactics is usually caused when the tactic is excessive, is targeted toward minorities, police are poorly trained in crowd management or when the relationship of the police with the community is strained or weak (Perez et al., 2003).

Modern literature (della Porta, 1998; della Porta & Reiter, 1998; D. Waddington, 2007a) claims that the policing of protests has become more coercive than oppressive and now includes a form of consensus, which has been built on negotiation (Gorringe & Rosie, 2008). As discussed in this chapter, the coercive approach does have its limitations and is not a strategy that is able to be implemented during a riot. According to Perez et al. (2003), there are weaknesses in the more coercive approaches, especially if they are found to be addressing "only the effects of blanket changes in levels of repressive force on the trajectory of collective action cycles" (p. 171). The occurrence of violence and rioting is dynamic and implies a vigorous relationship between the preparedness of the police, their control tactics and the response of the crowd to the application of these tactics.

In summary, the literature identifies that "no single response or level of preparation [by the police] can ensure de-escalation of every collective conflict" (Perez et al., 2003, p. 175). Rioting is, however, less likely to occur when the police act decisively to maintain a professional distance, minimize their communication with the crowd and avoid becoming involved in any discussion relating to the grievances of the protesters (Smelser, 1962). The literature also determines that the deployment of a large number of appropriately trained police officers does have a deterrent effect on the escalation of violence and rioting but if the police use violent or repressive tactics, it will not have a deterrent effect on the behavior of a crowd (Perez et al., 2003).

[5]This involves a small team of five or six officers forcefully pushing into the crowd, physically restraining the person and pulling them out of the crowd, to behind the police lines.

The coercive approach may also have another limitation and that is that it cannot be used for international summits such as the G8 meetings (King & Waddington, 2005).

A more balanced perspective was taken by Gorringe and Rosie (2008), who argued that the negotiated management approach could not be adopted carte blanche as a crowd control strategy but its use is influenced "by history, forms of police knowledge and modes of engagement" with the crowd (p. 187). The overarching, influencing factor that was not raised by Gorringe and Rosie (2008) was that the approach cannot be used by the police in specific forms of violent protest, such a riot. This means that the approach can only be used as a guideline, which is limited in practical terms for the police (Borch, 2013).

2.7 Conclusion

This chapter has attempted to explain a number of contentious areas in the literature that relates to the police response to riots. The first area which was discussed is the fact that, as with a number of social science topics, there is no clear definition of the term riot. An attempt to understand riots and how and why they start was the second area to be discussed. The third and fourth areas relate to the attempt to understand crowd behavior and the models developed to analyze crowd behavior. The last areas that were discussed relate to the police, their understanding of their role in responding to riots and the consequences of their actions.

As King and Brearley (1996) claimed, it is undeniable that the understanding of the behavior of crowds by the police and the control of violent crowds has changed. The response strategies and tactics to control violent crowds were not developed or adopted in a vacuum, but rather were influenced by a number of organizational and external factors (King & Brearley, 1996). The main factor that influenced the understanding of crowd violence by the police is the acceptance of the research that led to the development of the elaborated social identity model and the flashpoints model. The occurrence of violence is similar to other policing problems and requires a coordinated, multiagency response (King & Brearley, 1996).

Although the amount of available literature that relates to crowd control and the policing of large crowd events is growing, the topic of the policing of riots is characterized by some notable limitations (Davies & Dawson, 2015). The majority of studies that examine the police management of crowds use primarily qualitative methodologies rather than quantitative methodologies (Stott et al., 2008), and a number of studies have weaknesses in their data collection or sampling (Davies & Dawson, 2018).

The policing of pubic disorder and riots is different to any other role that the police undertake and it is a role that they cannot shelter from (P. Waddington, 1996). The following chapter examines the current approaches used by the police in response to riots in the context of the technologically, globalized world.

References

Allport, G., & Postman, L. (1947). *The Psychology of Rumor*. New York: Henry Holt.

Akram, S. (2014). Recognizing the 2011 United Kingdom riots as political protest: A theoretical framework based on agency, habitus and the preconscious. *British Journal of Criminology, 54*, 375–392.

Association of Chief Police Officers. (1992). *The new public order command level programmes*. Bramshill: National Police Training Centre.

Association of Chief Police Officers. (2010). *Manual of guidance on keeping the peace*. Wyboston: Specialist Operations Centre.

Bagguley, P., & Hussain, Y. (2008). *Riotous citizens: Ethnic conflict in multicultural Britain*. Oxford: Taylor & Francis Group Ltd..

Bateman, T. (2012). With the benefit of hindsight: The disturbances of August 2011 in historical context. In D. Briggs (Ed.), *The English riots of 2011: A summer of discontent* (pp. 91–110). Hook: Waterside Press Ltd.

Baudains, P., Braithwaite, A., & Johnson, S. (2013). Target choice during extreme events: A discrete spatial choice model of the 2011 London riots. *Criminology, 51*(2), 251–285.

Beckett, I. (1992). Conflict management and the police: A policing strategy for public order. In T. Marshall (Ed.), *Community disorders and policing: Conflict management in action* (pp. 129–139). London: Whiting & Birch.

Benyon, J. (1984). *Scarman and after: Essays reflecting on Lord Scarman's Report, the riots and their aftermath*. London: Pergamon Press.

Benyon, J. (1987). Interpretation of civil disorder. In J. Benyon & J. Solomos (Eds.), *The roots of urban unrest*. Oxford: Pergamon Press.

Bergesen, A., & Herman, M. (1997). Immigration, race, and riot: The 1992 Los Angeles uprising. *American Sociological Review, 63*, 39–54.

Body-Gendrot, S. (2013). Urban violence in France and England: Comparing Paris (2005) and London (2011). *Policing and Society, 25*(1), 6–25.

Bohstedt, J. (1994). The dynamics of riots: Escalation and diffusion/contagion. In M. Potegal & J. Knutson (Eds.), *The dynamics of aggression: Biological and social processes in dyads and groups* (pp. 257–306). Hove: Psychology Press.

Borch, C. (2013). Crowd theory and the management of crowds: A controversial relationship. *Current Sociology, 61*(5-6), 584–601.

Bohstedt J. (1983). *Riots and community politics in England and Wales*, 1790–1810. Cambridge, MA: Harvard University Press.

Bohstedt J. (1988). Gender, household and community politics: Women in English riots 1790–1810. *Past Present, 120*(1), 88–122.

Brearley, N., & King, M. (1996). Policing social protest: Some indicators of change. In C. Critcher & D. Waddington (Eds.), *Policing public order: Theoretical and practical issues* (pp. 101–116). Aldershot: Averbury.

Brewer, J.; Guekle, A., Hume, I., Moxon-Browne, E., & Wilford, R. (1988). *The police, public order and the state*. London: Macmillan.

Briggs, D. (2012d). What we did when it happened: A timeline analysis of the social disorder in London. *Safer Communities Special Edition on the Riots, 2*(1), 6–16.

Cantle, T. (2001). *Community cohesion: A report of the independent review team*. London: The Home Office.

Cerrah, I. (1998). *Crowds and public order policing*. Dartmouth: Ashgate.

Chen, M., & Bargh, J. (1997). Nonconscious behavioural confirmation processes: The self-fulfilling consequences of automatic stereotype activation. *Journal of Experimental Social Psychology, 33*(5), 541–560.

Clarke, K. (2011, September 5). Punish the feral rioters, but address our social deficit too. *The Guardian*. Retrieved from https://www.theguardian.com/commentisfree/2011/sep/05/punishment-rioters-help

Cronin, P., & Reicher, S. (2006). A study of the factors that influence how senior officers police crowd events: On SIDE outside the laboratory. *British Journal of Social Psychology, 45*(1), 175–196.

Davies, G., & Dawson, S. (2015). The 2011 Stanley Cup Riot: Police perspectives and lessons learned. *Policing: An International Journal of Police Strategies & Management, 38*(1), 132–152.

Davies, G., & Dawson, S. (2018). Spoonful of sugar or strong medicine: 'Meet and greet' as a strategy for policing large-scale public events. *Police and Society: An International Journal of Research and Policy, 28*, 697. https://doi.org/10.1080/10439463.2016.1259317

de Lint, W. (2005). Public order policing: A tough act to follow. *International Journal of the Sociology of Law, 33*(4), 179–199.

della Porta, D. (1995). *Social movements, political violence, and the state: A comparative analysis of Italy and Germany*. Cambridge: Cambridge University Press.

della Porta, D. (1998). Policing knowledge and protest policing: Some reflections on the Italian case. In D. Della Porta & H. Reiter (Eds.), *Policing protest: The control of mass demonstrations in western democracies* (pp. 228–252). Minneapolis, MN: University of Minnesota Press.

della Porta, D., & Fillieule, O. (2004). Policing social protest. In D. Snow, S. Soule, & H. Kriesi (Eds.), *The Blackwell companion to social movements* (pp. 217–241). Malden, MA: Blackwell.

della Porta, D., & Reiter, H. (1998). Introduction: The policing of protests in western democracies. In D. Della Porta & H. Reiter (Eds.), *Policing protest: The control of mass demonstrations in western democracies* (pp. 1–34). Minneapolis, MN: University of Minnesota Press.

Drury, J. (2000). Crowds, context and identity: Dynamic categorization processes in the 'poll tax riot'. *Human Relations, 53*(2), 247–273.

Drury, J., & Reicher, S. (1999). The intergroup dynamics of collective empowerment: Substantiating the social identity model of crowd behaviour. *Group Processes & Intergroup Relations, 2*(4), 381–402.

Drury, J., & Reicher, S. (2000). Collective action and psychological change: The emergence of new social identities. *British Journal of Social Psychology, 39*(4), 579–604.

Drury, J., & Stott, C. (2011). Contextualising the crowd in contemporary social science. *Contemporary Social Science, 6*(3), 275–288.

Drury, J., & Stott, C. (2001). Bias as a research strategy in participant observation: the case of intergroup conflict. *Field Methods, 13*(1), 47–67.

Drury, J., Stott, C., & Farsides, T. (2003). The role of police perceptions and practices in the development of "public disorder". *Journal of Applied Social Psychology, 33*(7), 1480–1500.

Earl, J., McCarthy, J., & Soule, S. (2003). Protest under fire? Explaining the policing of protest. *American Sociological Review, 68*(4), 581–606.

Feagin, J., & Hahn, H. (1973). *Ghetto revolts*. London: Macmillan.

Fogelson, R. (1971). *Violence in protest*. New York, NY: Doubleday.

Gilroy, P. (1991). *There ain't no black in the Union Jack*. Chicago, IL: University of Chicago Press.

Giner, S. (1976). *Mass society*. London: Martin Robertson.

Gorringe, H., & Rosie, M. (2008). It's a long way to Auchterarder! 'Negotiated management' and mismanagement in the policing of G8 protests. *The British Journal of Sociology, 59*(2), 187–205.

Gorringe, H., & Rosie, M. (2011). King mob: Perceptions, prescriptions and presumptions about the policing of England's riots. *Sociological Research Online, 16*(4), 17. Retrieved from http://journals.sagepub.com/doi/pdf/10.5153/sro.2521

Hall, A., & de Lint, W. (2003). Policing labour in Canada. *Policing and Society, 13*(3), 219–234.

Hedstrom, P., & Stern, C. (2008). *Rational choice and sociology. The New Palgrave Dictionary of Economics*. Basingstoke, United Kingdom: Palgrave Macmillan.

Her Majesty's Chief Inspectorate of Constabulary. (2009a). *Adapting to protest*. London: Her Majesty's Chief Inspectorate of Constabulary.

Her Majesty's Inspectorate of Constabulary. (1999). *Keeping the peace policing disorder*. London: Her Majesty's Inspectorate of Constabulary.

Hoggett, J., & Stott, C. (2010a). Crowd psychology public order police training and the policing of football crowds. *Policing: An International Journal of Police Strategies & Management, 33*(2), 218–235.

Hoggett, J., & Stott, C. (2010b). The role of crowd theory in determining the use of force in public order policing. *Policing and Society, An International Journal of Policy and Research, 20*(2), 223–236.

Horowitz, D. (1983). Racial violence in the United States. In N. Glazer & K. Young (Eds.), *Ethnic pluralism and public policy: Achieving equality in the United States and Britain*. Aldershot: Dartmouth Publishing Co Ltd..

Hough, M. (2007). Policing New Public Management and legitimacy. In T. Tyler (ed.), *Legitimacy and Criminal Justice*. New York: Russell Sage Foundation.

Hundley, J. (1968/1975). The dynamics of recent ghetto riots. *Detroit Journal of Urban Law, 45*, 627–639. (Reprinted as: Hundley, J. (1975). The dynamics of recent ghetto riots. In R. Evans (Ed.), Readings in Collective Behavior. Chicago: Rand McNally).

Jahoda, M. (1982). *Employment and unemployment: A social-psychological analysis*. Cambridge, England: Cambridge University Press.

Jefferson, T. (1990). *The case against paramilitary policing*. Milton Keynes: Open University Press.

Kaufman, L. (2002). A short history of radical renewal. In B. Shepard & R. Hayduk (Eds.), *From act up to the WTO* (pp. 35–41). New York, NY: Verso.

Kawalerowicz, J., & Biggs, M. (2014). *Anarchy in the U.K: Economic deprivation, social disorganization, and political grievances in the London riot of 2011* (Sociology Working Papers Number 2014-06). Oxford: University of Oxford: Department of Sociology.

Keith, M. (1993). *Race, riots and policing: Lore and disorder in a multi-racist society*. London: University of London Press.

King, M. (1963). *Why we can't wait*. New York, NY: Mentor.

King, M. (1997). Policing and public order issues in Canada: Trends for change. *Policing & Society: An International Journal of Research and Policy, 8*(1), 47–76.

King, M. (1998). Policing change in Eastern and Central Europe: Some contemporary concerns. *Innovation: The European Journal of Social Sciences, 11*(3), 277–285.

King, M., & Brearley, N. (1996). *Public order policing: Contemporary perspectives on strategy and tactics*. Leicester: Perpetuity Press.

King, M., & Waddington, D. (2004). Coping with disorder? The changing relationship between police public order strategy and practice - A critical analysis of the Burnley riot. *Policing & Society: An International Journal of Policy and Research, 14*(2), 118–137.

King, M., & Waddington, D. (2005). Flashpoints revisited: A critical application to the policing of anti-globalization protest. *Policing and Society, 15*(3), 255–282.

Kreps, G. (1973). *Decision making under conditions of uncertainty: Civil disturbance and organizational change in urban police and fire departments*. Columbus, OH: University of Delaware Disaster Research Center.

Le Bon, G. (1895/2002). *The crowd: A study of the popular mind* (Reprint ed.). Mineola, NY: Dover Publications.

Marx, G. (1970). Civil disorder and the agents of social control. *Journal of Social Issues, 26*(1), 19–57.

Mawby, R. (2002). *Policing images: Policing, communication and legitimacy*. Devon: Willan Publishing.

McCarthy, J., & McPhail, C. (1998). The institutionalization of protest. In D. Meyer & S. Tarrow (Eds.), *A movement society? Contentious politics for a new century* (pp. 83–110). Boulder, CO: Rowland and Littlefield.

McPhail, C. (1991). *The myth of the madding crowd, social institutions and social change*. New York, NY: Aldine de Gruyter.

McPhail, C., & Miller, D. (1973). The assembling process: A theoretical and empirical examination. *American Sociological Review, 38*, 721–735.

McPhail, C., Schweingruber, D., & McCarthy, J. (1998). Policing protest in the United States: 1960-1995. In D. Della Porta & H. Reiter (Eds.), *Policing protest: The control of mass demonstrations in western democracies* (pp. 49–69). Minneapolis, MN: University of Minnesota Press.

Moore, B. (1978). *The social bases of obedience and revolt*. London: Macmillan.

Moran, M., & Waddington, D. (2016). *Riots: An international comparison*. London: Macmillan Publishers Ltd.

Muddle, L. (2016). *The London riots 2011: Analyzing framing processes of the London riots*. Utrecht University. Retrieved from: https://dspace.library.uu.nl/bitstream/handle/1874/295601

Myers, D. (1997). Racial rioting in the 1960s: An event history analysis of local conditions. *American Sociological Review, 62*, 94–112.

National Advisory Commission on Civil Disorders. (1968). *Report of the National Advisory Commission on Civil Disorders*. Washington, DC: National Institute of Justice.

Newburn, T. (2016). Reflections on why riots don't happen. *Theoretical Criminology, 20*(2), 125–144.

Noakes, J., Klocke, B., & Gillham, P. (2005). Whose streets? Police and protester struggles over space in Washington, DC, 29-30 September 2001. *Policing and Society: An International Journal of Policy and Research, 15*(3), 235–254.

Olzak, S., & Shanahan, S. (1996). Deprivation race riots: An extension of Spilerman's analysis. *Social Forces, 74*, 931–961.

Olzak, S., Shanahan, S., & McEneaney, E. H. (1996). Poverty, segregation, and race riots: 1960 to 1993. *American Sociological Review, 61*, 590–613.

Otten, M., Boin, R., & van der Torre, E. (2001). *Dynamics of disorder: Lessons from two Dutch riots*. The Hague: Crisis Research Center, Lieden University.

Perez, A., Berg, K., & Myers, D. (2003). Police and riots, 1967-1969. *Journal of Black Studies, 34*(2), 153–182.

Quarantelli, E., Ponting, R., & Fitzpatrick, J. (1974). *Police department perceptions of the occurrences of civil disturbances*. Columbus, OH: Disaster Research Center, The Ohio State University.

Reicher, S. (1982). The determination of collective behaviour. In H. Tajfel (Ed.), *Social identity and intergroup relations*. Cambridge: Cambridge University Press.

Reicher, S. (1984). The St. Paul's riot: An explanation of the limits of crowd action in terms of a social identity model. *European Journal of Social Psychology, 14*(1), 1–24.

Reicher, S. (1987). Crowd behaviour as social action. In J. Turner, M. Hogg, P. Oakes, S. Reicher, & M. Wetherell (Eds.), *Rediscovering the social group*. Oxford: Blackwell Publishing.

Reicher, S. (1996). 'The Battle of Westminster': Developing the social identity model of crowd behaviour in order to explain the initiation and development of collective conflict. *European Journal of Social Psychology, 26*, 115–134.

Reicher, S. (2001). The psychology of crowd dynamics. In M. Hogg & R. Tindale (Eds.), *Blackwell handbook of social psychology: Group processes* (pp. 182–208). Oxford: Blackwell.

Reicher, S., & Potter, J. (1985). Psychological theory as intergroup perspective: A comparative analysis of "scientific" and "lay" accounts of crowd events. *Human Relations, 38*(2), 167–189.

Reicher, S., Stott, C., Cronin, P., & Adang, O. (2004). An integrated approach to crowd psychology and public order policing. *Policing: An International Journal of Police Strategies & Management, 27*(4), 558–572.

Reicher, S., Stott, C., Drury, J., Adang, O., Cronin, P., & Livingstone, A. (2007). Knowledge-based public order policing: Principles and practice. *Policing: A Journal of Policy and Practice, 1*(4), 1–13.

Rootes, C. (1999). *Environmental movements: Local national and global*. London: Frank Cass.

Rudé, G. (1981). *The crowd in history: A study of popular disturbances in France and England, 1730–1848*. London: Serif.

Scarman, L. J. (1981). *The Brixton disorders, April 10-12 1981: Report of an inquiry by the Rt. Hon. The Lord Scarman, O.B.E. (Cmnd. 8427)*. London: Her Majesty's Stationery Office.

Schneider, C. (2014). *Police power and race riots: Urban unrest in Paris and New York*. Philadelphia, PA: University of Pennsylvania Press.

Sheptycki, J. (2000). *Issues in transnational policing*. London: Taylor & Francis.

Sheptycki, J. (2005). Policing political protest when politics go global: Comparing public order policing in Canada and Bolivia. *Policing and Society: An International Journal of Policy and Research, 15*(3), 327–352.

Smelser, N. (1962). *Theory of collective behaviour*. New York, NY: Free Press.

Snyder, M., Tanke, E., & Berscheid. (1977). Social perception and interpersonal behaviour: On the self-fulfilling nature of interpersonal stereotypes. *Journal of Personality and Social Psychology, 35*(9), 656–666.

Spiegel, J. (1969). Hostility, aggression and violence. In A. Grimshaw (Ed.), *Racial violence in the United States*. Chicago, IL: Aldine Publishing Company.

Stephenson, J. (1979). *Popular disturbances in England 1700-1870*. London: Longman.

Stott, C. (2003). Police expectations and the control of English soccer fans at 'Euro 2000'. *Policing: An International Journal of Police Strategies and Management, 26*(4), 640–655.

Stott, C. (2009). *Crowd psychology & public order: An overview of scientific theory and evidence. A submission to the Her Majesty's Inspectorate of Constabulary Policing of Public Protest Review Team*. Liverpool: University of Liverpool.

Stott, C., Adang, O., Livingstone, A., & Schreiber, M. (2008). Tackling football hooliganism: A quantitative study of public order, policing and crowd psychology. *Psychology, Public Policy, and Law, 14*(2), 115–141.

Stott, C., & Drury, J. (1999). The intergroup dynamics of empowerment: A social identity model. In P. Bagguley & J. Hearns (Eds.), *Transforming politics: Power and resistance* (pp. 32–45). Basingstoke: Macmillan.

Stott, C., & Drury, J. (2000). Crowds, context and identity: Dynamic categorization processes in the 'poll tax riot'. *Human Relations, 53*(2), 247–273.

Stott, C., Drury, J., & Reicher, S. (2017). On the role of a social identity analysis in articulating structure and collective action: The 2011 riots in Tottenham and Hackney. *British Journal of Criminology, 57*, 964. https://doi.org/10.1093/bjc/azw036

Stott, C., Hoggett, J., & Pearson, G. (2012). Keeping the peace: Social identity, procedural justice and the policing of football crowds. *British Journal of Criminology, 52*(2), 381–339.

Stott, C., Hutchison, P., & Drury, J. (2001). 'Hooligans' abroad? Intergroup dynamics, social identity and participation in collective 'disorder' at the 1998 World Cup Finals. *British Journal of Social Psychology, 40*(3), 359–384.

Stott, C., & Reicher, S. (1998a). Crowd action as intergroup process: Introducing the police perspective. *European Journal of Social Psychology, 26*(4), 509–529.

Stott, C., & Reicher, S. (1998b). How conflict escalates: The intergroup dynamics of collective football violence. *Sociology, 32*(2), 353–377.

Stott, C. J., & Adang, O. M. J. (2004). 'Disorderly' conduct: Social psychology and the control of football 'hooliganism' at 'Euro2004'. *The Psychologist, 17*, 318–319.

Tajfel, H., & Turner, J. (1979). An integrative theory of intergroup relations. In S. Worchel & W. Austin (Eds.), *Psychology of intergroup relations*. Monterey, CA: Brooks-Cole.

Tarde, J. (1903). *The laws of imitation*. New York, NY: H. Holt and Company. Retrieved from https://archive.org/details/lawsofimitation00tard

Taylor, S. (1984). The Scarman report and explanations of riots. In J. Benyon (Ed.), *Scarman and after: Essays reflecting on Lord Scarman's report, the riots ad their aftermath*. Oxford: Pergamon Press.

Tilly, C. (1986). *The contentious French*. Cambridge, MA: Harvard University Press.

Tilly, C. (2000). Spaces of contention. *Mobilization, 5*(2), 135–151.

Tilly, C. (2003). *The politics of collective violence*. Cambridge: Cambridge University Press.

Torrance, J. (1986). *Public violence in Canada*. Kingston, ON: McGill-Queens University.

Treadwell, J., Briggs, D., Winlow, S., & Hall, S. (2012). Shopocalypse now: Consumer culture and the English riots of 2011. *British Journal of Criminology, 53*(1), 1–17.

Turner, J., Hogg, M., Oakes, P., Reicher, S., & Wetherell, M. (1987). *Rediscovering the social group: A self-categorization theory*. Oxford: Blackwell Publishers.

Turner, R., & Killian, L. (1987). *Collective behaviour* (3rd ed.). Englewood Cliffs, NJ: Prentice-Hall.

Tyler, T. (1990). *Why people obey the law*. New Haven, CT: Yale University Press.

Tyler, T. (2003). Procedural justice, legitimacy and the effective rule of law. In M. Tonry (Ed.), *Crime and justice: A review of research* (pp. 431–505). Chicago, IL: University of Chicago Press.

Tyler, T. (2007). *Legitimacy and criminal justice*. New York, NY: Russell Sage Foundation.

Tyler, T., & Huo, Y. (2002). *Trust in the law: Encouraging public cooperation with the police courts*. New York, NY: Russell Sage Foundation.

Van Ginneken, J. (1992). *Crowds, psychology, and politics, 1871-1899*. Cambridge: Cambridge University Press.

Waddington, D. (1992). *Contemporary issues in public disorder: A comparative and historical approach*. London: Routledge.

Waddington, D. (1996). Key issues and controversies. In C. Critcher & D. Waddington (Eds.), *Policing public order: Theoretical and practical issues* (pp. 1–36). Aldershot: Avebury.

Waddington, D. (2007a). *Policing public disorder: Theory and practice*. Devon: Willan Publishing.

Waddington, D. (2007b). Seattle and its aftershock: Some implications for theory and practice. *Policing, 1*(4), 380–389.

Waddington, D. (2013). A 'kinder blue': Analysing the police management of the Sheffield anti-'Lib Dem' protest of March 2011. *Policing and Society: An International Journal of Research and Policy, 23*(1), 46–64.

Waddington, D., Jones, K., & Critcher, C. (1989). *Flashpoints: Studies in public disorder*. London: Routledge.

Waddington, D., & King, M. (2005). The disorderly crowd: From classical psychological reductionism to socio-contextual theory – The impact on public order policing strategies. *The Howard Journal, 44*(5), 490–503.

Waddington, P. (1987). Towards paramilitarism: Dilemmas in policing public disorder. *British Journal of Criminology, 27*, 37–46.

Waddington, P. (1991). *The strong arm of the law: Armed and public order policing*. Oxford: Clarendon Press.

Waddington, P. (1993a). Dying in a ditch: The use of police powers in public order. *International Journal of the Sociology of Law, 21*(4), 335–353.

Waddington, P. (1994). *Liberty and order: Public order policing in a capital city*. London: University College London Press.

Waddington, P. (1998). Controlling protest in contemporary historical and comparative perspective. In D. Della Porta & H. Reiter (Eds.), *Policing protest: The control of mass demonstrations in western democracies* (pp. 117–140). Minneapolis, MN: University of Minnesota Press.

Waddington, P. (1999). *Policing citizens*. London: UCL Press.

Waddington, P. (2000). Orthodoxy and advocacy in criminology. *Theoretical Criminology, 4*(1), 93–111.

Waddington, P. (2003). Policing public order and political contention. In T. Newburn (Ed.), *Handbook of policing*. Cullompton: Willan.

Waddington, P. (2007). Editorial – Policing of public order. *Policing: A Journal of Policy and Practice, 1*(4), 375–379.

Wall, D. (1999). Mobilising Earth first! in Britain. In C. Rootes (Ed.), *Environmental movements: Local national and global* (pp. 81–100). London: Frank Cass.

White, D. (2006) A conceptual analysis of the hidden curriculum of police training in England and Wales. *Policing & Society: An International Journal of Research and Policy, 14*(4), 386–404.

Wilkinson, S. (2009). Riots. *Annual Review of Political Science, 12*, 329–343.

Winter, M. (1998). Police philosophy and protest policing in the Federal Republic of Germany, 1960-1990. In D. Della Porta & H. Reiter (Eds.), *Policing protest: The control of mass demonstrations in western democracies* (pp. 188–212). Minneapolis, MN: University of Minnesota Press.

Wright, A. (2002). *Policing: An introduction to concepts and practice*. Cullompton: Willan.

Chapter 3
An Analysis of the Current Police Response to Rioting

3.1 Introduction

Historically, protests and demonstrations have taken place as a response to industrial disputes or political events (Gravelle & Rogers, 2011). Protests and demonstrations have usually resulted from differences in social class and have attracted, as Gravelle and Rogers (2011, p. 112) describe, "individuals from a particular section of society." More recently, though, protests have involved better informed and more politically engaged, middle-class participants as well as "single issue" groups, such as environmentalists, animal rights proponents, and anti-globalizationists (Gravelle & Rogers, 2011). The change in the type of people who protest, the reasons for them protesting and the type of protest has demanded that the police review their crowd control techniques and implement accountability processes to ensure that the most appropriate response strategies are adopted (Gravelle & Rogers, 2011). Because the new form of protest includes elements of professionalization and comprises "hybrid protesters" (Button, John, & Brearly, 2002), an emphasis has been placed on ensuring that the actions taken by the police are "lawful, necessary, and proportionate" (Gravelle & Rogers, 2011, p. 112). These changes in protests, especially how protests are planned, organized and eventuate, according to Gravelle and Rogers (2011), indicate that "a new age of protesting may be upon us" (p. 113).

The response tactics used by most police agencies in western nations have been developed from experience and were able to be cultivated because protesters were usually a "known quantity" (Gravelle & Rogers, 2011). Tactics used by the police have included "'pushing and shoving', 'kettling,'" batons and shields, teargas, flash grenades, and specific firearms and ammunition, such as rubber or plastic rounds (Gravelle & Rogers, 2011, p. 113). With the new age of protests, the police, however, need to be able to balance their experience and use of strategies and tactics with new response strategies and tactics that have been shaped by human rights legislation (Gravelle & Rogers, 2011). The problems associated with the new form of protest became apparent to the police, according to Casciani (2009), during the

G. den Heyer, *Police Response to Riots*,
https://doi.org/10.1007/978-3-030-31810-9_3

G20 protests in London (2009) and in Pittsburgh (2009), where those participating came from all classes of society and were "lobbying on a plethora of issues, including climate change, the banking crisis, the recession, international business and capitalism" (Gravelle & Rogers, 2011, p. 113).

In addition to the change in protesting from influencing factors such as human rights, globalization and the use of social media have also influenced the form that protests take. The intensity of globalization and the escalation in the use of social media have created new opportunities for both police and protesters alike (Ellefsen, 2016). Both events have brought the actions of the police into the limelight and they have come under intense scrutiny from the public, media, judges, and politicians and this has created an environment for the police in which they cannot win.

In order to be able to understand the actions taken by protesters and why specific protests produced specific outcomes, the police need to view their response in the context of and in relation to the actions and reactions taken by protesters (Ellefsen, 2016). The police should be conscious of their actions both before the protest and while the protest is taking place as it is their actions that influence the actions that the protesters take and this in turn, subsequently affects the choices that both the police and protesters take in, what della Porta (2013) described as "a process involving innovation and adaptation" (p. 35). The actions that the police take during a disorder can lead protesters to react and adapt, which can change the level of threat that the police perceive, leading the police to reassess the tactics that are available and viable (Ellefsen, 2016). If the police include the reaction of the protesters to the tactics that they choose, this will make the outcome of using specific tactics more apparent and result in a reduction in the level of violence.

As noted in Chap. 2, extensive literature that examines the approach taken by the police to crowd management during protests and that identifies various options for the police to consider if they wish to improve their management of such events is available. However, no research has been conducted that would inform the police as to how they could improve their response to a riot, nor has any literature identified methods for managing protests that contain violent individuals or groups. As Her Majesty's Inspectorate of Constabulary (2011) noted, many commentators will claim that there is a need for the police to have better intelligence following a riot or a protest that has turned violent. However, as the Inspectorate highlighted, these events and the police response are "inherently messy events; complex and difficult" and intelligence "will never be perfect" (p. 5). Furthermore, even if the police were able to gather information, it would need to be tested for credibility and reliability, and this would create problems associated with the public's perception of the police in a democracy.

Violent protests or riots do not occur frequently, but when they do, they result in death, injury and extensive damage. The police response to violent protests has not changed completely nor has it become militarized (Wood, 2014). Wood (2014), noted that the majority of violent protests and riots usually initially involve "soft hat" policing strategies but as the police response becomes more organized, it may include a more militarized approach, of which Gillham, Edwards, and Noakes (2013) described as "strategic incapacitation."

It is clear that the policing of protests remains in a state of confusion and faces intensified public, media and political scrutiny (Wood, 2014). The issue for the police is how do they develop their capability further so that they can respond to riots and violent protest effectively while ensuring that the crowd control tactics that they use do not become over-militarized. The other issue is how do they manage closer public scrutiny.

This chapter comprises five sections. The first section discusses how the police have previously or traditionally responded to violent protests and riots. The second section examines the main factors that have been the catalyst for change in the police response to violent protest and riots. The third section investigates the influence of social media on the police response and the fourth section reviews the influence of police knowledge and the reactions of the police to the occurrence of a riot. The final section discusses crowd control strategies and examines the five types of public order policing.

3.2 The Traditional Response to Violent Protest and Riots

When the London Metropolitan Police was established in 1829, a military response to protest and disorder was adopted but by the 1950s and 1960s, the police had changed their handling of such events to one of "tolerance, compromise and accommodation" (Reiner, 1992). The police in London had used a "military structure and capacity" in the 1830s and 1840s and according to Silver (1971), that upon the passing of the Reform Bill of 1832, the Duke of Wellington stated that "[f]rom henceforth we shall never be able to carry on a government without the assistance and support of a military body. If we cannot have a regular army in such a state of discipline and efficiency as that the King can rely on them, we must and we shall have a National Guard in some shape or other" (p. 185).

Geary (1985), suggested that the policing of violent disorder in the UK had made a U-turn since 1829 and by the 1970s and 1980s, the police response had returned to a more "paramilitary" approach (Hills, 1995; Jefferson, 1987, 1990, 1993; Northam, 1988; P. Waddington, 1987, 1991, 1993a, 1993b) or as Reiner (1998), described, to a process of militarization. The return to this form of policing was brought about primarily by officers' concerns about the increase in protester violence and provocation (Reiner, 1998). Critics of the change in the police approach during this period based their censure on the militarized style of policing, not only because of the use of protective clothing and equipment but also because of the response structure and tactics used, the use of intelligence and the rapid deployment of large numbers of officers who had been trained in crowd control (Reiner, 1998). This also led to some critics arguing that the police crowd control squads were de facto "third forces" (Morris, 1985).

During the mid-1980s, the police approach became more pragmatic, but they kept the capability to implement more coercive actions (Reiner, 1998) or models of escalated force (McPhail, Schweingruber, & McCarthy, 1998). By the 1990s, the police had accepted the notion of negotiated management for controlling non-violent protests (McPhail et al., 1998). The change in the police response to disorder during this period was, according to Reiner (1998), a result of two factors. The first being the police reaction to specific disorder or riot events (industrial strikes, anti-nuclear and the anti-Vietnam war protests) and the second was the change in politics, of policing and of British society (Reiner, 1998).

The changes to the police approach of handling public disorder was slightly different in the USA, owing to the majority of riots being socially and racially based. The response to public disorder in the USA has always included a form of coercion, mass-arrest and the indiscriminate use of force (Kienscherf, 2014). Rioting began in the 1960s in New York City with the Bedford-Stuyvesant and Harlem riots beginning on 16 July and continuing through to 22 July 1964. The Los Angeles-Watts area riots followed in 1965, commencing 11 August until 16 August. Rioting in the USA continued almost every summer until 1968 (McPhail et al., 1998), spreading across the country; Chicago, Illinois, in 1965; Omaha, Nebraska, in 1966, and Newark, New Jersey, Detroit, Michigan, and Milwaukee, Wisconsin, in 1967, all differing in their level of violence, intensity and duration (McPhail et al., 1998, p. 54). A wave of rioting in 1968 followed the assassination of Martin Luther King Jr. Known as the Holy Week Uprising, extensive rioting occurred in Washington, DC, Chicago, Baltimore, Kansas City, Detroit, New York City, Pittsburgh, Cincinnati, Trenton, Wilmington, and Louisville.

A number of organizational and external factors brought about change in the police response to violent and non-violent protest in the 1970s. The first factor was the amount of public criticism of the actions taken by the police during the protests that took place in the 1960s (Kienscherf, 2014). The second factor related to the over-reaction of the police to the race and anti-war riots of the 1960s, with the insight of a number of more perceptive police leaders that saw that there was a need for change in how the police responded to violent and non-violent protests (Kienscherf, 2014; Perez, Berg, & Myers, 2003). The third factor was that by the early 1970s, various Commissions of Inquiry—the National Commission on Civil Disorder (Kerner Commission), the National Commission on the Causes and Prevention of Violence (Eisenhower Commission), and the National Commission on Campus Unrest (The Scranton Commission)—had all been established to examine the causes of urban unrest and violence (Kienscherf, 2014). The principal Commission was, however, the United States National Advisory Commission on Civil Disorders and they compiled a report in 1968, which was commonly referred to as the Kerner Commission. The Commission was established to investigate the police response to the 1967 race riots which had occurred across the country. The Commission found that the actions of the police were central in triggering more than half of the 24 riots that were examined in detail for the report (McPhail et al., 1998; National Institute of Justice, 1968). The Commission criticized the use of excessive force by the police, especially deadly force and found that the violence was often exacerbated, if not triggered by the actions of the police (McPhail et al., 1998; National Advisory Commission on Civil Disorders, 1968). The remaining factor that influenced a change in approach to the policing of protests was the decisions that were made by the courts that affected the rights of protesters (Kienscherf, 2014; McPhail et al., 1998). According to McPhail et al. (1998), "the courts were important in shaping the dimensions of the" change and for "setting the stage for, if not mandating, negotiated [crowd] management" (p. 58).

These factors changed in way that the police responded to protests in the mid- to late-1970s. A number of researchers described the change as a move away from an escalated force approach to a negotiated management approach (Kienscherf, 2014; McPhail et al., 1998; McPhail & McCarthy, 2005; Soule & Davenport, 2009). The changes made to the response to civil unrest were supported by the training given by the United States Army Military Police School (USAMPS), which delivered a civil disturbance orientation course (SEADOC) (Kienscherf, 2014). The 7-day course focused on how to counter urban riots and was delivered 56 times from February 1968 to April 1969 at Fort Gordon, Georgia (Kienscherf, 2014; McPhail et al., 1998).

A revised course (termed SEADOC II), which included the recommendations made by the Kerner and Eisenhower Commissions was introduced in May 1970 and continued until 1978 (Kienscherf, 2014). According to Kienscherf (2014), the revised course included strategic and tactical elements and a component called confrontation management, which was designed to prevent police officers from overreacting in the face of protester provocation. The course not only focused on riot control but also included education on managing a wider variety of protest activity. The tactical component emphasized the importance of a minimal use of necessary force (McPhail et al., 1998). The course provided the police with "more targeted and selective protest control tactics" and thereby created the basis for "the development of a negotiated management [crowd control] strategy" (Kienscherf, 2014, p. 12).

King (2013) claimed, however, that the negotiated management approach to crowd control imposed a normative structure on protest, resulting in protesters who did not follow the norm being identified as criminals and thereby, denied their right to political dissent. This implies that "the negotiated management strategy is not a more consensual approach to protest policing, but a 'multi-layered form of social control'" (King, 2013, p. 465). della Porta and Peterson (2005) made similar claims in their editorial in a special issue of the Policing and Society Journal when they observed that since the 1970s, many western governments had become more tolerant of protests and that protesting was "becoming institutionalized, or at least 'civilized', with a reduction in more radical forms of action" (pp. 233–234).

della Porta, in earlier research with Reiner (1998), also examined the change in police response to protest. These researchers claimed that the withdrawal of direct government intervention in the police response to protests appeared to have occurred at the same time that the police changed their response to protests. In other words, governments tended to leave the police to manage protests (della Porta & Reiter, 1998). The problem was that at the same time that governments were decreasing their intervention in the response to protests, the police were sensing that governments were leaving them to themselves to manage protests. The protests were generally the result of social or political problems and could only be resolved by the government (della Porta & Reiter, 1998).

One reason for the opposing trend in the police-government response to protests is that the police react to external demands, especially those made by the government (della Porta & Reiter, 1998). According to della Porta and Reiter (1998), the police seek to realize demands by the government, even if these demands affect democratic rights (see, for example, New Zealand Herald, 2000). della Porta and Reiter (1998), expanded on this by claiming that because of the relationship between the police and the government, "that if a government were to order a change in public order policies, the police would feel bound to comply" (p. 30). The claim may be technically correct but in the majority of western nations, there is a separation in the operational decision making between the police and the government and in the UK and their former colonies (including New Zealand and Australia), there is the notion of constabulary independence[1] (Jeffersen & Grimshaw, 1984).

The response taken by the police to public protest has changed markedly over the past few decades, with the majority of police forces around the world adopting protest-tolerant, negotiated management approaches (Human Rights Observer Team, 2006). The negotiated management approach usually includes the following five components: the protection of the basic right of free speech and peaceful assembly, tolerance of a reasonable level of community disruption, the initiation of ongoing communication with demonstrators, the use of arrest only whenever necessary and the use of force only to overcome resistance to arrest and to prevent death and serious injuries (Human Rights Observer Team, 2006, p. 4).

The question remains as to whether the new response philosophy is a genuine step in reforming the policing of protests or whether it is an attempt to legitimize police actions and improve public relations (Winter, 1998).

3.3 The Catalysts for Change in the Police Response to Violent Protests and Riots

A number of authors have claimed that the policing of protests changed after the violent protests during the 1999 World Trade Organization (WTO) conference in Seattle, USA (D. Baker, 2002; della Porta, Peterson, & Reiter, 2006; Noakes & Gillham, 2006; Noakes, Klocke, & Gillham, 2005; Vitale, 2005; Wood, 2014). The conference was overshadowed by a new type of violent protest (Gillham & Marx, 2000) that had more than 40,000 people participating (Seattle Police Department, 2000). The disruptive planning and tactics used by the protesters for "shutting down the WTO" had not been used previously, while the police response was seen as a failure, it was also seen as a watershed (termed "Pearl

[1] The most detailed exposition of constabulary independence came in the 1962 Royal Commission on the Police, which argued that chief constables should be given complete immunity from political influence in decisions to apply the law in particular cases—for example, in deciding whether to initiate a criminal investigation. More widely the report argued that a chief constable should have considerable room for discretion in areas such as the deployment of police resources (Muir, 2008).

Harbor" by Wood, 2014) that began a period of re-assessment of the strategies and tactics used by the police around the world when responding to violent crowds and protests (Gillham & Marx, 2000; Noakes & Gillham, 2006; Seattle Police Department, 2000; D. Waddington, 2007a).

According to Wood (2014), the violence that occurred during the Seattle protests justified the development of a new approach to protest policing, especially in the USA and Canada. The problem for police agencies is, however, that as soon as they develop new strategies to respond to protesters' actions, the large and increasingly diverse population of protesters change their actions again (O'Neill, 2004).

Prior to the protests in Seattle, the police perception of protesters was based primarily on the "history of the groups protesting" (cited in Noakes et al., 2005), which meant that the police responded to specific events or protests differently and based their response on the level of risk posed by the protesting group or the individuals within the group (Fillieule & Jobard, 1998; Jaime-Jimenez & Reinares, 1998; P. Waddington, 1998b, 1999). According to Tilly (2000), prior to Seattle, the police viewed protests on a continuum of perceived risk and this was based on the history of the personality of the protest group. The continuum consisted of three different types of protest, with contained protests being at one end, bad protests at the other end and transgressive protests in the middle. Contained protests are those where an identified protest group has obtained a permit to protest or have negotiated with the police (Noakes et al., 2005). The second type of protest is undertaken by transgressive groups or in other words, groups who are unfamiliar with the police, have a reputation for disorderly behavior or are likely to challenge or confront the police (Noakes et al., 2005). The third type of protesters are "Bad" protesters; those groups that the police identify as being radical or on the fringe or that include professional protesters (Fillieule & Jobard, 1998; Jaime-Jimenez & Reinares, 1998; P. Waddington, 1999).

The Seattle protests did not fit onto Tilly's (2000) continuum and they did not fit into any previous form of police response strategy. The main reason for the difference in the Seattle protests was the level of violence perpetrated by the protesters and that the protesters came from all around the world (della Porta & Peterson, 2005). The protesters were well organized and targeted their protests and vandalism toward specific international financial institutions which, according to della Porta and Peterson (2005), "not only challenged law and order, but also civil liberties" (p. 233).

The changing form of violent protest attracted the attention of a number of researchers who focused on the policing of these events (see for example, D. Baker, 2002, 2007; Gillham & Marx, 2000; D. Waddington, 2007a, 2009; P. Waddington, 1994, 1996, 2001). This early research was dominated by a debate on the use of tactics by the police, such as de-escalation and negotiating to manage the crowd (della Porta & Peterson, 2005). What was quickly realized by some researchers was that the policing of protests at international events, such as the G8 and G20 meetings needed to "be understood and researched as a distinctive category" within protest research (della Porta et al., 2006, p. 4; see also Ericson & Doyle, 1999; Gorringe & Rosie, 2008). The argument to consider the policing of protests of transnational meetings was based on the perspective that the policing of these events included extensive security preparations and involved government intervention (Gorringe & Rosie, 2008). What the researchers found with the police response to the protests at the G8 and G20 meetings was that the police had become more militarized and were not using the more tolerant approaches, such as that of negotiation (della Porta & Peterson, 2005).

The difference between the protests that occurred at the G8 and G20 meetings, according to Sheptycki (2005), was that the world had entered the era of globalization and the policing of political protests needed to be examined through a transnational lens. Wainwright and Ortiz (2006), in support of Sheptycki claimed that not only had the form of protesting changed, but the police response to these protests had changed as well. They noted that owing to this new form of violent protest the police response had become increasingly disciplined and militarized (Wainwright & Ortiz, 2006). These developments, according to P. Waddington (2007b), reinforced the need for a new response to such protests and that a new level of analysis was needed. With the comments made by these researchers in mind, the following sections of this chapter examine the protests at the 1999 Seattle WTO conference, the 2003 Miami FTAA meeting and the 2009 London G20 meeting and the effect that these have had on the police response to violent protests and riots.

3.3.1 1999 Seattle World Trade Organization Conference

The type of protest that occurred during the World Trade Organization conference, which was held in Seattle from November 29 to December 3, 1999, had not been seen in the city for many years and challenged the planning and the response by the Seattle Police Department (Wainwright & Ortiz, 2006). On November 30, 1999, non-violent protesters in Seattle were able to shut down the conference for 1 day, owing to the large number of protest participants and the action that they took of which, the police were not prepared for (de Armond, 2001). According to Noakes et al. (2005), the Seattle Police Department had negotiated a number of agreements with established, mainstream political groups who had stated prior to the start of the World Trade Organization conference that they would protest in Seattle. The police were not, however, able to negotiate agreements "with the grassroots wing of the global justice movement, which refused to agree to severe limits on their protests" (Noakes et al., 2005, p. 240).

It was the blockading of major intersections in downtown Seattle by the protesters that caused the police to lose control of security for the conference and this forced the police to cancel the opening day (Cockburn, St. Clair, & Sekula, 2000; Gillham & Marx, 2000; Herbert, 2007; Thomas, 2000). The initial success achieved by the protesters was, however, short-lived. Following the initial action taken by the protesters, the police response changed from one of being reactive to one of being proactive (National Lawyers Guild, 2004, cited in Starr & Fernandez, 2009), and this began the "battle for Seattle" (Thomas, 2000). The police attempted to disperse the protesters by using baton-charges and pepper spray, but instead of dispersing the protesters, it inflamed the situation (D. Waddington, 2007a). As the violence increased, the police retaliated by deploying tear gas and by using rubber bullets (Smith, 2001; D. Waddington, 2007a). The confrontation between the protesters and the police continued until the next day with order not being completely restored for another day (Seattle Police Department, 2000).

Prior to the WTO meeting, the city's streets had been designated for the use of both World Trade Organization conference delegates and protesters but following the disruption of the conference meeting by protesters, officials implemented a number of strategies to re-establish control, including the declaration of a civil emergency and the mobilization of 200 National Guard troops (Noakes et al., 2005). The police also cordoned a large area of the inner-city and used a number of less-than-lethal crowd dispersal tactics and weapons that included batons, pepper spray, bean bag projectiles, tear gas, baton-charges, and concussion grenades (Gillham & Marx, 2000; Seattle Police Department, 2000).

According to the police, the tactics used were consistent with their existing use-of-force policy and followed two of the guidelines that related to the continuum of force (Seattle Police Department, 2000). The two guidelines specified: "(1) that the force employed must be proportionate to the threat presented; and (2) that the officer never relinquishes the right to self-defense" (Seattle Police Department, 2000, p. 8).

In their report that was compiled after the action the police acknowledged that while they had planned for the WTO conference, their planning and deployment of staff was inadequate for responding to the situation that developed on November 30 (Seattle Police Department, 2000). The planning that had been undertaken by the police was founded on local, historical precedent of peaceful protest and their assumption of their success in managing the protests held during the 1993 Asia Pacific Economic Cooperation (APEC) Conference (Seattle Police Department, 2000).

Despite the Seattle Police Department having "received credible information of a serious threat to the Conference" 3 weeks prior to the World Trade Organization conference taking place (Seattle Police Department, 2000, p. 4), they did not plan for the violent protesting that occurred. According to the police, in response to this information, they approached a number of contiguous police agencies to ask them to commit to deploying more of their staff to assist with responding to the protests. They also established a small "flying squad" to identify and arrest violent protesters (Seattle Police Department, 2000). The police did not, however, plan for a worst-case scenario (Seattle Police Department, 2000). Given the large number of protesters entering the city in the days leading to the World Trade Organization conference, questions should have been raised by the intelligence staff.

Other weaknesses in the response taken by the police were in their command and control and in the deployment of their officers (Seattle Police Department, 2000). According to the report written after the action, command and control arrangements had failed early in the response, with the centralized Incident Commander in the Seattle Police Operations Center (SPOC) not having had a complete picture of the events and nor did the Commander know where the officers had been deployed (Seattle Police Department, 2000). The field Incident Commander had a span of control that was too wide to manage and this resulted in platoon commanders not being given command or direction (Seattle Police Department, 2000). These problems were compounded by the mutual aid agencies not having radios that had compatible frequencies, their officers not having personal riot protective equipment or receiving food and water while deployed (Seattle Police Department, 2000).

3.3.2 2003 Miami Free Trade Area of the Americas (FTAA) Meetings

On November 17, 2003, just short of 4 years after the Seattle World Trade Organization conference, protesters gathered to oppose the Free Trade Area of the Americas meetings in Miami (Starr & Fernandez, 2009). The police and the city council had based their planning for this event on the approach taken by the police in securing the 2000 Republican National Convention that had been held in Chicago. A number of different strategies were included to minimize the actions of the protesters who hoped to disrupt the meetings. The first strategy was to ensure that there was the capability to deploy a large numbers of police officers. More than 40 law enforcement agencies, seven of which were federal agencies (Starr & Fernandez, 2009) were deployed. A number of press conferences and media and community briefings were held to highlight that violent protesting was a criminal action (Starr & Fernandez, 2009). The briefings were also used to advise the community that downtown Miami would be in lock-down for the duration of the meeting (Starr & Fernandez, 2009). Another strategy employed was the passing of a city ordinance, which made it illegal for a broad range of items to be used as a weapon and for drawing public attention and disrupting the normal flow of traffic (Wainwright & Ortiz, 2006). The ordinance was designed specifically for the meetings and was only to remain in force for the duration of the meeting. Free speech zones were established and a no-go zone was created by erecting a fence around a 30-block area of downtown Miami (Starr & Fernandez, 2009; Wainwright & Ortiz, 2006).

A number of other proactive crowd control tactics were employed. These tactics included large-scale, pre-emptive arrests, the use of police intervention to remove violent and potentially violent individuals, the containment of protesters within the free-speech zones, the deployment of heavily armed police officers and the collection of intelligence from protesters (Starr & Fernandez, 2009; Wainwright & Ortiz, 2006).

The approach taken by the police and the city council in securing the meetings was described by the Miami Mayor as "the model for homeland defense" and became known as "the Miami Model" by protesters (Starr & Fernandez, 2009, p. 42). According to Starr and Fernandez (2009), the approach taken by the police not only minimized violent protesting but also limited the protest and the actions that the protesters took.

3.3.3 2009 London G20 Summit Meeting

From 28 March to 2 April 2009, more than 35,000 people participated in marches and protests that were held to coincide with the G20 Summit, which was held in London. The majority of the protests and protesters were peaceful, but there were a number of outbreaks of violence and vandalism in central London. The police, in response to the heightened threat of violence and damage to property, used a number of crowd management tactics, one of which was kettling.[2] The use of this tactic tragically led to a death of a protester and the force used by the police led to 145 complaints being laid with the Independent Police Complaints Commission (Gill & Sears, 2009). It was noted by Joyce (2010), that the use of kettling and the "acts of indiscipline by individual police officers seemed more appropriate to a former era of public order policing" and that the tactics adopted by the police during the G20 summit did not appear to support the argument that the police had moved away from escalated force, which had been a common aspect of the policing of protests during the late 1980s (p. 31).

On 15 April 2009, the Metropolitan Police Commissioner wrote to Her Majesty's Inspectorate of Constabulary requesting that a review of the response that the police took during the G20 protests be conducted (Murphy, 2009). The review resulted in two reports being published by the Inspectorate: Adapting to Protest on 5 July 2009 and Adapting to Protest—Nurturing the British Model of Policing in November 2009. Both reports examined a number of police strategic and tactical issues that related to the response to protests and to the delivery of public order policing in England and Wales. The report included a number of recommendations for the police (Gravelle & Rogers, 2011; Her Majesty's Inspectorate of Constabulary, 2011). The recommendations included the implementation of a "no surprise" communication policy that would advise of the actions that the police could take, enabling the protesters to make informed choices and that the police should establish a positive image with the media to foster public support (Gravelle & Rogers, 2011).

The two reports that were written in 2009 that examined the policing of riots substantiated the 1999 report produced by the Inspectorate, which had examined the policing of riots in the 1990s. The earlier report found that the number of protests were increasing and that the "nature of potential disorder" was broadening to include "environmental and associated issues" (Her Majesty's Inspectorate of Constabulary, 1999, p. 5). The problem for the police during the late 1990s was that the majority of forces were using outdated "strategies, tactics and equipment" which were based on the reactive experiences of the police when responding to the riots that occurred in 1980s and early 1990s (Her Majesty's Inspectorate of

[2] Kettling (also known as containment or corralling) is used by the police for controlling large crowds during demonstrations or protests. It involves the establishment of cordons of police officers who then move to contain a crowd within a limited area. Protesters are left only one choice of exit, which is controlled by the police (Davenport, 2009).

Constabulary, 1999; King, 2006). The Inspectorate reports warned that the problem had not dissipated, but had in fact, evolved even further, owing to a number of factors influencing the way that public order policing was being undertaken. The primary factor was a result of the increase in the scale and geographical spread of violent protests in 2009 and 2010 (Her Majesty's Inspectorate of Constabulary, 2011).

The weaknesses in the police response to the protests held during the G20 summit and the increasing occurrence of violent protests led to Her Majesty's Inspectorate of Constabulary to publish a third report in 2011, which evaluated the change in the protest environment and examined whether the policing of protests had changed since the publication of their earlier reports in 2009. The later report measured the changes that had been made in the policing of protests against the recommendations that were outlined in the two 2009 Inspectorate reports. The 2011 report found that:

1. there had "been clear changes in the care and effort invested in planning processes" prior and during the occurrence of violent protests and riots;
2. the police gave due consideration of the law;
3. the police considered the law prior to the use of public order tactics;
4. the police established dialogue with protest groups; and
5. "the wide array of communication initiatives intended to reach out to potential protesters, counter protesters, affected communities and the wider public" (Her Majesty's Inspectorate of Constabulary, 2011, p. 17).

The report also claimed that "[t]he investment made by forces in community engagement before, during and after events has been impressive and undoubtedly assisted in achieving operational objectives and maintaining the peace, as well as enhancing community and public confidence" (Her Majesty's Inspectorate of Constabulary, 2011, p. 17).

3.3.4 The Effect that Transnational Protests Have Had on the Policing of Violent Protest

The anti-globalization or transnational protests, such as those that occurred in Seattle, London and Miami, Melbourne's World Economic Forum in 2000, Melbourne's G20 summit in 2006 and Sydney's APEC meeting in 2007 all have a primary place in the history of the policing of riots (Sheptycki, 2005). Prior to the protests in Seattle, Miami and London, the police had become more tolerant of minor infringements of the law in order to allow protesters to exercise their right to protest (della Porta & Zamponi, 2013). The police were using the negotiated management approach to manage protest crowds because this approach had been successful in decreasing the number and intensity of confrontations between protesters and the police (Gilham & Noakes, 2007). This trend, however, was reversed in the 2000s with the approach only being adopted at anti-globalization protest events rather than at transnational protests (della Porta & Zamponi, 2013).

The policing of these events had become "increasingly ambiguous," with the police needing to balance the security requirements of internationally protected persons with the rights of individuals to protest (D. Baker, 2016). These protests provided a basis on which to develop new methods to police mass protest (D. Baker, 2016).

In the early 2000s, Noakes and colleagues, in two separate articles, claimed that the actions of anti-globalization protesters in Seattle in 1999 were the catalyst in the "innovative and arguably more repressive police policies for the handling of major political demonstrations in North America and Western Europe." These policies were based on the "new penology" approach for dealing with offenders (Noakes et al., 2005; Noakes & Gillham, 2006, cited in D. Waddington, 2007a, p. 118). The penology approach, according to P. Waddington (2007b), increased the focus on the security of the public and did not include any examination of the occurrence of crime. This implies that in the context of the policing response to violent protest, "the introduction of innovative techniques for dealing with 'transgressive' (uncooperative and potentially violent) as opposed to 'contained' (responsible and law-abiding) protesters" (p. 119) was adopted as a response strategy. According to Noakes et al. (2005) and Noakes and Gillham (2006), the majority of police agencies in western nations have adopted strategic and tactical crowd control management techniques that have been influenced by the "penology" approach to manage protests. The techniques that have been adopted have included the use of negotiated management to contain protesters to specific areas and strategic incapacitation[3] techniques for maintaining control of protesters (D. Waddington, 2007a).

The major challenges for the police when policing protests at international meetings or summits are the presence of a large numbers of protesters, the violent intent of some protesters and the diverse range of actions taken by protesters (Human Rights Observer Team, 2006). As a result of protester actions, the police have moved away from responding with the strategy of negotiated management and have responded with more of a militarized, coercive and punitive response (Human Rights Observer Team, 2006).

One of the main techniques that the police use to incapacitate protests is kettling (Donson, Chesters, Welsh, & Tickle, 2004). The use of kettling has led to sections of the public no-longer believing that the police are separated from politics and "perceive them to be as aligned with politicians and the political will of government" (Gravelle & Rogers, 2011, p. 114). The use of techniques such as kettling led Mitchell and Staeheli (2005) to claim "that mass protests have become so 'routinized' and 'neutralised' by the police as to render them virtually ineffectual" (cited in D. Waddington, 2007a, p. 138), and to protesters "being resentful and defiant," increasing the likelihood of violence (D. Waddington, 2007a, p. 138).

D. Baker (2016) suggested that using a strategy of negotiating with protesting groups could still be used in the lead-up to an event, however, during transnational

[3] Following the Seattle riots, researchers created the phase 'strategic incapacitation' to describe the policing of transnational events which included such strategies as no-protest zones, the use of less-than-lethal force by the police, mass arrest and intelligence gathering (Gilham & Noakes, 2007).

events, the police usually use protest or exclusionary zones to manage protesters. The establishment of protest or exclusionary zones is usually enforced by a large number of police officers who have been fitted-out in riot-safety equipment and this can have a psychological effect on protesters and can create the perception that the police will use force (D. Baker, 2016; della Porta et al., 2006; Farnsworth, 2004; Waddington & King, 2005). The deployment of riot officers is often used to deter violent protest and vandalism (D. Baker, 2016). Sheptycki (2005) and Waddington and King (2005) claimed that a high-end police response to protests at international events is an aberration or exception but is a move "away from escalated force and towards negotiated management." This means that the high-policing approach is the opposite to the trend of using crowd management techniques, which involves the use of escalated force and proactive policing strategies and tactics (Sheptycki, 2005, p. 329). Escalated force and proactive policing strategies and tactics enable the police to portray the desire to be more accountable and democratic (Gorringe & Rosie, 2008).

There were a number of reasons for the change in the police response to the actions of anti-globalization protesters. The first reason was that the protesters rejected the negotiated management model of protest and adopted the use of confrontational tactics. Protesters adopted these tactics in the mid- to late 1990s and this meant that the response taken by the police was more likely to be repressive (Fernandez, 2009; Gorringe & Rosie, 2008; Noakes & Gillham, 2006). One of the reasons why the negotiated management approach was rejected by the anti-globalization movement was its broad base. Having a broad base means that divisions would be formed when coordinating protest strategies because the movement is non-hierarchical and leaderless (D. Waddington, 2007a). The lack of structure to a protest means that the police cannot negotiate with a specific individual or group, which subsequently results in a conservative police response, consisting of the deployment of a large number of officers and the use of containment tactics (D. Waddington, 2007a). In the UK, containment tactics became known as strategic incapacitation (Noakes et al., 2005; D. Waddington, 2007a). The use of the tactic was problematic and aggravated the relationship between protesters and the police (Noakes et al., 2005). Its use caused extensive backlash from the public when it was used during the protests against the World Bank and the International Monetary Fund in 2000 and during the anti-war demonstration in New York in February 2003 (Mitchell & Staeheli, 2005).

The second reason for the change in the police response centers upon the perception that the police held of protesters. The change in perception formed as a result of the threat that anti-globalization protesters posed. According to Fernandez (2009), the police developed "more sophisticated modes of control" to respond to the more confrontation tactics of protesters that were "neither purely repressive nor entirely negotiated" (p. 15). The police also used "an effective mixture of hard- and soft-line tactics including the use of new 'non-lethal weapons' as well as laws, codes, regulations, and public relations strategies that attempt[ed] to control protest spaces directly and indirectly" (Fernandez, 2009, p. 15).

The change also came about as a result of the 2001 terrorist attacks on the World Trade Center in New York. Although the attacks did not relate to anti-globalization protests the security of public events and protests became more planned and structured (Fernandez, 2009).

3.3.5 Conclusion

The police have learned lessons from their previously aggressive and confrontational approach in responding to violent protesters (D. Baker, 2002). In addition, an increase in the level of collective and individual accountability, intense scrutiny from the public, the establishment of internal investigation departments and internal reviews (Sarre, 2001), and an increase in the recording of the actions taken by police officers on mobile phones have all led the police to review their disorder response tactics. These environmental changes have meant that there are high political stakes involved in providing security for transnational meetings and summits and this leaves the police with very few options to accommodate the protesters' right to protest (D. Waddington, 2007a). This has led to the "impersonal and unyielding" policing of such events and has resulted in the use of indiscriminate police tactics; causing further protester "resistance and defiance" (D. Waddington, 2007a, p. 384).

Several of the protest response tactics used by the police have become central to the security framework used for the security of transnational meetings (Noakes & Gillham, 2004). These tactics include:

- the establishment of no protest zones from the erection of large concrete and metal fence barriers;
- the disruption of safe spaces, such as convergence centers where protesters could congregate to sleep, eat and acquire information;
- the use of less-lethal weapons to incapacitate protesters so that the police can retake control;
- the use of electronic surveillance technology to provide real-time information on demonstrators' activities; and
- pre-emptive arrests of protester leaders and large numbers of protesters (McCarthy & McPhail, 1998; Noakes et al., 2005; Starr & Fernandez, 2009).

The study of the policing of anti-globalization protesters at transnational meetings demonstrates that the police have been able to react quickly to the continually changing forms of violence and actions (Fernandez, 2009). The police appear to have learned more from the protests in Seattle than the protesters have. They have been able to prevent protest action at subsequent transnational meetings (de Armond, 2001). The ability to learn from earlier events forms is what researchers term "police knowledge," and it is this factor that has played a principal role in determining the policing response to violent protest (della Porta, 1995, 1998; King, 2006; D. Waddington, 2007a). In this regard, it is the police, the perception of governments, public opinion and the police interaction with the protesters that forms the context in which the police response to protests is developed and it is this that transforms into police knowledge (della Porta & Reiter, 1998). Therefore, police knowledge is "the main intervening variable between structure and action" (della Porta & Reiter, 1998, p. 22), and will determine the response taken by the police in any given event.

3.4 The Influence of Social Media on the Police Response to Protests

The establishment of various forms of social media has fundamentally changed the way that a large proportion of the public communicates and shares information (S. Baker, 2012a). The implementation of Facebook in 2004 and Twitter, 2 years later, has made communication mobile and instant, broadening "the spatial and temporal configuration of contemporary public life" (S. Baker, 2012a, p. 44). The changes in communication have given rise to an emerging social trend that has been termed the "mediated crowd" (S. Baker, 2012a, p. 44). The mediated crowd has been described as a number of individuals who have formed a crowd virtually, rather than gathering physically into a crowd in a specific location (S. Baker, 2012a). The virtual and the physical are not, however, mutually exclusive and people are able to move between the two or participate in both at the same time (S. Baker, 2012a). This means that a mediated crowd differs from a traditional crowd because of their mobility and use of technology and because they are able to inform a community instantly and affect a mass mobilization from a wide geographical area (S. Baker, 2012a).

The problem for the police is the scale and the speed that a mediated crowd is able to gather in a physical location or locations (S. Baker, 2012a). As a result of the speed and scale of a mediated crowd gathering in the 2011 London riots, social media became one of the main areas of focus for research into the cause of the riots (S. Baker, 2012a). The possible cause of the 2011 London riots led to one publication terming the riots as "The Blackberry Riots" as it was claimed that the BlackBerry Messenger (BBM) service enabled users to invite their contacts to gather at a specific location, leading to the formation of crowds who ultimately rioted ((The) Economist, 2011). Eddo-Lodge (2011) also discussed the role that the social media played in the 2011 London riots and claimed that Facebook and the BBM were the primary forms of communication that were used to incite violence and that Twitter was used to communicate "regular reports and updates of a credible and false nature" (p. 45).

Social media was also used extensively by climate change protesters in the UK to advise and connect with "other like-minded individuals" (Gravelle & Rogers, 2011, p. 113). The campaigners used social media to create discussion blogs, upload videos of their protests, and distribute the interviews of individual protesters (Lewis, 2009). The use of social media by the protesters enabled them to influence the way that the public viewed their campaign. These practices often placed the police at a disadvantage, especially in relation to specific events and "before an official explanation or response to the same incident was forthcoming" (Gravelle & Rogers, 2011, p. 113), from the police.

Another problem for the police in relation to the use of social media and enabling technology is that they have created the citizen journalist. Citizen journalism is a term defined by Allan and Thorsen (2009) as "the spontaneous actions of ordinary people, caught up in extraordinary events, who felt compelled to adopt the role of a news reporter" (cited in Greer & McLaughlin, 2010, p. 1045). Peat (2010), expanded on this description with "armed with cellphones, BlackBerries or iPhones, the average Joe is now a walking eye on the world, a citizen journalist, able to take a photo, add a caption or a short story and upload it to the Internet for all their friends, and usually everyone else, to see" (cited in Greer & McLaughlin, 2010, p. 1045).

The problem of citizen journalists for the police stems not only from the fact that they are able to record or capture images of the actions taken by the police but that they are able to circulate the images quickly and to a large number of people including the media. As discussed above, the climate change protesters in the UK circulated images of the policing of the event before the police command was able to be briefed about a specific incident and before a statement about the incident could be released. Protesters are, therefore, able to control the direction of the media and the public perception of the police, which is usually to depict the police as incompetent, disorganized or aggressive.

As a result of the ability of citizen journalists being able to collect potential news, media organizations have created a facility for the images of incidents and events to be uploaded immediately, which allows the images to be considered for use as scheduled and breaking-news items in the mainstream media (Glaser, 2004; Pavlik, 2008; Reich, 2008; Wallace, 2009). According to Deuze (2008), citizen journalist images, can in turn, generate more "information and images, fuelling 'endless remixes, mashups and continuous edits'" and images can be photo-shopped to suit the perceptive of the media article or publication (p. 861). Subsequently, the facts of the incident can be lost to the heat of sensationalism and the method used to portray the incident usually places the police in a position from which they are unable to recover from in the eyes of the public.

3.4.1 *Case Study: The 2009 London G20[4] and the Rise of the Citizen Journalist*

The examination of the policing of the 2009 London G20 was important for three reasons. The first was that there had been concern about the use of policing tactics that were employed during the protests in 2008 and the second reason was that the policing of the G20 would be scrutinized by independent monitors (Greer & McLaughlin, 2010). The third reason was the number of people recording the events (Greer & McLaughlin, 2010), which was further exacerbated by the police use of

[4] This case study draws extensively on the comments and analysis of Greer and McLaughlin (2010).

crowd containment tactics within confined areas, resulting in a "captive audience" of bystanders and passers-by (Greer & McLaughlin, 2010). A "hyper-mediatized, high-surveillance context" was created, in which there was no ability to control information or communications by the police or media organizations (Greer & McLaughlin, 2010, p. 1050).

The incident that became the measure for gauging the state of policing of the G20 protests were the actions taken by a police officer that had led to the death of a part-time newspaper agent who was making his way home. The event was televised the following weekend and was "accompanied by the first calls for a public inquiry" (Greer & McLaughlin, 2010, p. 1050). The call for a public inquiry into the policing of the protest gained momentum with the release of real-time video footage of the actions taken by the police officer that led to newspaper agent's death and the establishment of a campaign website by the agent's family (Greer & McLaughlin, 2010). The website called for an investigation into "(1) the overall policing of G20 and (2) the actions of officers attached to specialist units" (Greer & McLaughlin, 2010, p. 1051).

The problem for the police and for politicians was the media's initial response to the death and the tactics that the police used during the protest. The media focused on the videos that emerged of the death and the tactics that the police used and this attention subsequently evolved into criticism of the police and their use of "violence" (Greer & McLaughlin, 2010). The media highlighted "two major issues that challenged not only the police handling of the G20 protests but also the credibility of the [London Metropolitan Police Service] MPS:

1. the problem of police violence as indicated by the sheer number of videoed incidents and witness statements that were coming to light;
2. the possibility that the MPS statement was intended to mislead on the events surrounding Ian Tomlinson's death" (Greer & McLaughlin, 2010, p. 1051).

According to Greer and McLaughlin (2010), "the 'story' of G20 was re-ordered and re-interpreted within" the context of a change in focus from protester to police violence, which led to questions being asked about the public order policing strategy and the tactics that were used by the MPS (p. 1053). The re-ordering and re-interpreting of the policing of the G20 protests also led to the identification of a number of other weaknesses and problems in the police response to the violent protest. These weaknesses and problems have been summarized as:

1. the extensive criticism of the MPS
2. the need for the MPS to develop more positive relations with the media
3. protest groups using more sophisticated technology
4. the implications of the increase in the number of the citizen journalists for the policing of protests
5. the number of public inquiries that were established to critique and examine the police response to the G20 protests
6. the raising of wider questions about public order policing strategies and tactics, such as deploying untrained officers to protests, "the concealment of police

identification numbers, the use of indiscriminate heavy-handed 'containment' (especially 'kettling') and 'distraction tactics' and the role of the Territorial Support Group (TSG)" (Greer & McLaughlin, 2010, pp. 1053–1054).

3.5 The Relevancy of Elaborated Social Identity Model and Flashpoints Model in the Police Response to Protests

As discussed in Chap. 2, the Elaborated Social Identity Model (ESIM) assumes that a protest crowd will react as a group to "any police use of force perceived as indiscriminate and/or illegitimate" (D. Waddington, 2013, p. 47). This means that as a crowd becomes unified it becomes easier for proponents of disorder to encourage other crowd members to challenge the police (Drury & Reicher, 2000). As a result of these assumptions, the model has provided "four specific principles" that have become central to the development of a doctrine of crowd management (D. Waddington, 2007b), and these have been used to form the basis for an effective public order policing response (Drury & Reicher, 2000). The four principles are:

1. education of the police about the crowd (understanding the various "social identities," values, beliefs and objectives of the different sections of the crowd);
2. facilitation of protesters (assisting protesters to achieve their legitimate aims);
3. communication with the crowd (maintaining contact and employing negotiation, both prior to and during the event, with the intention of forging agreements, and avoiding any misunderstandings or unpleasant surprises); and
4. differentiation of the crowd (resisting the tendency to treat all members of the crowd in uniform manner, regardless of whether they are "guilty" or "innocent") (Reicher et al., 2007; Reicher, Stott, Cronin, & Adang, 2004, cited in D. Waddington, 2013, p. 47).

The Elaborated Social Identity Model has been used successfully in a number of cities in Sweden where the police used an approach called Dialogue Policing (Holgersson & Knutsson, 2011). Dialogue Policing involves two parts. The first part includes pre-event discussions (or dialogue) with protest organizers with the intention of identifying expectations, explaining any protest or route restrictions and assisting the protesters to achieve their legitimate objectives (D. Waddington, 2013). The second part includes the immersion of Dialogue Police[5] into a crowd during a protest (D. Waddington, 2013). Immersion into a crowd enables the Dialogue Police to explain the actions of the police to protesters and provides information to police commanders as to any potential violence or risk (D. Waddington, 2013).

[5]Dialogue police officers are specific assigned during dangerous or potentially dangerous public events that are trained in dialogue, de-escalation, and non-confrontation tactics (see for example The National Police Board, 2010).

3.6 Police Knowledge and the Reaction of the Police to the Occurrence of a Riot

As a result of rioting and violent protesting becoming more socially and politically salient, one of the more important requirements for the police is to ensure that they have the capability and capacity to be able to effectively respond and manage larger-sized crowd events (Police Executive Research Forum, 2015). The capability and capacity of the police depends upon the police being able to "act deliberately and with thought, developing tactics and techniques for controlling those who challenge authority" (cited in Fernandez, 2009, pp. 6–7; Morris & Mueller, 1992; Tarrow, 1998; Giugni, McAdam, & Tilly, 1999).

One approach that the police can take to plan for and manage their capability and capacity to effectively respond to riots and violent protests is to assess the level of risk that violence may occur and the likelihood that violence may occur. The level of risk involved in conducting policing activities, however, has not previously been calculated (Waddington & Wright, 2008). Waddington and Wright (2008), claimed that while the police do identify hazards, they do not estimate the risk involved in operational policing and do not consider the risk in the use of force. Waddington and Wright (2008, p. 486) also claimed that owing to the rare use of force used by the police it is "almost impossible to isolate risk."

This perception is now outdated. Since the early 2000s, the majority of police forces in the UK, Australia, and New Zealand have used different force escalation models and various threat assessment processes for the deployment of resources to security events. The risk assessment processes used by these police agencies has been reinforced by the use of intelligence-led policing and the engagement of intelligence analysts.

The issue of risk, however, is only one factor involved when the police are making strategic decisions about violent protest and riot response. The actual choices and decisions made by the police, according to della Porta (1998), depends upon the culture of the specific police agency and their organizational structure. Decision-making is further complicated by the political structure of the government and the "reality" of the situation (della Porta, 1998). What della Porta (1998) means by the term reality is the police understanding of the actions that protesters take, the resources available and the other commitments or business-as-usual problems that also need to be managed. The police understanding or perception of the situation is what della Porta (1998) refers to as police knowledge or the "images held by the police about their role and the external challenges they are asked to face" (pp. 228–229). This implies that the strategic and tactical options that could be used by the police in response to violent protest are linked to the police understanding of protesters and that of their role (della Porta, 1998). The constraining factor for the police is that in any response, while applying the law, they usually attempt to portray themselves as being neutral (della Porta, 1998). It is, however, the protesters' perception of how the law is being applied by the police that will determine the outcome of the police response.

One of the major weaknesses in the police knowledge of how to respond to violent protest and riots is that they do not have a common or recognized approach that they can take toward those individuals or groups that are involved (Joyce, 2010). This is different for permitted protests, where the police are able to negotiate with legitimate or contained protesting groups (Joyce, 2010). The problem for the police arises with transgressive protest groups, who are often anti-authoritarian, unwilling to negotiate with the police and will undertake protest actions that includes vandalism and confronting the police (Joyce, 2010). This means that legitimate protests that include transgressive protest groups or individuals are usually managed by a more proactive policing approach, which is one based on the prior experience or knowledge of the police (Joyce, 2010).

There are two other factors involved in police knowledge that influence the strategic decision making by the police in relation to their response. The first is that the occurrence of a riot will often catch the police by surprise and subsequently the rioters will be perceived by the police as challenging their authority and legitimacy (Wood, 2014). This leads the police to reflect upon the effectiveness of their response strategies and will often lead to an evaluation and assessment of their capacity and their capability to respond to such events. The second factor is that the police response will result in criticism from the public and the media and often from politicians, which can result in the public questioning their legitimacy, meaning, and identity (Winter, 1998). Winter (1998) states that this implies that decision-making by the police is not only influenced by the factors that comprise police knowledge but also by the reaction of the public and that the police response to riots takes place in two stages; the first is the police response and the second is the public reaction following the police response.

3.7 Crowd Control Strategies

In the late-1990s and then again in the early-2000s, Donatella della Porta and colleagues completed extensive research on the approaches that the police took in response to protests (della Porta et al., 2006; della Porta & Reiter, 1998). Wood (2014) claimed that this research identified that the protest response strategies adopted by the police were a result of the political system and the police organization and its culture. These factors were, however, constrained by police knowledge of the protesters and their intentions during an event (Wood, 2014). The earlier research described a model that was developed based on the interactions between the police, the public and protesters within the police interpretation of their operating environment and this was used to explain why the police use different protest response strategies (Wood, 2014). At about the same time, a second researcher also concluded that the policing of protests was based on a number of factors, "including time, place, space and the characteristics of the people involved in the protest" (Hall, 1998, p. 226). The della Porta and Reiter (1998) model maintains that the police response strategies are determined on two levels, with the first level comprising five influencing variables:

1. Organizational features of the police;
2. Configurations of political power;
3. Public opinion;
4. Police occupational culture; and
5. Police interactions with protesters (della Porta & Reiter, 1998).

The second level of the model is the concept of police knowledge, which is the constraint or the controlling parameter of the first level[6] of influencing variables. Police knowledge is, however, an outcome of the structure utilized by a police agency and the political environment in which it operates (della Porta et al., 2006).

The theory developed by della Porta and colleagues provides a comprehensive framework for examining the policing of illegitimate and violent protests. The theory was supported by P. Waddington (2007b), who emphasized that political influence is the most important determinant in the development of police response strategies and tactics. According to P. Waddington (2007b), the police may even "die in a ditch" to achieve the implicit objectives of the government of the day (p. 18). Consequently, the police may deploy strategies based on implicit or explicit political pressure (D. Waddington, 2007a), to resolve actions taken by protesters such as those taken during the 2011 Wall Street Occupation protests.

The political influence on the decisions made by the police was also identified by Jeffersen and Grimshaw (1984). These researchers proposed that senior police develop their protest response strategies within the context of three specific "audiences":

1. Legal—the courts, police authorities, and the UK Home Secretary;
2. Democratic—politicians and the community (at large); and
3. Occupational—peers of all ranks and other policing organizations (Jeffersen & Grimshaw, 1984).

The theory of different audiences that influence the decisions made by the police is useful according to P. Waddington (2007b), as it "also provides a useful basis for explaining the on-the spot decisions made by commanding officers caught up in the heat of public order events" (p. 20).

An alternative model to that developed by della Porta and colleagues was proposed by D. Waddington (1992), who claimed that the theories that relate to the policing of protests can be differentiated on a continuum. At one end of the continuum are theories that are "police-centric" or those developed by the police and at the opposite end are the theories or perspectives that are radical/Marxist (Sheptycki, 2005). Between the poles of the continuum there are a number of social

[6] Police knowledge was defined by della Porta and Reiter (1998) as "the police's perception of external reality, which shapes the concrete policing of protest on the ground" (p. 2).

and political theories that explain the policing of protest and these can be used to develop a model that can predict how and when legitimate protests will turn into a riot (see Jefferson, 1990; Marx, 1998; Waddington et al., 1987). According to D. Waddington (1992), the police-centric theories provide an explanation as to how the police make decisions about "what is to be done" during the response to a protest, while the radical/Marxist theories are about the repression of protest by the police.

Linking the della Porta and colleagues research with D. Waddington's continuum, de Lint (2005) claimed that the police have a range of tactics for responding to violent protests all of which will be applied differently because of the form that a protest takes, the perceived threat posed by a protest and the experience of the police. The police tactics used may, however, be examined further and a clear differentiation between the forms of protest may be identified, especially if the protests are viewed as being a "political challenge to authority" (de Lint, 2005, p. 192).

Using the idea of D. Waddington's (1992) continuum, de Lint (2005) used a matrix to demonstrate that the strategic and tactical responses to a riot that the police use could comprise of a number of options, depending on whether there is agreement by the protesters to the authority of the police. This means that the police response can be plotted on the matrix according to the three intersecting dimensions of "the politics of law, the politics of enforcement, and the politics of consent"[7] (de Lint, 2005, p. 182). The matrix has been presented in Fig. 3.1 and shows the politics of law on the horizontal axis and the politics of order (and enforcement) on the vertical axis. This structure results in the five ideal types of public order policing: consent policing, high stakes policing, conflict policing, disordered policing, and crisis policing (de Lint, 2005, p. 183), which has been presented in Fig. 3.1 (Table 3.1).

An alternative perspective as to how the police develop their response strategies has been proposed by Starr et al. (2011). According to these researchers, police protest response tactics "are in effect mass and individual psychological operations, serving to marginalize, isolate, delegitimize, and demonize dissenters and dissent" and the researchers claim that this is a form of political violence (p. 21). This view is based, however, on historical studies of totalitarian regimes and not on the policing of protests in democratic western countries (Starr et al., 2011). The weakness in our understanding of the policing of protests is, as Starr et al. (2011) suggested, that researchers have not considered the multiplicity of the effects that the response tactics used have on society other than on the immediate victims.

[7] de Lint (2005, p. 182) defines each of these variables as: The politics of law—the legitimacy of rulemaking or the legislative function; the politics of consent—the legitimacy of rule following or the value of strong compliance with the polity; the politics of enforcement—the legitimacy of the enforcement function.

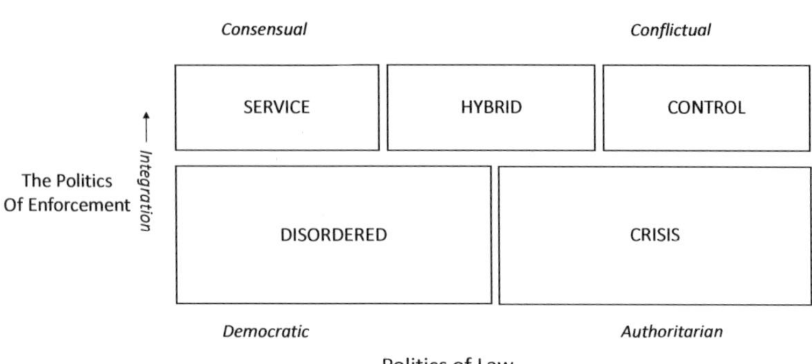

Fig. 3.1 Five types of public order policing (*Adapted from* de Lint, 2005, *p. 183*)

Table 3.1 Five types of public order policing defined

	Type of public order policing	Definition
1	Service policing	This type of police response is based on consent and is professional, knowledgeable, representative, and effective in maintaining public order maintenance. The form of order maintenance tactics will be appropriate to the circumstances.
2	Control policing	This response is professional, knowledgeable, representative, and effective in a protest environment where there is exclusivity and division. The crowd control tactics are more about maintaining public order in exceptional circumstances or divided rule.
3	Hybrid policing	This response uses dual control strategies (information-coercion) to maintain public order. The response gives the appearance of service policing and is capable of limiting violence but uses informational or communications resources. The police, however, maintain the capability to use force to manage the dissenting protesters (Iron fist in velvet glove).
4	Disordered policing	Disordered policing is under-professionalized, under-representative, inexpert, and ineffective order maintenance in an environment of public consent or in circumstances favorable for integrative policing. Police are not legitimate because they introduce disintegration through faulty or unprofessional enforcement practices, including quick resort to coercive force and rule breaking, and organizational and operational misalignments.
5	Crisis policing	Crisis policing is disintegrative policing in a disputed ground context or where there is political fracture. The response resorts to explicit protection of the executive function of the government of the day and is expressed in routine violations of civil rights.

Adapted from de Lint (2005, *p. 183*)

3.7.1 The Application of the Police Response Models

The della Porta and Reiter (1998) model has been used to examine the difference in the use of police protest response strategies in Europe and in the USA and has been used to question the changes in the police response to more proactive and accommodating styles in the 1980s and 1990s (Wood, 2014). The application of the model to the protests that occurred in Europe and the USA in the 1980s and 1990 resulted in the identification of police response strategies that are transformative and change over time (Wood, 2014), which indicates the importance of recognizing the interaction between the police and the protesters as this forms the basis for the police response (Scholl, 2013).

To measure whether the police have successfully responded to a protest depends upon whether the protesters have been able to make their point peacefully (Her Majesty's Inspectorate of Constabulary, 2011). To achieve this objective, police leadership is required in addition to understanding the purpose of the police, the existence of an operational plan, appropriately trained officers, communication prior to the event and the use of discretion (Her Majesty's Inspectorate of Constabulary, 2011). The use of discretion is one of the most important policing strategies involved in public order, as protests can become violent or turn into riots if the protesters perceive that the police have violated their rights or have overreacted to an incident (Klein, 2012). The perception of protesters, however, needs to be tempered with the research findings of Favre and Fillieule (1994), who claimed that demonstrations seldom become violent because of the actions that the police take. The researchers claimed that only 5% of the protests that they had studied had become violent and turned into a riot that had included vandalism and attacks on people (Favre & Fillieule, 1994).

The importance of the interaction between the police and the protesters is also applicable in a riotous situation. Based on comparative research that examined the 1992 Los Angeles riots and the 2005 French riots, Simiti (2012) found that riots were not coherent or unified events but were usually fragmented and nonlinear in form. While Moran and Waddington (2016) claimed that riots were "volatile, discontinuous and comprise often very contradictory elements," and usually occurred as "a number of different and spatially dispersed incidents" (p. 33). This implies that riots are "a continuous but fragmented process of forming and dissolving, during which multiple shifts occur from planned to spontaneous, non-violent to violent, collective to individual actions and vice versa" (p. 33).

The time-tested response to protests and riots is to deploy a large number of police officers. The problem for the police, however, is getting the balance right between deploying too many officers and not deploying enough should violence occur. The deployment of too many officers can actually trigger violence within the protest (Klein, 2012).

The deployment of a large number of officers to a protest is the usual approach as the police prepare for worst-case scenarios (D. Waddington, 1992). This enables the police to control a situation, although some commenters claim that such an approach is militarized and does not make use of information-gathering, intelligence, or covert surveillance and ultimately, riot technology becomes the weapon used by the police to dominate public order (D. Baker, 2002; Marx, 1998; Wood, 2014). One of the roles of the police is to control and maintain public order (Hall, 1998). This implies that the police will develop and implement a response strategy based on how they perceive the threat posed by the protesters (D. Baker, 2011).

According to P. Waddington (1991), the traditional approach of the policing of protests has failed and there is therefore a need to look for more appropriate crowd control strategies. A number of researchers of protests and riots have noted that the role of the police is important in understanding how collective violence is triggered (see for example Bergesen, 1982; Giugni & Wisler, 1998; Koopmans, 1993; Marx, 1979; McCarthy & McPhail, 1998; McPhail et al., 1998; Rasler, 1996; Salert & Sprague, 1980). The problem is that any research that examines rioting that has occurred since the 1990s has not directly examined the methods that the police use when responding to protests and riots and nor has the effect of repression used by the police on protesters been examined (see for example, Bergesen & Herman, 1997; Myers, 1997; Olzak & Shanahan, 1996; Olzak, Shanahan, & McEneaney, 1996; Perez et al., 2003). A small number of these studies have suggested that repression is an important factor in the understanding of the occurrence of protest violence and the triggering of riots. The likelihood that repression is an influencing factor in our understanding of the occurrence of riots has been identified by a number of researchers (Francisco, 1995, 1996, 1997; Mason & Krane, 1989; Moore, 1995; Olivier, 1990, 1991; Perez et al., 2003; Rasler, 1996), but their view is balanced by a number of earlier researchers who claimed that high levels of police repression can reduce violence (Hibbs, 1973; Muller, 1985; Tilly, 1978).

The likelihood that the repression of protesters by the police can contribute to violence, specifically in relation to racial riots, was supported by the findings of the Kerner Commission (National Advisory Commission on Civil Disorders, 1968; Useem, 1997). However, the relationship between repression and the occurrence of protester violence is not well understood and specific police behavior has not been examined to identify those behaviors that result in violence and under what specific environmental and social conditions (Perez et al., 2003).

In 2003, Perez et al. published their findings on their examination of riots that had occurred in the USA from 1967 to 1969; specifically those that had occurred in Boston and San Francisco. According to these researchers, the rioting that occurred in both of these cities was characterized by the excessive or selective use of force by the police, which failed to control the riots and actually led to the escalation of the confrontations (Perez et al., 2003). The researchers claimed that all of the confrontations examined and especially those in San Francisco were "initiated by police repression rather than student aggression" and that the use of excessive force by the police did not subdue the riots (Perez et al., 2003, p. 160). The research formed the basis for identifying three criteria under which the use of physical repression by the police may escalate protest violence. The three criteria are as follows:

1. When the repression is excessive and/or based on race or is racially selective;
2. When police have poor training in crowd control management or lack understanding of the threat level of the protest; and

3. When police–community relations are strained or lacking in formal connections and channels for feedback (adapted from Perez et al., 2003, p. 155).

The research completed by Perez et al. (2003), and the subsequent development of the three criteria, although important in the context of protests that are based on racial infringements either by the police or another social institution, has limitations for the police when responding to violent protests or riots. The first limitation is that the criteria stated are time and location specific because they are based on research that examined racial riots in two US cities in the late 1960s. Society and policing were different during the late 1960s, especially as the Vietnam War and other major political changes were taking place during this period. The second is that the criteria are based on the police response and "police knowledge" at that time. The third limitation is that the research does not take into account the improvements in the police understanding of protest strategies, tactics and organizational structures.

3.7.2 The Police Response to Violent Protest: Change on the Horizon

The approach taken historically by the police to violent protests in democratic countries is to usually avoid confrontation by using negotiation and accommodation (P. Waddington, 1998b). In the majority of protests, the police have formed passive cordons for the protesters to occupy or travel in and the compliance of the protesters is usually secured by negotiation and not by force (P. Waddington, 1991). The view that the police usually take an accommodating approach to protesters is supported by Waddington and Wright (2008), who claimed that even if protesters seek to breach the cordon the normal response of the police is to hold-the-line and if there is a need, push the crowd back. These traditional tactics gave rise to the use of shields. Shields help maintain a cordon and can be used to push back the crowd (P. Waddington, 1991).

By using such tactics the police have been able to use non-confrontational response tactics because these tactics have given them the ability to manage a crowd, but as protests have become more politically based and violent, the police have been pressured to use more confrontational tactics (P. Waddington, 1998b). Following the 1960s riots in the USA and the violent industrial protests and pickets in the UK in the 1980s, the police response to protests was interpreted as a shift toward "paramilitarism" (Reiner, 1998; P. Waddington, 1998b). This view was supported by Joyce (2010), who claimed that the changes to policing and the use of special equipment and tactics provided the police with the capability of delivering a more aggressive approach when responding to protests. This approach was called escalated force but as a result of using the approach during the 1984–1985 English miners' strikes and the damage done to their public image, the police moved to a negotiated management approach (Joyce, 2010). During this period, the management of violent protests in the UK became centralized and a national system that was capable of deploying officers from across the country was used (P. Waddington, 1998b).

The argument that the police had become more paramilitarized during the 1980s was based on four factors. The first factor, especially in the UK, was that the police were adopting protest response strategies and tactics that were used in the British colonies (Northam, 1985, 1986, 1988; P. Waddington, 1998b). The second factor was that the police had regular and frequent contact with their colleagues in other countries including both democratic countries and post-conflict countries "from whom some or all the tactics now in use may have been learned" (P. Waddington, 1991, p. 214). The third factor was the adaption in the early 1970s of the Police Support Units (PSU) to a public order role rather than a civil defense role and the fourth factor was the change in the type of equipment used by the police in their response to violent protests (P. Waddington, 1991). The police started to use the long shield in 1976 and protective helmets, overalls, and tear gas in 1981 (P. Waddington, 1991). This equipment was introduced primarily for officer protection and not for crowd control. According to Waddington (1991), the provision of protective equipment built on the tradition of holding-the-line in a cordon and pushing back the crowd if there was a need.

The police, according to P. Waddington (1991), have responded to each escalation in violent protest and riots and the violence used against them by providing officers with personal protective equipment in an effort to reduce the number of officer injuries. The provision of protective equipment has enabled officers to undertake their roles more effectively and has allowed them to maintain strategic response requirements, such as securing cordons (P. Waddington, 1991). The provision of protective equipment, however, has not stopped officers being injured or increased the effectiveness of deployed officers after a riot has commenced (P. Waddington, 1991).

Changes occurred in how the police respond to violent protest in the 1980s and the form and nature of public order events changed again in the late 2000s (Hughes, 2010). According to Hughes (2010), the police in the UK were becoming more legalistic in the implementation of their command strategies and tactics. Hughes's (2010) point was that such strategies and tactics needed to be flexible but should be applied consistently as an event unfolds. The suggestion was that the then, new Association of Chief Police Officers (ACPO) Manual on Public Order would "provide the framework for managing and deploying operations at a local, regional and national level" (Hughes, 2010, p. 17).

A similar change also appeared to be taking place in the USA. The only difference was that in the USA, the police were more legalistic in their response to violent protest (Starr et al., 2011). According to Starr et al. (2011), the policing of protests in the USA had the appearance of Low Intensity Operations (LIO or Low Intensity Warfare) and that the police focused on order maintenance. They went on to claim that "LIO falls short of full-scale warfare, mainly to avoid the appearance of repression" and that they rely on "the use of less-than-lethal weapons, public relations campaigns, and the extensive gathering of intelligence" (Starr et al., 2011, p. 60).

P. Waddington (1991) described the police as failing "to appreciate the nature of the task of quelling serious disorder" and claimed that they were "blinded by their traditional image" of being non-confrontational and were actually "out of touch with reality" (p. 159). This perspective, however, is not supported by other researchers, and Noakes and Gillham (2006) suggested that the police response to violent protests during this period was driven by the adoption of "penology" strategies, which allowed the protests to reach a "negotiated" level before the police responded in a manner only to "reduce uncertainty and maintain order" during the protest event (p. 115).

Violently confronting the police during a protest is a no-win situation (D. Baker, 2016). The police have, historically, relied on the deployment of large numbers of officers to control crowds and violent protest but they are the enforcement institution of the state and are capable of using the resources of the state to achieve the maintenance of order (D. Baker, 2016). The police now not only rely on traditional response strategies and tactics but use intelligence, surveillance and other technology along with approaches such as negotiated management and strategic incapacitation.

The negotiated management of protests was discussed in Chap. 2 and was one of the strategies adopted by the police to manage protests in the late twentieth century. The strategy involved the establishment of a permitting system and the police negotiating the form and route of the protest with the protest organizers. The police generally support protest permitting systems as they call for protesters to negotiate their intentions with the police prior to an event, which from a policing perspective, creates a more predictable protest (D. Baker, 2011). According to D. Waddington (1998a), the use of a negotiated management strategy assists with the institutionalization of protesting because it ensures that the police maintain control of the event. As a result, the permitting system provides a framework to minimize the level of disruption for the public but also enables the police and the protesters to achieve a peaceful demonstration (D. Waddington, 1998a).

The downside of negotiated management for the police is that they need to facilitate the aims of the protesters while not treating the protesters as homogenous (Reicher et al., 2004). This means that the police need to develop comprehensive planning procedures and contingent deployment capabilities. A weakness of the strategy is that it focuses extensively on the protest event and needs the protesters to have an identifiable leadership with whom the police can negotiate (Gorringe & Rosie, 2008). The leaders need to be able to make decisions that would be acceptable to the protesters and that ensure that the protesters are organized in a manner that safeguards them from the police reverting to a more proactive crowd management approach (Noakes & Gillham, 2006; Vitale, 2005).

It has been argued by some researchers that the negotiated management strategy has been replaced by strategic incapacitation (Gillham, 2011; Gillham et al., 2013), which according to Kienscherf (2014), was the outcome of the police seeking to remove the constraints of the protest permitting systems and negotiated management. The catalyst for the use of strategic incapacitation was the riots that took place during the 1999 WTO meeting in Seattle, in which protesters demonstrated that they were not going to respect the permitting system or negotiate with police (Kienscherf, 2014).

The use of the strategic incapacitation protest response tactic has been identified as one of the factors that make up a part of a modern militarized response to policing protests (Noakes & Gillham, 1999). Other researchers claimed that the tactic was supported by the public and the media in the past because the protesters' actions were not viewed as being legitimate (Gilham & Noakes, 2007), and because the protesters were reluctant to negotiate with the police (Gorringe, Rosie, Waddington, & Kominou, 2011). Earl and Soule (2006) proposed that the police had a tendency to explain away the use of the tactic as being the most reasonable method for allowing protesters to achieve their objective while enabling them to maintain control of the crowd and minimize disorder.

The tactic comprises two stages. The first stage is the gathering of and the analysis of intelligence to preempt protester violence or offending (Wood, 2014). The information obtained also assists the police with the development of a deployment plan and the use of other crowd management techniques. If a protest does become violent, the police can implement pre-planned tactics, such as mass-arrest, the deployment of less-than-lethal weapons and riot control officers (Wood, 2014). The tactic also works in combination with other control tactics that have been used more frequently by the police since the 1999 Seattle protests. Other tactics used include:

- no-protest zones that include the installation of large concrete and metal fence barriers;
- the surveillance and control of safe protest spaces;
- the use of "kettling" of protesters;
- the use of less-lethal weapons;
- the use of electronic surveillance technology to provide real-time information on demonstrators' activities, and
- the use of preventative or preemptive arrests of "high-risk" protesters (Gorringe et al., 2011; Wood, 2014).

An alternative view of strategic incapacitation was offered by Kienscherf (2014). This researcher claimed that because strategic incapacitation distinguishes between violent and non-violent protesters it complements the negotiated management strategy rather than replaces it. As Kienscherf (2014) noted, the proactive strategies used by the police when planning for a protest, such as surveillance or intelligence gathering, work alongside the existing permitting systems.

3.7.3 The Police Use of Force and Crowd Control Tactics

The police response to managing a violent protest or crowd requires officers to maintain close physical proximity to protesters and to restrain the crowd from moving forward. They may actually push the crowd back or use crowd dispersal tactics (P. Waddington, 1991). To restrain the crowd or push them back often involves the police using long or round shields and physically pushing or shoving individuals (P. Waddington, 1991). As a result, this becomes a highly charged physical environment and, as Moran and Waddington (2016) identified, can easily lead to "a self-fulfilling prophecy of violence and disorder" (p. 22). One of the most provocative actions that the police can display is the high-profile presence of riot response-equipped officers, which could intensify the situation with the protesters further if the deployed police officers have not been able "to become situationally adjusted to the prevailing mood of the crowd," leading to an increase in the "likelihood of officers behaving in an ill-disciplined, idiosyncratic, or indiscriminate manner" (Moran & Waddington, 2016, p. 23). The possibility of officers not becoming situationally adjusted increases when an officer is not from the same geographical area in which the riot is taking place or if their usual police role is a specialized position, such as an organized crime investigator (Moran & Waddington, 2016).

Waddington and Wright (2008) claimed that there are two ways that the amount of force used by the police could be considered as being excessive. The first way is the extent to which the police have used the force in a specific situation or circumstance that may be thought to "be disproportionate to the resistance shown by the adversary or adversaries" (Waddington & Wright, 2008, p. 487). The second way is how the force is applied (Waddington & Wright, 2008). In this case it is not the amount of force used by the police, but whether the amount of force used was justified in the specific circumstances (Waddington & Wright, 2008). The use of force can be divided into two further parts: the capacity of the police to use force and how often the police use force (Waddington & Wright, 2008).

The application of force by the police and the perception of its use at any given time is inherently complex (Hall, 1998). This means that the use of force may be avoided if officers base their judgment on whether to use force in the circumstances at the time rather than basing their judgment on the characteristics of the individual or the crowd involved (Hall, 1998). As Hall (1998) identified, it is the officer's or the police commander's threat assessment of the situation at the time and the probability of the violence or disorder continuing that should form the basis for deciding on the application of force and the level of the force to be applied.

The threat of an individual or the crowd becoming violent or disorderly is also a challenge to the authority of the police and the rule of law (P. Waddington, 1991). The better option in this type of situation is, according to Waddington (1991), for the police to disperse the crowd, by force if necessary, rather than arresting large numbers of offenders. This advice is based on the view that the most sensible strategy to manage violent crowds is to disperse it as "a dispersed crowd is no longer a crowd, and lacking coherence, loses its awesome potential for violence and destruction" (P. Waddington, 1991, p. 162). A second benefit of taking this approach is that the crowd would be broken up into smaller groups, which would then allow the police to arrest those identified as offenders. According to P. Waddington (1991), the police do not implement the dispersal approach when a crowd becomes violent but instead, use the tactic of slowly moving forward with the officers being protected by large, drawn shields. This attracts the crowd and then draws them to the police cordon (P. Waddington, 1991).

The use of the crowd dispersal tactic is only one approach to managing a violent crowd. Research demonstrates that the interpretation of a situation should form the basis for the response taken by the police (della Porta, 1998; della Porta & Reiter, 1998; Earl & Soule, 2006). The use of this more tolerant but generic approach has been observed in the USA and the UK and emphasizes a non-confrontational strategy and a commitment to avoiding "trouble" (P. Waddington, 1994; Warner & McCarthy, 2014).

While there are a number of strategies that can be used for managing violent crowds, strategies can be classified into two categories, depending on their orientation: high-profile orientation or low-profile orientation (Davies & Dawson, 2018). The high-profile orientation response consists of reactive police response strategies and tactics that rely on an oppressive police presence (Davies & Dawson, 2018). The response also relies on the strict enforcement of the law and crowd management tactics, such as strategic incapacitation and the assumption that if offenders are removed from a crowd then the violence will not escalate (Gilham & Noakes, 2007; Wahlström, 2011). The response also requires the police to remove disruptive offenders quickly (Westley, 1957), and when the crowd is out-of-control, more physical or coercive tactics, such as kettling, stun grenades, teargas or non-lethal weapons can be used (Wahlström, 2007).

In contrast to the use of high-profile orientation strategies are those that make up the low-profile orientation. Low-profile orientation strategies are based on the assessment and analysis of the level or the possibility of violence being perpetrated by a crowd. This is determined by the level of communication and negotiation with the crowd (Adang & Cuvelier, 2001; Gorringe, Stott, & Rosie, 2012). The strategies are known by a number of different names, such as "negotiated management," "dialogue policing," "low-profile policing," "Meet and Greet," "The Madison Method," and "The Cardiff Approach" and are based on lowering the possibility of crowd violence occurring by communication with the police (Davies & Dawson, 2018, p. 2). The weakness in the low-level orientation strategies from the police perspective is that the police must be genuine in their communication endeavors and their willingness to assist the crowd (Davies & Dawson, 2018).

3.7.4 Conclusion

The discussion in this chapter clearly indicates that there are numerous factors influencing how a protest crowd behaves, whether they will become violent and how the police will respond to changes in crowd behavior. As a result of this complexity there is not a one-size-fits all police response to managing a crowd should they become violent or turn to rioting (Davies & Dawson, 2015; della Porta, 1998). As a result of the various factors that influence crowd behavior, the management of a crowd should be based on the features of a crowd (Davies & Dawson, 2018) and the information gathered from intelligence. The initial police response to a planned, low-risk protest should be one that involves a low-profile policing approach (see for example Adang & Cuvelier, 2001; Davies & Dawson, 2018; Gorringe et al., 2012; Stott, 2003; Stott, Adang, Livingstone, & Schreiber, 2008; Wahlström, 2011). The problem for the police, however, is when the protest is not one of low risk but intelligence warns that there is a high risk of crowd violence or vandalism occurring.

One option to respond to a high-risk protest is for the police to deploy a sufficient number of officers to the event and have an appropriate number of officers on standby (Davies & Dawson, 2018; della Porta, 1998). Having an appropriate number of officers deployed and on standby will ensure that the police are not limited in their ability to deter potential violent individuals and that they will be able to respond to any threat of violence or escalating violence (Davies & Dawson, 2015).

3.8 The Militarization of the Police Response to Protests

A number of researchers have claimed that since the early 2000s, the policing of protests has become increasingly militarized (D. Baker, 2007, 2011; Davies & Dawson, 2015; della Porta, 2016; P. Waddington, 2003; Wood, 2014). One group of researchers, della Porta et al. (2006), provided a convincing argument in that since the turn of the century the police in Europe have reverted to using more proactive tactics in controlling protests. This view was supported by D. Baker (2011), who argued that the police show "an inclination to use force, construct no-go areas, discourage presence at protests by tactics of warnings and threats of violence, utilize riot technology, and accumulate extensive intelligence of demonstrators," which "has reignited confrontation between [the] police and protesters" (p. 145). Recent examples of the militarization of the police response to protests, according to researchers, are the eviction of the 2011 Occupy Wall Street Protest in Manhattan, New York, and the 1997 Vancouver APEC, the 1999 Seattle WTO and the 2014 Fergusson protests (Kienscherf, 2014; Wood, 2014).

The change in the police response to protests occurred, according to Fernandez (2009), because of an increased fear of violence held by the community and the unwillingness of the police to "allow protest[s] as a consequence of 9/11" (p. 4). D. Baker (2016), however, claimed that changes are occurring because the role of the police is to respond to and control violence in the community and because the police feel that they need to respond to and control threatening or violent protesters as they fear that if they do not, they will appear as not being capable (Earl, McCarthy, & Soule, 2003). The police "believe that they must 'win' the situation in order to maintain control and authority" and that any appearance of the police not being able to control a protest could lower the public's confidence in the police and could provide the basis for challenging the authority of the police during future protests (Earl, 2003; Earl & Soule, 2006).

The weakness in existing research as to whether there has been an increase in a militarized response to protests is that any research available has been based on permitted protests only and it was only Myers-Montgomery (2016) who differentiated between permitted and unpermitted protest. The majority of research does not examine protests that are mobile, that increase in size quickly and do not have a clear leadership structure. The literature only focuses on protests that are predictable and not riots that are unpredictable. Myers-Montgomery (2016) claimed that the police response to unpermitted protests has become more militarized and this has occurred for the following reasons:

(a) unpermitted protests present a threat to the police's ultimate goal of order and control;
(b) the militarized response is encouraged by the police leadership; and
(c) the individual officers take personal pride and pleasure in being equipped with the specialized equipment and weapons (p. 278).

A word of warning on the militarization of the police was, however, conveyed by P. Waddington (2007b), who noted that while it could be argued that the police response to protests had become more militarized there was a danger in portraying the changes "too stereotypically" (pp. 2–3). P. Waddington (2007b) claimed that there are a number of examples of large, international protests where the police response has not been militarized, but have been one of negotiation and non-confrontational, such as during the subsidiary G8 meetings held in Derby, Sheffield and those held in Edinburgh prior to the Gleneagles meeting.

According to della Porta and Reiter (1998), any analysis of the effect of the militarization of the police response to protests will result in two different findings. The first finding, which is supported by a number of researchers, is that militarization could be positive owing to hierarchical control structures and could assist in preventing police actions that are violent toward the protesters (della Porta & Reiter, 1998). The second finding is that an increase in militarization increases the potential for the police to overreact to any protester violence (della Porta & Reiter, 1998; Reiner, 1991).

3.9 The Police Organization

Since the late-1960s, police from all around the world have faced investigations into their response to emergencies, disasters, protests, terrorist attacks, and riots (Wood, 2014). Such events usually generate comments pertaining to community confidence, litigation, changes in policy and police reform (Wood, 2014). Over the same period, police organizations have faced changes in management, introduced community policing, problem-oriented policing and intelligence-led policing and have placed an emphasis on the use of information and communication technology (Wood, 2014). They have also faced a more attentive public and media (Wood, 2014). These changes have resulted in the police focusing on prevention and compliance, the identification and management of risk and how they are perceived by politicians and the public (de Lint & Hall, 2009; Ericson & Haggerty, 1997; Maguire, 2000; O'Malley, 1992). To understand how these changes have affected the police organization and the policing of protests and riots, "we need to go beyond political rhetoric about the police as the tool of the elites, or as omnipotent masterminds" and move to a position where we view police organizations as complex, political, with specific cultural histories that contain active and "reflexive" personnel (p. 7).

There are two major internal challenges for the police in responding to protests and they have come about as a result of the changes in the operating environment since the late 1960s. The first challenge is their neo-military organizational and rank structure. The rank structure according to Mawby (2002) creates different perceptions "between the 'command team' and the 'rank and file' as to what 'real policing' should constitute in public order situations" (p. 163). This difference is exacerbated as command teams are usually located in an agency's headquarters, which is not where the protest is located and cannot therefore, appreciate how fluid the event is and how fluid the control of such an event is. As a result of the structure of the response and the nature of the event, officers are often not able to be appropriately supervised or controlled, especially when the protest or riot is fast moving or mobile (King & Waddington, 2005). The second challenge arises from the adoption of risk management techniques and the perspective of executive-level police officers to normal operational events. These factors, according to King and Waddington (2004), have created a view that is held by the police executive that the police response to a protest is reactive, or in other words, the response will intensify "according to the level of violence of the protesters" (p. 121).

3.10 The Police Response to Industrial Action

The response of the police to an industrial-action protest can have a significant role in how the protest is perceived by the public and on the outcome of the dispute (D. Baker, 2002). Industrial-dispute protests are unusual events, which often require special tolerance to some actions that are undertaken during a protest (P. Waddington, 1998b). D. Baker (2002) argued that the capacity and the capability for the police to make appropriate strategic and tactical choices in relation to their management of industrial-action protests challenges their independence and impartiality and their resource levels and commitment.

When responding to an industrial-action protest, the police need to ensure that their crowd management tactics are not overly aggressive. Overly aggressive tactics have been used previously by the police during these protests and this has drawn criticism from politicians, unionists and the media (D. Baker, 2002).

3.11 The Police Response to a Political Rally

In response to the "anti-Lib Dem" protest held during the Liberal Democrat's Conference in Sheffield in March 2011, the South Yorkshire Police, following the principles of the Elaborated Social Identity Model (ESIM), announced the security strategy it intended to use (D. Waddington, 2013). The police had anticipated that there would be between 5000 and 10,000 protesters at the protest and that they would deploy approximately 1000 officers, including officers from contiguous constabularies to assist with controlling the crowd (D. Waddington, 2013). The security of the conference, which was to be held in City Hall "would involve erecting a part-concrete, part metallic fence (what the media quickly dubbed a 'ring of steel'), varying between 6 and 8 ft in height, which was designed to protectively surround the centrally located conference venue" (The Star, 24 February, 2011, cited in D. Waddington, 2013, p. 47). The intention of this level of security was to "'sterilise' a huge area of the Barker's Pool pedestrian precinct positioned directly in front of 'the conference venue'" (The Star, 24 February, 2011, cited in D. Waddington, 2013, p. 47).

To ensure that the physical security parameters were understood by the protesters, the police also deployed a Police Liaison Team (PLT), whose role it was, was to mix with crowd (Waddington, 2013). The purpose of these officers was to ensure that there was a communication link between the police and the crowd (D. Waddington, 2013). The police also monitored social media to "counter any potentially 'inflammatory messages' relating to the protest" (The Star, 24 February, 2011, cited in D. Waddington, 2013, p. 47).

There were two reasons why the police adopted a more balanced response to the Sheffield political protests. The first was as a result of the publication of the Adapting to Protest report (Her Majesty's Chief Inspectorate of Constabulary, 2009a, 2009b), which recommended that the police adopt more tolerant approaches to managing political protests (D. Waddington, 2013). The second reason was to ensure that the police met the requirements that were documented in the 2010 Manual of Guidance on Keeping the Peace published by the Association of Chief Police Officers (D. Waddington, 2013). Both of these documents were developed from the findings of an examination of the crowd control tactics used by the police during the 2009 G20 protests in London and because of the claims made by protesters that the police were using excessive violence (Greer & McLaughlin, 2010).

The success of the planning and response to the Li Dem Conference protests taken by the South Yorkshire Police, according to D. Waddington (2013), "serves to validate Reicher et al.'s (2004, 2007) emphasis on education, facilitation, communication, and differentiation as essential components of effective public order policing" and supported the findings and recommendations contained in the Inspectorate of Constabulary reports and the Association of Chief Police Officers Manual of Guidance (p. 62).

3.12 UK Public Surveys of Police Riot Responses

The triggers and the reasons for the spread of the 2011 UK riots and the response tactics taken by the police caused extensive debate amongst British academics and politicians (Borch, 2013). Both asked "what were the reasons behind the events and how might such massive violence and looting be prevented in the future?"

(Borch, 2013, p. 585). To assist with understanding the reasons for the riots, the Guardian newspaper, in partnership with the London School of Economics, published a report based on "interviews with 270 people who were directly involved in the riots in London, Birmingham, Manchester, Salford, Liverpool and Nottingham" (Lewis, Newburn, Taylor, Mcgillivray, et al., 2011, p. 3). The research concluded that "Although rioters expressed a mix of opinions about the disorder, many of those involved said they felt like they were participating in explicitly anti-police riots" (Lewis & Newburn, 2012). According to Lewis and Newburn (2012), the interviewees claimed that the police and the style of policing experienced in the main cities in the UK were "the most significant cause of the riots."

The findings of the 2011 riot research substantiates the results obtained from a survey that was undertaken between 29 May and 4 June 2009 by Ipsos MORI, who were commissioned by Her Majesty's Chief Inspectorate of Constabulary to conduct a survey to gather information as to the opinion of the public "in relation to the [2009 London] G20 protests and policing of large-scale protests in general" (Her Majesty's Chief Inspectorate of Constabulary, 2009a). The survey included questions relating to the policing of the 2009 London G20 and similar high-profile protests and the findings were based on the comments from 1726 respondents in England and Wales (Her Majesty's Chief Inspectorate of Constabulary, 2009a).

The survey found that opinion was divided between those respondents "who felt the police dealt with the protests well and those who did not" (Her Majesty's Chief Inspectorate of Constabulary, 2009a, p. 27). Only 7% of the survey participants believed that the police had dealt with the G20 protests very well, while 39% believed that the police handled the protests fairly well. This means that under half (46%) of the respondents (46%) believed that the police dealt with the G20 protests either very or fairly well (Her Majesty's Chief Inspectorate of Constabulary, 2009a). In comparison, one-third (33%) of the respondents had the view that the police did not handle the G20 protests very well and 12% stated that the police did not handle the protests well at all (Her Majesty's Chief Inspectorate of Constabulary, 2009a). This means that 45% of the respondents stated that the police did "not do very well/ not at all well" (Her Majesty's Chief Inspectorate of Constabulary, 2009a). According to Her Majesty's Chief Inspectorate of Constabulary (2009a), although the opinions of the survey respondents were closely balanced, at the margins of the responses, a larger percent of the respondents were negative (12%) than were positive (7%).

In the second section of the survey, participants were asked for their views on the police using force against protesters (Her Majesty's Chief Inspectorate of Constabulary, 2009a). The responses indicated that the participants had "a willingness to accept that, in some circumstances, use of force against protesters is justified" (Her Majesty's Chief Inspectorate of Constabulary, 2009a, p. 28). When presented with opposing statements about the use of force, respondents were "twice as likely to select a situation where the police may need to use force against protesters as necessary to keep public order, as opposed to a situation where the police should never use force" (Her Majesty's Chief Inspectorate of Constabulary, 2009a, p. 28).

The final section of the survey comprised questions that related to the confidence held in the police. Approximately, two-thirds (65%) of the survey respondents were confident that the police would manage large-scale protests effectively in the future, 54% stated that they were fairly confident and 11% were very confident. There were, however, 27% who claimed that they were not confident that the police would be able to manage a large-scale protest in the future (Her Majesty's Chief Inspectorate of Constabulary, 2009a).

3.13 Conclusion

This chapter has discussed and summarized the strategies and tactics that the police use to respond to violent protests and riots. The major points from the discussion are that the policing of protests and riots remain in a state of confusion, exacerbated by media, social media and political scrutiny (Wood, 2014). Another factor is that while the police have generally accepted the principles of negotiated management they have retained the capability to respond to a protest or riot in a more militarized fashion should the need arise. It is this capability that is the most contentious for the public, some academics and politicians.

In the late 1980s, academics examined the causes of violent protests and riots and this led to the development of the Elaborated Social Identity Model and the Flashpoints Model. The results of the examination pointed to the changes in the police response to protests from being reactive (escalated force), based on threat and the use of force to a more proactive (negotiated management) approach that relies on communication and negotiation (Stott, 2009). The problem for the police is that there is a continuing debate as to how the police will be able to deliver the strategy of "negotiated management" effectively at the tactical level (Hall & De Lint, 2003; McCarthy & McPhail, 1998; McPhail et al., 1998).

A number of academics claim that the form of response to protests and the actions used by the police are some of the main triggers for a protest to turn violent (Bergesen & Herman, 1997; Kawalerowicz & Biggs, 2014; Myers, 1997; Olzak et al., 1996; Olzak & Shanahan, 1996; Perez et al., 2003; Schneider, 2014). This is supported by the application of the Elaborated Social Identity Model, which emphasizes that a proactive police response can and does "have the capacity to negatively impact upon crowd dynamics" (Stott, 2009, p. 8). This also poses difficulty for the police because again the literature is contradictory with a number of researchers (Adang & Cuvelier, 2001; della Porta & Reiter, 1998; Hall & de Lint, 2003; Sheptycki, 2002), claiming that the two approaches—the police being proactive and negotiated management "can actually be applied simultaneously by different police forces or units within the same country and even within the same event" which would achieve different results (Stott, 2009, p. 8).

The management of a crowd and the response to any protest or riot is, however, controlled by the police; the police determine what is acceptable or unacceptable protester behavior (D. Baker, 2002) and will undertake crowd control and public order on their terms (P. Waddington, 1994). Undertaking crowd control on their own terms, according to D. Baker (2002), results from the police being in a position of superiority and they are therefore in a stronger position to negotiate the ground rules for any protest. The position of being able to control protest crowds came about from advances made in technology. The advances made it possible to employ the negotiated model of responding to protests in the UK in the late 1980s (D. Baker, 2002).

The advances made in technology, supported by intelligence and video surveillance, enabled the police to use more communicative strategies and tactics (King & Brearley, 1996). The position of strength held by the police has also come about because of the improvements in crowd management capability and the use of more sophisticated equipment. According to D. Baker (2002), the establishment and deployment of mobile police officers, equipped with "flame-retardant clothing, riot shields, armored personnel vehicles and CS gas have created new forms of superiority" (pp. 21–22). These advancements and because the police have the capacity and capability to use a number of different forms of coercive actions and tactics have meant that the police can "win" protest confrontations without having numerical superiority (D. Baker, 2002). There is, however, evidence that the most effective means for managing protests is for the police response to include facilitation and a differentiated approach to the use of force (Stott, 2009).

How the public perceive the police response to violent protests and riots will depend on the pressures that influence the development of police strategy (D. Waddington, 2013). D. Waddington (2013) noted that some of these pressures are implicit in that the police are legally required to act to control disorder but other pressures can be subtle and can include interference from local politicians, community groups, and the media. This implies that the police either accept these influencing factors and adapt their public order strategies or resist these factors and face the possibility of imposed political direction. Accepting the influencing pressures, according to D. Waddington (2013), gives the police its ethos while resisting such pressures enforces the police belief, value-system and occupational sub-culture.

The theory that public image influences the development of public order response policies is opposed by Reiner (1998). This opposition is based on the fact that the police are committed to maintaining the principle of minimal force, under-enforcing the law and the use of discretion (Reiner, 1998). According to Reiner (1998), the police seek to "preserve tranquility" rather than to enforce "the strict letter of the law" (p. 46). This implies that the police primarily use persuasion to ensure protester compliance and to avoid violence, which appears to work in the majority of protests (Reiner, 1998). When the police do fail in containing a violent protest, it is "mainly because of errors of judgment rather than the underlying paramilitary capacity" (Reiner, 1998, p. 46).

To assist the police to minimize the occurrence of errors during their response, the majority of police forces have implemented processes for gathering information as to the composition of the crowd involved in any organized protest (Stott, 2009). This information forms the basis for the police response strategy and ensures effective facilitation of a crowd. It also enables the police to communicate effectively should they need to use force as a part of their response.

This chapter has revealed the complexity of the policing of protests, especially in relation to the legitimacy of the use of police strategies, tactics and use of force (Stott, 2009). An effective police response to an organized protest must incorporate a negotiated approach and the proactive management of the crowd and should use strategies and tactics that link the response to a "continuous 'dynamic risk assessment'" process (Stott, 2009, p. 1).

References

Adang, O., & Cuvelier, C. (2001). *Policing Euro2000: International police co-operation, information management and police deployment*. Ubbergen: Tandem-Felix.

Allan, S., & Thorsen, E. (2009). *Citizen journalism: Global perspectives*. New York, NY: Peter Lang.

Baker, D. (2002). The changing Australian prototype of policing, pickets, and public order. *International Journal of Comparative and Applied Criminal Justice, 26*(1), 1–28.

Baker, D. (2007). From batons to negotiated management: The transformation of policing industrial disputes in Australia. *Policing: A Journal of Policy and Practice, 1*(4), 390–402.

Baker, D. (2011). A case study of policing responses to camps for climate action: Variations, perplexities, and challenges for policing. *International Journal of Comparative and Applied Criminal Justice, 35*(2), 141–165.

Baker, D. (2016). Paradoxes of policing and protest. *Journal of Policing, Intelligence and Counter Terrorism, 3*(2), 8–22.

Baker, S. (2012a). From the criminal crowd to the 'mediated crowd': The impact of social media on the 2011 English riots. *Safer Communities, 11*(1), 40–49.

Bergesen, A. (1982). Race riots of 1967: An analysis of police violence in Detroit and Newark. *Journal of Black Studies, 12*, 261–274.

Bergesen, A., & Herman, M. (1997). Immigration, race, and riot: The 1992 Los Angeles uprising. *American Sociological Review, 63*, 39–54.

Borch, C. (2013). Crowd theory and the management of crowds: A controversial relationship. *Current Sociology, 61*(5-6), 584–601.

Button, M., John, T., & Brearly, N. (2002). New challenges in public order: the professionalisation of environmental protests and the emergence of the militant environmental activist. *International Journal of the Society of Law, 70*, 17–31.

Casciani, D. (2009). *Eyewitness: Two days of protests*. Retrieved from http://news.bbc.co.uk/1/hi/uk/7980400.stm

Cockburn, A., St. Clair, J., & Sekula, A. (2000). *5 Days that shook the world*. London: Verso.

Davenport, J. (2009, April 3). Police defend 'corralling' thousands of protesters for eight hours in City. *Evening Standard*. Retrieved from https://www.standard.co.uk/news/police-defend-corralling-thousands-of-protesters-for-eight-hours-in-city-6915861.html

Davies, G., & Dawson, S. (2015). The 2011 Stanley Cup riot: Police perspectives and lessons learned. *Policing: An International Journal of Police Strategies & Management, 38*(1), 132–152.

Davies, G., & Dawson, S. (2018). Spoonful of sugar or strong medicine: 'Meet and greet' as a strategy for policing large-scale public events. *Police and Society: An International Journal of Research and Policy, 28*, 697. https://doi.org/10.1080/10439463.2016.1259317

de Armond, J. (2001). Netwar in the emerald city: WTO protest strategy and tactics. In J. Arquilla & D. Ronfeldt (Eds.), *The future of terror, crime and militancy* (pp. 201–235). Santa Monica, CA: Rand Corporation.

de Lint, W. (2005). Public order policing: A tough act to follow. *International Journal of the Sociology of Law, 33*(4), 179–199.

de Lint, W., & Hall, A. (2009). *Intelligent control: Developments in public order policing in Canada*. Toronto, ON: University of Toronto Press.

della Porta, D. (1995). *Social movements, political violence, and the state: A comparative analysis of Italy and Germany*. Cambridge: Cambridge University Press.

della Porta, D. (1998). Policing knowledge and protest policing: Some reflections on the Italian case. In D. della Porta & H. Reiter (Eds.), *Policing protest: The control of mass demonstrations in western democracies* (pp. 228–252). Minneapolis, MN: University of Minnesota Press.

della Porta, D. (2013). *Clandestine political violence*. Cambridge: Cambridge University Press.

della Porta, D. (2016). The policing of protest repression, bargaining, and the fate of social movements. *African Studies, 56*(1), 97–127.

della Porta, D., & Peterson, A. (2005). Editorial. *Policing and Society: An International Journal of Policy and Research, 15*(3), 233–234.

della Porta, D., Peterson, A., & Reiter, H. (2006). *The policing of transnational protest*. Aldershot: Ashgate.

della Porta, D., & Reiter, H. (1998). Introduction: The policing of protests in western democracies. In D. della Porta & H. Reiter (Eds.), *Policing protest: The control of mass demonstrations in western democracies* (pp. 1–34). Minneapolis, MN: University of Minnesota Press.

della Porta, D., & Zamponi, L. (2013). Protest and policing on October 15th, Global Day of Action: The Italian case. *Policing and Society: An International Journal of Policy and Research, 23*(1), 65–80.

Deuze, M. (2008). The changing context of news work: Liquid journalism and monitorial citizenship. *International Journal of Communication, 2*, 848–865.

Donson, F., Chesters, G., Welsh, I., & Tickle, A. (2004). Rebels with a cause, folk devils without a panic, policing tactics and anti-capitalist protests in London and Prague. *Internet Journal of Criminology*. Retrieved from http://orca.cf.ac.uk/60834/1/Rebel%20with%20a%20cause%20folk%20devils%20%20%20%20%20.pdf

Drury, J., & Reicher, S. (2000). Collective action and psychological change: The emergence of new social identities. *British Journal of Social Psychology, 39*(4), 579–604.

Earl, J. (2003). Tanks, tear gas, and taxes: Toward a theory of movement repression. *Sociological Theory, 21*(1), 44–68.

Earl, J., McCarthy, J., & Soule, S. (2003). Protest under fire? Explaining the policing of protest. *American Sociological Review, 68*(4), 581–606.

Earl, J., & Soule, S. (2006). Seeing blue: A police centred explanation of protest policing. *Mobilization, 11*(2), 145–164.

(The) Economist. (2011, August 13–19). Technology and order: The Blackberry riots. *The Economist*, 22.

Eddo-Lodge, R. (2011). Twitter didn't fuel the Tottenham riot. *The Guardian*. Retrieved 26 November, 2017, from https://www.theguardian.com/commentisfree/2011/aug/08/tottenham-riot-twitter

Ellefsen, R. (2016). Relational dynamics of protest and protest policing: Strategic interaction and the coevolution of targeting strategies. *Police and Society: An International Journal of Research and Policy, 28*, 751. https://doi.org/10.1080/10439463.2016.1262366

Ericson, R., & Doyle, A. (1999). Globalization and the policing of protest: The case of APEC 1997. *British Journal of Sociology, 50*(4), 589–608.

Ericson, R., & Haggerty, K. (1997). *Policing the risk society*. Toronto, ON: University of Toronto Press.

Farnsworth, K. (2004). Anti-globalisation, anti-capitalism and the democratic state. In M. Todd & G. Taylor (Eds.), *Democracy and participation: Popular protest and new social movements* (pp. 55–77). London: Merlin.

Favre, P., & Fillieule, O. (1994). La manifestation comme indicateur de l'engagement politique. In P. Perrineau (Ed.), *L'Engagement politique, declin ou mutation?* (pp. 115–139). Paris: Presses de la Foundation Nationale des Sciences Politiques.

Fernandez, L. (2009). *Policing dissent*. Piscataway, NJ: Rutgers University Press.

Fillieule, O., & Jobard, F. (1998). The policing of protest in France: Toward a model of protest policing. In D. della Porta & H. Reiter (Eds.), *Policing protest: The control of mass demonstrations in western democracies* (pp. 70–90). Minneapolis, MN: University of Minnesota Press.

Francisco, R. (1995). The relationship between coercion and protest: An empirical evaluation in three coercive states. *Journal of Conflict Resolution, 39*, 263–282.

Francisco, R. (1996). Coercion and protest: An empirical test in two democratic states. *American Journal of Political Science, 40*, 1179–1204.

Francisco, R. (1997). Why are collective conflicts stable? In C. Davenport (Ed.), *Paths to state repression* (pp. 149–172). New York, NY: Rowman and Littlefield.

Geary, R. (1985). *Policing industrial disputes: 1893 to 1985*. Cambridge: Cambridge University Press.

Gilham, P., & Noakes, J. (2007). More than a march in a circle: Transgressive protests and the limits of negotiated management. *Mobilization, 12*(4), 341–357.

Gill, C. & Sears, N. (2009). *Watchdog receives 145 complaints over G20 police as protester struck by officer demands compensation*. Mail Online, 16 April, London: Daily Mail Online. Retrieved from https://www.dailymail.co.uk/news/article-1170010/Watchdog-receives-145-complaints-G20-police-protester-struck-officer-demands-compensation.html

Gillham, P. (2011). Securitizing America: Strategic incapacitation and the policing of protest since the 11 September 2001 terrorist attacks. *Sociology Compass, 5*(7), 636–652.

Gillham, P., & Marx, G. (2000). Complexity and irony in policing and protesting: The World Trade Organization in Seattle. *Social Justice, 27*, 212/236.

Gillham, P. F., Edwards, B., & Noakes, J. (2013). Strategic incapacitation and the policing of Occupy Wall Street Protests in New York City, 2011. *Policing and Society: An International Journal of Policy and Research, 23*(1), 81–102.

Giugni, M., McAdam, D., & Tilly, C. (1999). *How social movements matter*. Minneapolis, MN: University of Minnesota Press.

Giugni, M., & Wisler, D. (1998). Political coalitions, face-to-face interactions, and the public sphere: An examination of the determinants of repression with protest event data. *CBSM Working Paper Series, 1*(4), 1–37.

Glaser, M. (2004). The new voices: Hyperlocal citizen media sites want you (to write)! *Online Journalism Review*. University of Southern California. Retrieved from http://ojr.org/ojr/glaser/1098833871.php

Gorringe, H., & Rosie, M. (2008). It's a long way to Auchterarder! 'Negotiated management' and mismanagement in the policing of G8 protests. *The British Journal of Sociology, 59*(2), 187–205.

Gorringe, H., Rosie, M., Waddington, D., & Kominou, M. (2011). Facilitating ineffective protest? The policing of the 2009 Edinburgh NATO protests. *Policing and Society: An International Journal of Policy and Research, 22*(2), 115–132.

Gorringe, H., Stott, C., & Rosie, M. (2012). Dialogue police, decision making, and the management of public order during protest crowd events. *Journal of Investigative Psychology and Offender Profiling, 9*(2), 111–125.

Gravelle, J., & Rogers, C. (2011). Policing public protests and corporate social responsibility. *International Journal of law, Crime and Justice, 39*, 111–120.

Greer, C., & McLaughlin, E. (2010). We predict a riot? Public order policing, new media environments and the rise of the citizen journalist. *British Journal of Criminology, 50*(6), 1041–1059.

Hall, A., & de Lint, W. (2003). Policing labour in Canada. *Policing and Society: An International Journal of Policy and Research, 13*(3), 219–234.

Hall, P. (1998). Policing order: Assessments of effectiveness and efficiency. *Policing and Society: An International Journal of Research and Policy, 8*, 225.

Her Majesty's Chief Inspectorate of Constabulary. (2009a). *Adapting to protest*. London: Her Majesty's Chief Inspectorate of Constabulary.

Her Majesty's Chief Inspectorate of Constabulary. (2009b). *Adapting to protest: Nurturing the British model of policing*. London: Her Majesty's Chief Inspectorate of Constabulary.

Her Majesty's Inspectorate of Constabulary. (1999). *Keeping the peace policing disorder*. London: Her Majesty's Inspectorate of Constabulary.

Her Majesty's Inspectorate of Constabulary. (2011). *The rules of engagement: A review of the August 2011 disorders*. London: Her Majesty's Chief Inspectorate of Constabulary.

Herbert, S. (2007). The battle of Seattle revisited: Or, seven views of a protest-zoning state. *Political Geography, 26*(5), 601–619.

Hibbs, D. (1973). *Mass political violence*. New York, NY: Wiley.

Hills, A. (1995). Militant tendencies. *British Journal of Criminology, 35*, 450–458.

Holgersson, S., & Knutsson, J. (2011). Dialogue policing: A means for less crowd violence. In T. Madensen & J. Knutsson (Eds.), *Preventing crowd violence* (pp. 191–215). London: Lynne Rienner.

Hughes, M. (2010, December). Call to order. *Police Review, 118*(6111), 16–17.

Human Rights Observer Team. (2006). *Final report: G20 protests*. Melbourne, VIC: Federation of Community Legal Centres (Victoria) Inc.

Jaime-Jimenez, O., & Reinares, F. (1998). The policing of social protest in Spain: From dictatorship to democracy. In D. della Porta & H. Reiter (Eds.), *Policing protest: The control of mass demonstrations in western democracies* (pp. 166–187). Minneapolis, MN: University of Minnesota Press.

Jeffersen, T., & Grimshaw, R. (1984). *Controlling the constable: Police accountability in England and Wales*. London: Muller/Cobben Trust.

Jefferson, T. (1987). Beyond paramilitarism. *British Journal of Criminology, 27*, 47–53.

Jefferson, T. (1990). *The case against paramilitary policing*. Milton Keynes: Open University Press.

Jefferson, T. (1993). Pondering paramilitarism: A question of viewpoints. *British Journal of Criminology, 33*, 374–388.

Joyce, P. (2010). The policing of protest. *Policing Today, 15*(3), 31–33.

Kawalerowicz, J., & Biggs, M. (2014). *Anarchy in the U.K: Economic deprivation, social disorganization, and political grievances in the London riot of 2011* (Sociology Working Papers Number 2014-06). Oxford: University of Oxford: Department of Sociology.

Kienscherf, M. (2014). Beyond militarization and repression: Liberal social control as pacification. *Critical Sociology, 42*(7-8), 1–16.

King, M. (2006). From reactive policing to crowd management? Policing anti-globalization protest in Canada. *Jurisprudencija, 79*, 40–58.

King, M. (2013). Disruption is not permitted: The policing and social control of occupy Oakland. *Critical Criminology, 21*(4), 463–475.

King, M., & Brearley, N. (1996). *Public order policing: Contemporary perspectives on strategy and tactics*. Leicester, England: Perpetuity Press.

King, M., & Waddington, D. (2004). Coping with disorder? The changing relationship between police public order strategy and practice - A critical analysis of the Burnley riot. *Policing and Society: An International Journal of Policy and Research, 14*(2), 118–137.

King, M., & Waddington, D. (2005). Flashpoints revisited: A critical application to the policing of anti-globalization protest. *Policing and Society: An International Journal of Policy and Research, 15*(3), 255–282.

Klein, A. (2012). Policing as a causal factor – A fresh view on riots and social unrest. *Safer Communities, 11*(1), 17–23.

Koopmans, R. (1993). The dynamics of protest waves: West Germany, 1965 to 1989. *American Sociological Review, 58*, 637.

Lewis, P. (2009). Climate campers get a lesson in citizen journalism. *The Guardian*. Friday 28th August. Retrieved from: https://www.theguardian.com/media/2009/aug/27/climate-camp-citizen-journalism

Lewis, P., & Newburn, T. (2012). Introducing phase two of Reading the Riots: Police, victims and the courts. *The Guardian*. Retrieved from https://www.theguardian.com/uk/2012/jul/01/introducing-phase-two-reading-riots

Lewis, P., Newburn, T., Taylor, M., Mcgillivray, C., Greenhill, A., Frayman, H. & Proctor, R. (2011). *Reading the riots: Investigating England's summer of disorder*. London: London School of Economics.

Maguire, M. (2000). Policing by risks and targets: Some dimensions and implications of intelligence-led crime control. *Policing and Society: An International Journal of Policy and Research, 9*(1), 315–336.

Marx, G. (1979). External efforts to damage or facilitate movements: Some patterns, explanations, outcomes, and complications. In M. Zald & J. McCarthy (Eds.), *Dynamics of social movements* (pp. 94–125). Boston, MA: Winthrop Publishers.

Marx, G. (1998). Some reflections on the democratic policing of demonstrations. In D. della Porta & H. Reiter (Eds.), *Policing protest: The control of mass demonstrations in western democracies* (pp. 253–269). Minneapolis, MN: University of Minnesota Press.

Mason, T., & Krane, D. (1989). The political economy of death squads: Towards a theory of the impact of state-sanctioned terror. *International Studies Quarterly, 33*, 175–198.

Mawby, R. (2002). *Policing images: Policing, communication and legitimacy*. Devon: Willan Publishing.

McCarthy, J., & McPhail, C. (1998). The institutionalization of protest. In D. Meyer & S. Tarrow (Eds.), *A movement society? Contentious politics for a new century* (pp. 83–110). Boulder, CO: Rowland and Littlefield.

McPhail, C., & McCarthy, J. (2005). Protest mobilization, protest repression, and their interaction. In C. Davenport, H. Johnston, & C. Mueller (Eds.), *Repression and mobilization* (pp. 3–32). Minneapolis, MN: University of Minnesota Press.

McPhail, C., Schweingruber, D., & McCarthy, J. (1998). Policing protest in the United States: 1960 -1995. In D. della Porta & H. Reiter (Eds.), *Policing protest: The control of mass demonstrations in western democracies*. Minneapolis, MN: University of Minnesota Press.

Mitchell, D., & Staeheli, L. (2005). Permitting protest: Parsing the fine geography of dissent in America. *International Journal of Urban and Regional Research, 29*(4), 796–813.

Moore, W. (1995). Rational rebels: Overcoming the free-rider problem. *Political Research Quarterly, 48*, 417–454.

Moran, M., & Waddington, D. (2016). *Riots: An international comparison*. London: United Kingdom, Macmillan Publishers Ltd.

Morris, A., & Mueller, C. (1992). *Frontiers in social movement theory*. New Haven, CT: Yale University Press.

Morris, T. (1985). The case for a riot squad. *New Society, 29*(November), 373–374.

Muir, R. (2008). *What do we mean by police independence*. Open Democracy UK: Power & liberty in Britain. 11 December. Retrieved from: https://www.opendemocracy.net/blog/email/rick-muir/2008/12/11/what-do-wemean-by-police-independence.

Muller, E. (1985). Income inequality, regime repressiveness, and political violence. *American Sociological Review, 50*, 674–701.

Murphy, M. (2009, April 15). Police to review 'kettling' tactics. *The Financial Times*. Retrieved from https://www.ft.com/content/db331250-29ee-11de-9d01-00144feabdc0

Myers, D. (1997). Racial rioting in the 1960s: An event history analysis of local conditions. *American Sociological Review, 62*, 94–112.

Myers-Montgomery, J. (2016). Militarized police and unpermitted protest: Implementing policy that civilizes the police. *Cultural Studies, 16*(3), 278–286.

National Advisory Commission on Civil Disorders. (1968). *Report of the National Advisory Commission on Civil Disorders*. Washington, DC: National Institute of Justice.

National Lawyers Guild (2004). *Know your rights*. Retrieved from www.nlg.org/resources/know_your_rights.htm.

New Zealand Herald. (2000, December 12). *Operation Jiang case of overkill*. Retrieved from http://www.nzherald.co.nz/nz/news/article.cfm?c_id=1&objectid=164942.

Noakes, J. & Gillham, P. (1999). Police and protestor innovation since Seattle. *Mobilization, 12*(4), 335–340.

Noakes, J. & Gillham, P. (2004). Policing protest in the US and Europe: The failure of negotiated management and the emergence of selective incapacitation post-Seattle. Paper presented at the conference on Policing Political Protest After Seattle, Fiskebackskil, Sweden, 1–5 May.

Noakes, J., & Gillham, P. (2006). Aspects of the 'new penology' in the police response to major political protests in the United States, 1999-2000. In D. della Porta, A. Peterson, & H. Reiter (Eds.), *The policing of transnational protest* (pp. 97–115). Burlington, VT: Ashgate.

Noakes, J., Klocke, B., & Gillham, P. (2005). Whose streets? Police and protester struggles over space in Washington, DC, 29-30 September 2001. *Policing and Society: An International Journal of Policy and Research, 15*(3), 235–254.

Northam, G. (1985, October 31). People may be violent … they are not enemies to be destroyed. *The Listener*.

Northam, G. (1986, July 17). Plastic bullets: A shot in the dark which could prove fatal. *The Listener*.

Northam, G. (1988). *Shooting in the dark*. London: Faber.

O'Malley, P. (1992). Risk, power and crime prevention. *Economy and Society, 21*(3), 252–269.

O'Neill, K. (2004). Transnational protest: States, circuses and conflict at the frontline of global politics. *International Studies Review, 6*(2), 233–251.

Olivier, J. (1990). Causes of ethnic collective action in the Pretoria-Witwatersrand Triangle, 1970-1984. *South African Sociological Review, 2*, 89–108.

Olivier, J. (1991). State repression and collective action in South Africa, 1970-84. *South African Journal of Sociology, 22*, 109–117.

Olzak, S., & Shanahan, S. (1996). Deprivation race riots: An extension of Spilerman's analysis. *Social Forces, 74*, 931–961.

Olzak, S., Shanahan, S., & McEneaney, E. H. (1996). Poverty, segregation, and race riots: 1960 to 1993. *American Sociological Review, 61*, 590–613.

Pavlik, J. (2008). *Media in the digital age*. New York, NY: New York University Press.

Peat, D. (2010, February 1). Cellphone cameras making everyone into a walking newsroom. *Toronto Sun*.

Perez, A., Berg, K., & Myers, D. (2003). Police and riots, 1967-1969. *Journal of Black Studies, 34*(2), 153–182.

Police Executive Research Forum (2015). *Lessons learned from the 2015 civil unrest in Baltimore*. Washington, DC: Police Executive Research Forum.

Rasler, K. (1996). Concessions, repression, and political protest in the Iranian revolution. *American Sociological Review, 61*, 132–152.

Reich, Z. (2008). How citizens create news stories: The 'news access' problem reversed. *Journalism Studies, 9*(5), 739–758.

Reicher, S., Stott, C., Cronin, P., & Adang, O. (2004). An integrated approach to crowd psychology and public order policing. *Policing: An International Journal of Police Strategies & Management, 27*(4), 558–572.

Reicher, S., Stott, C., Drury, J., Adang, O., Cronin, P., & Livingstone, A. (2007). Knowledge-based public order policing: Principles and practice. *Policing: A Journal of Policy and Practice, 1*(4), 1–13.

Reiner, R. (1991). *Chief constables: Bobbies, bosses or bureaucrats*. Oxford: Oxford University Press.

Reiner, R. (1992). *The politics of the police* (2nd ed.). Kernel Hempstead: Harvester Wheatsheaf.

Reiner, R. (1998). Policing, protest, and disorder in Britain. In D. della Porta & H. Reiter (Eds.), *Policing protest: The control of mass demonstrations in western democracies* (pp. 35–48). Minneapolis, MN: University of Minnesota Press.

Salert, B., & Sprague, J. (1980). *The dynamics of riots*. Ann Arbor, MI: ICPSR.

Sarre, R. (2001). The policing of public order in Australia. *Police Practice and Research: An International Journal, 2*(1–2), 53–70.

Schneider, C. (2014). *Police power and race riots: Urban unrest in Paris and New York*. Philadelphia, PA: University of Pennsylvania Press.

Scholl, C. (2013). *Two sides of a barricade: (Dis)order and summit protest in Europe*. Albany, New York: SUNY Press.

Seattle Police Department. (2000). *After action report: World Trade Organization Ministerial Conference Seattle, Washington November 29–December 3, 1999*. Seattle, WA: City of Seattle.

Sheptycki, J. (2002). Accountability across the policing field: Towards a general cartography of accountability for post-modern policing. *Policing and Society: An International Journal of Policy and Research, 12*(4), 323–338.

Sheptycki, J. (2005). Policing political protest when politics go global: Comparing public order policing in Canada and Bolivia. *Policing and Society: An International Journal of Policy and Research, 15*(3), 327–352.

Silver, A. (1971). Social and ideological bases of British elite reactions to domestic crises 1829-32. *Politics and Society, 1*, 179–201.

Simiti, M. (2012). The volatility of urban riots. In S. Seferiades & H. Johnson (Eds.), *Violent protest, contentious politics and the neoliberal state* (pp. 133–147). Farnham: Ashgate.

Smith, J. (2001). Globalizing resistance: The battle of Seattle and the future of social movements. *Mobilization: An International Journal, 6*(1), 1–19.

Soule, S., & Davenport, C. (2009). Velvet glove, iron fist, or even hand? Protest policing in the United States, 1960-1990. *Mobilization, 14*(1), 1–22.

Starr, A., & Fernandez, L. (2009). Legal control and resistance post Seattle. *Social Justice, 36*(1), 41–60.

Starr, A., Fernandez, L., & Scholl, C. (2011). *Shutting down the streets: Political violence and social control in the global era*. New York: New York University Press.

Stott, C. (2003). Police expectations and the control of English soccer fans at 'Euro 2000'. *Policing: An International Journal of Police Strategies and Management, 26*(4), 640–655.

Stott, C. (2009). *Crowd psychology & public order: An overview of scientific theory and evidence. A submission to the Her Majesty's Inspectorate of Constabulary Policing of Public Protest Review Team*. Liverpool: University of Liverpool.

Stott, C., Adang, O., Livingstone, A., & Schreiber, M. (2008). Tackling football hooliganism: A quantitative study of public order, policing and crowd psychology. *Psychology, Public Policy, and Law, 14*(2), 115–141.

Tarrow, S. (1998). *Power in movement: Social movements and contentious politics*. New York, NY: Cambridge University Press.

Thomas, J. (2000). *The battle in Seattle*. Golden, CO: Fulcrum Publishing.

Tilly, C. (1978). *From mobilization to revolution*. Reading, MA: Addison-Wesley.

Tilly, C. (2000). Spaces of contention. *Mobilization, 5*(2), 135–151.

The National Police Board (2010). *Dialogue police: Experience3s, observations and opportunities*. Stockholm, Sweden.

Useem, B. (1997). The state and collective disorders: The Los Angeles Riot/Protest of April, 1992. *Social Forces, 76*, 357–377.

Vitale, A. (2005). From negotiated management to command and control: How the New York Police Department polices protests. *Policing and Society: An International Journal of Research and Policy, 15*(3), 283–304.

Waddington, D. (1992). *Contemporary issues in public disorder: A comparative and historical approach*. London: Routledge.

Waddington, D. (1998a). Waddington versus Waddington public order theory on trial. *Theoretical Criminology, 2*(3), 373–394.

Waddington, D. (2007a). Seattle and its aftershock: Some implications for theory and practice. *Policing: A Journal of Policy and Practice, 1*(4), 380–389.

Waddington, D. (2007b). Seattle and its aftershock: Some implications for theory and practice. *Policing, 1*(4), 380–389.

Waddington, D. (2009). A North American example: The 2001 Cincinnati riot and a subsequent peace making initiative. In D. Waddington, F. Robard, & M. King (Eds.), *Rioting in the UK and France: A comparative analysis* (pp. 203–215). London: Routledge, Taylor & Francis Group.

Waddington, D. (2013). A 'kinder blue': Analysing the police management of the Sheffield anti-'Lib Dem' protest of March 2011. *Policing and Society: An International Journal of Research and Policy, 23*(1), 46–64.

Waddington, D., & King, M. (2005). The disorderly crowd: From classical psychological reductionism to socio-contextual theory – The impact on public order policing strategies. *The Howard Journal, 44*(5), 490–503.

Waddington, D., Jones, K., & Critcher, C. (1987). Flashpoints of public disorder. In: G. Gaskell and R. Benewick, R. (Eds.), *The Crowd in Contemporary Britain*. London, England: Sage.

Waddington, P. (1987). Towards paramilitarism: Dilemmas in policing public disorder. *British Journal of Criminology, 27*, 37–46.

Waddington, P. (1991). *The strong arm of the law: Armed and public order policing*. Oxford: Clarendon Press.

Waddington, P. (1993a). Dying in a ditch: The use of police powers in public order. *International Journal of the Sociology of Law, 21*(4), 335–353.

Waddington, P. (1993b). The case against paramilitary policing considered. *British Journal of Criminology, 33*(3), 353–373.

Waddington, P. (1994). *Liberty and order: Public order policing in a capital city*. London: University College London Press.

Waddington, P. (1996). Public order policing: Citizenship and moral ambiguity. In F. Leishman, B. Loveday, & S. Savage (Eds.), *Core issues in policing* (pp. 114–129). Harlow: Longman Group Limited.

Waddington, P. (1998b). Controlling protest in contemporary historical and comparative perspective. In D. della Porta & H. Reiter (Eds.), *Policing protest: The control of mass demonstrations in western democracies* (pp. 117–140). Minneapolis, MN: University of Minnesota Press.

Waddington, P. (1999). *Policing citizens*. London: UCL Press.

Waddington, P. (2001). Negotiating and defining "public order". *Police Practice and Research: An International Journal, 2*(1-2), 3–14.

Waddington, P. (2003). Policing public order and political contention. In T. Newburn (Ed.), *Handbook of policing*. Cullompton: Willan.

Waddington, P. (2007b). Editorial – Policing of public order. *Policing: A Journal of Policy and Practice, 1*(4), 375–379.

Waddington, P., & Wright, N. (2008). Police use of force, firearms and riot – Control. In T. Newburn (Ed.), *Handbook of policing* (2nd ed., pp. 465–496). Cullompton: Willan Publishing.

Wahlström, M. (2007). Forestalling violence: Police knowledge of interaction with political activists. *Mobilization: An International Quarterly, 12*(4), 389–402.

Wahlström, M. (2011). *The making of protest and protest policing - Negotiation, knowledge, space, and narrative*. Göteborg Studies in Sociology, No. 47. Göteborg: Göteborg University. Retrieved from https://gupea.ub.gu.se/handle/2077/25025

Wainwright, J., & Ortiz, R. (2006). The battles in Miami: The fall of the FTAA/ALCA and the promise of transnational movements. *Environment and Planning D: Society and Space, 24*(3), 349–366.

Wallace, S. (2009). Watchdog or witness: The emerging forms and practices of video-journalism. *Journalism, 10*(5), 684–701.

Warner, C., & McCarthy, J. (2014). Whatever can go wrong will: Situational complexity and public order policing. *Policing and Society: An International Journal of Research and Policy, 24*(5), 566–587.

Westley, W. (1957). The nature and control of hostile crowds. *The Canadian Journal of Economics and Political Science, 23*(1), 33–41.

Winter, M. (1998). Police philosophy and protest policing in the Federal Republic of Germany, 1960-1990. In D. della Porta & H. Reiter (Eds.), *Policing protest: The control of mass demonstrations in western democracies* (pp. 188–212). Minneapolis, MN: University of Minnesota Press.

Wood, L. J. (2014). *Crisis and control: The militarization of protest policing*. Toronto, ON: Pluto Press.

Chapter 4
The 2005 Riots in France

4.1 Introduction

The worst rioting since 1968 occurred in France in late October 2005, where rioting spread to more than 300 cities and towns across the country (Katz, 2008). The riots followed the deaths of two teenagers of North African and Malian descent, who were attempting to avoid an identity check undertaken by the police. The rioting began to subside after the third night, but after the police threw a teargas grenade into a mosque while prayers were being said, they ignited again.

After the throwing of the tear gas grenade, the Minister of Interior gave a radio interview, where he minimized the incident (Schneider, 2014). Reaction to the interview resulted in more rioting, which spread quickly throughout a large number of banlieues in Paris (Koff & Duprez, 2009). French officials supported the perspective of the Minister of the Interior and claimed that the media had exaggerated the level of violence and the extent of the damage that the rioting had caused (Koff & Duprez, 2009). These officials also refuted the use of the term "riot," preferring to define the violence as a "disorder" (Koff & Duprez, 2009).

The riots occurred over 21 nights, injuring 201 police officers and 26 fire fighters, with no official figures on the number of rioters injured. Despite the injuries, local hospital emergency wards did not report an increase in the number of admissions during the period that the riots took place (Mucchielli, 2009). An extensive amount of damage was also caused from the rioting. More than 9000 vehicles and 30,000 rubbish containers were burnt (Mucchielli, 2009). Government buildings and institutions were targeted and this made these riots different to earlier riots that had been experienced in France. Hundreds of public buildings, such as schools, sports facilities, town halls, local council administration buildings and police stations were vandalized or burnt. The public transport system was also targeted and more than 140 buses were burnt and in addition, more than 20 places of worship were damaged (Mucchielli, 2009).

G. den Heyer, *Police Response to Riots*,
https://doi.org/10.1007/978-3-030-31810-9_4

The purpose of this case study is to examine the police response to the riots that occurred across France for 21 nights in late October and early November 2005. This case study will use empirical data to examine the police response and will only discuss the possible reasons for the riots where they are relevant to the context of the police response. Research that has analyzed and documented the 2005 riots in France is scarce and as a result, this examination of the police response is limited when compared to the other case studies that have been presented in this book.

The case study will comprise six sections. The first section will present the background and context of the 2005 riots. The second section will present a chronology of the October–November 2005 riots and the third section will discuss the police response. The fourth section of the case study provides a critique of the police response and the fifth section briefly discusses the main operational problems that became apparent while the critique of the police response was being examined. The conclusions drawn from the examination will be presented in the final section.

4.2 Background and Context

The word "riot" was not used in France until 1990. The term was first used to describe the violence in the "Mas du Taureau neighbourhood of Vaulx-en-Velin (a suburb of Lyon) after the death of a boy in a crash between a motorcycle and a police car and then again several months later in the Val Fourré neighbourhood of Mantes-la-Jolie, in the Paris region, where a boy died in the local police station" (Mucchielli, 2009, p. 732). In contemporary France, the term "riot" refers to urban civil disorder, primarily in the banlieues (Jobard, 2009a).

The October–November 2005 riots were far from being the first and only one of their kind in France (Jobard, 2009a). Riots in the past have occurred in a series of cycles. The first cycle occurred shortly after the Second World War, the second began in May 1968, with another beginning in 1981 (Mucchielli, 2009). Since 1981, riots have occurred every few years in France.

The death of a member of the public has often been the trigger for the onset of rioting. Jobard (2014), stated that rioting following the death of a member of the public has been happening "as early as the eighteenth century in France" (Nicolas, 2008 cited in Jobard, 2014, p. 4). Rioting has taken place not only as a result of the death of a member of the public but also as a result of a rumor that such a death followed the actions of the police (Jobard, 2009, 2014).

Riots involving the immigrant population and residents of economically and socially deprived urban areas have been occurring in France, especially in Paris and the surrounding suburbs since the beginning of the 1980s (Jobard, 2009). It was in these suburbs that confrontations between Algerian workers and the police had occurred during the 1954–1962 Algerian War of Independence (Blanhard, 2007 cited in Jobard, 2009, p. 27). Even if the frequent number of cases of civil disorder involving Algerian migrants is discounted, there have still been a large number of riots in France (Jobard, 2009, p. 35).

Rioting in France has generally followed a pattern, occurring over two or three consecutive nights on local estates and rarely in city centers. They have included looting, the burning of a large number of vehicles and the infrequent use of deadly weapons (Jobard, 2014). One riot that had similar features to the October–November 2005 riot occurred in the summer of 1981, where cars were stolen, used for joyriding and then burnt (Duprez, 2009; Jobard, 2014; Wieviorka, 2005).

There has been a history of rioting in areas such as in Vaulx-en-Velin, a suburb of Lyon, "the Sapins neighbourhood in Rouen in January 1994" and in the La Duchère neighborhood in Lyon, in October 1995 (Berestycki, Nadal, & Rodriguez, 2015, pp. 445–446). The most devastating riot during this period was in Vaulx-en-Velin in October 1995, where more than 200 people took part. Rioting also spread to a number of suburbs in Lyon, but it did not spread across the country (Berestycki et al., 2015, pp. 445–446).

According to Mucchielli (2009), urban riots have been occurring in France on a regular basis since the mid-1990s, with confrontations between the police in Paris and the youth in the banlieues becoming more violent (Schnieder, 2014). Ten to fifteen riots in a number of banlieue towns occurred in the first half of the 1990s, and in the majority of these instances, police interaction with the minority community was the immediate cause of the violence (Jobard, 2014). Eleven riots occurred between September 1995 and December 2003 within the housing project areas of Fontenelles (Nanterre, September 1995), the Saint-Jean district of Châteauroux (May 1996), Dammarie-lés-Lys in the Seine-et-Marne département (December 1997), the Mirail district in Toulouse (December 1998), Vauvert, in the Gard (May 1999), the Grande Borne and Tarterêts neighborhoods in Grigny and Corbeil-Essonnes respectively (September 2000), the Borny neighbourhood of Metz (July 2001), Vitry-sur-Seine (December 2001), les Mureaux, Yvelines (January 2002), the Hautepierre neighborhood in Strasbourg (October 2002), and the last in the Monclar neighborhood in Avignon (December 2003) (Mucchielli, 2009, p. 732; Jobard, 2014, p. 6). All of these riots consisted of nightly confrontations with the police and the burning of vehicles and sometimes, the looting of local shops (Jobard, 2014; Wieviorka, 2005).

Although rioting in France may result from police shootings—whether lawful, unlawful, or accidental, it is more often the result of lethal traffic crashes that have occurred after the police have chased youths who were trying to escape arrest in a stolen vehicle. Riots have also been triggered by the outcomes of judicial investigations or trials where local youths have felt that the police officers involved have been unjustly cleared or too leniently sentenced (Waddington, King, & Jobard, 2009, p. 5).

Schnieder (2014) discussed at length the actions of the police and their connection to a riot and maintained that the majority of riots in France since the 1990s have come about because of police violence. Schnieder (2014) also claimed that a study of riots by a French judge found that each occurrence of youth violence was triggered by the actions of the police and a second study found that "16 out of 24 incidents of urban unrest were caused by the killing of young people by police or prison authorities, and almost half of those youths were chased to their deaths by police after they fled identity checks" (Schneider, 2014, p. 132).

Rioting did not follow the riot in Monclar in December 2003 and the French Government was of the opinion that urban violence had diminished. Then the October–November 2005 riots occurred (Mucchielli, 2009), which a French sociologist described as "les emeutes de la mort," which means "the riots of death" (Berestycki et al., 2015, p. 446). The 2005 riot, however, was not the last of the rioting that France would experience. A 2-day riot occurred in Villiers-le-Bel in 2007 which spread to neighboring cities but did not spread across the country (Berestycki et al., 2015, pp. 445–446).

After the 1990 riots, the French authorities changed the way that they responded to riots. The first change occurred in 1993 when legislation that was designed to deter juvenile crime was introduced (Jobard, 2009). This resulted in an increase in the number of paramilitary police units in the cities and the number of violent confrontations between youths and the police (Jobard, 2009). Public policy was changed in the early 2000s, which emphasized urban renewal, but the change in policy was implemented during a period of reductions in state-subsidized employment schemes and this led to increased tension in the community (Jobard, 2009), and poor social conditions in the banlieues (Entzinger, 2009).

The changes implemented by the French authorities brought the relationship of the police with the community, especially with youth, to the forefront. The police had responded to the riots in the banlieues by implementing militarized tactics, such as deploying surveillance teams, plain-clothed officers and riot police, which resulted in repression (Moran & Waddington, 2016). The government, in 2002, introduced community policing (called police de proximité) with the hope of strengthening the relationship of the police with the community (Jones & Wiseman, 2006). Unfortunately, this was shorted-lived and was abolished in 2003 with the election of a new Minister of Interior who claimed "that the community police had undermined traditional police functions (investigation and arrest) and that it was time to 're-establish a balance" (Moran & Waddington, 2016, p. 52). According to the minister, "balance" meant a focus on a "culture of results," where arrest rates were viewed as a measure of success" (Moran & Waddington, 2016, p. 52). The minister's change in focus prompted the police to change their strategic service delivery approach to one that was more repressive rather than preventative and to one that emphasized the enforcement of legislation pertaining to gangs (Moran & Waddington, 2016; Mohammed, 2009).

An emphasis on the pro-active policing of gangs came about because of the view held by the French authorities that "youth gangs" were the main instigators of the banlieue riots (Mohammed, 2009). Mohammed (2009) claimed that the view held at the political level was that the gangs were responsible for the riots and the solution was one of law and order rather than a social or economic one, which meant that the grievances within the banlieues could be ignored.

4.2.1 Conclusion

In France, the occurrence of rioting has been numerous and repetitive (Jobard, 2014), so much so that they have become an established tradition (Loch, 2009). The more modern form of rioting in France extends "from the first unrest in Lyon and Paris in the early 1990s, through to continually recurring, flare-ups in the peripheries of large cities up to the major conflagration of Autumn 2005, which introduced new dimensions in duration and geographical extent" (Loch, 2009, p. 791). Rioting in France has been evolving since the early 1980s (Jobard, 2014) primarily as a result of the form of policing that the French authorities have adopted. Given the history of rioting in France, the Autumn 2005 riots was not a new phenomenon; however, from a historical point of view, the riots were more about state violence than about popular revolt (Canet, Pech & Stewart, 2008). Jobard (2009) claimed that the 2005 riots were different in that they "were considerably more disruptive and enduring than their predecessors, insofar as they spread far beyond their city of origin" and "lasted for an unprecedented 20-day period" (p. 35). This difference is important for policing as the police need to be able to plan and implement a coordinated and sustainable, national approach based on tactics that can be implemented at the community level.

4.3 The 2005 Riots in France

4.3.1 Introduction

In late fall 2005, rioting in France occurred on an unprecedented scale (Moran & Waddington, 2016), and at a level that the country had never experienced before. According to Mestries (2007), the riots that swept through the suburbs of France were the "most serious popular rebellion since 1968" (p. 117). Despite France having experienced violent disorders periodically since the 1980s, the country had not previously experienced such a level of violence on a national scale (Koff, 2009). The Clichy-sous-Bios riots were triggered by the death of two youths who were electrocuted as they tried to evade police officers in the Parisian suburb of Clichy-sous-Bois (Canet, Pech, & Stewart, 2008). The deaths of the two youths reignited the tension that existed in the minority community in the Parisian suburbs. The tension existed because of high unemployment, racial prejudice and police harassment (Canet et al., 2008). Tension escalated further when the Minister of Interior visited the Parisian suburb of Argenteuil to see whether the new measures taken against urban violence were working (BBC News, 2005b). During the visit, the minister said that crime-ridden neighborhoods should be "cleaned with a power hose" and described violent offenders as "gangrene" and "rabble" (BBC News, 2005c). As a result of these comments, the minister was pelted with stones and bottles by those living in the neighborhood (BBC News, 2005b).

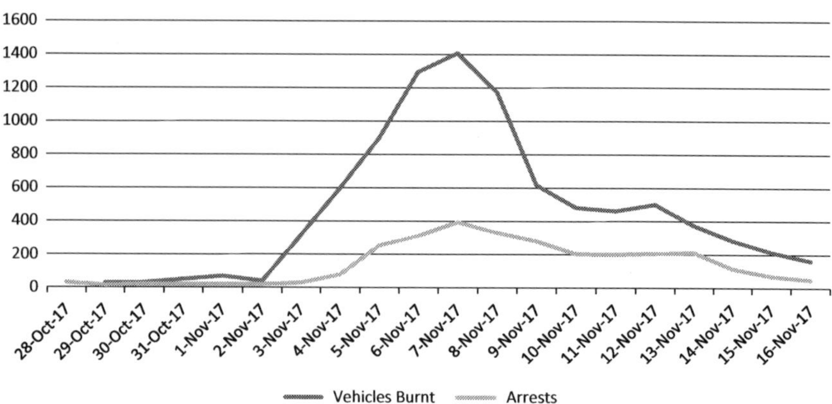

Fig. 4.1 Number of vehicles burned and people arrested during the riots in France, October 29 to November 16, 2005

For more than three weeks, in late October and early November, young people in the suburbs and small towns (known as banlieues in France) rioted—burning cars, damaging buildings, and confronting the police (Moran & Waddington, 2016; Sahlins, 2006). The effect was spectacular (Jobard, 2009). More than "10,000 cars were set alight over the course of the riots and conservative estimates put the financial cost" of the riots at approximately 200 million euros (Jobard, 2008; 2009; Moran & Waddington, 2016; Mucchielli, 2009, p. 39). Moran and Waddington (2016) claimed that between 13,000 and 15,000 people were involved in the riots with more than "11,000 police officers deployed on a daily basis" and "over 5,000 arrests were made in total" (Moran & Waddington, 2016, p. 39). The number of vehicles burned and people arrested by day has been presented in Fig. 4.1. Table 4.1 lists this information by location for the 20 days of the riots.

According to Crampton (2005), the incident that triggered the riots began at 5.20 pm on Thursday, 27 October 2005, in Clichy-sous-Bois when the police were called to a construction site to investigate a possible break-in. Three teenagers, who were returning from a soccer match, but were not carrying their identification papers, saw the police, who were conducting an identity check, chose to climb a wall to hide in a power substation (Chrisafis, 2012; Crampton, 2005; Mestries, 2007). There is some controversy over whether the three youths were actually chased by the police or whether they had fled before the police had started to chase them. An analysis of the radio calls that were made by the police at the construction site revealed that the police knew that the youths had scaled the wall and entered the power station site (Crampton, 2005). At approximately 5.50 pm, the police detained six youths at the construction site (Crampton, 2005), and they were subsequently taken to the police station at Livry-Gargan. While the detained youths were being questioning at the Livry-Gargan police station, power blackouts occurred (Crampton, 2005; Chrisafis, 2012). Two of the three youths that had climbed the wall into the power station were fatally electrocuted. The third youth received extensive electrical

Table 4.1 The number of vehicles burned and the number arrested in each location per day—28 October to November 16, 2005

	Date	Number of vehicles burned	Number of arrests	Locations	Reference
1	28–31 October	59	60	Clichy-sous-Bois	Aljazeera (2005a)
2	31 October	N/A	N/A	Montfermeil	Aljazeera (2005a)
3	1 November	69	N/A	Seine-Saint-Denis	Fox News (2005)
4	2 November	40	N/A	Seine-Saint-Denis, Seine-et-Marne, Val-de-Marne, Val-d'Oise, Hauts-de-Seine	Fox News (2005)
5	3 November	315	29	Île-de-France, Dijon, Rouen, Bouches-du-Rhone, Planoise	Fox News (2005)
6	4 November	596	78	Île-de-France, Dijon, Rouen, Marseille	Fox News (2005)
7	5 November	897	253	Île-de-France, Dijon, Rouen, Marseille, Evrenux, Roubaix, Tourcoing, Hem, Strasbourg, Rennes, Nantes, Nice, Toulouse, Bordeaux, Pau, Lille	LeMonde (2005b)
8	6 November	1295	312	Île-de-France, Nord, Eure, Eure-et-Loir, Haute-Garonne, Loire-Atlantique, Essonne	LeMonde (2005c)
9	7 November	1408	395	274 towns in total. Île-de-France, Nord-Pas-de-Calais, Midi-Pyrénées, Rhône-Alpes, Alsace, Franche-Comté, Angers.	Aljazeera (2005b)
10	8 November	1173	30	Paris region, Lille, Auxerre, Toulouse, Alsace, Lorraine, Franche-Comté, Angers	AFX News (2005)
11	9 November	617	280	116 towns in total. Paris region, Toulouse, Rhône, Gironde, Arras, Grasse, Dole, Bassens	CNN International.com (2005)
12	10 November	482	203	Toulouse, Belfort	BBC News (2005e)
13	11 November	463	201	Toulouse, Lille, Lyon, Strasbourg, Marseille	CBS News (2005)
14	12 November	502	206	Paris, Saint-Quentin, En Île-de-France, à Maisons-Alfort (Val-de-Marne), Rennes (Ille-et-Vilaine)	LeMonde (2005d)
15	13 November	374	212	Lyon, Toulouse, Carpentras, Dunkirk, Amiens, Grenoble	LeMonde (2006)
16	14 November	284	115	Toulouse, Faches-Thumesnil, Halluin, Grenoble	The Economist (2005)

(continued)

Table 4.1 (continued)

	Date	Number of vehicles burned	Number of arrests	Locations	Reference
17	15 November	215	71	Saint-Chamond, Bourges	LeMonde (2005e)
18	16 November	163	50	Paris region, Arras, Brest, Vitry-le-François, Romans-sur-Isère	LeMonde (2005f)
19	**20 nights**	**8973**	**2888**	**TOTAL**	

Source: Author

burns but was able to climb back over the wall to evade the police. The deaths of the two youths provoked rioting later that evening in Clichy-sous-Bois, where the tragedy had occurred (Koff & Duprez, 2009). Rioters, which included bands of 10–15 youths, some as young as 12 years old (ABC News, 2005), destroyed 15 vehicles on the first night of the violence (BBC News, 2005b), and caused the death of a photographer. The photographer was beaten to death by the rioters in Epinay-sur-Seine, Seine-Saint-Denis (Hopquin, 2005).

Canet et al. (2008) claimed that there were three phases to the 2005 riots in France. The first phase was the containment of the riots to the Clichy-sous-Bois area for five days from 27 October to 1 November. According to Lapeyronnie (2006, cited in Koff, 2009), the start of the riots was "mundane," in that "the violence began like so many episodes in the past" (Koff, 2009, p. 780). Koff is implying that the violence started because of the deaths of the two minority youths and as a result of the poor relationship between the police and youths in the area. Events such as these had been seen a number of times in the past in cities "such as Lyon, Toulouse, Lille and Strasbourg," but unlike any of the previous riots, the 2005 riots spread "from one Paris suburb to another" (Koff, 2009, p. 780).

While the riots of 27 October were a result of the deaths of the youths, the rioting which began on the evening of 28 October occurred after the Minister of Interior made a "statement denying any involvement of the police in the two deaths" (Mucchielli, 2009, p. 736). As a result of this statement, a number of low-level confrontations between the youth of Clichy and Montfermeil and the police took place (Schneider, 2014). More than 500 people took part in a march on the morning of October 29 in Clichy but there was little violence (Mucchielli, 2009). Later in the day, however, rioting occurred in the Seine-Saint-Denis administrative region (BBC News, 2005c).

Rioting occurred again on the night of 30 October and at approximately 5.00 pm the police chased a group of youths into a mosque (Schneider, 2014). However, the mosque was in use and the police were prevented from entering. A police officer threw a tear-gas grenade into the mosque "asphyxiating hundreds of families attending the sermon" (Mucchielli, 2009, p. 736; Schneider, 2014, p. 182). Again, the Minister of Interior claimed that "the police had not committed any wrong" (Schneider, 2014, p. 182), and these comments provoked more anger in the minority community (BBC News, 2005b).

On 30 October, the Minister of the Interior stated, at a media conference, that there would be a zero-tolerance approach taken towards the rioters and that he had arranged for police reinforcements to be sent to the Clichy-sous-Bois area (BBC News, 2005b). The police reinforcements included "17 companies of riot police (C.R.S.) and 7 mobile police squadrons (escadrons de gendarmerie mobile)" (Wikipedia, 2017). The minister also stated that he believed that the rioters were racailles (Koff, 2009) or scum (Kaufman, 2005) and that most of the violence was caused by organized gangs (Ena, 2005).

According to Koff (2009), the comments made by the minister caused the rioting "to spread to other cities and even beyond the national borders to Belgium and Germany" (Koff, 2009, p. 781). It seems probable that the throwing of the tear-gas grenade into the mosque was responsible for the violence spreading (Waddington et al., 2009). The incident with the grenade and the minister's "denial had a catalytic effect, causing rioting to spread initially to other Zones Urbaines Sensibles (ZUS) or 'sensitive urban zones' in the 93rd Department of Seine-Saint-Denis." By 7 November, the rioting had spread from suburb to suburb and eventually to more than "280 cities nationwide," galvanizing the prime minister to declare a state of emergency (Waddington et al., 2009, pp. 4–5). The riots resulted in more than 9000 vehicles being burnt, hundreds of public and commercial buildings being destroyed (worth more than 200 million euros), over 5000 rioters being arrested with 800 being imprisoned, and 125 policemen wounded (Schneider, 2014, p. 182).

The second phase of the riots began during the evening of October 31, with the riots spreading from the Clichy-sous-Bois area to other Zones Urbaines Sensibles around Paris, especially in the town of Seine-Saint-Denis (Mucchielli, 2009). By November 1, the riots had spread to other départements in the Paris area, starting with the Yvelines (Mantes-la-Jolie and Trappes, then to Achères, Carrières-sur-Seine, Chanteloup-les-Vignes, Chatou, Les Mureaux, Poissy, and Sartrouville) and to towns and suburbs in the Hauts-de-Seine, Val-de-Marne, Essonne, Seine-et-Marne and the Val-d'Oise (Mucchielli, 2009, pp. 736–737).

During the evening of November 2, rioters attacked and looted a police station at Aulnay-sous-Bois, while the police at La Courneuve reported being shot at (BBC News, 2005b). Overnight, 177 vehicles were also burnt in the Aulnay-sous-Bois area (BBC News, 2005b). By November 3, the third phase of the rioting began with the rioting spreading "beyond the Paris region to the eastern city of Dijon and parts of the south and west [of France], with 400 vehicles burnt" (BBC News, 2005b).

The riots during the evening of November 3 resulted in a number of cars in "the metropolitan areas of Rouen, Lyon, Rennes, Soissons and in the Département du Nord" (Mucchielli, 2009, p. 737) being burnt. The tenor of the riots changed during the evening of November 4, "when those ZUS well-known for their tradition of rioting came to the fore, especially the 'heavy' places, the large working-class neighbourhoods of the regional metropolises of Lille, Toulouse, Strasbourg, Rennes, Rouen and Bordeaux" (Mucchielli, 2009, p. 737). Mucchielli (2009) claimed that almost every mid-size city in France with a Zones Urbaines Sensibles was affected by the riots, with rioting occurring in more than 40 départements (suburbs) in one city.

The second death occurred on November 4 after a person was knocked unconscious by a rioter as they were trying to extinguish a fire in a trash bin near their home at Stains, Seine-Saint-Denis (LeParisien, 2009). In two days, the number of towns across the country that were affected by the riots reached more than 300 (Mucchielli, 2009) and by November 7, the riots had reached its peak, with more than 1400 vehicles being destroyed.

On November 6, the French government held an emergency meeting to discuss the riots and an extra 2600 police officers were deployed as a result (BBC News, 2005b). On November 7, the French Premier claimed that more than 18,000 police officers and more than 1500 reserve officers had been deployed to respond (BBC News, 2005b). As a result of the spread and the intensity of the riots, on November 8, the French President declared a state of emergency and the Cabinet authorized a range of emergency powers to tackle the unrest, which included giving local authorities the power to impose curfews and restrict people's movements (BBC News, 2005b; LeMonde, 2005a; Mestries, 2007). The authorization of the extra powers was the first time that the 1955 legislation had been enacted on mainland France (BBC News, 2005b). The declaration exposed the mistrust between the government and the minority youth who lived in the improvised suburbs of France and were suffering from high unemployment, discrimination and poor access to public services (Laban-Mattei, 2015). The riots continued to spread and a school in Belfort was burned and violence was suffered in Toulouse, Lille, Strasbourg, Marseille, and Lyon (LeMonde, 2005a).

Emergency powers came into force from midnight November 8 in more than 30 towns and cities, including the Parisian suburbs (BBC News, 2005b; Mestries, 2007). The police claimed that the level of violence had dropped from November 9 but the riots remained widespread across France (BBC News, 2005b). Also on November 9, the Minister for Interior issued an order to deport any foreigners who were convicted of being involved in the riots (Morice, 2006).

On the night of November 10, the violence increased around Paris and on November 11, the number of arson cases and attacks on the police increased with more attacks on electrical substations (MYTF1 News, 2005). One of the attacks on the electrical substations caused a blackout in the northern part of Amiens (MYTF1 News, 2005). Also, on November 11, the Parisian Council announced a ban on all public meetings from 9 am on Saturday November 12, to 7 am on Sunday November 13 that were likely to provoke disturbances (BBC News, 2005b). Just hours before the curfew for minors was about to start, the police in Lyon fired teargas to disperse rioters on Place Bellecour; the first rioting to occur in a major city centre (BBC News, 2005a). On November 12, a nursery school was set alight in the southern town of Carpentras (BBC News, 2005c).

On November 13, in response to the increase in violence in the city of Lyon, the Lyon Council enacted a ban on all public meetings (BBC News, 2005c). The BBC News (2005b) reported that the French authorities described the situation across France as being "much calmer," with a decrease in the number of vehicles set alight overnight. Thirteen vehicles, however, were set alight in central Paris, compared with only one on the night before and firebombs were thrown at the treasury in Bobigny and at an electrical transformer in Clichy-sous-Bois; the neighborhood where the disturbances had started (BBC News, 2005c). A day-care center in Cambrai, along with a tourist agency in Fontenay-sous-Bois, was also attacked and 18 buses were damaged by arson at a depot in Saint-Étienne (BBC News, 2005c).

On 16 November, the French parliament approved a 3-month extension of the state of emergency (BBC News, 2005d; Mestries, 2007). Extending the law enabled local authorities to impose curfews, conduct house-to-house searches and ban public gatherings (BBC News, 2005d). On 17 November, the French police declared that throughout France, the situation had returned to normal and stated that 98 vehicles had been set alight the night before, which corresponded to the usual number (BBC News, 2005d; Canet et al., 2008; Hargreaves, 2005). Mucchielli (2009) claimed that the rioting began to decrease on the eighteenth night of the disorder but decreased at different rates, depending on the region. Despite the decrease, during the evening of November 17, a Roman Catholic church was burnt and a vehicle was rammed into an unoccupied police station in Romans-sur-Isère (BBC News, 2005d).

Since the 2005 riots there have been other riots in France (Waddington et al., 2009), such as those that occurred in the Parisian banlieue of Villiers-le-Bel in November 2007, in Grigny in May 2007 and in a number of small towns in October 2007 and in June and October 2008 (Waddington et al., 2009).

The 2005 French riots followed a pattern which was similar to the other riots discussed in this book, in that they were the result of the actions of the police and that they occurred in a number of locations over a number of days. There are five factors, however, that not only make the French riots different but make them stand out in comparison to the riots discussed in the other case studies. The first difference was their scale and duration (Canet et al., 2008), and the second was the role that the media played. According to Cozens (2005), a leading TV news executive admitted to censoring the coverage of the riots in fear of encouraging support for far-right politicians, while a public television station stopped reporting the numbers of vehicles burned, apparently in order not to encourage "record making" between delinquent groups. The problem of record breaking came to light when it was found that protesters were using the Internet to get other cities to join the rioting, with the ultimate goal of making the evening newscast (ABC News, 2005).

The third difference was that there was hardly any use of firearms during the riots. Other than the two shots fired at police officers in La Courneuve on 3 November, no other firearm incidents were recorded. The fourth difference was that while there was a lot of damage to vehicles and property there were few reports of looting (Canet et al., 2008). The last difference between the riots that was noted was that all of the riots occurred in towns that had no prior history of rioting occurring (Jobard, 2009).

4.4 The Police Response to the Riots

This section of the chapter discusses the police response to the 2005 riots in France. The major problem with undertaking a discussion such as this is that there has been very little written about the police response. No examination of the police response has been undertaken by the government or a research institute as there has been for the other case studies presented in this book. Furthermore, while there is an adequate amount of literature available that comments on the police and their relationship with the community prior to and after the riots, there is no literature available that discusses the tactics that were used by the police in their response to the 2005 riots. Most French scholars and researchers (Duprez, 2009; Koff, 2009; Mucchielli, 2009), discuss the role of the police briefly and do not present an in-depth examination of the actions that the police took during the riot. These authors concentrate primarily on the socioeconomic and marginalization issues in the banlieues (Koff, 2009). As a result of the absence of literature, the presentation of how the police responded to the riots does not follow a similar format to the other case studies discussed in this book but takes a more strategic approach in discussing the police response to the riots.

According to Mouhanna (2009), the October–November 2005 riots are a part of a series of civil disorders that have occurred regularly in the banlieues since the early 1980s and of which, have increased in frequency since the early 1990s. Mouhanna (2009), examined whether the police authority was in any way responsible for triggering the riots and wanted to ascertain what lessons the police could draw from the riots. The crux of this discussion is to examine the police response to the riots, taking into consideration the perpetually tense relationship that the police had with the youths who live in the banlieues.

One of the reasons for the tense relationship is because of the type of policing undertaken in the banlieues. The police keep the banlieues "under control" through the "prevalence of patrolling officers" undertaking "intensive and extensive controls," including "stop-and-search operations" (Mouhanna, 2009, p. 174). While there may be a degree of rationality in young people having some resentment of the police, the resentment held by the youth and the adults living in the banlieues is much stronger and appears to be more permanent than the resentment held by youths and adults who do not live in the banlieues. According to Mouhanna (2009), what is being witnessed "in the banlieues, is a situation of permanent hostility on the part of people objecting to the siege-like presence of the police and their [the police] apparent indifference to the need to maintain any reasonable relationship with local residents" (p. 174).

Three distinctive characteristics are noticeable when the policing system in France is compared to policing in non-continental, European nations (Roché & de Maillard, 2009). The first feature is that the police system in France comprises different levels; public, national, or a combination of public and national (Roché & de Maillard, 2009), with the largest component being public. There are three types of police organizations in France: National, Municipal, and Gendarmerie, which employ more than 260,000 officers. Individually there are 146,000 National Police and 18,000 Municipal Police (Malochet, 2010), and 100,488 Gendarmeries (Gendarmerie Nationale, 2016). The Gendarmerie also has a further 25,000 officers in reserve (Gendarmerie Nationale, 2016).

There are two main police organizations—the Gendarmerie (a civil police force with a military history, which is responsible for policing predominantly rural areas) and the National Police that is responsible for policing urban areas (Roché & de Maillard, 2009). Both organizations are part of the Ministry of Interior, but the

Gendarmerie also undertakes duties for the Ministry of Defence. The national forces operate at the local level but are accountable to the Minister of Interior through the local Prefect (the local representative of the state) (Roché & de Maillard, 2009, p. 35). The third police organization, the Municipal Police, "have fewer legal powers than the national forces" and are accountable to the local mayor (Roché & de Maillard, 2009, p. 35).

In relation to the policing of protests, demonstrations and riots, the resources of the police are even more disjointed (Roché & de Maillard, 2009). Both the National Police and the Gendarmerie have officers who are trained to respond to riots and are deployed in units. The units in the National Police are called "CRS (Compagnies Républicaines de Sécurité)" and the riot units in the Gendarmerie are called "EGM (Escadrons de Gendarmerie Mobile)" (Roché & de Maillard, 2009, p. 35). When these units respond to a riot, the Compagnies Républicaines de Sécurité comes under the authority of the departmental head of the National Police and the Escadrons de Gendarmerie Mobile, comes under the control of the central government (Roché & de Maillard, 2009).

The French policing system has some advantages and some disadvantages. The main advantage of having a national or centralized policing system is that the training is uniform, communication procedures are standardized and there is the capability to deploy large numbers of officers from across the country to respond to an incident or event (Roché & de Maillard, 2009). According to Roché and de Maillard (2009), France has benefited from its centralized policing system and has been able to "create a riot monitoring system" that is capable of measuring the social climate and tension in the community (Roché & de Maillard, 2009). Owing to the remoteness of a centralized structure, decision-makers in police organizations do not understand the social issues or the tension in the relationship of the local police with its community to a level that would enable them to be able to respond to individual banlieues with a more community-focused, policing-ethos rather than from the use of repressive policing methods. The major advantage of having a centralized policing system during the 2005 riots was that the police had extensive experience in responding to them. According to Roché and de Maillard (2009), the police had more than 25 years of experience of responding to riots.

There are a number of disadvantages in having a centralized policing system. These include the "lack of flexibility and coordination" in any response to an emergency, the interference of central or state level politics (Roché & de Maillard, 2009, p. 35), and the lack of accountability by central managers for local policing issues.

The final aspect of policing to be discussed in this section is the accountability of the French police to the community. Any attempt by the government to introduce policing reform in order to improve police accountability and their relationship with the minority community has been resisted on the grounds that the police themselves are only truly qualified to comment on issues pertaining to policing and law enforcement (Mouhanna, 2009, p. 177). Furthermore, as the French police are "only accountable to a single central authority," they "consider the public unfit to cooperate with them on aspects of local security" (Mouhanna, 2009, p. 177). The views held by the French police, together with their centralized governance, control and character have a number of important implications for the management of public order and response (Mouhanna, 2009, p. 177). The first is that police officers are recruited from across the nation and are not deployed to their home town region (Mouhanna, 2009). This means that they often do not have a cultural tie with the area that they are deployed to, which is often a banlieue. The second is that officers are routinely required to implement proactive policing strategies that "primarily target people who are racially and socially marked out as young men of migrant origin" (Mouhanna, 2009, p. 178). The third, which is an extension of the second, is that police will often cordon an entire neighborhood for several days and will stop and question everyone within the restricted area (Mouhanna, 2009). The last implication is that the police rely extensively on "fire-brigade" reactive policing (Mouhanna, 2009) rather than a more victim or prevention-centric form of service delivery.

Reactive policing provokes a violent cycle "of resentment and retaliation" (Mouhanna, 2000, cited in Mouhanna, 2009, p. 178), and provides a basis for underlying and permanent conflict to develop (Mouhanna, 2009). This means that confronting the police is a main motivator for rioters (Koff, 2009; Mucchielli, 2009), especially when the trigger for the rioting has been the death of a minority community member caused by the actions of the police. According to Koff (2009), the tension between the police and the youths of the banlieues cannot be over-emphasized and is one of the key factors in explaining the violence in the autumn 2005 riots.

Another dimension to be considered in this discussion is the use of the police by the French government (Mouhanna, 2009). The control of the police forces by the Minister of Interior has been reinforced gradually "as part of a politically opportunistic strategy adopted in 2002 by the then Minister of Interior" (Mouhanna, 2009, p. 174). At the same time, the Minister of Interior was able to influence the approach taken by the police when responding to the riots. This influence together with the fact that the gendarmerie has had extensive experience in responding to different forms of disorder and rioting has led to a more reactive style of policing in France (Mouhanna, 2009).

The strategy used by the French police to respond to riots is based on a technique called space saturation. This technique involves deploying riot police in large numbers to project a threatening police presence, which makes it possible for the police to limit the size and the consequence of an incident (Mouhanna, 2009). This usually enables the police to take control and suppress the riots within a very short time frame (Mouhanna, 2009). However, the downside of this is that it has influenced the development of riot response units at the city level, which are made up of non-specialized police officers (Mouhanna, 2009, p. 175). The officers in these units have been trained to respond to riots and disorders and to focus on arresting offenders rather than engaging with the community (Mouhanna, 2009).

The large size of the national riot response capability enabled the police to deploy more than 11,000 officers on each night of the 2005 autumn riots and allowed for a contingency of reserve forces (Mouhanna, 2009; Mucchielli, 2009). The deployed officers included the Compagnies Républicaines de Sécurité and Escadrons de Gendarmerie Mobile who were supported by the municipal police, the investigation police and the surveillance police (renseignements généraux) (Roché & de Maillard, 2009). Although the police had the resources and the capability to respond to the riots, it appears that they were slow in doing so. The response was slow for two reasons. The first was that the riots were occurring only in the banlieues and the disorder initially only included the torching of vehicles. The second reason was because riots such as these had usually only lasted for two or three nights. The slow reaction of the police would explain why there were not a large number of arrests made during the first week of the riots.

Jobard (2009), claimed that at first there was not the political support for the police to respond to the riots in their usual, repressive manner. Political support was lacking because the Minister of Interior did not have the backing of the majority of the Members of Parliament until the end of the first week of the rioting and it was then that the Minister of Interior implemented a more arrest-oriented form of policing (Jobard, 2009).

Sanctions by the Minister of Interior enabled the police to change their response. Three strategies were implemented by the police as a part of their new response. The first strategy was to increase the number of riot officers and riot control units. According to Roché and de Maillard (2009), at the height of the riots, 14 public order units with approximately 80 officers in each unit had been mobilized. The increase in the number of officers available enabled large numbers of police to be deployed; "in Aulnay-sous-Bois, the number of agents [officers] went from about 150 on the 2nd November and to 300 on the 3rd November evening (Roché & de Maillard, 2009, p 38).

The second strategy adopted by the police was a change in riot control tactics. According to Roché and de Maillard (2009), the police initiated a new tactic at the département level (district level) from the evening of November 3, that "focused on containing the riots" which was to be achieved by the police entering the neighborhoods where the riots were occurring (p. 38). Dividing the existing Compagnies Républicaines de Sécurité units into a number of smaller units that enabled a more effective use of the resource was the main tactic. The Compagnies Républicaines de Sécurité were more effective when operating in smaller units because it meant that they could deploy officers to more of the sites where the rioting was occurring (Roché & de Maillard, 2009, p. 38). The new tactic gave the police more visibility, which gave assurance to the public (Roché & de Maillard, 2009). The tactic also ensured that offending rioters were arrested, which balanced with the directive that the officers were to avoid direct confrontations and violence. This also enabled the police to gather information about the offenders and the riots (Roché & de Maillard, 2009).

The third strategy that the police adopted was to change the responsibility for the command and control of the deployed units and officers from the département level to the local level (Roché & de Maillard, 2009). The change in the level of responsibility was adopted as there were too many riots to be able to coordinate them all at the département level and the demand from the district commissioners at the local level was more of a tactical nature than of a strategic one. The district commissioners were "given the operational capacity to organize units (by using both public security forces, Compagnies Républicaines de Sécurité and gendarmerie mobile)" within their district and the authority to speak on behalf of the police to the media (Roché & de Maillard, 2009).

The response to the riots before and after the tactical changes made by the French police "supports the view that there has been a decrease in the intensity of use of force by the police in European democracies" (Fillieule & della Porta, 2006). This was demonstrated by the lowering of the delegation of authority to the local level. However, the change in strategy and having the ability to deploy a large number of officers may have been too late to have had any effect on the riots. As noted by Roché and de Maillard (2009), the changes adopted "paralleled a decline in the intensity" in the riots (p. 39). This decline was seen in Aulnay, where on November 2, there were 103 interventions, while on November 3, there were only 75 interventions and 20 interventions on November 4 (Roché & de Maillard, 2009). The decline in the number of riots, according to Roché and de Maillard (2009), supported Carter's (1987), claim "that a large increase in police staff has a deterrent effect on riots" mainly because it makes the perpetration of violence riskier for rioters (Roché & de Maillard, 2009). The increase in the number of police and the change in tactics appear to have influenced the rioters (Roché & de Maillard, 2009).

The response taken by the municipalities to the riots differed to the response that the central government took. While the municipalities supported the National Police, the municipal police did not respond directly to the riots. They primarily undertook initiatives that decreased the level of tension amongst the rioters and also "assumed control of the security of the parts of the town not affected by the riots" (Roché & de Maillard, 2009, p. 39). The municipal police were supported by social workers, voluntary organizations and members of the public, who organized patrols to initiate discussions with the rioters and they occupied public spaces to minimize the probability of a riot occurring (Roché & de Maillard, 2009, p. 39; Body-Gendrot, 2013)). It is unknown as to what effect the mobilization of the community had on the riots, despite the increase in the number of police deployed and their change in response tactics, but it does reveal that there was a level of resilience at the community level (Roché & de Maillard, 2009). According to Roché and de Maillard (2009), if there was any weakness in the community response, it was only because they were not coordinated and did not know "how to communicate with potential rioters" (p. 39).

The final strategy to be discussed, which may have influenced the rioters was the introduction of a curfew and the November 8 declaration of a state of emergency. These factors enabled the authorities at the local level "to prohibit the circulation of individuals and vehicles at certain times and in certain places; to temporarily close entertainment halls and social meeting places; to place some individuals under house arrest; and to make it possible to order searches at night and even to pursue fleeing suspects into private residences" (Mucchielli, 2009, p. 734). These measures were for an initial period of 12 days and also included censorship of the press (Silverstein & Tetreault, 2006). Such a wide range of powers would have deterred a number of potential rioters and would have had an effect on the riots continuing.

To conclude, the rioting in more than 300 locations across France caused surprise and concern as they involved the most serious violence to occur in France since 1968 (Mucchielli, 2009). The occurrence caused apprehension, especially amongst the municipality authorities, who knew that they could not afford to pay for the policing services that were required to respond to the riots (Mouhanna, 2009). As Mouhanna

(2009), highlighted, the occurrence of riots in such a large number of locations stretched the French security system and revealed weaknesses in the system.

Roché and de Maillard (2009) claimed that the form and the structure of the police system and the way that it is embedded into the governance structure of the state determines whether a response to a crisis is successful. This success, however, depends on the coordination of the police at the local level and their relationship with the media and the community (Roché & de Maillard, 2009). The French authorities and the police did not score highly in relation to any of these success factors because of the centralization and politicization of the national security system which affected the approach taken in responding to the riots (Mouhanna, 2009; Roché & de Maillard, 2009).

4.5 The Critique of the Police Response

In a democracy or a republic, the maintenance of public order is an essential aspect of government and is traditionally considered as one of the tasks of the police (Roché & de Maillard, 2009, p. 34). The police, however, are regarded as the enemy in France, especially in the banlieues. The repetitive and aggressive identity checks that the police have conducted in the banlieues has resulted in tension and a very weak relationship with the community. These factors have played a part in triggering the majority of the riots that occurred in the 1990s (Moran & Waddington, 2016).

This section of the chapter will examine the police response to the riots and will evaluate the command of the police, their planning and their communication. Koff (2009) claimed that the 2005 riots could be best described as a series of local, rather than national disorder events. Two factors about the riots should be mentioned. The first is that the occurrence of the riots changed the political view of ethnic conflict in France when it became clear that one of reasons for the rioting was the poverty in the banlieues (Koff, 2009). The second was that the riots were primarily directed at the police, who the protesters considered an enemy in their neighborhoods (Koff, 2009).

The riots spread to hundreds of municipalities by late October and November (Roché & de Maillard, 2009). The spread and the intensity of the riots placed pressure on the authorities to such a level that a state of emergency was declared by the government and legislation was enacted that had not been used previously on the French mainland but only during civil unrest in Algeria in the 1950s (Roché & de Maillard, 2009). Enacting the legislation meant that curfews and the searching of the homes of offenders could be imposed (Roché & de Maillard, 2009).

The response by the police in the first few days of the riots could explain, in part, why the riots spread to other locations (Roche, 2006, cited in Roché & de Maillard, 2009). It is clear that the police, in the first days of the riots, were unable to foresee the occurrence of future events and did not have the information that would enable them to plan a response to such a mobile form of rioting (Roché & de Maillard, 2009). The police, according to Roché and de Maillard (2009), were unable to develop a response to the riots as the surveillance police did not have any credible intelligence and the public security police had received conflicting information as to the identity of offenders and the locations of the riots. The lack of information created uncertainty amongst police decision makers and they were unsure as to which response strategy they should implement (Roché & de Maillard, 2009).

Not being able to obtain the information needed for decision making is a problem with a centralized structure, especially at the département (regional) level (Roché & de Maillard, 2009). According to Moran and Waddington (2016), centralizing the coordination of the response at the départemental rather than at the local level and the structuring of the police into separate services caused "confusion and disorganization" (p. 63) during the response to the riots. The allocation of the resources used to respond to the riots was determined at the départemental level and as a result, the local police commissioners were not able to develop a response plan because they were not told as to how many officers would be available for deployment in their area (Roché & de Maillard, 2009).

Weaknesses at the local level were exacerbated by the lack of communication between the Prefect and the Commissioner and the deployment of different police services to the same area. The deployment of more than one police service to an area occurred without any of the services knowing about the deployment of the others (Roché & de Maillard, 2009). This meant that police services often did not have any knowledge of their role in relation to the roles that other police services would perform (Moran & Waddington, 2016). This would not have happened if the role that each service would perform had been defined prior to their deployment (Roché & de Maillard, 2009).

The final problem at the département level to be discussed is in relation to officers being deployed to areas of which they had little knowledge of. This often resulted in officers becoming lost in large neighborhoods (Roché & de Maillard, 2009) and led to an ineffective police response. As a result of the inadequate response, the police transferred the tactical command for the riots from the département level to the local level and it was only after this that the police gained control of the riots (Moran & Waddington, 2016).

4.5.1 The French Police

In order to understand the response taken by the national police it is necessary to discuss its structure. There are a very large number of public police officers in France, with the country having the third highest ratio of police officers to population in Europe (Duprez, 2009). Both the National Police and the Gendarmerie are structurally complex systems with each institution being comprised several distinct units that compete for resources and political power (Duprez, 2009). In the National Police, there are a number of different divisions that undertake three broad functions: public order, organized crime and community policing (Duprez, 2009).

The management and the administration of the National Police are organized and governed centrally (Moran & Waddington, 2016). This means that officers, once they have finished their recruit training are deployed to locations (usually the banlieues), which are not usually their home town, for 2 years (Moran & Waddington, 2016). This means that the suburbs are patrolled by officers that do not have any association with the community and often do not have an incentive to develop any long-term relationship with them (Moran & Waddington, 2016).

The police, in the 1980s, introduced beat policing and local youth action committees to strengthen their relationship with the community (Duprez, 2009). However, beat policing was not successful as police managers were not receptive to its implementation and had doubts as to its effectiveness (Duprez, 2009). Another problem was its resourcing. Beat officers were often taken from their primary role and reassigned to critical incidents or to major events (Duprez, 2009).

In 1998, to develop the relationship of the police with the community, the French government introduced community policing (policing de proximité), which was based on the Northern European model (Duprez, 2009). Community policing was first introduced into the banlieues to communicate that public safety was a priority for the government (Duprez, 2009). The introduction of community policing provided the catalyst for introducing a number of other changes in areas such as recruitment, the initial and in-service training of officers, and in the assignment, transfer and career paths of officers (Duprez, 2009). The introduction of the earlier beat policing and community policing programs was met with resistance from the majority of officers and supervisors and by mid-1999, the programs had ceased. By 2002, they were officially discontinued (Duprez, 2009). Following the national elections in 2002, the police returned to the operational structures and systems that were used in the early 1980s, which included a separation of the police from the community and the implementation of repressive force and identity checks (Duprez, 2009).

The changes to the police following the elections in 2002 resulted in a "muscular" police force that was only interested in maintaining public order (Duprez, 2009). This type of policing and the nonexistent relationship of the police with the community may have been one of the factors that led to the rioting, its escalation and its spread (Moran & Waddington, 2016). This view is supported by Duprez (2009), who claimed that the relationship of the police with the community was the crux of the riots, as the deaths of the two youths were the events that triggered the riots.

The police response to the riots was based principally on the maintenance of order and there was no strategy to include the community or gang leaders. Gang involvement in the riots was very limited, although they appeared to publicize their actions to encourage competition between banlieues (Koff, 2009). Gangs appeared to be communicating by text messages to provide warning as to the location of the police (Koff, 2009). Fortunately, the problem of electronic communication and competition between gangs and groups of youths was tempered by the mainstream media, who censored news videos of riots and only released the daily total of cars burnt (Koff, 2009).

While the police organizational and structural factors provide a partial explanation for the riots (Duprez, 2009), these must be considered within the context of the wider political response to the riots and the social problems that the youth in the banlieues faced. The government did not take the rioting seriously until after the riots had spread to other banlieues on the third night. The initial lack of political support did not help the police with their response and did not encourage the police to work with the community to minimize the risk of the riots continuing and spreading across the country.

4.6 Discussion

The critique of the police response to the October–November 2005 riots provides an opportunity to understand the reasons for the actions that the police took and to examine whether there are any lessons that could be learned from their actions. The riots did not have any ideological structure, nor was there any organization at the local or national level (Mucchielli, 2009). There was no cultural element involved in the riots, but they did follow the traditional pattern of protest; one that is based on deprivation and exclusion (Koff & Duprez, 2009). The riots may have, however, been less about the uprising of the youth from the banlieues and more about the government and the police response to the riots (Koff & Duprez, 2009).

The riots exposed a major weakness in the government's understanding of the problems faced by people living in the banlieues. Koff and Duprez (2009) claimed that it was not, however, just a lack of understanding of the problems in the banlieues but was more to do with the lack of communication between the officials at the various levels of government. The riots began in the same way that many others had begun before; from the actions of the police, who were not wanted in the banlieues and spread as a result of the statements made by politicians (Roy, 2005). Koff and Duprez (2009) claimed that the reason for the spread of the riots was because of the daily presence of the police in the banlieues and their violence. The authors also claimed that the reason for the spread of the riots was because national officials did not show any interest in communicating with community groups or leaders, which subsequently led to members of the community feeling abandoned by their local authorities. The national authorities did, however, enact curfews and attempted to mediate with the rioters. They also met with residents of the neighborhood to discuss how the violence could be brought under control (Koff & Duprez, 2009).

One of the reasons why the riots started was because the community felt anger towards the police. Schneider (2014) supported this view and discussed the results of a survey interview of banlieue youth, which was undertaken by the French Press Agency two years after the riots. The results of the survey indicated that the initial reason for the riots occurring was because the young people of the banlieues were angry with the police and second reason was because of the comments that the Minister of Interior made (Schneider, 2014). The youths' anger with the police increased during the riots because the police were deployed in large numbers to banlieues, which were not experiencing any violence, to undertake identity checks and to provoke local youth (Mucchielli, 2009).

According to Jobard (2009), the riots only spread to other towns and banlieues as a result of the Interior Minister refusing to apologize for the tear gas canister being thrown into the mosque. The riots that followed the mosque incident changed from those that were experienced in the first three days, where youths confronted the police, to more of a hit-and-run or guerrilla style (Jobard, 2009). This was actually the distinguishing feature of the riots; not just because they spread quickly to more than 300 locations across the country, but because they took a similar form in each of the locations (Duprez, 2009). This new form of riot was enabled by the response that the police took. The police deployed static Compagnies Républicaines de Sécurité units to areas where the violence was occurring but did not make a large number of arrests. The downside to this strategy was that because offending youths were not arrested and taken off the streets, they were able to continue their violence in areas that were cordoned by the police. The result was that there was no cost for the youths for their involvement in the violence and there was no legal incentive for them to stop committing acts of violence (Jobard, 2009).

The form of policing conducted prior to the riots did not help to strengthen the poor relationship that the police had with the community (Koff & Duprez, 2009). Since the 1980s, crime prevention has been based on "social prevention," which has focused on intervention rather than the effects of delinquency (Koff & Duprez, 2009). Research has found that this form of policing, along with the use of arbitrary identity checks increases tension between the police and ethnic youths (Mucchielli, 2009). A number of strategies were introduced to relieve the tension including the establishment of youth clubs and the introduction of a form of community policing. However, these strategies were short-lived and the police returned to a repressive policing approach, which was supported by the Minister of Interior (Koff & Duprez, 2009).

4.7 Conclusion

The most salient feature of the riots that occurred in France from the early 1990s is their similarity; youth from the banlieues confronting the police over a number of nights and the setting alight of vehicles (Jobard, 2014). The difference in the October–November 2005 from the earlier riots is how quickly they spread and how widely they spread across the country. Jobard (2014) claimed that the 2005 riots were a point of change in comparison to the riots of the 1990s, as they occurred in rural banlieues rather than in city banlieues. Another point of difference in the 2005 riots was their contagiousness and as they spread across the country, they changed from being a local political problem to a national political problem (Koff, 2009). Unlike the previous riots, the rioters tended to band together in small, mobile groups in order to bait the police rather than directly confronting them (Mucchielli, 2009).

According to Jobard (2008), the level and the duration of the French riots left their mark on the developed nations of the world. Not only because of the type of tactics used by the rioters or because buildings and institutions were being targeted for vandalism or destruction but because the perpetrators of the riots were essentially second-generation immigrants which implied that this type of riot could occur in any developed country that had a large immigrant population.

The initial response taken by the French police to the riots appears to have been a cordon and contain approach and it is presumed from the information available that this approach was adopted for two reasons. The first reason was that the authorities and the police thought that the 2005 riots would follow a similar pattern to earlier riots and would stop after a few days. The second reason was, because the police thought that the riots would stop after a few days, they did not deploy a large number of officers to control the riots and arrest offenders. The result of the police cordoning the areas where the riots were occurring in an effort to stop them from spreading and by not arresting rioters meant that the youth were able to remain "free to continue their activities unhindered in smaller territories surrounded by police forces" (Jobard, 2009b cited in Schneider, 2014, p. 15).

The initial police response changed, however, after the tear gas grenade was thrown into the mosque. Following this incident and with the riots spreading quickly across the country, the police became more proactive in their response and confronted and arrested a number of the rioters. Only 2888 rioters were arrested over the 21 days of rioting (see Table 4.1 for the number arrested each day). This is not a significant number considering the number of people who participated in the rioting and the amount of damage involved.

The police did not gain control of the riots at any time or in any location, nor did they implement any community or communication strategies that included reaching out to the neighborhoods affected by the riots in order to obtain their assistance in gaining control of the riots. Even following the declared state of emergency on November 7, the police did not change their form of response, but relied principally on containing each riot and arresting the offenders that they were able. The riots appeared to come to an end on November 17, with the number of vehicles being burned each day returning to "normal" (BBC News, 2005e). Some commentators claimed that the declaration of the state of emergency was the catalyst for the riots ceasing (Koff & Duprez, 2009), while others claimed that the turning of the weather was the sole reason why the riots ceased (Jobard, 2008).

References

ABC News (2005, November 4). *Paris riots in perspective*. Retrieved from http://abcnews.go.com/International/story?id=1280843.

AFX News (2005, August 11). *France plans curfews to curb spiralling riots*. Retrieved from https://web.archive.org/web/20051125191659/http://www.forbes.com/home/feeds/afx/2005/11/08/afx2323455.html.

Aljazeera (2005a, November 14). *Timelne: France riots*. Retrieved from http://www.aljazeera.com/archive/2005/11/2008410121424989730.html.

Aljazeera (2005b, November 7). *Police shot, wounded in France unrest*. Retrieved from https://web.archive.org/web/20051125132150/http://english.aljazeera.net/NR/exeres/6727FE6C-C8E3-491A-B272-A902E3F3F500.htm.

BBC News (2005a). *Assault protest stops traffic*. Retrieved October 18, 2005, from http://news.bbc.co.uk/2/hi/uk_news/england/west_midlands/4354554.stm.

BBC News (2005b). *Timeline: French riots*. November 14. Retrieved February 19, 2016, from http://news.bbc.co.uk/2/hi/europe/4413964.stm.

BBC News (2005c). *Riot erupts in French city centre.* November 13. Retrieved May 3, 2017, from http://news.bbc.co.uk/2/hi/europe/4430540.stm.

BBC News (2005d). *France extends laws to curb riots.* November 16. Retrieved May 3, 2017, from http://news.bbc.co.uk/2/hi/europe/4441246.stm.

BBC News (2005e, November 10). *-Curfew for riot-hit French towns*. Retrieved from http://news.bbc.co.uk/2/hi/europe/4423584.stm.

Berestycki, H., Nadal, J., & Rodriguez, N. (2015). A model of riots dynamics: Shock, diffusion and thresholds. *Networks and Heterogeneous Media, 10*(3), 443–475.

Blanhard, E. (2007). The Paris police and Algerians in Paris (1944–1956). *Colonial context and equality of rights, the impossible implementation of ordinary policing*. (unpublished) Leeds, United Kingdom: University of Leads.

Body-Gendrot, S. (2013). Urban violence in France and England: Comparing Paris (2005) and London (2011). *Policing and Society, 25*(1), 6–25.

Canet, R., Pech, L. & Stewart, M. (2008). *France's burning issue: Understanding the urban riots of November 2005*. November 18. Retrieved from https://ssrn.com/abstract=1303514.

Carter, G. (1987). Local police force Size and the severity of the 60's Black riots. *Journal of Conflict Resolution, 31*(4), 601–614.

CBS News (2005, November 10). *Chirac seeks to learn lessons from unrest*. Retrieved from https://web.archive.org/web/20051126060706/http://www.cbsnews.com/stories/2005/11/10/ap/world/mainD8DPR93GD.shtml.

Chrisafis, A. (2012, October 31). *French teens electrocution case linked to 2005 riots reopens*. The Guardian. Retrieved from https://www.theguardian.com/world/2012/oct/31/french-electrocution-deaths-case-reopens.

CNN International.com (2005, November 9). *Unrest flares amid the curfew*. Retrieved from https://web.archive.org/web/20051125223614/http://edition.cnn.com/2005/WORLD/europe/11/09/france.riots/index.html.

Cozens, C. (2005). *French TV boss admits censoring riot coverage*. November 10. Retrieved May 3, 2017, from https://www.theguardian.com/media/2005/nov/10/france.tvnews.

Crampton, T. (2005). *Behind the furor, the last moments of two youths*. The New York Times, November 7. Retrieved April 30, 2017, from http://www.nytimes.com/2005/11/07/world/europe/behind-the-furor-the-last-moments-of-two-youths.html?_r=0.

Duprez, D. (2009). Urban rioting as an indicator of crisis in the integration model for ethnic minority youth in France. *Journal of Ethnic and Migration Studies, 35*(5), 753–770.

Ena, C. (2005, November 7). *Rioting threatens France's tourism image*. USA Today. Retrieved from https://usatoday30.usatoday.com/travel/world/2005-11-07-france-tourism_x.htm.

Entzinger, H. (2009). Different systems, similar problems: The French urban riots from a Dutch perspective. *Journal of Ethnic and Migration Studies, 35*(5), 815–834.

Fillieule, O., & della Porta, D. (2006). *Police et Manifestants*. Paris: Presses de Sciences Po.

Fox News (2005, November 2). *Riots plague Paris suburbs for sixth night*. Retrieved from http://www.foxnews.com/story/2005/11/02/riots-plague-paris-suburbs-for-sixth-night.html.

Gendarmerie Nationale (2016). *Memogend 2016*. Retrieved from http://www.gendarmerie.interieur.gouv.fr/Notre-communication2/Publications-Documentations/MemoGend.

Hargreaves, A. (2005). *An emperor with no clothes*? November 28. Retrieved from: http://riots-france.ssrc.org/Hargreaves/.

Hopquin, B. (2005, November 9). *Après la mort de Jean-Claude Irvoas, des habitants affligés*. Le Monde. Retrieved from http://www.lemonde.fr/societe/article/2005/11/09/apres-la-mort-de-jean-claude-irvoas-des-habitants-affliges_708368_3224.html.

Jobard, F. (2008). The 2005 French urban unrests: Data-based interpretations. *Sociology Compass, 2*(4), 1287–1302.

Jobard, F. (2009a). An overview of French riots: 1981–2004. In D. Waddington, F. Robard, & M. King (Eds.), *Rioting in the UK and France: A comparative analysis* (pp. 27–40). New York: Willan Publishing.

Jobard, F. (2009b). Rioting as a political tool: The 2005 riots in France. *Howard Journal, 48*(3), 235–244.

Jobard, F. (2014). *Riots in France: Political, proto-political or anti-political*. Retrieved March 27, 2017, from https://hal.archives-ouvertes.fr/halshs-01118328/document.

Jones, A. & Wiseman, R. (2006, March 31). *Policing and terrorism: The French (dis)connection and the lessons for America*. Retrieved from http://www.lacp.org/Articles%20-%20Expert%20-%20Our%20Opinion/060321-TheFrench(DIS)connection-AJ.htm.

Katz, M. (2008). Why don't American cities burn very often? *Journal of Urban History, 34*(2), 185–208.

Kaufman, G. (2005). *Violence continues across France: President vows to crack down on rioters*. July 7. Retrieved from: http://www.mtv.com/news/1513131/violence-continues-across-france-president-vows-to-crack-down-on-rioters/.

Koff, H. (2009). Understanding 'La Contagion': Power, exclusion and urban violence in France and the United States. *Journal of Ethnic and Migration Studies, 35*(5), 771–790.

Koff, H., & Duprez, D. (2009). The 2005 riots in France: The international impact of domestic violence. *Journal of Ethnic and Migration Studies, 35*(5), 713–730.

Laban-Mattei, O. (2015, March 16). *French police go on trial for teen deaths that kicked off riots*. France 24. Retrieved from http://www.france24.com/en/20150316-french-police-officers-trial-clichy-sous-bois-riots-electrocution.

Lapeyronnie, D. (2006). Revolte primitive dans les banlieues francaises'. *Déviance et Société, 30*(4), 431–448.

LeMonde (2005a, February 14). *Le Conseil d'Etat refuse de suspendre l'état d'urgence*. Retrieved from http://www.lemonde.fr/societe/article/2014/02/14/le-conseil-d-etat-refuse-de-suspendre-l-etat-d-urgence_4854780_3224.html.

LeMonde (2005b). *1 295 véhicules ont brûlé cette nuit*. http://www.lemonde.fr/economie/article_interactif/2007/08/17/crise-des-subprimes-le-point-de-vue-de-deux-economistes_944553_3234.html.

LeMonde (2005c, November 6). *1 295 véhicules ont brûlé cette nuit, le plus lourd bilan depuis le début des émeutes*. Retrieved from http://www.lemonde.fr/web/article/0,1-0@2-3226,36-707066@51-704172,0.html.

LeMonde (2005d, November 12). *Incidents pour la seizième nuit consécutive en France, la police en alerte*. Retrieved from http://www.lemonde.fr/web/article/0,1-0@2-3226,36-709528@51-704172,0.html.

LeMonde (2005e, November 15). *Le retour au calme semble se confirmer dans les banlieues*. Retrieved from http://www.lemonde.fr/web/article/0,1-0@2-706693,36-710208@51-707207,0.html.

LeMonde (2005f, November 16). *La tendance à l'apaisement se confirme*. Retrieved from http://www.lemonde.fr/web/article/0,1-0@2-3226,36-710597@51-704172,0.html

LeMonde (2006, February 19). *Les protestations contre les caricatures dégénèrent en violences interconfessionnelles au Nigeria*. Retrieved from http://www.lemonde.fr/europe/article/2006/02/19/les-caricatures-provoquent-des-violences-interconfessionnelles-au-nigeria_742933_3214.html.

LeParisien (2009, June 12). *Emeutes de 2005: Cinq ans de prison pour l'agresseur de Le Chenadec*. Retrieved from http://www.leparisien.fr/faits-divers/emeutes-de-2005-cinq-ans-de-prison-pour-l-agresseur-de-le-chenadec-12-06-2009-546697.php#xtref=https%3A%2F%2Fwww.google.fr%2F.

Loch, D. (2009). Immigrant youth and urban riots: A comparison of France and Germany. *Journal of Ethnic and Migration Studies, 35*(5), 791–814.

Malochet, V. (2010). *Les polices municipales: points de repères. Note rapide*. Institut d'aménagement et d'urbanisme, Septembre 2010. Retrieved from http://www.iau-idf.fr/fileadmin/Etudes/etude_734/NR_515_web.pdf.

Mestries, F. (2007). *The French autumn riots of 2005 and the crisis of republican integration*. Retrieved from http://meme.phpwebhosting.com/~migracion/rimd/revistas/rev9/e7.pdf.

Moran, M., & Waddington, D. (2016). *Riots: An international comparison*. London: Macmillan Publishers Ltd.

Mohammed, M. (2009). Youth gangs, riots and the politicisation process. In D. Waddington, F. Robard & M. King (Eds.), *Rioting in the UK and France: A comparative analysis* (pp. 157–172). London, United Kingdom: Routledge Taylor & Francis Group.

Morice, A. (2006, February 13). *Comprendre avant de juger: à propos des émeutes urbaines en France.* Retrieved from http://atouteslesvictimes.samizdat.net/archives/index-8405.html.

Mouhanna, C. (2000). Les services publics et la question jeune: de la crainte au rejet? In F. Bailleau & C. Gorgeon (Eds.), *Prevention et Securite. Vers un Nouvel Ordre Social?* Paris: Editions de la Delegation Interministerielle a la ville.

Mouhanna, C. (2009). The French police and urban riots: Is the national police force part of the solution or part of the problem? In D. Waddington, F. Robard, & M. King (Eds.), *Rioting in the UK and France: A comparative analysis* (pp. 173–182). London: Routledge Taylor & Francis Group.

Mucchielli, L. (2009). Autumn 2005: A review of the most important riot in the history of French contemporary society. *Journal of Ethnic and Migration Studies, 35*(5), 731–751.

MYTF1 News (2005). *Banlieues: Les violences se stabilisent – Société.* Retrieved from http://lci.tf1.fr/france/2005-11/violences-stabilisent-4860108.html.

Nicolas, J. (2008). *La rébellionfrançaise. 1661–1789.* Paris, France: Gallimard.

Roché, S., & de Maillard, J. (2009). Crisis in policing: The French rioting of 2005. *Policing, 3*(1), 34–40.

Roche, S. (2006). *Le Frisson de l' 'Emeute, Violences Urbaines et Banlieues.* Paris, France: Le Seuil.

Roy, O. (2005). *The nature of the French riots.* November 18. Retrieved from: http://riotsfrance.ssrc.org/Roy/.

Sahlins, P. (2006). *Civil unrest in the French Suburbs.* November 2005. Retrieved from: http://riotsfrance.ssrc.org/.

Schneider, C. (2014). *Police power and race riots: Urban unrest in Paris and New York.* Philadelphia: University of Pennsylvania Press.

Silverstein, P. & Tetreault, C. (2006, June 11). *Postcolonial urban apartheid.* Retrieved from http://riotsfrance.ssrc.org/Silverstein_Tetreault/.

The Economist (2005, November 14). *An underclass rebellion.* Retrieved from http://www.economist.com/node/5138990.

Waddington, D., King, M., & Jobard, F. (2009). Introduction and overview: The British and French Riots. In D. Waddington, F. Robard, & M. King (Eds.), *Rioting in the UK and France: A comparative analysis* (pp. 3–12). London: Routledge Taylor & Francis Group.

Wieviorka, M. (2005, November 18). *Violence in France.* Retrieved from http://riotsfrance.ssrc.org/Wieviorka/.

Wikipedia (2017). *Reaction to the 2005 French riots.* Retrieved from https://en.wikipedia.org/wiki/Reactions_to_the_2005_French_riots.

Chapter 5
The 2011 Riots in London

5.1 Introduction

The December 2011 report of the August 2011 English riots prepared by the House of Commons Home Affairs Select Committee claimed that these riots were "unprecedented in the modern era" (citied in Moran & Waddington, 2016, p. 116). The Committee's opinion was based on the fact that several rioting incidents had occurred in different locations at the same time and because the form that the rioting took had never happened before. The riots occurred between 6 and 11 August 2011 and while they started in a London borough, they spread across a number of London boroughs and then on to several major towns and cities, such as Birmingham, Coventry, Leicester, Derby, Wolverhampton, Nottingham, West Bromwich, Bristol, Liverpool, Manchester, and Salford.

Five people died as a result of the rioting and at least 16 people were injured, with more than £200 million worth of damage to property (BBC News, 2011c). By 15 August, more than 3000 arrests had been made across England and a further 1100 people had been charged with various criminal offences relating to the riots (BBC News, 2011d). Briggs (2012c) professed that the damage sustained during the riots and the number of people arrested was not surprising "given the scale and unprecedented rapidity of the spread of the disturbances, and the initial picture of an inadequate law enforcement response to maintain public order and protect people and property …. But even as the smoke cleared, there seemed to be little idea of how it started and what to do to prevent it occurring again" (p. 17).

The initial and most vociferous criticism, which was aided by the media, centered on what was perceived to be as an inefficient response to the riots by the police (Klein, 2012a). The Daily Mail newspaper claimed that the disorder had spread because the police did not take control of the violence and that "officers allowed the impression to take hold that the streets [had] been surrendered to thousands of yobs" (Daily Mail, 2011). The newspaper also alleged that if the police had been more proactive earlier on in the riots, the disorder would not have spread as it did and far

G. den Heyer, *Police Response to Riots*,
https://doi.org/10.1007/978-3-030-31810-9_5

less damage would have been caused (Daily Mail, 2011). Muddle (2014) claimed that the police were criticized more than was necessary for the looting and the violence; furthermore, Klein (2012a) maintained that the argument of police ineffectiveness was disingenuous, as the criticism of the police was not in relation as to whether they were providing the wrong kind of policing, just that there was too little policing in the first few days of the riots.

There have been a number of enquiries and reports conducted as to cause of the riots, the behavior of the rioters and the response of the police and their training (The Secretary of State for the Home Department, 2011). Each report has provided some insight, but none of the reports, despite the considerable amount of work and evidence-gathering undertaken, has provided a complete picture of the issues involved or the variables that influenced the causes or the triggers of the disorder (The Secretary of State for the Home Department, 2011).

The purpose of this case study is not to provide a complete picture of the riots but instead to examine the response taken by the police. This case study will examine the riots that occurred in the London boroughs in 2011 and the response of the Metropolitan Police Service. The case study will comprise six sections. The first section will provide the background and the context in which the riots occurred and the second section will present a chronology of the August 2011 riots. The third section discusses the police response in detail and the fourth section provides a critique of the response within a framework of seven operational issues that were identified in an analysis of the police response to the riots. The fifth section discusses the operational issues within the context of what they mean for policing and the conclusions are presented in the final section.

5.2 Background and Context

In the UK, urban or civil disorder and riots are not a new occurrence (Her Majesty's Inspectorate of Constabulary, 2011), with a number of notable, modern, major riots transpiring in 1981, 1985, 1991, 2001, and 2005. It is against this backdrop of civil disorder that the August 2011 riots took place.

The earliest of these riots occurred in Brixton, which is located in the borough of Lambeth in South London and occurred over the evenings of 10–12 April 1981, with a few minor confrontations with the police taking place on 13 April. At the time that the riots broke out, the Brixton community, which was largely made up of people of African-Caribbean descent, was experiencing a recession and high levels of unemployment (Wain & Joyce, 2012). As with a number of the other riots discussed in this book, the Brixton riot was a response to a police operation called "Swamp 81" which was established as a response to the significant increase in street crime, especially mugging and robbery (Her Majesty's Inspectorate of Constabulary, 2011; Wain & Joyce, 2012). Wain and Joyce (2012) proclaimed that there was another reason as to the cause of the riot. Wain and Joyce (2012) claimed that the reason for the cause of the riot was because of the community's misperception of the actions taken by the police during an incident that involved the stabbing of an African-Caribbean youth. The police were assisting the injured youth but the assistance was perceived by on-lookers and later by members of the community that the police were assaulting the youth.

The Brixton riots also appeared to be the catalyst for the riots that occurred later in 1981 in a number of major metropolitan areas across England. Between 3 and 5 July, and on 27 and 28 July, riots occurred in Toxteth (Liverpool), between 8 and 12 July in Moss Side (Manchester), and on the 10 and 11 July in Handsworth (Birmingham) (Her Majesty's Inspectorate of Constabulary, 2011).

The Moss Side riots were the most serious in this sequence of disorder events. Moss Side was triggered by a racial incident, which involved a group of white youths taunting a small group of minorities and this led to shops being vandalized and incidents of arson (Hytner, 1981; Wain & Joyce, 2012). The initial response to the rioting taken by the police was to keep a low profile, but the victims of the riot accused the police of taking "no profile," which led, on subsequent nights, to a more aggressive response by the police and allegations that the police were using excessive force and that they were arresting people indiscriminately (Hytner, 1981; Wain & Joyce, 2012).

As a result of the 1981 series of riots, the government commissioned Lord Scarman to examine the cause of the riots and the police response to the disorder. Lord Scarman's report noted that prior to the riots, there were shortcomings in the relationship of the police with the community, especially with members of ethnic minorities (Scarman, 1981). This finding was supported by Hytner (1981), who claimed that young people were resentful of the police and that the feeling of resentment was the result of the youth being harassed by the police in the form of the liberal use of stop and search powers. These stops were usually undertaken by younger police officers and often included physical confrontations and racial abuse (Hytner, 1981).

The negative view taken of the police, however, was not only confined to the younger members of the Moss Side community but was also held by older members of the ethnic community (Hytner, 1981). This negative view was not only a result of the young people's relationship with the police but was also because the form of policing delivered was perceived as being intimidatory and based on racial prejudice that was not only directed toward young people but to all members of the ethnic minority community (Moss Side Defence Committee, 1981, p. 3).

However, the findings of Lord Scarman, the opinions of Hytner (1981), and the Moss Side Defence Committee (1981) were in contrast to the findings of two other studies which had been undertaken at the same time. The first study, taken by the Home Office, consisted of a survey of the residents of Moss Side following the riots. The study found that the majority of the West Indian community had a satisfactory relationship with the police (Tuck & Southgate, 1981). The second study, based on a survey of the residents of Handsworth in Birmingham, also undertaken by the Home Office, found that 77% of the residents had never been stopped, searched or arrested during the previous 12 months (Field & Southgate, 1982, p. 51).

The final riot in 1981 that occurred in Handsworth was also influenced by the relationship of the police with the African-Caribbean community but also, according to Scarman (1981), contained a "copy-cat element."

The second sequence of riots in England occurred in 1985. The first of these riots was on 28 and 29 September and also took place in Brixton. The second riot in 1985, occurred on 6 October, on the Broadwater Farm Estates area of Tottenham, North London. The September 1985 Brixton riot was caused by the accidental shooting and wounding of a Jamaican woman during a police search of her house in Brixton. Rumors spread across the community that the police had shot and killed the woman and as a result, members of the community formed a protest outside the local police station (Daily Telegraph, 2011). The protest eventually led to a number of skirmishes between some members of the ethnic minority and the police (Parry, Tirbutt, & Rose, 1985). Local shops were looted, more than 55 cars were burnt, 149 people were arrested and one person was killed during the riots (Parry et al., 1985).

The October 1985 Tottenham riot also followed a police search of a private residence and the death of the African-Caribbean occupant. The occupant had died of heart failure during a police search of her home on the day before the riot. The death, together with the tension that existed between the local youth and the police and the aftermath of the Brixton riot the week before, triggered the Tottenham riots (Parry et al., 1985).

The day following the death of the occupant, community members demonstrated outside the Tottenham police station. During this protest, violence between local youths and the police escalated, leading to riot police being deployed (Parry et al., 1985). Rioting, including the throwing of bricks and Molotov cocktails by youth and the setting alight of vehicles and buildings also occurred on the Boardwater Farm Estates (Parry et al., 1985).

It was during this period of the riot that the London Fire Brigade responded to a fire, a short distance away from the vicinity where most of the rioting was occurring. The fire fighters came under attack from a large group of youths. A police unit of a Sergeant and ten Constables were dispatched to assist the fire fighters (Bain, 2010), but the unit was not prepared for the violence and nor were they trained in how to control a riot (Bain, 2010). The violence forced the police to withdraw but one officer stumbled and was set upon by 30–50 people with machetes and knives (Bain, 2010), resulting in the death of the officer. The officer, PC Blacklock, was the first constable to be killed in a riot since 1833 (Newman, 1986).

The 1991 riots all occurred at the end of August and the beginning of September and in a number of different cities: Birmingham, Cardiff, Dudley, Leeds, Newcastle upon Tyne and Oxford. Each riot was triggered by a different incident; cars stolen by youths in Oxford, blackout looting in Handsworth, an inner-city area of Birmingham, and an ethnic dispute in Cardiff (King & Brearley, 1996). According to King and Brearley (1996), the police response to the rioting was different in each city: preemptive in Oxford, preventive in Cardiff, and proactive in Birmingham.

The 2001 riots also occurred in Oldham, Harehills, and Bradford. The first riot took place between 26 and 28 May in Oldham, a town in greater Manchester and followed a long period of ethnic tension and attacks between groups from local communities and South Asian-Muslim members of the community. The riots were described as the worst ethnically motivated riots in the UK since 1985 (Cantle, 2006; Carter, 2002). The Oldham riots were violent, with petrol bombs used by more than 500 Asian youths against riot police and numerous shop windows were broken and cars set alight (BBC News, 2001a). According to Islam Online (2001), at least 20 people were injured and 37 people were arrested.

The second riot in 2001 occurred on 5 and 6 June in Harehills, a multiethnic district of Leeds. According to Wainwright, Psarias, and Spencer (2001), the riot was triggered by the wrongful and allegedly, heavy-handed arrest of an Asian man. The riot initially involved more than 100 youths but increased to more than 200 by the end of the night. A hoax phone call to the police alleged that a number of police officers had been injured by a petrol bomb and this lured officers into a street which had been barricaded by burning furniture (BBC News, 2001b). It was within this area that the riot took place (Herbert, 2001) and resulted in more than 26 cars being burnt and two police officers and two journalists severely injured (BBC News, 2001b; Wainwright et al., 2001).

The 2001 Bradford riots were short in length but were intense and began on 7 July and ended on 9 July. They arose from heightened tension between the Asian community and a group from the white community (Bagguley & Hussain, 2008). Tension escalated when a number of far-right groups confronted members of the minority community during a march through the city and following the stabbing of an Asian man (Bagguley & Hussain, 2008). The riots involved an estimated 1000 youths, with groups of between 30 and 100 white youths attacking the police and Asian-owned businesses and vehicles (Bagguley & Hussain, 2008). The police deployed 500 officers initially, but this number increased to approximately 1000 officers as the riot progressed.

The 2005 riots occurred on the 22 and 23 October in the Lozells and Handsworth area of Birmingham (Her Majesty's Inspectorate of Constabulary, 2011), and was initiated because of tension between two ethnic minorities communities; Caribbean and British Asian, following an alleged gang rape of a teenage black girl by a group of South Asian men (BBC News, 2005). During a public meeting held on Saturday 22 October to discuss the alleged rape, a young man was stabbed and later died (Muir & Butt, 2005). The riot involved running battles between groups of between 30 and 50 youths (Muir & Butt, 2005).

The last disorder event to be discussed in this overview is the 2009 London G20 Summit protests, which were not riots in the same sense as those discussed above but involved a similar response by the police. The protests took place between 28 March and 2 April 2009, in London, where approximately 35,000 people participated in marches, sit-ins, and protester camps (McVeigh, Lewis, & Jha, 2009). The first event, March for Jobs, which was held on 28 March was not violent, although one person was arrested for climbing over the railing into the Houses of Parliament (McVeigh et al., 2009). The second protest, held on 1 April outside the Bank of England, comprised approximately 5000 people (MacLean & Holton, 2009). This protest consisted of a number of confrontations with the police and resulted in a number of smashed windows and the police "kettling" the crowd (BBC News, 2009b).

Although the police described the G20 as one of the largest, most challenging and complicated public order operations they had ever planned for, or responded to (BBC News, 2009a), few protesters were arrested. Only 100 protesters were arrested on 2 April after the police ended the protester camps (O'Neill, 2009).

The policing of the G20 events may have been used as a model for responding initially or lack thereof, to the 2011 London riots. The actions of the police during the

G20 event raised four issues and it is important that these issues are not overlooked. The first was the public and political reaction to the policing of the protests and the large number of complaints made to the Independent Police Complaints Commission (BBC News, 2009c). The second was the comments made by the then Metropolitan Police Commissioner. The Commissioner was concerned that the video footage revealed that some actions taken by the police were disturbing and needed to be investigated. The Commissioner also voiced that there was a need for reassurance that the use of containment, or the kettling tactic "remains appropriate and proportionate" (BBC News, 2009c). The third issue was the death of a protester from the strike of a police baton during the protest outside the Bank of England on 1 April and the last issue was the request by the Commissioner for the Chief Inspector of Constabulary to review the tactics for the policing of public events. These issues would have deeply demoralized the police in relation to their understanding and use of existing standing procedures and tactics when responding to civil disorder riots.

5.3 The 2011 London Riot (The Riot and Chronology)

The events that triggered the 2011 riots were very similar to the triggers of the 1985 riots in Brixton and Tottenham; because of the tense relationship between the police and the ethnic community, owing to the police use of tactics, such as stop and search. The 2011 riots followed the death of a man shot dead by the police on 4 August (BBC News, 2011a). Not satisfied with the police response and the lack of clarity over the shooting, a protest march was arranged by Broadwater Farm residents and was to take place outside the Tottenham Police Station on the afternoon of Saturday 6 August (Briggs, 2012b). Approximately 300 people gathered outside the police station to demand justice and to protest the discrimination that was demonstrated by the police toward the ethnic community (Briggs, 2012b). However, the marchers became agitated when a senior police officer was not available to talk to the crowd and at approximately 8 pm the crowd started to confront the police officers standing outside the police station. A bus was set alight, shops and businesses were ransacked and looted, and police cars and buildings were vandalized and set alight (Briggs, 2012b). The police were not prepared for the number of incidents or the level of violence and as a result, the rioting spread to other parts of the district on 6 August (Lewis et al., 2011; Metropolitan Police Service, 2012).

According to Her Majesty's Inspectorate of Constabulary (2011), the disorder that occurred during the riots "constituted the most widespread outbreaks of disorder seen in England for a generation" (p. 13), and while the shooting may have acted as a trigger to the initial riot, the clarity of the triggering event ended there (The Secretary of State for the Home Department, 2011, p. 15).

On Sunday 7 August, the rioting and disorder spread to five districts/boroughs of London: Brixton, Enfield, Islington, Oxford Circus, and Wood Green and by Monday 8 August, had also spread to Battersea, Bromley, Camden, Croydon, Ealing, East Ham, Hackney, Harrow, Lewisham, Peckham, Stratford, Waltham

Forest, and Woolwich and to other major cities, such as Birmingham, Bristol, Gloucester, Gillingham, and Nottingham (BBC News, 2011b; Briggs, 2012c).

According to the Metropolitan Police Service (2012), the speed and the scale of the escalation of the rioting, together with the rapid intensification of the disorder placed pressure on the resources and the response of the police. The major problem for the police was that as they responded to the disorder in one geographical location another incident of disorder would occur in another location and this stretched the resources of the police across London. The public perceived the police response as lacking (Metropolitan Police Service, 2012). The perception increased in intensity by day three as it "became clear that social networking was being used to coordinate groups in direct conflict with the police" and as result, the disorder and riot offending spread across 22 of London's 32 boroughs (Metropolitan Police Service, 2012, p. 14; Her Majesty's Inspectorate of Constabulary, 2011).

As a result of an increase in the number of police officers responding to the riots, the riots were brought under control in all of the districts of London by Tuesday 9 August. However, the rioting continued in Nottingham, Birmingham, Leicester, parts of greater Manchester and in Merseyside (BBC News, 2011b). The riots, violence, and disorder took the form of arson, criminal damage, looting, and intensive conflicts with police (Briggs, 2012c).

It was believed that two incidents may have triggered the riots. The first was the protest march to Tottenham Police Station and the second was the unsubstantiated rumor that a 16-year-old girl had been injured by the police during the march (Muir, 2011). The rioting and its connection with the shooting death was more tenuous outside of Tottenham. According to Kawalerowicz and Biggs (2014), a large number of rioters were motivated by their dislike and distrust of the police. Rioters substantiated this view during interviews with researchers where they voiced their frustrations about other social issues, such as economic deprivation and the cutting of social programs. The rioters also voiced their attraction to looting (Lewis et al., 2011; Morrell, Scott, McNeish, & Webster, 2011).

The number and the range of social problems facing the ethnic community of Tottenham may have been the trigger for the initial riots but the actual causes were wide and varied, or as Kawalerowicz and Biggs (2014) described "not strictly black and white" (p. 6). Furthermore, the initial incident, according to Kawalerowicz and Biggs (2014), was "only tangentially connected with rioting on the following days" (p. 6). This discussion and analysis becomes even more complicated when the makeup of those who were arrested in the riots is examined. In a synopsis of the arrestees, 47% were classified as black, 32% as white, 11% as mixed, and 8% as South Asian (Home Office, 2011). No one ethnic group formed a majority of those arrested but the number of black youths arrested was overrepresented in comparison to the population, while white youth were underrepresented (Kawalerowicz & Biggs, 2014).

It was estimated that 13,000–15,000 people participated in either the rioting or the looting across England during the 4 days, which caused the loss of homes and businesses, the deaths of five people and cost approximately one-half billion pounds (Briggs, 2012c; Her Majesty's Inspectorate of Constabulary, 2011). The one-half billion pounds was made up of £300 million of property damage, £80 million in lost business and retail sales, police response of £50 million, £43.5 million to clean up, £300 million in insurance claims, and £250 million in lost tourism revenue (Briggs, 2012c).

During the 4 days of rioting more than 5000 crimes were recorded by the police across the country, which included 1860 arson and criminal damage offences, 1649 burglaries, 141 incidents of disorder and 366 incidents of violence against the person (Riots Communities and Victims Panel, 2012a). These crimes resulted in more than 4000 of the suspected rioters being arrested across England by late 2011 and of those arrested, the majority were male and 90% had a criminal record or were known to police (Briggs, 2012c; Riots Communities and Victims Panel, 2012a). Of those people arrested, at least 84 "had committed 50 or more previous offences each" and "three-quarters were aged 24 or under" (Riots Communities and Victims Panel, 2012a). In London, by mid-September 2011, 1715 of the offenders had been identified and arrested, 462 were found guilty of their specific offences and 315 had been sentenced (Briggs, 2012c). Of the rioters identified, 763 were arrested for burglary, 459 for violent disorder and 229 for theft (Ministry of Justice, 2012).

An analysis of those arrested revealed that two-thirds of the rioters had special educational needs and had missed almost 1 day a week of school. The rioters had an average of 11 previous convictions and were likely to live in low-income neighborhoods. Of the those brought before the court, 70% were living in 30% of the most deprived postcodes in the country and "of the 66 areas that experience riots, 30 were in the top 25 percent most deprived areas in England" (Riots Communities and Victims Panel, 2012a, p. 9).

In a second report completed by the Riots Communities and Victims Panel (2012b), the panel found that the riots were "characterised by opportunistic looting" of stores that stocked specific desirable, high value brands (p. 9). This finding was also supported by the fact that more than 50% of offences recorded by the police were "acquisitive in nature" and that the rioters were not a homogenous group, but were actually undertaking separate actions, depending on what they wanted to achieve (Riots Communities and Victims Panel, 2012b). According to the panel, there were five different types of people present at the riots. The five types have been presented in Table 5.1.

Table 5.1 The five types of people who participate in riots

Type of person	Definition
Organized criminals	Identifiable offenders, often from outside of the geographical area of the riot
Violent aggressors	Individuals that committed the more serious violence and crimes
Late night shoppers	People who deliberately travelled to the location of riot in order to loot
Opportunists	People who were drawn into riot areas through curiosity or a sense of excitement and then became "caught up in the moment"
Spectators	People who did not partake in the disorder but who came to just watch the rioting

Adapted from Riots Communities and Victims Panel (2012b, p. 19)

The report found that while the riots were similar in each geographical area they were subtly different in form and the action of each riot or disorder varied, depending on the city and the location of the disorder within that city (Riots Communities and Victims Panel, 2012b; The Secretary of State for the Home Department, 2011). This similarity and difference, according to the Riots Communities and Victims Panel (2012b), made it very difficult to draw any general conclusions as to the reasons for the riots or their trigger.

5.4 The Police Response to the Riots

The disorder events that occurred over the 4 days in August 2011 were unprecedented in the capital's history (Metropolitan Police Service, 2012) and incomparable to earlier riots "in terms of the speed, scale and geographical spread of disorder" and this tested the ability and the capacity of the police service to respond and regain control (Her Majesty's Inspectorate of Constabulary, 2011). The riots were described by one journalist as "the worst disturbances of their kind since the 1995 Brixton riots" (Lewis, 2011), while other reporters compared the riots to the Broadwater Farm riot of 1985 (BBC News, 2011c). In some respects, the riots did share similar features of previous examples of violent civil disorder in the UK, but "the speed of events," as described by Her Majesty's Inspectorate of Constabulary (2011, p. 16), were "unprecedented."

The major issue that became apparent early in the event was the perception that was held by the public that the police were slow to react. According to a number of researchers, people saw little decisive action from the police (Hatherley, 2011; Klein, 2012b; Newburn, 2012) and became fascinated with the media images of the violence and disorder (Body-Gendrot, 2011; Lewis et al., 2011). This motivated people to go and see what was happening and for others, it gave them a chance to join the looters (Briggs, 2012b). Briggs (2012b) also claimed that the environment had enabled some offenders to carry out specific, targeted looting activities under the guise of being a part of the disorder crowd.

The use of social media during the riots and its capability exacerbated the opportunity for offending, violence, and looting. This situation was further intensified when people saw from the live media coverage that the police were not taking any enforcement action in relation to the rioting (Briggs, 2012b). To impede the crowd-control strategies and tactics used by the police, Twitter and YouTube were used to update protesters and media sources by providing up-to-date information on the locality of the riot police officers (Sagrans, 2011; Newnham & Bell, 2012). YouTube was also used to upload footage of the protests and to report on the location of the police and their response activities and provided a basis for criticizing the police for their alleged acts of excessive violence toward individual protesters (Newnham & Bell, 2012).

The major issue for the police during their initial response to the riots was balancing the resources they had available with how they would respond to the looting and violence and their duty to protect people and property from the threat of harm or injury. This, especially in the heat of the moment, is defined as the policing dilemma (Her Majesty's Chief Inspectorate of Constabulary, 2009). Policing in the UK, as in all democratic societies, is by consent. The acceptance of this principle is important at every level when the police respond to public disorder, as the level of response must be seen as conciliatory with the philosophy of policing by consent (Her Majesty's Chief Inspectorate of Constabulary, 2009). However, the policing of public order and riots also requires careful interpretation of the law and how it is applied. This issue of interpretation in relation to maintaining The Queen's Peace was identified by Lord Scarman in his report on the 1981 riots, who noted that "it is well recognised that successful policing depends on the exercise of discretion and on how the law is enforced" (quoted in Her Majesty's Chief Inspectorate of Constabulary, 2009, p. 5). It is within this context of consent and law that the response of the police is discussed and in particular, the response taken by the London Metropolitan Police Service to the 2011 London riots.

The discussion in this section relies extensively on the Metropolitan Police Service (2012) report, entitled "4 Days in August: Strategic Review into the Disorder of August 2011." The report is a review of the response of the Metropolitan Police Service to the pan-London disorder of August 2011, which was called Operation Kirkin. The report is used extensively, as it is the only document that includes a comprehensive discussion and presentation of the actions taken by the Metropolitan Police Service. An analysis of the actions taken by the police is supported by academic and other specific references, wherever available. The objective of the strategic review of Operation Kirkin was "to develop a detailed understanding of the MPS [Metropolitan Police Service] response to significant public disorder in London between Thursday 4 August and Friday 19 August 2011, in order to inform future policing operations by ensuring organizational learning is recognised and developed for the future" (p. 11).

Following the shooting of Mark Duggan on Thursday 4 August, consideration of the resources required for the delivery of the policing plan were made at various times (p. 35). A Commander was appointed on Thursday evening to take overall control of the critical incident (p. 26). It was clear that the incident needed to be investigated and priority given to engaging with the community so the Haringey Borough Commander, a Chief Superintendent, was appointed to immediately attend the scene to lead the community response of the borough (p. 27). According to the Metropolitan Police Service (2012), the police had considered engaging with the community immediately following the shooting and had maintained an emphasis on community engagement from the occurrence of the shooting through to the march on Tottenham Police Station on the evening of Saturday 6 August. The report also stated that the police sought independent involvement and advice by engaging with the Independent Advisory Group members and Key Individual Networks[1] and also sought community intelligence from the Safer Neighbourhoods Teams[2] and local

[1] Key Individual Networks are a list of key individuals with the local community.

[2] These are mixed teams of officers and Police Community Support Officers that are deployed to a set geographical location where they are expected to be known by their local community.

partners (p. 30). By Thursday evening, the police had developed a community engagement structure, which included a governance framework (p. 27).

On Thursday, establishing a policing plan for the Broadwater Farm Estate was given consideration and it was at this time that the local police commander requested that additional police staff from the Metropolitan Police Service Central be made available (p. 35). These resources were to include police officers that had been trained in the policing of public order and later on Thursday evening, a policing plan was developed for the area (p. 35). The plan for the Estate was to be low-key and for a Police Support Unit[3] to be on standby at Tottenham police station (p. 35).

It was at this early stage, on Thursday evening and Friday morning that the Temporary Commissioner and Temporary Deputy Commissioner were briefed and a separate briefing was held for the management board and the Gold Group on Friday morning (p. 27). Following the management board meeting, the Tottenham Police Commander directed that the policing strategy for the area would remain "reassuring and calm" (p. 35). Local police officers held planning meetings and an e-mail was sent on Friday to community representatives and council partners about the shooting. A community assessment to measure the level of tension in the community was also undertaken on the Friday. The tension was measured against three categories: "experienced," "evidenced," and "potential" and on a scale of 1–6, of which 6 equates to no raised tension. Each was graded at 5 at the time, which indicated that tension levels were above normal and were thought to be localized in nature (p. 28).

As a result of the increase in tension within the community and because a pre-season football match was to be held at the Tottenham Hotspur Football Club grounds on Saturday 6 August, the police increased their resources. Violence or disorder at the Broadwater Farm Estate was not expected at this stage (p. 35). Thirty Constables, a Police Support Unit, and ten mounted officers were made available (p. 35). The policing plan for the area, with agreement from the duty Chief Inspector, allowed for the redeployment of an Inspector, one Sergeant and seven Constables from the football match to the Estate if any disorder occurred (p. 35). These resources were deployed to the Tottenham Police Station during the march on Saturday evening.

Early on Saturday morning, the police received information that there would be a march to the Tottenham Police Station as a response to the shooting on Thursday 4 August (p. 28). Later that morning, the police held a meeting with their key strategic partners and it was agreed that the march would be facilitated "with a low-key approach" (p. 28). A second meeting was held later in the day with the Independent Advisory Group and community representatives where it was made known that tension in the community was increasing (p. 29). It was at this second meeting that the issue was raised "that the Duggan family were unhappy with the lack of contact [from the police that] they had received" (p. 29).

As a response to the perception held by the community, a march, led by a member of the Black Independent Advisory Group and family and friends of Mark Duggan ascended on the Tottenham Police Station at approximately 5.30 pm on Saturday 6

[3] A squad of approximately 25 officers trained in public disorder.

August. Members of the family asked the police for an explanation for the shooting, but the Inspector on duty was unable to provide an explanation that satisfied the crowd. It was also at this time that attempts were made to contact a more senior police officer but owing to a number of other policing commitments that evening, a Superintendent was not available until later in the evening. Some of the family group members and others left the area outside the police station at about 8.30 pm (p. 32). Two incidents of missiles being thrown from the crowd prior to the family leaving were recorded, but as soon as the family left (at approximately 8.30 pm), the situation intensified with multiple missiles being thrown at the police station and two police vehicles were set on fire (p. 32). These actions changed the interpretation of the police of the crowd gathering in peaceful protest to one of serious public disorder (p. 32).

A critical incident was declared by the police on Saturday at 5.35 pm, at which time the Chief Inspector left the football match and made his way to the Tottenham Police Station to take command of the policing operation (p. 36). Upon his arrival at the police station, the Chief Inspector requested that additional resources be mobilized to the area (p. 36). The extra resources included the redeployment of officers from the football match, two Sergeants and 14 Constables from another operation and a Police Support Unit from the Commissioner's Reserve in Central London (p. 36). The Police Support Unit, which was held in reserve, were deployed, wearing high visibility jackets, rather than public order protective equipment and arrived outside the police station, at approximately 6.45 pm, where the crowd had gathered (p. 36). In total, over 50 officers were mobilized to Tottenham Police Station during the protest march (p. 36).

Following the outbreak of disorder, the Police Support Unit, deployed in full personal protective equipment and a cordon of officers were put in place across the road from the police station to control the movement of the large number of people (p. 39). Local police were deployed to the south of the police station and they were to clear and maintain a safe operating area outside the station (p. 37). However, with the mounting violence and the frequency of missile attacks on police lines it became clear that more public order officers were needed (p. 42). A request was made to the Commissioner's Reserve for another Police Support Unit (p. 37). In addition to this response, the chief inspector activated the Metropolitan Police Service—Service Mobilisation Plan (SMP).[4]

Upon activation of the SMP, all London boroughs are sent a message instructing them to either identify available resources (amber message) or to mobilize resources (red message) (p. 40). The activation of the SMP resulted in the Commander of the Metropolitan Police Service's Public Order Command establishing a Special Operations Room and the instruction was given by the Commander for the SMP to be elevated to phase red (p. 40). However, these instructions were not followed and the amber message was instead sent to other boroughs (p. 41). The phase red SMP message was finally sent at approximately 9.33 pm (p. 41).

[4]The SMP is activated in times of increased demand for resources and provides a mechanism for deploying additional public order trained officers to spontaneous major events.

The activation of the SMP resulted in nine Public Support Units (approximately 225 officers) being deployed and they arrived at Tottenham Police Station at approximately 10.40 pm (p. 41). The Support Units were assisted by a dog section, an additional specialist team of officers equipped with armored vehicles, traffic officers and four Public Support Units (approximately 100 officers) which came from four contiguous police forces (Essex, Kent, Surrey and Thames Valley) (p. 41).

The crowd was growing in size and the violence was rapidly escalating and this challenged the police officers who were attempting to control the situation (p. 42). At this stage, the police formed a single line cordon and made several short shield advances to distance the crowd because a number of petrol bombs had been thrown (p. 43). While the majority of the crowd continued to focus their attention on the police, a number of individuals started to loot nearby shops (p. 43). It was at this stage that a central command structure was established (p. 43).

By midnight, the mobilization plan was in full operation (p. 43), but weaknesses in the tactical plan became evident. The original plan was to isolate the rioters, but the scale and intensity of the disorder prevented the available resources from achieving this (p. 45). The battle to gain control over the riot was not achieved until early Sunday morning and this was the main reason as to why the police were unable to deploy officers to the looting that was taking place at Tottenham Hale Retail Park and Wood Green (p. 45). However, by 3.00 am, deployments were made to both locations and multiple arrests were made (p. 45).

At 7.00 am on Sunday morning (7 August), the Temporary Commissioner chaired an emergency management board meeting where the Temporary Commissioner and his deputy were updated on the operational plans and this enabled them to set a strategic direction for policing the riots (p. 50). During the meeting and as a result of the previous night, the management board mobilized an additional 33 Public Support Units to complement the already on-duty borough officers (p. 50). The additional units meant that an extra 825 officers trained in riot control, equivalent to the total complement of police officers in a large London borough, were available for deployment should violence erupt on Sunday (p. 50). The police also deployed further public order support assets, such as the Mounted Branch (a horse unit), Dog Section and officers trained in the use of firearms and they informally sought mutual aid support from neighboring forces (p. 50). In response to the request for assistance, four Public Support Units (approximately 100 officers) were supplied from Kent, Surrey, Thames Valley, and Essex Police (p, 50).

Behind the scenes, the police appointed an Assistant Commissioner to lead a team across London to cope with the demands of community engagement (p. 51). While it was realized that the majority of local community engagements were going to be undertaken at the borough level, these engagements would be coordinated centrally by specialists (p. 51). The team also provided briefings to the Independent Advisory Group who were encouraged to offer advice to police commanders (p. 51). This process was designed to build the trust of the community and to foster confidence in the police decision-making process (p. 51). Other boroughs that were most likely to be impacted by the riots in the Tottenham area (Lambeth; Hackney, Croydon, Southwark, Tower Hamlets, Lewisham, Waltham Forest, and Newham Boroughs) were instructed to review their community engagement procedures as well as their local policing plans (p. 51).

A social media monitoring function that fed into the Metropolitan Police Intelligence Bureau (Met Intelligence Bureau/MIB) was established. The objective of the monitoring function was to develop and maintain a community tension assessment across London and the information gathered would form part of the national community tension assessment (p. 51). To provide a platform to implement the social monitoring function, an intelligence management structure was implemented on Sunday. The management structure would receive and develop relevant information and intelligence that indicated the locations where disorder and other criminality would take place (p. 51). The intelligence gathered was then passed to the Operational Command Team to assist in the deployment decision-making (p. 51).

The earliest disorder that took place on the second night (Sunday) was in Enfield town centre, which later spread to Enfield Retail Park (p. 49). The disorder was on a smaller scale compared to the rioting that occurred on Sunday in other London boroughs, but it stood out as an area that attracted younger males, many of whom were known to be linked to gangs (p. 49). The nature of the offending was more of criminal damage rather than of burglary, which suggested that the disorder at this stage remained expressive rather than purely acquisitive despite the shops being the primary target, which were subsequently looted as the night progressed (p. 49). The disorder extended to other parts of North London, including Lambeth, Hackney, Lewisham, and Peckham as well as the Tottenham area and continued until the early hours of Monday morning (p. 50). The disorder was more destructive with arson and looting being the main forms of offending and this increased the strain on the police and the London Fire Brigade (p. 50).

During the evening of the third day, Monday, the disorder had spread throughout London (p. 63). Twenty-two of the 32 London boroughs recorded serious incidents of disorder, with the first starting in Hackney just before 5.30 pm (p. 63). The disorder included widespread looting and violent skirmishes with the police (p. 63). The major difference in the disorder that took place on Monday evening in Croydon compared to the disorder that took place over the previous evenings was that people travelled across London to partake in the disorder (p. 63). While Croydon suffered from an influx of individuals, Hackney was the exception, with the disorder being localized in two specific areas only (p. 63).

The borough of Croydon experienced sustained disorder on a considerable scale on Monday evening and was the scene of some of the most iconic images of the rioting. It was also the area where one of the two murders was committed during the riots (p. 49). The borough suffered a relentless display of violence, fires were deliberately preplanned and opportunistic burglary and theft took place (p. 74). Vehicles filled with petrol bombs were intercepted by the police, police vehicles were damaged and set alight, retail stores were looted and there were reports of the presence of firearms (p. 74). The borough recorded more crime than any other borough during Monday evening with the disorder centering on retail areas. In comparison to other boroughs, offences were concentrated within relatively confined areas (p. 49).

The disorder carried on into the morning of the next day (Tuesday 9th August) and was of similar duration to the disorder on the two previous days. On the third day, the police were overwhelmed by the spread and scale of the disorder (p. 63) and it became clear that too few police resources had been deployed. Officers completed extended tours of duty in order to maintain a level of response but under the circumstances they were unable to suppress the level of crime and violence that was occurring across London that night (p. 63).

The police management board convened a meeting on Monday morning and decided to nearly double its resources, mobilizing 61 Public Support Units or approximately 1525 officers and additional staff to support these units (p. 64). It was also decided at the meeting that mutual aid would be formally requested from other forces, which would increase the amount of resources for the ongoing operation (p. 64). The level of resources to be mobilized reflected the fact that the disorder had spread to five other boroughs and that a greater number of officers would be required to police any disorder should it occur in multiple locations over the course of Monday night (p. 64).

The management board held a second meeting on Monday evening and resolved to increase the number of officers available for deployment, which would result in 16,000 officers being deployed rather than the 13,000 officers initially deployed and would include another 50 Police Support Units (approximately 1250 officers) (p. 92). Following a discussion at the meeting, the members realized that developing tactical plans and basing resourcing decisions on the previous day's experience was no longer applicable. The Temporary Commissioner decided that a more appropriate response/policing plan would need to be developed overnight that would take into account the additional resources that had been made available (p. 92). It was proposed that the additional staff and the Police Support Units would be allocated to individual boroughs as they would present a high visibility patrol and an effective mobile response to any incidents that occurred (p. 92).

On the third day, another major issue arose. The volume of information and intelligence was so immense that it was overwhelming. Four hundred and eighty-four reports had been received from the intelligence unit on the first day of the disorder, which overwhelmed the ability of the decision makers in the operational command team (p. 65). As a result, the intelligence process and the management structure was adapted to triage incoming intelligence material (p. 65). It was proposed that the new process that was developed would be a more effective way of evaluating the material quickly and would provide the flexibility to alter the triage criteria in a response to both the volume of intelligence received and the changing intelligence requirements of the operational command team and the various types of incidents (p. 65).

By Monday, it was realized that a management structure would be required to coordinate the resources that were needed to engage with a community the size of London (p. 66). Managing the engagement of the community was divided into two strands, each led by a commander who would recognize the differing needs of the business community and the public (p. 66). An emphasis was placed on using the police corporate messaging system Neighbourhood Link, to deliver information to the community and to businesses (p. 66).

Day 4, Tuesday 9 August, saw the disorder across London dissipate and the restoration of order (p. 92). Officers that were deployed to specific boroughs were briefed to ensure that they provided a high visibility patrol and that they would respond to any incidents as required (p. 92). Officers were to disperse any groups of youths that were forming and were to engage with local communities and reassure them (p. 92).

A police recovery phase was implemented on Tuesday. Operation Withem was established to coordinate the investigation of all crime relating to the disorder and the community engagement management structure was streamlined to bring residential and business engagement back together under one senior lead (p. 93). The change was introduced because it was believed that a single coordinator would be better placed to oversee the use of and the management of information in a consistent fashion (p. 93).

In summary, the disorder saw 5100 individual offences recorded across 66 London local authorities by the ten police forces involved, with 68% of these offences being recorded by members of the Metropolitan Police Service (p. 17). An analysis of these offences revealed that 50% of all offences involved some form of acquisitive crime, 36% involved criminal damage, while violent offences were less common at 7% (p. 18). The number and the percentage of arrests by the day of the riots has been presented in Table 5.2, and the number and percentage by crime type for the 5 days of the riots has been presented in Table 5.3.

Table 5.2 The number and percentage of arrests by day during the London riots

Day and date	Number of arrests[a]	Percentage of total arrests[b]
Saturday August 6	54	2.5
Sunday August 7	232	10.0
Monday August 8	1477	64.0
Tuesday August 9	446	19.5
Wednesday August 10	90	4.0
Total	*2299*	*100.0*

[a]Information obtained from Baudains, Braithwaite, and Johnson (2013)
[b]Percentage are rounded

Table 5.3 The number and percentage of crime types for the 5 days of the London riots

Offense type	Number of offenses	Percentage of offenses
Burglary	1359	59.1
Theft	262	11.4
Criminal damage	147	6.4
Violence against person	10	4.5
Robbery	40	1.7
Other	387	16.8
Total	*2299*	*100.0*

[a]Information obtained from Baudains, Braithwaite, and Johnson (2013)

5.5 The Critique of the Police Response

The previous section of this chapter has presented a chronology of the police response to the riots over the 4 days in August 2011. The chapter has provided the basis for a high-level critique of the police response and for the identification of weaknesses in the response that may have influenced the course that the riots took. Four strategic weaknesses are discussed in the first section of this chapter, followed by an examination of the police response to the riots at the operational level under the following six headings: Service Mobilization Plan, Command, Tactical, Community Engagement, Intelligence, and Final Comments.

The London Metropolitan area experienced over 5000 protests in 2010 (Her Majesty's Chief Inspectorate of Constabulary, 2009), yet the events of August 2011 and, in particular, the first three nights of the disorder, saw the Metropolitan Police Service's riot response, tactics, and structures tested to the limit of its capability (Metropolitan Police Service, 2012). The major difference in the 2011 disorder, compared to all previous disorders, was the speed, geographical distribution, and the scale of the escalation in violence (Metropolitan Police Service, 2012).

The differences in the 2011 riots were also noted by Her Majesty's Inspectorate of Constabulary (2011), who claimed that police training, tactics and equipment "had been developed largely to deal with set-piece, single-site confrontations between police and protesters" (p. 4). The Inspectorate went on to state "that the police were, therefore, not well prepared for the widespread, fast moving and opportunistic criminal attacks on property, loosely organised using social media" (p. 4).

The first weakness of a strategic nature became evident on the evening of Saturday 6 August. A review held during the evening of the events, which led to the initial riots, revealed that it was clear that the death of Mark Duggan acted as a trigger (The Secretary of State for the Home Department, 2011) to the disorder and that the lack of perception as to the level of tension within the community was the catalyst (Klein, 2012a).

The second weakness was that the service mobilization plan did not foresee the number of officers that would be needed to control the level of violence that occurred in Tottenham on the evening of Saturday 6 August 2011. Subsequent analysis that was undertaken by the Metropolitan Police found that 13 Police Support Units (approximately 750 public disorder trained officers) would have been needed to clear the street of protesters outside the Tottenham Police Station on the evening of Saturday 6 August (Metropolitan Police Service, 2011a). With the privilege of hindsight, there were not enough officers deployed to Tottenham on Saturday, nor were they deployed quickly enough to respond to the unfolding incident (Metropolitan Police Service, 2011a). It was this vacuum that created the perception that the police could not contain or control the rioting in Tottenham and this led to the disorder spreading across London (Riots Communities and Victims Panel, 2012a). In retrospect, it is not known whether a more significant police response (of 13 Police Support Units) would have prevented the disorder from spreading across London and England on the subsequent days (Metropolitan Police Service, 2011a).

The third weakness related to the public's perception of the police response following the deployment of officers to the disorder. According to the Metropolitan Police Service (2011b), there was criticism from the public of what appeared to be a lack of reaction by the police to the disorder and in some instances, members of the public claiming that officers stood by as offences took place. Briggs (2012a) claimed that there was "severe criticism against the police for being too timid" during the riots (p. 388). Briggs continued to note that the lack of initial response by the police was a result of the police being "in an awkward position, with little strategic leadership, low morale because of impending austerity cuts to the force," and that officers were "worried about accountability should they act improperly under the lens of the media" (p. 389).

The police replied to the criticism in a report, which was published in late 2011 and was titled "Strategic Review of MPS response to disorder: Early learning and initial findings." The report identified three reasons why the police reaction was perceived to be ineffective:

- The need to protect other emergency services, such as London Fire Brigade, engaged in saving life;
- To prevent further disorder spreading and thereby preventing further risk to life; and
- To facilitate the arrival of more police resources (Metropolitan Police Service, 2011b, p. 4).

These reasons can, however, sound as though they are justifications for the response taken by the police. If the police did not have the number of officers available or these officers could not be deployed quickly it seems to be within reason that the three reasons stated are reasonably accurate. Klein (2012a) believed, however, that even if the police had the appropriate number of officers deployed and that they were attempting to contain the riots, it would have been unlikely that the damage to property could have been contained or the proliferation of the riots avoided. The problem was that there was a great deal of copycat activity (The Secretary of State for the Home Department, 2011), by the rioters who "were not a homogeneous group of people all acting for the same reasons" and were capable of acting differently, individually or in groups, "depending on why they decided to riot and what they wanted to get out of it" (Riots Communities and Victims Panel, 2012a, p. 10).

Other weaknesses in the police response that will be discussed and are intertwined with the three weaknesses discussed above are; the difficulty that the police had in responding to the death of Mr. Duggan, the expectations of the community as a result of the death, the ineffective leadership delivered by the police and the operational errors made (Klein, 2012a). These errors, which were exacerbated by the media and social media, led to the lack of confidence in the initial response by the police. This in turn, created an environment where people felt encouraged to test the response of the police in other areas of London and later, across England (Riots Communities and Victims Panel, 2012a). The Riots Communities and Victims Panel (2012a) later concluded that the actions taken by local police influenced the public's perception at a national level.

The remainder of this section of the chapter discusses six operational issues that were identified when analysing the police response to the riots.

5.5.1 Service Mobilization Plan

A critique of the actions of the police and a number of reports that examined the riots, including reviews carried out by the Metropolitan Police Services (Metropolitan Police Service, 2011a, 2011b) found that there were a number of problems with the response of the police on the evening of Saturday 6 August. The problems can be traced to the failure of some aspects of the Service Mobilization Plan (SMP). The SMP had been established to provide a procedure and a framework for deploying additional, appropriately trained officers "to spontaneous public disorder, terrorism or civil emergency incidents" (Metropolitan Police Service, 2012, p. 108). The framework for sending messages within the SMP was designed to alert all geographical areas within the police organization to either make officers who were trained in public order policing available at times of "heightened demand" or to mobilize these resources immediately to areas experiencing public disorder. Unfortunately, during the evening of Saturday 6 August, an incorrect message was sent (Metropolitan Police Service, 2011a, 2011b; Moran & Waddington, 2016). The message was sent as an "amber" coded message, which is a request for area command staff to make resources available, rather than a "red" coded message, which requires commanders to immediately mobilize resources (Moran & Waddington, 2016). This error led to an inadequate number of officers being mobilized to control the disorder and the officers not being made available quickly enough (Metropolitan Police Service, 2011a, 2011b, 2012).

The second failing of the SMP was that it was based on the modus operandi of previous riots and was not flexible or dynamic enough to provide a platform for the police to be able to respond and deploy resources rapidly to the escalating levels of violence, such as that which was experienced on 6 August (Metropolitan Police Service, 2012). According to the Metropolitan Police Service (2012), at the time of the initial riots, the SMP provided "a phased response to deliver a full mobilisation within three hours of activation, comprising 380 public order trained officers" (p. 109), which history would determine as being an adequate level of additional resources. The phased approach allocated disorder resources proportionately across London according to information and intelligence received (Metropolitan Police Service, 2012).

Based on the events of August 2011, the questions that need to be asked are: what is the number of officers that would need to be deployed to control the disorder in Tottenham on Saturday evening and how quickly could these officers be deployed to the site of the disorder? Any attempt to answer these questions would need to bear in mind that even if the police could have deployed the required number of officers could they have controlled the rapidly escalating, new form of violent rioting that was taking place, especially when a large percentage of rioters only wanted to engage violently with the police?

In the context of this discussion, the Metropolitan Police Service (2012) declared that they could not quell the disorder using the SMP-phased approach. They explained that after the riots an assessment was undertaken "to determine the levels of resource which would have been required to contain the disorder and clear Tottenham High Road. It was assessed to be in excess of 25 PSUs, in other words, in excess of 750 public order trained officers" (Metropolitan Police Service, 2012, p. 109). It would not be possible to have such a large number of officers trained in public order on stand-by across London.

The other point to be made in this discussion is that any response or deployment plan, such as the SMP, while it can identify and plan for a deployment for most of the situations or events that the police may encounter, it has a number of physical and technological limitations. The first limitation is that the police have a set obligation (business as usual) of providing a service for the community. There are times in any given 24-h period when the resources of the police are limited (Metropolitan Police Service, 2012). This is because of their usual business obligations and the result of resourcing a 24-h roster. In other words, at any given time, police staff will be rostered to work the next shift, have days off, be on sick leave or taking annual leave. The Metropolitan Police Service (2012) claimed that these limitations resulted directly from the boroughs rostering staff to "a shift pattern that matches resources to territorial policing demand" and that the changes to the activation of the SMP provides at any given time, a minimum number of officers trained in public order to be on duty to mobilize nine Public Support Units (p. 109). Changes have since been made to the SMP since the 2011 riots and it includes the requirement for the mobilized resources to proceed to a forward mustering point rather than mustering in the boroughs. The change recognizes the necessity to quickly assemble trained, equipped and fully briefed officers (Metropolitan Police Service, 2012), at a location close to the disorder rather than having officers assemble in their home borough and then proceeding to the location of the disorder.

In summary, the lessons learned from 2011 are now reflected in the SMP. However, there are still a number of practical difficulties relating to the implementation of the updated SMP, in particular, whenever a large-scale response or a large number of officers need to be deployed. The revised SMP does not have the capability to deploy a large number of public order officers to an incident (Metropolitan Police Service, 2012) quickly or to a location that is distant from central London. To minimize the risk of the police not having the capability to deploy a large number of public order officers, the police have increased the number of officers trained in public order and have established a policy that ensures that a minimum number of local, appropriately trained officers are available to assist in a rapid deployment to large scale civil disorder events (Metropolitan Police Service, 2012).

5.5.2 Command

The first report that examined the operational command structure that was in place for policing the riots found that it worked effectively (Metropolitan Police Service, 2011a). This was despite the limited number of specifically trained, Public Order Commanders available to fill the operational response positions (Metropolitan Police Service, 2011a). However, this being said, there were a number of command decisions or actions that were either not taken early enough during the initial response phase or were not taken at all.

The first of the decisions that were not taken early enough was the request for assistance from other forces. According to Her Majesty's Inspectorate of Constabulary (2011), the requests that were made to the other forces for assistance during the evening of Saturday 6 August were often ad hoc or informal and the call for national assistance was not made early enough, resulting in a delay in deploying officers from other forces. The delay in requesting assistance may have meant that the police missed an opportunity to take control earlier during the riots.

Two points need to be made to counter this argument. The first point is that no matter what planning was undertaken and no matter what processes the police had in place, no model of response would have been adequate to guide the police in their reaction to such a rare and unexpected escalation of violence such as that which occurred on 6 August. The second point supports the first point made, in that no matter what deployment process the police had in place, even if it was modeled on a worst-case scenario, no organization could deploy such a large number of appropriately-trained, public order officers in only a few hours to such a rapidly moving event. The best that the police could do would be to develop processes and procedures to contain the initial event that would enable "a level of response which would provide commanders with the widest range of options to deal with disorder" (Her Majesty's Inspectorate of Constabulary, 2011, p. 59). An approach such as this would enable operational flexibility and would allow the Inspectors who were commanding the Public Support Units and responding to the event to be a part of the command decision-making process (Metropolitan Police Service, 2012).

In addition to command decisions not being made early enough, the riots highlighted a problem in the software that was used in the command centre of the Metropolitan Police Service Special Operations Room (SOR) (Metropolitan Police Service, 2012). Although the software had been used for commanding and managing the police response to a number of other events during the 2011 riots, the software was not capable of managing a dynamic incident and did not allow commanders to monitor specific events or the deployment of staff. Nor was the software capable of allowing the SOR to communicate in real-time with ground commanders (Metropolitan Police Service, 2012). According to the police, "[t]he scale of the disorder and the number of officers deployed in response to it exacerbated these challenges" (Metropolitan Police Service, 2012, p. 8).

5.5.3 Tactics

A number of important operational and tactical lessons were learnt from responding to the riots, especially as it was a fast-moving disorder and resources were limited. The riots highlighted problems with the planning process. The plans that were in place were not flexible or dynamic enough for the police to respond to an emerging or evolving disorder event (Her Majesty's Inspectorate of Constabulary, 2011). As a result of the limited availability of resources during the first 2 days of the riots, it was evident that the police "mixed and matched tactics to suit the resources they had" available at the time and the specific geographical locations (Her Majesty's Inspectorate of Constabulary, 2011, p. 61). In other words, the police often had to do the best that they could with what they had at the time.

As well as offering important lessons, the 2011 riots can provide a foundation from which the police can move forward. The response of the police to a riot is usually based on how they have responded to riots in the past and it is proposed that the lessons learned from the 2011 riots can be used to develop and implement deployment and tactical plans that can be used by the police in the future to counter fast moving disorder events. As Her Majesty's Inspectorate of Constabulary (2011) suggested, the police "need to build on these experiences and develop a range of tactics that are not wholly dependent on overwhelming police numbers to ensure" control of any disorder (p. 61). However, any tactic developed must be based on clear, strategic response objectives and on the police resources that are available (see Wain and Joyce (2012) for an overview of the evidence presented by Her Majesty's Inspectorate of Constabulary to the Home Affairs Committee on 29 November 2011 in regard to new police public disorder tactics).

The August 2011 riots highlighted three tactical weaknesses in the police response. The first weakness was that the police were not able to deploy their resources quickly enough to the locations in which they were needed and the second was the actual number of officers needed to take control of the disorder. According Her Majesty's Inspectorate of Constabulary (2011), the police estimated that they needed "to outnumber rioters by three or five to one if they are to make arrests and disperse groups – a much higher level of resource than is needed to hold a line and protect territory" (p. 7). The police, of course, never reached this number of officers to deploy until Monday 8 August, and as a result, the use of arrest—a deterrent tactic—was not able to be used until the Saturday or Sunday night (Her Majesty's Inspectorate of Constabulary, 2011). Unfortunately, this was one of the reasons why the police were perceived as backing off from the violence or as taking a soft approach to the offending (Riots Communities and Victims Panel, 2012a). Being able to deploy a significant number of officers quickly is important as this tactic offers the opportunity to prevent and contain disorder and dampen its impact on the community or to stop violence from escalating (Her Majesty's Inspectorate of Constabulary, 2011).

The second tactical weakness pertains to the use of methods that were not suitable for dealing with highly mobile crowds and offenders. The police have in the past relied heavily on the use of crowd dispersal methods to scatter and diffuse crowds but this did not work during the 2011 riots (Her Majesty's Inspectorate of Constabulary, 2011). When they used this method in the 2011 riots, the crowd dissipated quickly, but simply reformed in another location (Her Majesty's Inspectorate of Constabulary, 2011). This phenomenon was brought under control on Monday evening by the use of arrest, which was used once more officers were available.

5.5.4 Community Engagement

Community engagement played a major part in the police response to the riots. The importance of community engagement can be seen by the initial activity taken to reassure the community and to gather the information needed to complete a Community Impact Assessment. This was undertaken on the evening of Thursday 6 August. However, the sudden appointment of a senior officer to lead the community assessment, which can be viewed as giving community engagement the importance that it deserves, can also be seen as a process to right a wrong. This view is based on the fact that during the week prior to the riots, the police had mounted an operation targeting the Pembury Estate and the Pembury Boys gang (one of the most prominent gangs in London), in which 23 arrests were made and firearms, drugs, cash, and mobile phones were seized (Angel, 2012). According to Harding (2012), the police should have known that the implementation of this operation would mean that tensions would increase within the community.

A senior officer was appointed quickly to command the police-community engagement process and this was supported by a number of people who had experienced the 1981 Brixton riots. However, one member of the community who had experienced the Brixton riots reportedly said that the police should have expected trouble in August as August is historically known as "the riot month" (Briggs, S. 2012), and therefore, the police should have considered appointing a senior officer in preparation for the possibility of any rioting occurring in August. Appointed a senior officer to coordinate the police engagement with the community prior to any rioting occurring in August was given further credence by the Black Police Officers Association, who claimed that the police service had not retained its "collective memory" (Briggs, S., 2012), in regard to handling issues with minority communities. The police, however, claimed in response that while the riots raised important questions about the effectiveness of their community engagement framework, the practice of community engagement is a strategy which is "embedded in their [police] ethos" but they had to respond to the riots using the resources and the processes that were available at the time (Metropolitan Police Service, 2012). This comment implies that community engagement was not the first priority of the police when the riots started on the Saturday evening.

The police had, however, engaged members of the Black Independent Advisory Group to partake in the management of the response from the evening of Thursday 4 August and with the advice from these members in mind, issued media statements that would reassure local communities (Metropolitan Police Service, 2012).

The police also implemented processes to obtain relevant information that could be used to inform a Community Impact Assessment. The Metropolitan Police Service use the Community Impact Assessment to monitor tension in a community (Metropolitan Police Service, 2012). The assessment is completed at both the borough (or local) level and at the organizational (force) level and is used to make decisions regarding the allocation of resources and determine the level of community engagement that is required (Metropolitan Police Service, 2012).

A Community Impact Assessment was initiated by the police on the evening of Thursday 4 August, but the engagement of the police with the community in Haringey (the borough in which Tottenham was located) was already viewed as being in place and possessing a "structure, appropriate governance and relevant actions in place to progress it" (Metropolitan Police Service, 2012, p. 27). It was also suggested by the police that the tension in the community before the violence began on Saturday evening "was at a relatively low level" meaning that Haringey was appropriately resourced (Metropolitan Police Service, 2012, p. 100). According to the police, the assessment level was the same for all of London's boroughs at this time (Metropolitan Police Service, 2012).

As well as an inaccurate reading of the level of tension in the community, two other weaknesses in the Community Impact Assessment processes were revealed. The first weakness was the inconsistency of reporting by the individual boroughs to the centralized Community Engagement team and the second was that the team did not receive sufficient information or intelligence upon which to develop a comprehensive picture (Metropolitan Police Service, 2012). As both of these weaknesses are fundamental to the community assessment process, it calls into question its ability to be able to provide a robust assessment of the level of a community's engagement (Metropolitan Police Service, 2012).

The police also held a meeting with five Black Independent Advisory Group and community representatives on the afternoon of Saturday 6 August (Metropolitan Police Service, 2012). The police shooting was discussed during the meeting but there was no indication from any of the attendees of the possibility of a riot occurring that evening although comments were made that the family of the victim were not happy with the lack of police contact (Metropolitan Police Service, 2012). The point to be emphasized here is that community intelligence was not "provided to police regarding the possibility of imminent disorder arising out of levels of tension reaching a critical state" (Metropolitan Police Service, 2012, p. 98). The lack of any indication or information leads to the impression "that the reach of the MPS into Haringey's communities was neither as far reaching or current as it needed to be" and that the breadth of individuals representing the community within the Independent Advisory Group was too narrow (Metropolitan Police Service, 2012, p. 98).

Members of the Independent Advisory Group were confused as to their role in liaising with members of the community during the riots. The confusion lay in whether the members were responsible for advising the police about their actions or whether they were responsible for "improving community relations with police by mitigating concerns and proactively advising on community issues as they arise" (Metropolitan Police Service, 2012)? While the police acknowledged that it was their responsibility to manage their relationship with the community, it became clear during the riots that individual members of the Independent Advisory Group had definite boundaries, outside of which they would not take any responsibility for. The Independent Advisory Group members were reluctant to offer advice to the police or to provide information to the police about any activities taking place within the community (Metropolitan Police Service, 2012). While this may have been an extreme action taken by some members, it may have been as a result of their confidence in their relationship with the police or with specific individuals within the police organization. This raises questions as to the value of the input and advice from the Independent Advisory Groups during the planning for a police response to an incident or event. The weakness in understanding the role that Independent Advisory Groups play demonstrates a deficiency in the grasp of the dynamics of the relationship between the police and the community during an incident. This matter needs further research.

The last topic to be discussed in relation to community engagement is the use of social media by the police and the public. The police, by not taking advantage of social media, missed an opportunity to engage more effectively with the community (Metropolitan Police Service, 2012). The police acknowledge that the use of social media and the internet is a new phenomenon and that they were risk-averse in their use of social media during the riots. They noted that social media could have been used to communicate instantly with the public, especially to respond to incorrect information and "to improve public safety and confidence" (Metropolitan Police Service, 2012, p. 100).

The riots demonstrated that social media was clearly being used as "a planning and communication medium by people intent on causing disruption" (Metropolitan Police Service, 2012, p. 105). The monitoring of the use of social media by the police during the riots would have provided a significant opportunity to collect information as to the intention of the rioters (Metropolitan Police Service, 2012). The police recognised that their collection systems during the riots were tested to their limits and that they did not have the resources available to monitor social media in real time (Metropolitan Police Service, 2012). According to Baker (2012b), the police recognised this weakness and have now integrated social media services into their response strategies. They have also developed methods to collect information from social media, which has a positive impact on the intelligence process.

To conclude, the public want to know why the police make certain decisions (Riots Communities and Victims Panel, 2012b), especially when there has been a shooting of a member of the public by the police. When sensitive events occur, it is important for the police to explain their reasons for any action taken or for the lack of action taken. This is especially true where police "actions are likely to lead to a perceived feeling – accurate or otherwise – of abandonment in communities" (Riots Communities and Victims Panel, 2012b, p. 104).

The police need to be proactive in engaging with the community and ensuring that relationships are established and maintained. The Metropolitan Police Service recognize the importance of effective community engagement and as a part of continuous improvement, are evaluating the composition of and their use of Independent Advisory Groups and Key Individual Networks. They will determine whether these entities will continue to be part of their framework for engaging and communicating effectively with the community (Metropolitan Police Service, 2012).

5.5.5 Intelligence

One of the criticisms of the police during the riots was that they were not equipped to respond to "the technological tactics of this new 'mediated crowd' phenomenon" (Baker, 2012b, p. 184). It appears that there was a failure in the intelligence gathering process owing to the police using dated methods to collect information. The collection methods were not able to integrate with the new forms of communication used by the rioters (Baker, 2012b). This resulted in the police not being able to deploy their resources quickly enough or deploy their resources to where the violence and disorder was occurring. Some critics have even gone as far as to suggest "that better use of new social media could have made the police much more effective in anticipating and policing" the riots (Baker, 2012b, p. 184).

The police acknowledged that the independent advice and community intelligence sources did not achieve their purpose in identifying whether tensions existed within the Broadwater Farm Estate or in the wider community, which lead to the riots on Saturday 6 August or whether "there existed within the community large numbers of individuals prepared to engage with or take advantage of that disorder" (Metropolitan Police Service, 2012, p. 96).

As well as the failure of the police to monitor and use social media, two weaknesses were found in the management of the intelligence gathering process. The first weakness pertained to the large amount of information and intelligence becoming available during the riots and the difficulty in evaluating such large quantities of information and establishing the credibility of their sources (Metropolitan Police Service, 2012). These issues were compounded by the inconsistency in the reporting of the tension experienced in the community and boroughs from the police officers deployed (Metropolitan Police Service, 2012). These problems were "partially resolved by the introduction of a standardised template and central recommendations for minimum standards of engagement" with the community (Metropolitan Police Service, 2012).

Another weakness was the gap in the gathering of intelligence and the analysis processes that were used for the policing of public order events. A specialised intelligence unit that prepared and supported the planning for an event and the execution of an operation existed (Metropolitan Police Service, 2012), and while the police used this model initially, it became apparent that the model was not appropriate for the disorder that occurred on the evening of Saturday 6 August, especially when the level of violence began to escalate. The intelligence response model had been developed for peaceful protests or for a group of protesters confronting the police and not the type of protest that evolves into a riot. The police were forced to adapt the model during that evening (Metropolitan Police Service, 2012). The revised intelligence model had limited success in predicting and preventing disorder and looting in some locations, and it did not predict that the violence would be replicated in other boroughs the next day (Metropolitan Police Service, 2012).

5.5.6 *Gangs*

The involvement of gangs in various aspects of the riots, especially in relation to the organization of looting is discussed at length in the literature (Baudains, Braithwaite, & Johnson, 2013; Harding, 2012; Lewis et al., 2011; Morrell et al., 2011; Riots Communities and Victims Panel, 2012a). According to Harding (2012), as the riots unfolded, gangs took the opportunity to loot in the areas that lacked a police presence. Harding also claimed that the gangs "actively monitored police activity on an hourly basis," which enabled them to take advantage of any emerging policing vacuum (2012, p. 202).

The incidence of gangs taking advantage of riots, just like social media, is a new phenomenon that should be included in any future riot response plans. The potential involvement of gangs in riots would need to be factored into the community engagement process and the Independent Advisory Group needs to be cognizant of the role that gangs can play.

5.5.7 *Final Comments*

Briggs (2012a) claimed that the failings of the police in the days leading up to the riots and during the initial hours of the disorder seem in some ways familiar, especially given the history of the relationship of the police with the community in the Haringey borough. However, in a public survey conducted by Her Majesty's Inspectorate of Constabulary (2011), more than 85% of the respondents thought that the actions of the police helped to bring the riots to an end. This was tempered, however, by 60% of the respondents saying that the police could have bought the riots to an end more quickly (Her Majesty's Inspectorate of Constabulary, 2011). The results of the survey indicated that this was not the view of the majority of the survey participants. Just under half (49%) thought that the police did not use enough force, while 43% thought that the force used by police was "about right" (Her Majesty's Inspectorate of Constabulary, 2011).

What ultimately bought the riots under control was the increase in the number of police officers deployed and the deployment of officers from other forces (Her Majesty's Inspectorate of Constabulary, 2011; The Secretary of State for the Home Department, 2011). To be able to deploy large numbers of police officers quickly means that officers deployed from other forces must be trained to the same standard and be able to use the same tactics and equipment (Her Majesty's Inspectorate of Constabulary, 2011). If officers are all trained to the same standard and their deployment processes are streamlined, this will ensure that all officers who are deployed as a squad, even if they are deployed from different forces, will be able to understand commands and tactics and be able to work together as a disciplined unit.

While the initial response to the riots by the police was hesitant, the police were able to deploy and mobilize enough assets to regain control of the streets (Her

Majesty's Inspectorate of Constabulary, 2011). What is debatable is that if the number of officers had been increased earlier, could some of the disturbances have been avoided (The Secretary of State for the Home Department, 2011) or minimized? As the Secretary of State for the Home Department correctly pointed out, the initial focus of the police, when responding to a riot, should be to increase the number of officers deployed, whether this is from the force where the riot is occurring or whether it is from other forces. Having sufficient resources available enables the police to respond adequately to large scale disorders and rioting and increases their effectiveness. Having adequate resources gives the police a range of tactical options that will help control any violence. As the report by Her Majesty's Inspectorate of Constabulary (2011) pointed out, every riot is different and a "one size fits all" response does not work. The response to attacks on police cordon lines for example, "needed to be different to the tactics employed to combat small groups of highly mobile looters" (Her Majesty's Inspectorate of Constabulary, 2011, p. 59).

Her Majesty's Inspectorate of Constabulary (2011) does, however, accept that there are differences in the way that the police respond to riots at the strategic, operational, and tactical levels and this may require a prioritization process that balances the police response to disorder with the delivery of other police services. One option is to ensure that other policing priorities receive equal recognition and that appropriate and robust response models and frameworks are in place to ensure that a national approach can be taken (Her Majesty's Inspectorate of Constabulary, 2011). Taking a national approach would ensure that there was consistency in the response to a riot and such an approach would "set out clear expectations around the importance to be attached to [the] early resolution of disorder; details of the planning required to ensure forces are prepared for national disorders (e.g. how officers will be mobilised); and the circumstances in which a range of tactics (including the use of vehicles, water cannon and attenuating energy projectiles) can be considered" (Her Majesty's Inspectorate of Constabulary, 2011, p 83). If such an approach was taken then all police forces, the Home Office and chief police officers would need to co-operate. An agreement would need to be reached on the maintenance of the capability so that large incidents of civil disorder could be responded to and to determine what is affordable and how this capability would be balanced against other policing requirements (Her Majesty's Inspectorate of Constabulary, 2011).

5.6 Discussion

There have been a number of suggestions as to the causes and triggers of the 2011 riots. According to the police, the actions of a group of youths that were angered by the lack of action taken by the police during the community march to the Tottenham Police Station on the evening of Saturday 6 August was the trigger for the disorder (Moran & Waddington, 2016). This claim is in contrast to Reicher and Stott (2011), who argued that the "flashpoint" or trigger occurred when the police allegedly knocked a young black woman to the ground as they were dispersing the crowd from outside the police station. This incident and a subsequent allegation that the police repeatedly hit the woman while she was on the ground, was, according to Reicher and Stott, the "flashpoints" for the riot. The police disputed the allegations (Metropolitan Police Service, 2012), but Reicher and Stott maintained that all of those who witnessed the incident agreed that this was the actual trigger for starting the riots (cited in Moran & Waddington, 2016).

The report written by the Home Affairs Select Committee adopted a more strategic perspective as to the cause of the riots and claimed that the death of Mark Duggan was the most significant factor leading to the start of the rioting (quoted in Riots Communities and Victims Panel, 2012b). The panel went on to claim that the sensitivity of the community in relation to the police shooting was only accentuated by the police failing to adequately communicate with the family but the causes of the riots were far deeper and were "partly caused by a combination of high youth unemployment and toxic relations with local police" (Riots Communities and Victims Panel, 2012b, p. 21).

The panel also discussed the reasons as to why the riots spread across London and did not remain just in the Haringey–Tottenham area. The panel noted, based on an extensive survey of residents and people involved in the riots across London, that "the sole trigger for disturbances in their area was the perception that the police could not contain the scale of rioting in Tottenham and then across London" (Riots Communities and Victims Panel, 2012b, p. 22). The perceptions of a vacuum in the police response to the initial riot in Tottenham encouraged rioters in other boroughs to test the reaction of the police as they believed that "they would be able to loot and damage without being challenged" (Riots Communities and Victims Panel, 2012b, p. 22).

Bateman (2012) offered a third opinion as to what triggered the 2011 riots. Bateman's (2012), view took a more academic and historic perspective and claimed that the 2011 riots could be compared to the Brixton riots of 1981, in that both involved confrontations between members of the minority black community and the police. Bateman (2012), also suggested that there were similarities in all of the riots in the UK from the late 1970s, including St. Pauls in 1980, Toxteth in 1981, Brixton in 1985, and Broadwater Farm in 1985. The similarities that Bateman (2012) suggested are not only a feature of disorder events in the UK but are also a feature of riots in other countries. Angel (2012), for example, maintained that all of the major riots in the USA since Watts in 1965 have been triggered by "perceived police brutality and racism" (p. 25). The history and the similarity in the causes of the riots led Bateman to claim that there was "no doubt [that] antagonistic relations between minority ethnic communities and the constabulary contributed to an underlying mood of resentment that made it more likely that police intervention would lead to a broader disturbance" (p. 100). Kelly and Gill (2012) expanded on the perspective that the police had a poor relationship with the community. These researchers claimed that the "excessive use of stop and search powers and dispersal orders to prevent groups meeting in public spaces – were among their main reasons for rioting" but conceded that the motivations behind the looting were more complex (p. 221).

There is no doubt that the resentment of the police held by the minority community in the Tottenham area was one of the major contributing factors to the 2011 riots. A survey of the residents of Tottenham undertaken by Bateman (2012) revealed that there was "widespread anger with the police that fuelled the unrest," with many residents emphasizing that "they believed that they were participating in 'explicitly anti-police riots'" (p. 101).

The finding of Bateman's research was supported by Klein (2012a), who claimed that "in Tottenham, as in other parts of London, relations between the police and the community, particularly the black community" were tense (p. 135). However, the resentment held of the police and their actions extended beyond the black community with more than 85% of the 270 informants interviewed after the riots expressing their dislike and distrust of the police (Lewis et al., 2011). The tense relationship was not only a result of the police operation conducted in the weeks leading up to the riots and the police shooting, but because there was "historic mistrust of the police among young black men, with widespread allegations of deliberate and persistent harassment" (Klein, 2012a, p. 135; see also Riots Communities and Victims Panel, 2012b, p. 19). This historical grievance, according to Klein (2012a), together with the use of social media, incited a segment of the minority community that had experienced alleged police harassment through the police use of stop and search to riot and this led to the disorder in Tottenham spreading across London and other cities. The mutual distrust and dislike of the police resulted in rival gangs putting aside their differences (Klein, 2012a). A participant of a youth riot said, "this is not about postcode war, it is 'us' against 'them' and 'forget our beef with each other and let's get the police" (Briggs, 2012d). The involvement of gangs in the London riots and in the majority of violence and disorder incidents that occurred in communities that had strong gang affiliations was acknowledged by the police (Harding, 2012).

The main difference between the 2011 riot and earlier twentieth century riots was the scale and the speed that the violence evolved in the 2011 riot (Baker, 2012b). Baker (2012b) explained that social media, in part, was to blame for the "contagion" (Baker, 2011 cited in Baker, 2012b). The police acknowledged Baker's (2012b) view that social media was used to advise other potential participants and that "'waves' of extra rioters appeared in areas which were already experiencing rioting" and that rioters were attracted to those areas that were already experiencing looting owing to the limited police presence (Riots Communities and Victims Panel, 2012a, p. 5).

A number of factors have been identified as influencing the cause of the 2011 riots. The extensive reductions made to youth services in London that had been implemented earlier in the year were thought to be a factor in triggering the riots (Newnham & Bell, 2012; Stott, Drury, & Reicher, 2017). In parallel to the closure of youth centres and the reduction in youth services, a number of protests had taken place as a reaction to the large increase in university fees and cuts in tertiary education funding (Newnham & Bell, 2012). According to Stott et al. (2017), by February 2011, "eight [Tottenham] youth centres had been closed and other services such as after-school clubs and employment support removed" (p. 5). The youth centre closures left "many young people feeling aggrieved" and nowhere to spend their leisure time other than on the streets (Stott et al., 2017, p. 5), and this resulted in an increase in the number of youths being stopped and searched and consequently bringing them into contact with the police. In June 2011, the police conducted 1614 stop-and-searches in Haringey, of which 91.4% of those stopped not being arrested (Moore, 2012), while in Hackney, the number of black youths being stopped and searched was three times higher than the number of white youths (Human Rights and Equalities Commission, 2010).

The communities in the contiguous boroughs of Haringey and Hackney appear to have had similar relationships with the police, which according to Stott et al. (2017) crystallized "in antagonistic encounters that served as precursors to generalized violence" where attacks on police and property was systematic (p. 13). The theory of Social Disorganization implies such an outcome. Social Disorganization theory suggests that riot-related events occur in locations where social cohesion is low and in particular, in areas "that have higher population churn rates, greater ethnic diversity, and that are more deprived" (Baudains et al., 2013, p. 257).

There is political pressure on the police to maintain low levels of crime on inner-city housing estates (Moran & Waddington, 2016), and this results in the police using enforcement approaches that are viewed, especially by young people and minority community members, as repressive and not taking into consideration the social "structural and cultural factors at stake in the equation" (Moran & Waddington, 2016, pp. 126–127). The tense relationship between the police and minority youth exacerbates the problem, "contributing to the further deterioration of the already poor police-public relations that invariably frame riots such as those witnessed in 2011" (Moran & Waddington, 2016, pp. 126–127). The police, however, argued that their policies and operations did take into account the political pressure and community issues and the impact that these have on their day-to-day relationship with the community (Metropolitan Police Service, 2012). In an attempt to maintain low crime levels on the estates prior to the riots, the police implemented various operational strategies that placed more emphasis on specific crimes and community problems, such as drugs, youth and firearms by using specialized crime and surveillance teams (Moran & Waddington, 2016). Some benefits were experienced from using this approach such as a reduction of crime committed on the estates while the downside was the increased use of "stop-and-search" that resulted in the perception that the tactic was abused (Moran & Waddington, 2016). According to Moran and Waddington (2016), the police carried out 6894 stops in Tottenham and the surrounding area of Haringey between April and June 2011, of which only 87 resulted in convictions.

The use of stop-and-search is not just about the number conducted but is about the quality of the search and how the search is conducted (Moran & Waddington, 2016). Poor-quality searching has an impact on the relationship of the police with the community, at both the individual and the community level. In a survey undertaken by the Riots Communities and Victims Panel (2012b), of those who had been in contact with the police in the previous 12 months, one in four (25%) were unhappy with the way that they were treated while in some areas it was nearly as high as one in three (33%). High levels of dissatisfaction with the police affect not only the relationship that the police have with the community but also with youth within the community and as Waterton and Sesay (2012) correctly pointed out, over time, the legitimacy of the police will be eroded and their relationship with young people typified by opposition and conflict.

The last issue that influenced the start of the riots was the increase in community "resentment and distrust resulting from a recent history of deaths relating to police raids or detention in police custody" (Moran & Waddington, 2016, p. 130). According to Moran and Waddington (2016), the level of resentment and distrust of the police held by the community "challenged the legitimacy of the police as the representatives of justice and order" (p. 130). The challenge of legitimacy has a negative effect on policing by public consent, which poses a problem for the police when they respond to public disorder, such as that experienced during the August 2011 riots.

The August 2011 riots were not the usual public protest where the police exercise their discretion to ensure that protesters are able to protest legitimately and that members of the public can go about their lawful business. In lawful protests, police "act as arbiter, balancing the rights of protesters against the rights of the wider public, the business community and local residents" (Her Majesty's Inspectorate of Constabulary, 2011, p. 5). It is difficult for the police to balance the rights of the protesters with those of the public as they need to respond to protesters with an appropriate level of force that protects the public without being excessive.

A report by Her Majesty's Inspectorate of Constabulary (2011) examined the level of force used by the police. The Inspectorate claimed that "in order to use appropriate levels of force swiftly, decisively and with confidence, officers need to know that they are both acting lawfully and that they are likely to have a substantial level of support from most people in the communities that they police" (p. 86). There are both strategic and tactical elements in this claim that police decision makers need to consider. The tactical element that needs to be considered is that public order officers need to be trained in the application of force within the context of the law. There are three strategic elements that create the capability for the police to respond to disorder while providing assurance to both the community and the organization. The first element is that the police need to have established a level of trust with the community and that the community has confidence in the actions of police. The second element provides the political framework for the tactical element in that the police organization offers support for their officers when they are taking lawful actions. The final element, which is essential for responding to a riot such as that experienced in August 2011 (but was not identified by the Inspectorate), is that the police should have policies, plans and structures in place or that are able to be put in place to ensure that the police can respond with political and public support and confidence.

An analysis of the response to the August 2011 riot provides an avenue for lessons to be learned for future responses to any such disorder, especially in the beginning of a disorder (The Secretary of State for the Home Department, 2011). As the Secretary of State for the Home Department (2011) noted, the police gave the appearance that they were reacting to a legitimate event such as responding to a student or political demonstration. This form of response, according to The Secretary of State for the Home Department (2011), is a result of the training that is given to respond to a riot being "sterile," focusing on "the delivery of rehearsed tactics in pre-determined scenarios," such as for example, "taking a junction where rioters disperse when challenged" (p. 19). Providing Public Order Squad supervisors and commanders with practical training that incorporates the use of scenarios requiring problem solving combined with operational response tactics will further the capability of the police. Practical training will allow the response of the police to be "flexible and reactive to emerging threats" (Her Majesty's Inspectorate of Constabulary, 2011, p. 63). Enhanced training will also provide the police with the capability of responding to fast moving and escalating riots and disorder (Her Majesty's Inspectorate of Constabulary, 2011).

The second area that should be considered in relation to lessons learned is the relationship of the police with the community. This relationship needs to be expanded to include programs that build the public's confidence in the police and this will result in the community's support for the police during a disorder or riot. However, the relationship of the police with the community is complex and community resilience is beyond the ability of the police to solve. This requires political intervention and the assistance of social agencies.

One program that could be expanded upon to improve the relationship of the police with the community is the Independent Advisory Group. The group was established in 1999 as a result of the Stephen Lawrence Inquiry and had an initial membership of 35 members from the community (Metropolitan Police Service, 2011a). The purpose of the group "was to provide informed critical feedback" to the police and became the principal method of measuring tension in the community (Metropolitan Police Service, 2011a, p. 7). The group was to measure the level of community response to and the views of, "all aspects of policing, particularly at times of incidents" that were "likely to have an impact on community confidence" (Metropolitan Police Service, 2011a, p. 8).

While the police rely upon the group for independent advice, group members have very little understanding as to their role in assisting the police and the community or their effectiveness in doing so. There is no understanding as to how the composition of the group should reflect the ethnicity of the community. There is no doubt that the group has been an avenue for individuals, communities and the police to communicate with each other (Metropolitan Police Service, 2011a), but research needs to be undertaken to investigate whether the use of advisory groups is appropriate and whether they enable the police to build on any successes.

Extending the role of the Safer Neighbourhood Teams would improve the relationship of the police with the community. These teams were established in 2004 and were operating in every London ward by April 2006 (Metropolitan Police Service, 2011a). The Metropolitan Police Service deployed approximately 4000 officers and Community Support officers to these teams, which were "dedicated to the needs of each specific neighbourhood" (Metropolitan Police Service, 2011a, p. 8). The strength of the structure and the approach of the team model is that it is at the "grass roots level" and that the "policing priorities for each area are decided in partnership with local stakeholders – the public, crime and disorder reduction partnerships, local authorities and other local organisations" (Metropolitan Police Service, 2011a, p. 8). This means that the Safer Neighbourhood Teams can easily be extended so that they are present during a disorder event. This would mean that they could act as a point for community liaison and as a conduit for the flow of information (Metropolitan Police Service, 2011a, 2011b).

Improving the relationship of the police with the community would change how riots are viewed (Stott et al., 2017). Stott et al. (2017) claimed that if the police had a resilient relationship with the community then the importance of police interaction with the community increases and any causes of rioting would not be attributed to historical social issues. This would mean that the interactions of the police with the community would "produce changed social relations and changed social understandings" (Stott et al., 2017, p. 9). The chance of a riot being triggered by the actions of the police would be minimized, but should a riot occur, it would be for a specific reason and within a geographical area rather than spreading across a city or a country.

5.7 Conclusion

The August 2011 riots highlighted four important issues for the future of the policing of riots. The first is that it is important to understand the evolving nature of public order policing and the organizational requirements of the police when responding to a riot. The next two issues are more hypothetical but form the foundation for the development of strategy. As the police and policy makers contemplate the task of the policing of riots; how do police prevent the loss of control of the streets and how do they regain it once it has been lost (Wain & Joyce, 2012)?

How the police respond to rioting is based on how they responded to riots in the past and the form that the previous riots took within the context of the law. Responding in the same manner as in the past is problematic, as the root of a problem can change or evolve. The difference between the August 2011 riots in comparison to earlier riots was "a perception that the police could not contain the scale of rioting in Tottenham and then across London" and this triggered the spread of disturbances (Riots Communities and Victims Panel, 2012a, p. 12). The vacuum in the police response enabled the rioters to believe "that they would be able to loot and damage without being challenged by the police" (Riots Communities and Victims Panel, 2012a, p. 12).

The perception that the police could not contain the August 2011 riots was initially based on two significant changes that occurred after the riots of the 1980s. The first change was the level of violence that was expressed toward the police and that such actions did not appear to concern the public, the police or the judiciary (see Prasad, 2011; Topping & Bawdon, 2011), and the second change was the introduction of social media and the citizen journalist (Greer & McLaughlin, 2010). These changes, together with other pivotal events, such as the investigation and reports of the police handling of the G20 summit in London in April 2009, the student demonstrations in November 2010 and the Trades Union Congress Day of Action in March 2011 all attracted scrutiny as to the style of policing that would be adopted to police peaceful protest in London (Metropolitan Police Service, 2011a). These earlier events also influenced the frameworks and tactics that the police use for responding to riots. It is important to note that these events were pre-planned marches and protests for which the police were able to develop contingency plans should disorder occur (Metropolitan Police Service, 2011a). The August 2011 riots did not provide the police with an opportunity to pre-plan and as a result, the police had to use their existing frameworks and tactics for something for which they were not designed (Metropolitan Police Service, 2011a).

The tactics used by the police when disorder has broken out provides the potential for either defusing or accelerating acts of violence (Riots Communities and Victims Panel, 2012a). To ensure that the actions of the police are perceived by the community as being neutral, the police must have a robust and multipronged community relationship program in place. The program should include officers that are appointed as Community Police Officers and that meetings with the community are held to include Police Liaison Officers, staff from local authorities and volunteer organizations, and minority advisory groups that represent all ethnicities in the community. Having such an engagement program should build the trust and the confidence of minority communities (Wain & Joyce, 2012) and should provide a mechanism for delivering information to the community, especially when there is an "information vacuum" (Riots Communities and Victims Panel, 2012a) and when community tensions are high.

While there may not have been any fore knowledge of the scale, the level of violence or precedence of the August 2011 riots, it is possible that this type of riot or evolutions of it could be seen again. An evolutionary response model and associated deployment plans would need to be developed to respond to this type of disorder. The development of a dynamic and flexible response process that is grounded in an established community relationship would enable police commanders to understand the consequences of their decisions. The August 2011 riots amplified police tactical errors "against structural policing deficits" which created a perception that the police did not have the capacity to respond to the riots with adequate resources (Klein, 2012a, p. 127). The Home Affairs Committee (2011) observed that the loss of control of the streets by the police was the "single most important reason" that explained the spread of disorder.

References

Angel, H. (2012). Viewpoint: Were the riots political? *Safer Communities, 11*(1), 24–32.

Bagguley, P., & Hussain, Y. (2008). *Riotous citizens: Ethnic conflict in multicultural Britain.* Oxford, England: Taylor & Francis Group Ltd.

Bain, T. (2010). *A history of policing in England and Wales from 1974: A turbulent journey.* Oxford, UK: Oxford University Press.

Baker, S. (2012b). Policing the riots: New social media as recruitment, resistance, and surveillance. In D. Briggs (Ed.), *The English riots of 2011: A summer of discontent* (pp. 169–192). Sherfield on Loddon Hook, UK: Waterside Press Ltd.

Bateman, T. (2012). With the benefit of hindsight: The disturbances of August 2011 in historical context. In D. Briggs (Ed.), *The English riots of 2011: A summer of discontent* (pp. 91–110). Sherfield on Loddon Hook, UK: Waterside Press Ltd.

Baudains, P., Braithwaite, A., & Johnson, S. (2013). Target choice during extreme events: A discrete spatial choice model of the 2011 London riots. *Criminology, 51*(2), 251–285.

BBC News. (2001a). *Hague calls for race apology*. 28 May 2001. Retrieved November 26, 2016, from http://news.bbc.co.uk/news/vote2001/hi/english/newsid_1355000/1355606.stm.

BBC News. (2001b, June 6). *No excuse for Leeds riot.* Retrieved from http://news.bbc.co.uk/2/hi/uk_news/1372301.stm.

BBC News. (2005, October 18). *Assault protest stops traffic*. Retrieved from http://news.bbc.co.uk/2/hi/uk_news/england/west_midlands/4354554.stm.

BBC News (2009a). The *challenge of policing the G20*. 30 March 2009. Retrieved from http://news.bbc.co.uk/2/hi/uk_news/7971212.stm.

BBC News. (2009b, April 1). *Live: G20 summit build-up*. Retrieved from http://news.bbc.co.uk/2/hi/business/7973178.stm.

BBC News. (2009c, April 21). *Minister is proud of G20 police*. Retrieved from http://news.bbc.co.uk/2/hi/uk_news/politics/8009939.stm.

BBC News. (2011a, August 7). *Riots in Tottenham after Mark Duggan shooting protest*. Retrieved from http://www.bbc.com/news/uk-england-london-14434318.

BBC News. (2011b, August 11). *England riots: Maps and timeline*. Retrieved from http://www.bbc.co.uk/news/uk-10321233.

BBC News. (2011c, August 15). *England riots: Broken society is top priority – Cameron*. Retrieved from http://www.bbc.com/news/uk-politics-14524834.

BBC News. (2011d, August 15). *England's week of riots*. Retrieved from http://www.bbc.co.uk/news/uk-14532532.

Body-Gendrot, S. (2011, August 15). *Disorder in world cities: Comparing Britain and France*. Retrieved from https://www.opendemocracy.net/ourkingdom/sophie-body-gendrot/disorder-in-world-cities-comparing-britain-and-france.

Briggs, D. (2012a). Concluding thoughts. In D. Briggs (Ed.), *The English riots of 2011: A summer of discontent* (pp. 381–402). Sherfield on Loddon Hook, UK: Waterside Press Ltd.

Briggs, D. (2012b). Frustrations, urban relations and temptations: Contextualising the English riots. In D. Briggs (Ed.), *The English riots of 2011: A summer of discontent* (pp. 27–42). Sherfield on Loddon, Hook, UK: Waterside Press Ltd.

Briggs, D. (2012c). Introduction. In D. Briggs (Ed.), *The English riots of 2011: A summer of discontent* (pp. 9–26). Sherfield on Loddon Hook, UK: Waterside Press Ltd.

Briggs, D. (2012d). What we did when it happened: A timeline analysis of the social disorder in London. *Safer Communities, 2*(1), 6–16.

Briggs, S. (2012). Rurality and the riots: From the panel to the village pub. In D. Briggs (Ed.), *The English Riots of 2011: A Summer of Discontent* (pp. 303–326). Sherfield on Loddon Hook, United Kingdom: Waterside Press Ltd.

Cantle, T. (2006). *Review of community cohesion: Challenging local communities to change Oldham*. Manchester, England: Oldham Metropolitan Borough Council.

Carter, H. (2002). *Oldham council hits out over riot report's criticism*. The Guardian, 29 June.

Daily Mail. (2011, November 29). *How police abandoned streets to riot mobs: Officers gave impression of surrender.* Daily Mail. Retrieved from http://www.dailymail.co.uk/news/article-2067178/How-police-abandoned-streets-riot-mobs-Officers-gave-impression-surrender.html#ixzziltNc5HXw.

Daily Telegraph. (2011, April 29). *Woman whose shooting sparked Brixton riots*. Daily Telegraph. Retrieved from http://www.telegraph.co.uk/news/uknews/law-and-order/8483471/Woman-whose-shooting-sparked-Brixton-riots.html.

Field, S., & Southgate, P. (1982). *Public disorder: A review of research and a study in one inner city area*. Home Office Research and Planning Report, Research Study No. 72. London: Her Majesty's Stationery Office.

Greer, C., & McLaughlin, E. (2010). We predict a riot? Public order policing, new media environments and the rise of the citizen journalist. *British Journal of Criminology, 50*(6), 1041–1059.

Harding, S. (2012). Street government: The role of the urban street gang in the London riots. In D. Briggs (Ed.), *The English riots of 2011: A summer of discontent* (pp. 193–214). Sherfield on Loddon Hook, UK: Waterside Press Ltd.

Hatherley, O. (2011, August 12). *Something has snapped, and it has been a long time coming*. Retrieved from http://www.versobooks.com/blogs/660-something-has-snapped-and-it-has-been-a-long-time-coming.

Her Majesty's Chief Inspectorate of Constabulary. (2009). *Adapting to protest*. London, England: Her Majesty's Chief Inspectorate of Constabulary.

Her Majesty's Inspectorate of Constabulary. (2011). *The rules of engagement: A review of the August 2011 disorders*. London, England: Her Majesty's Chief Inspectorate of Constabulary.

Herbert, I. (2001, June 6). Arrest of Asian over disc sparked Leeds riot. *The Independent*. Retrieved from http://www.independent.co.uk/news/uk/this-britain/arrest-of-asian-over-tax-disc-sparked-leeds-riot-9156046.html.

Home Office. (2011). *An overview of recorded crimes and arrests resulting from disorder events in August 2011*. London, England: Home Office.

Human Rights and Equalities Commission. (2010). *Stop and think: A critical review of the use of stop and search powers in England and Wales*. London, UK: Equality and Human Rights Commission.

Hytner, B. (1981). *Report of the Moss Side enquiry panel to the leader of the Greater Manchester Council*. Manchester, England: Moss Side Enquiry Panel.

Islam Online. (2001, June 13). *Reasons behind the ethnic riots in Oldham*. Retrieved from http://islamonline.net/english/views/2001/06/article6.shtml.

Kawalerowicz, J., & Biggs, M. (2014). *Anarchy in the UK: economic deprivation, social disorganization, and political grievances in the London riot of 2011*. Sociology Working Papers Number 2014-06. University of Oxford: Department of Sociology.

Kelly, Z., & Gill, A. (2012). Reading the riots through gender: A feminist reflection on England's 2011 riots. In D. Briggs (Ed.), *The English riots of 2011: A summer of discontent* (pp. 215–234). Sherfield on Loddon Hook, UK: Waterside Press Ltd.

King, M., & Brearley, N. (1996). *Public order policing: Contemporary perspectives on strategy and tactics*. Leicester, England: Perpetuity Press.

Klein, A. (2012a). More police, less safety? Policing as a causal factor in the outbreak of riots and public disturbances. In D. Briggs (Ed.), *The English riots of 2011: A summer of discontent* (pp. 127–146). Sherfield on Loddon Hook, UK: Waterside Press Ltd.

Klein, A. (2012b). Policing as a causal factor – A fresh view on riots and social unrest. *Safer Communities, 11*(1), 17–23.

Lewis, P. (2011, August 7). *Tottenham riots: weren't to be violent like they were, then suddenly all hell broke loose*. The Guardian. Retrieved from https://www.theguardian.com/uk/2011/aug/07/tottenham-riots-peaceful-protest.

Lewis, P., Newburn, T., Taylor, M., Mcgillivray, C., Greenhill, A., Frayman, H., et al. (2011). *Reading the riots: Investigating England's summer of disorder*. London, England: London School of Economics.

MacLean, W., & Holton, K. (2009). *G20 protestor smash windows and clash with police*. Reuters, 2 April 2009. Retrieved from: http://uk.reuters.com/article/uk-g20-protests-idUKTRE53101020090402.

McVeigh, T., Lewis, P., & Jha, A. (2009, March 28). *G20 protest: Thousands march for jobs, justice and climate*. The Guardian. Retrieved 2016 from https://www.theguardian.com/world/2009/mar/28/g20-protest-police-rainbow-alliance.

Metropolitan Police Service. (2011a). *Operation Kirkin strategic review interim report*. Retrieved from https://tottenhamdefencecampaign.files.wordpress.com/2012/01/interimreportkirkin.pdf.

Metropolitan Police Service. (2011b). *Strategic review of MPS response to disorder: Early learning and initial findings*. Retrieved from http://content.met.police.uk/cs/Satellite?blobcol=urldata&blobheadername1=Content-Type&blobheadername2=Content-Disposition&blobheadervalue1=application/pdf&blobheadervalue2=inline;+filename%3D%22367/144/CO553-11Initial_Findings.pdf%22&blobkey=id&blobtable=MungoBlobs&blobwhere=1283531305435&ssbinary=true.

Metropolitan Police Service. (2012). *4 Days in August. The Metropolitan Police Service strategic review of the disorder of 2011*. London, England: Metropolitan Police.

Ministry of Justice. (2012). Statistical bulletin on the public disorder of 6th–9th August 2011.

Moran, M., & Waddington, D. (2016). *Riots: An international comparison*. London, UK: Macmillan Publishers Ltd.

Moore, S. (2012). *Number of stop and searches halved in Haringey*. Tottenham and Wood Green Journal, 6 August 2012. Retrieved from: http://www.tottenhamjournal.co.uk/news/crime-court/number_of_stop_and_searches_halved_in_haringey_1_1469742.

Morrell, G., Scott, S., McNeish, D., & Webster, S. (2011). *The August riots in England: Understanding the involvement of young people*. London, England: NatCen.

Moss Side Defence Committee. (1981). *The Hytner myths*. Manchester, England: Moss Side.

Muir, H. (2011). *Tottenham riots: Missteps in the dance of police and a frustrated community*. Retrieved September 5, 2016, from https://www.theguardian.com/uk/2011/sep/05/tottenham-riots-police-community.

Muddle, L. (2014). *The London riots 2011: Analyzing framing processes of the London riots*. Retrieved from https://dspace.library.uu.nl/bitstream/handle/1874/295601/Eindversie%20scriptie.pdf.

Muir, H., & Butt, R. (2005). *A rumour, outrage and then a riot. How tension in a Birmingham suburb erupted*. The Guardian, 24 October 2005. Retrieved from: https://www.theguardian.com/uk/2005/oct/24/race.ukcrime.

Newburn, T. (2012, March 1). *Cuts to police numbers*. Retrieved from https://blogs.lse.ac.uk/politicsandpolicy/2011/08/22/police-relationship-conservatives/.

Newman, K. (1986, July). *Police-public relations: The pace of change*. Police Foundation Lecture. Retrieved from https://web.archive.org/web/20110721071915/http://www.police-foundation.org.uk/files/POLICE0001/speeches/1986%20Sir%20Kenneth%20Newman.pdf.

Newnham, J., & Bell, P. (2012). Social network media and political activism: A growing challenge for law enforcement. *Journal of Policing, Intelligence and Counter Terrorism, 7*(1), 36–50.

O'Neill, S. (2009, April 11). *Metropolitan police chiefs ordered to justify tactics at G20 protests*. The Times.. Retrieved from http://www.timesonline.co.uk/tol/news/uk/crime/article6073436.ece.

Parry, G., Tirbutt, S., & Rose, D. (1985, September 30). *Riots in Brixton after police shooting*. The Guardian, Retrieved from https://www.theguardian.com/theguardian/2009/sep/30/brixton-riots-1985-archive.

Prasad, R. (2011, December 5). *Rioter profile: I saw an opportunity to take stuff, so I entered the shop*. The Guardian. Retrieved from https://www.theguardian.com/uk/2011/dec/05/rioter-profile-opportunity-take-stuff.

Reicher, S., & Stott, C. (2011). *Mad mobs and Englishmen*? London, United Kingdom: Constable & Robinson. Kindle Edition.

Riots Communities and Victims Panel. (2012a). *5 Days in August: An interim report on the 2011 English riots*. Retrieved from http://webarchive.nationalarchives.gov.uk/20121003195935/http:/riotspanel.independent.gov.uk/wp-content/uploads/2012/04/Interim-report-5-Days-in-August.pdf.

Riots Communities and Victims Panel. (2012b). *After the riots: The final report of the riots communities and victims panel*. Retrieved from http://webarchive.nationalarchives.gov.uk/20121003195935/http:/riotspanel.independent.gov.uk/wp-content/uploads/2012/03/Riots-Panel-Final-Report1.pdf.

Sagrans, E. (2011). *Just getting started: Did UK students ignite a movement*? Retrieved from: http://www.movements.org/blog/entry/did-students-in-the-ukignite-a-lasting-movement/.

Scarman, L. J. (1981). *The Brixton disorders, April 10–12 1981: Report of an inquiry by the Rt. Hon. The Lord Scarman, O.B.E.* (Cmnd. 8427). London, UK: Her Majesty's Stationery Office.

Stott, C., Drury, J., & Reicher, S. (2017). On the role of a social identity analysis in articulating structure and collective action: The 2011 riots in Tottenham and Hackney. *British Journal of Criminology, 57*(4), azw036. https://doi.org/10.1093/bjc/azw036

The Secretary of State for the Home Department. (2011). Policing large scale disorder: Lessons from the disturbances of August 2011. In *The government response to the sixteenth report of the home affairs committee session 2010-12 HC 1456*. London: The United Kingdom Government.

Topping, A., & Bawdon, E. (2011, December 5). *It was like Christmas: A consumerist feast among the summer riots*. The Guardian. Retrieved from https://www.theguardian.com/uk/2011/dec/05/summer-riots-consumerist-feast-looters.

Tuck, M., & Southgate, P. (1981). *Ethnic minorities, crime and policing: a survey of the experiences of West Indians and whites*. Home Office Research and Planning Report, Research Study No. 70. London: Her Majesty's Stationery Office.

Wain, N., & Joyce, P. (2012). Disaffected communities, riots and policing: Manchester 1981 and 2011. *Safer Communities, 11*(3), 125–132.

Wainwright, M., Psarias, C., & Spencer, S. (2001, June 7). *Riot began as planned ambush, say police*. The Guardian. Retrieved from https://www.theguardian.com/uk/2001/jun/07/race.world.

Waterton, S., & Sesay, K. (2012). Out of touch—a youth perspective. *Criminal Justice Matters, 87*(1), 28–29.

Chapter 6
The 2014 Riots in Ferguson

6.1 Introduction

The fatal shooting of a young African American man by a white police officer in Ferguson, Missouri on ninth August 2014, sparked one of the worst riots ever seen in the greater St. Louis County area (Institute for Intergovernmental Research, 2015). Waves of protesting and rioting followed the shooting. The first wave, from 9 to 24 August 2014 was widespread and involved acts of vandalism and looting (Kienscherf, 2014; New York Times, 2014). The second wave, from September 23 to September 29, centered on the call for the resignation of the Chief of the Ferguson Police. The third wave was a result of the police officer who shot the African American man not being indicted for the death. The fourth and last wave of protesting and rioting took place on the first anniversary of the shooting.

St. Louis, Missouri and the wider area does not have a history of violent disorder or of rioting (Newburn, 2014). Even following the widespread race-based riots of the 1960s, the assassination of Dr. Martin Luther King and the assault of Rodney King, rioting did not occur in the St. Louis area (Newburn, 2014). This changed however, following the death of the young African American man. The death prompted violent demonstrations and disorder with the police responding with tear gas and rubber bullets (New York Times, 2014). Even after the responsibility for the response changed from the St. Louis County Police Department to the Missouri State Highway Patrol and the deployment of the Missouri National Guard to assist the police with the response, the level of violence and disorder continued (New York Times, 2014).

Ferguson is one of 89 municipalities in St. Louis County and is a small community of approximately 21,000 people (United States Department of Justice, 2016). While the population of Ferguson has been relatively stable in recent decades, the ethnic demographic of the population has changed dramatically during this time (United States Department of Justice, 2016). In 1990, the demographics of the community was made up of 74% white and 25% African American (United States

G. den Heyer, *Police Response to Riots*,
https://doi.org/10.1007/978-3-030-31810-9_6

Department of Justice, 2016). However, by 2010, this composition had changed to 67% African American and 29% white, while the composition of the Fergusson police agency was 95% white (The Economist, 2014).

The Ferguson Police Department is one of approximately 60 police departments in the St. Louis City and County region (Norton, Hamilton, Braziel, Linskey, & Zeunik, 2015). According to the United States Department of Justice (2016), the 60 departments possess widely differing resources and provide differing standards of protection across a significantly diverse, geographic and demographic county and as a result, police services across St. Louis County are widely differentiated. Fifty-eight municipalities make up the county of St. Louis. Both St. Louis City and County provide their own police services while 14 municipalities of the county contract their policing services from neighboring municipalities, 18 municipalities contract the St. Louis County Police Department to provide policing services to their municipalities and the remaining municipalities in the county have their policing services provided by their own single, small police agency (Norton et al., 2015).

A large number of police agencies responded to the Ferguson riots and this caused difficulties in coordinating resources and tactics. The initial police response to the protests and riots led to criticism from the public, politicians and the media about the deployment and use of military-type equipment and the use of, what they perceived to be, military tactics (Kienscherf, 2014). Criticism of the police response to the unrest led to a major debate "about the militarization of American police" (Kienscherf, 2014, p. 2).

An initial examination of the events which lead to the unrest and the form that the police response took presents the police in a light where it would not be hard to be critical of the police approach and as Gene O'Donnell of the John Jay College of Criminal Justice claimed "it is hard to point to anything that [the] Ferguson police did that was not wrong" (cited in The Economist, 2014). Mr. O'Donnell substantiated his statement by noting that the police "left Mr Brown's body on the street for four hours," "withheld the name of the officer who shot him" and "they confronted peaceful demonstrators and rioters alike with a stunning show of force—armoured cars with snipers on top—and precious little tact" (The Economist, 2014).

The purpose of this chapter is to examine the police response to the disorder and the riots in Ferguson, Missouri in August 2014 and to look beyond the rhetoric from commenters to find the reasons as to why the police responded as they did. The examination is undertaken in the form of a case study and comprises five sections. Similar to previous chapters, the first section provides the background and the context in which the riots occurred. It also outlines the chronology of the August 2014 events. The second section discusses the police response in detail and the third section provides a critique of the response within a framework of six operational issues that were identified in an analysis of the police response to the riots. The fourth section discusses the operational issues within the context of what they mean for policing and the conclusions are presented in the final section.

6.2 Riots and Chronology

There were four separate waves to the riots that occurred in Fergusson. The first and most violent wave occurred between 9 and 25 August 2014. The waves of protest and rioting that followed have been presented in Table 6.1 along with their start and finish dates and the reasons why the disorder occurred.

On Saturday 9 August 2014, a police officer in Ferguson, Missouri confronted two African American youths walking in the middle of the street. During this incident, the police officer shot and killed one of the unarmed youths. Following the shooting, rumors spread through the community that the youth who had been shot had his hands up in surrender. This accusation was later found to be incorrect, but the widely circulated account contributed to a large gathering of members of the African American community at the site of the shooting, where a memorial was constructed on the spot where the youth had died (Follman, 2014). Later in the evening, the memorial was damaged by the police (Follman, 2014).

The damage to the memorial and the belief held by the community that the youth who had been shot by the police was surrendering to the officer led to a peaceful protest and a candlelight vigil on the evening of Sunday 10 August. It was following the vigil that the disorder began (Follman, 2014). Bottles were thrown at the police (Bennett, 2014), nearby businesses were looted, and vehicles were vandalized (Yang, 2014). Approximately 150 police officers wearing protective riot equipment, responded to the disorder, cordoned the area, and blocked rioters from accessing the city of Ferguson (Chicago Tribune, 2014; Follman, 2014; Yang, 2014). The disorder continued until the crowd was dispersed at approximately 2.00 am. Twelve businesses were vandalized or looted and a convenience store and a gas station were set on fire (Barker, 2014; Bennett, 2014; Chicago Tribune, 2014). The violence led to 32 arrests, mainly for assault, burglary and theft and two police officers suffered minor injuries (Piper, 2014; The St. Louis American, 2014).

On Monday evening 11 August, a large crowd gathered at the convenience store that had been set on fire during the previous night. As darkness fell, the crowd began to shout obscenities and made threats, such as “kill the police” (Press Association, 2014). The crowd also began to throw rocks and other projectiles at the police with

Table 6.1 Details of the four separate Ferguson riots

Wave	Start date	Finish date	Number of days	Reason for disorder
1	August 9	August 25	16	Shooting of Michael Brown
2	September 23	September 29	4	Calling for resignation of Chief of Police
3	November 24	December 2	8	Police Officer not indicted for the shooting
4	August 9[a]	August 11	2	Anniversary of initial 2014 shooting

Source: Author
[a]2015

one projectile shattering on the ground and erupting into flames (Wulfhorst & Malone, 2014). The police used tear gas and stun grenades to control the disorder and to disperse the crowd (Wulfhorst & Malone, 2014). Forty-seven people were arrested during the disorder (Shoichet, Brumfield, & Smith, 2014).

A similar series of events occurred on the evenings of 12, 13 and 14 August. Protesters gathered on Florissant Avenue, carrying signs and walking with their arms raised, chanting 'don't shoot' as a response to the rumor that the youth who had been shot by the police had his hands raised in an attempt to surrender at the moment that he was shot (Suhr & Salter, 2014). During the protest, bottles were thrown at the police, which prompted the police to use tear gas and rubber bullets to disperse the crowd (Shoichet et al., 2014; Suhr & Salter, 2014). During the stand-off with the police a protester was shot in the head (non-fatally) by an unknown party (Lussenhop, 2014).

On 13 August, owing to the increasing level of violence and with protesters throwing Molotov cocktails at the police (The Associated Press, 2014), more than 70 SWAT officers were deployed to assist with dispersing the crowd (Shoichet et al., 2014). This night saw the police use smoke bombs, flash grenades, rubber bullets, and tear gas in an attempt to control the protesters (Suhr & Salter, 2014).

By Friday 15 August, according to Peters (2014), the protests were undertaken in "an almost celebratory manner." However, the mood changed later in the evening and early the next morning, the crowd of more than 200 people started to throw rocks at the police and nearby stores were looted (CBS St. Louis, 2014). The crowd was eventually dispersed by the police using tear gas and rubber bullets (CBS St. Louis, 2014).

As a result of the continuing violence, on Saturday 16 August, the Governor of Missouri declared a state of emergency in Ferguson and imposed a curfew, making it illegal to be on the streets of the town after midnight (Ellis, Hana, & Prokupecz, 2014). However, hundreds of protesters remained in the streets after the curfew took effect, even though the police had used loudspeakers to warn the protesters to disperse before the curfew began (Reuters, 2014). At midnight, when the curfew took effect protesters clashed with the police with police tactical units using smoke canisters and tear gas to clear the area (Vinograd, 2014). One protester was shot by an unknown assailant during the melee and seven were arrested (Reuters, 2014; The Telegraph, 2014; Vinograd, 2014).

A midnight curfew was imposed for the second night, which was Sunday 17 August (The Telegraph, 2014). At around dusk on Sunday evening, a large number of people, including families and children, gathered on Florissant Avenue to peacefully protest the shooting (The Telegraph, 2014). However, a small group within the crowd threw a number of Molotov cocktails at the police and directed gunfire at the police (The Telegraph, 2014). A small group began to loot the stores (The Telegraph, 2014). The police responded by dispensing tear gas and smoke canisters (The Telegraph, 2014).

The evening of 18 August also saw several hundred protesters gathered on Florissant Avenue and again, as the time for the curfew approached, a number of participants started to throw bottles at the police and charge the police line (Brown,

Johnson, Angelucci, & Murray, 2014). Seventy-eight protesters were arrested (Cook, 2014). As a result of the continuing violence and the resources of the police being stretched from enforcing the curfew, the Missouri State Governor issued an executive order, calling in the National Guard to "help restore peace and order and to protect the citizens of Ferguson" (Hartmann, 2014). The Governor then announced that there would be no curfew on the night of August 18 (Berman, 2014).

Forty-seven arrests were made on Tuesday 19 and six people were arrested on Wednesday 20 August for disorder related offences (i24news, 2014). The violence started to decrease on the evening of Wednesday 20 August and as a result, the National Guard were withdrawn on Thursday 21 August (Zagier, 2014). The last of the arrests for the first wave of protests were made on Saturday 23 August when three people were arrested for disorder during a peaceful protest (Reuters, 2014).

A second series of protests occurred on Tuesday 23 and continued until Sunday 28 September 2014, with the protesters calling for the resignation of the Chief of the Ferguson Police. During the evening of 23 August, several hundred-people gathered outside the Ferguson Police Headquarters and demanded that the Chief of Police resign (Bruton & Duchon, 2014). The Chief of Police attempted to address the crowd, but bottles and rocks were thrown at the Chief and at the 50 police officers who were controlling the crowd (Bruton & Duchon, 2014). Eight protesters were arrested for charges such as failure to disperse and resisting arrest (Bruton & Duchon, 2014).

A similar sequence of events occurred during the evenings of Saturday 27, Sunday 28 and Monday 29 September. During the Saturday 27 protests, a police officer was shot in the arm, but no arrests were made (Coleman, 2014). On Sunday 28 August, a large crowd gathered outside the police headquarters and began to throw bottles and stones at the police (Coleman, 2014). Eight arrests were made during this confrontation (Coleman, 2014).

On Monday 29 September, protesters gathered again in front of the police headquarters, while members of the clergy gathered in the parking lot (Samuels, 2014). At approximately 11 pm, the crowd were told to disperse but as the police approached the crowd gunshots were heard (Samuels, 2014). The crowd dispersed following the sound of gunshots and no further action was taken by the police.

Protesters gathered again in front of the police headquarters on Thursday 2 October. More than 12 people were arrested during the assembly for noise related offenses and for resisting arrest (Stewart & Reilly, 2014). While on Monday 13 October more than 50 people were arrested for staging a peaceful act of disobedience (Davey & Blinder, 2014).

The third wave of protests occurred throughout the night of November 24–25 following the grand jury decision not to indict the officer for the shooting that occurred on August 9. Looting and vandalism ensued with more than a dozen buildings being burnt. A number of vehicles were also burnt (Wulfhorst, Wallis, & McAllister, 2014). In response, the police dispersed tear gas and 61 people were arrested for burglary and trespass offenses (Li & Sheehy, 2014).

6.3 The Police Response

According to the Institute for Intergovernmental Research (2015), more than 50 law enforcement agencies were involved in the police response to the Ferguson riots but the principal agencies that responded were the St. Louis County Police Department, the St. Louis Metropolitan Police Department, the Missouri State Highway Patrol, and the Ferguson Police Department (p. XIII).

This section of the case study discusses the police response to the protests and riots from immediately after the shooting on Saturday, August 9, 2014 through until midnight on Monday, August 25, 2014; the day of Mr. Brown's funeral.

The discussion in this section relies extensively on the Institute for Intergovernmental Research (2015) report entitled "After-action assessment of the police response to the August 2014 demonstrations in Ferguson, Missouri." The report summarized the independent review of the activities undertaken by the police for the 17 days following the death of Michael Brown and included a synopsis of "how the police managed the mass demonstrations in Ferguson." The report provided a number of findings and documented the lessons that had been learned, of which, may be beneficial to law enforcement" (p. IX). The report claimed that "the demonstrations that followed the shooting … were more than a moment of discord in one small community; they have become part of a national movement to reform our criminal justice system and represent a new civil rights movement" (p. IX).

The shooting of Michael Brown occurred at approximately 12.02 pm in a street within the Canfield Green Apartments complex in Ferguson (p. 6). At approximately 1.17 pm two Captains from the St. Louis Police Department completed an assessment of the scene of the incident and the resources that were present to establish whether there was a need to request further resources from contiguous police agencies (p. 7). By 1.30 pm privacy screens had been erected around the body, uniform police officers had been deployed to cordon and protect the scene and investigators and crime scene technicians had begun their investigation (p. 7).

At the same time, a crowd of approximately 200 people had gathered around the cordoned scene area (p. 7). According to officers at the scene, the size and response of the crowd was unprecedented in St. Louis County (p. 7). A number of officers who had discussed how quickly the crowd had assembled noted that "the pulse of the situation was different" (p. 7). According to the Institute for Intergovernmental Research (2015), the catalyst for the growing crowd and their mood was the "presence of Mr. Brown's body" and "the number of emergency vehicles" (p. 8).

The large crowd in the area "continued to encroach into the cordoned area" and as officers attempted to move them back from the cordons, members of the crowd became increasingly abusive, with some "stating that officers should be killed" (p. 8). The growing number of people made the scene increasingly chaotic and it was difficult for the officers to "protect the scene" and ensure that the evidence was preserved (p. 8). Unfortunately during which time, Mr. Brown's body laid, unmoved for 4 h (p. 9).

The first officers to arrive at the scene were from the Ferguson Police Department and the St. Louis County Police Department but it was soon realized that more officers would be needed to protect the scene and assist with the investigation (p. 9). At approximately 1.55 pm the Captain of the St. Louis County Police Department, who was at the scene, called for assistance[1] and at 1.58 pm an officer from the Ferguson Police Department contacted the St. Louis County Police Department Bureau of Communications to request additional canine officers to assist with crowd control (p. 9). Following these requests for assistance more than 50 officers were dispatched or self-deployed from 29 different police agencies (p. 9).

Officers who arrived at the scene included "15 troopers from the Missouri State Highway Patrol and 20 members of its Special Weapons and Tactics (SWAT) team" (p. 9). These officers arrived at one of two staging areas, the first was outside a local restaurant, approximately 0.3 miles from the scene and the second "was on Glen Owen Drive, approximately 0.2 miles" from the scene (p. 9).

At approximately 2.15 pm, a Sergeant from the St. Louis County Police Department called a Code 2000 "for an additional 25 officers to be dispatched to the scene" (p. 9).[2] However, according to the Institute for Intergovernmental Research (2015), it was not known as to how many officers arrived at the scene following this call (p. 9). The confusion as to the number of officers who had arrived at the scene and the number of officers who were already at the scene arose because officers had self-deployed and records were not kept at the staging areas (p. 9).

As a result of the hostility of the crowd and the number of gunshots fired, a Bearcat armoured vehicle was dispatched to the scene at approximately 2.43 pm (p. 10). By 3.15 pm tactical officers from the St. Louis County Police Department, the St. Louis Police Department and the Florissant Police Department, under the command of a Captain from the St. Louis County Police Department had arrived at the scene (p. 10).

At approximately 4.00 pm, Mr. Brown's body was removed from the scene while the area remained cordoned to allow crime technicians to finish processing and packaging evidence (p. 10). By 4.49 pm, the police reported that the size of the crowd was still growing and that further assistance was required (p. 10). In response to the calls for assistance more officers arrived at the scene and by 6.33 pm the crime scene investigators and technicians had begun to leave the scene (p. 10).

At 7.00 pm, Canfield Drive was reopened to the public (p. 11). However, by 8.40 pm the crowd had increased in size and as a result, the police vehicles parked "on Canfield Drive were surrounded by protesters" (p. 11). The police interpreted the number of people in the area as being threatening and a decision was made to recall all police officers to the staging areas (p. 11). At approximately 9.03 pm all

[1]The Captain called a Code 1000 which is the code for general assistance. According to the Institute for Intergovernmental Research (2015) there is some confusion as to the time between the two calls for assistance, but as there was no documentation on the timing, the information provided was from their interviews with officers at the scene (p. 9).

[2]A Code 2000 call is part of the Code 1000 Plan that allows for additional officers to assist (p. 9).

police department personnel had "left the staging area while observing more people walking toward the area of the shooting" (p. 11).

The crowd remained around the West Florissant Avenue and Canfield Drive area, but some gathered outside the Ferguson Police Department Headquarters (p. 11). By early Sunday morning, 10 August "the crowds began dissipating," and the St. Louis County Police Department handed responsibility for control back to the Ferguson Police Department (p. 11).

By mid-afternoon Sunday 10 August, large, hostile crowds were amassing at three locations: Canfield Drive, in the area of the shooting; West Florissant Avenue, near a popular, local restaurant; and South Florissant Road, in front of the Ferguson Police Department Headquarters (p. 11). The crowd on West Florissant was estimated to be of between 700 and 800 people but the major problem for the police was that the dynamics of the crowd had changed from one of where people were observers to one where they were demonstrators (p. 11). The crowd in front of the police headquarters were chanting and eventually blocked the road by sitting on the street (p. 12).

As result of the size of the gatherings, especially on West Florissant Avenue, a Code 2000 was called and assistance was requested from both the St. Louis County Police Department and the St. Louis Police Department tactical units (p. 12). The Missouri State Highway Patrol responded to the request by dispatching a Captain, 12 Troopers and their SWAT team (p. 12).

The Chief of the St. Louis Police arrived by late-afternoon and took command of the police response to the protesting and the looting "at the Canfield Green Apartments and with the growing crowds on West Florissant" (p. 12). The command was initially joint, with the Chief of Ferguson Police having command of the police response at the Ferguson Police Headquarters and the Chief of the St. Louis Police having command at the Canfield Green Apartments (p. 12).

By the early evening, the size of the crowd had grown to approximately 1000 people and businesses on West Florissant Avenue near Canfield Drive had been looted and set ablaze (p. 12). The protesters in this area had started to throw missiles at the police officers and their vehicles (p. 12). In an "attempt to gain control of the situation, several agencies" (p.12) (such as the St. Louis Police Department, the Missouri State Highway Patrol and the St. Charles County Police Department) had "deployed armoured vehicles and canine" units (p. 12).

Later in the evening of Sunday, a command post was established at a police sub-station in a strip mall on West Florissant Avenue (p. 13). According to the Institute for Intergovernmental Research (2015), the Incident Command System (ICS) had been partially implemented but there was uncertainty as to whether the Ferguson Police Department or the St. Louis County Police Department was in command or "whether it was a joint command" (p. 13). This uncertainty caused confusion among the responding officers and for the additional resources that had been requested from contiguous police departments (p. 13). The officers who responded from the other police departments received "mixed messages on arrest procedures" and as to "the circumstances under which officers could or should appropriately respond" to rioters and looting (p. 13).

According to the Institute for Intergovernmental Research (2015), the lack of information provided by the police, the extensive use of social media and texting by the public and the criticism of the police by the media, all "contributed to the development of a narrative that Mr. Brown had been shot while trying to surrender or run away" (p. 14). The lack of information caused crowds to form in the area and increased the tension in the community.

The size of the crowd and the increasing level of violence led the police officers of St. Louis County to claim that they did not have the resources to control the civil disobedience and they called another Code 1000 at 8.25 pm and then immediately after, a Code 2000 (p. 14). Assistance was sought from the "St. Louis Police Department SWAT team, the Missouri State Highway Patrol SWAT team and the St. Charles County multijurisdictional SWAT team" (p. 14). These teams started to arrive at approximately 10 pm (p. 14).

Following the arrival of the SWAT teams, protesters were ordered to disperse (p. 15). However, this instruction was unheeded by crowd, even after the use of smoke canisters. In retaliation to the use of smoke canisters, the crowd began to throw missiles at the police and gunfire was heard (p. 15). In an attempt to gain control of the situation and to disperse the crowd, the police deployed CS tear gas (p. 16). Following the use of the CS tear gas, "many protesters dispersed, although small pockets remained" (p. 15).

In the early hours of Monday 11 August, "there were still large groups of protesters and looters" in the area and they did not leave until between 3 and 4 am (p. 15). Protests during the day of 11 August were peaceful and at approximately 6 pm, "community members joined together" with the large crowds gathered at Canfield Green Apartments to pray for justice (p. 15). Although the police cordoned the area around the apartments, they did not enter the area as "Canfield [Green] Apartments became a no-police zone" and "became a safe haven for criminals" (p. 15).[3]

Later that evening, "the group of protesters became even larger than previous nights" and although the majority of protesters were demonstrating peacefully, others were aggressive, threw objects, such as Molotov cocktails, set fires and looted businesses (p. 16). As a result of the violence, the police deployed armored vehicles to protect the officers and deployed tear gas, pepper ball projectiles, bean bag rounds and Stingerballs (p. 16). The use of these forms of non-lethal weaponry gave rise to the first instance of criticism from the community, which was contradictory, with a number of people alleging that the force used by the police was excessive, while local "business owners complained that the police waited too long to disperse the crowds, resulting in more damage to and looting of their businesses" (p. 16). Some members of the community claimed that the use of the weaponry and the armored vehicles was evidence of police militarization (p. 16).

There was more confusion in the police response during that evening as it was not clear as to who was in command and the arrest procedures that should be followed. The confusion as to who was in command stemmed from a Code 2000,

[3] Residents complained that the police had "abandoned" Canfield Green Apartments.

which was called by the Chief of the Ferguson Police Department but it was the Chief of the St. Louis County Police Department who was the primary incident commander (p. 17). Fortunately, this confusion did not delay the arrival of further assistance. The confusion in relation to the arrest procedures resulted from the lack of information or direction about the process to be used, which should have been provided by the commander. As no advice was provided, officers followed the procedures used by their own departments, depending on which jail was used by the arresting officer and this exacerbated the confusion (p. 17).

On Tuesday 12 August, owing to "images in the media," the Chief of the St. Louis Police Department withdrew his department's support and resources from the police response to the protests (p. 17). The Chief stated that he also "had concerns about his two responsibilities as chief to protect the community and to keep it safe and to protect his officers" (p. 17).

A regular pattern of protesting was seen during the day of Tuesday, where the protests were peaceful, but as soon as it became dark, the protests became violent (p. 17). It was also noted that the size and the dynamics of the crowd changed after it became dark (p. 17). The police claimed that these changes arose from participants arriving "from the surrounding St. Louis metropolitan area and beyond" (p. 17).

The Ferguson Police Department, the St. Louis County Police Department and the Missouri State Highway Patrol all responded to the riots on Tuesday night (p. 17). Armored vehicles and less-than-lethal weapons were used to respond to the violence and to disperse the crowd (p. 18). According to the Institute for Intergovernmental Research (2015), the main difference in the protests during the evening of 12 August and the protests held in the early morning hours of 13 August was that "protesters from outside the region – including increasing numbers of those intent on exploiting the demonstrations – arrived in Ferguson" (p. 17). Police intelligence also supported this claim. Intelligence suggested that "some individuals might be attempting to promote aggressive law enforcement responses and actions with the purpose of focusing public attention away from the action of protests and more upon the police response to those actions and more upon the police response to those actions" (pp. 18–19).

The police reported that potential offenders had embedded themselves within the peaceful demonstrators "solely with the intent to loot businesses" (p. 19). According to the police, "burglaries and thefts increased in locations away from the protest areas, presumably by offenders taking advantage of the diverted police presence" (p. 19). The first of a new form of deliberate criminal offending also occurred on 12 August; hackers (p. 19). A number of municipal government websites were hacked by the group Anonymous and on 13 August, the St. Louis County Police Communications Unit was hacked (p. 19).

To differentiate the peaceful demonstrations or protests from those that resulted in violence, Ferguson city officials, on 13 August, requested "that protests and vigils for Mr. Brown be held during the daytime" (p. 19). Although some members of the community "viewed this as an attempt to restrict First Amendment Freedoms, the officials claimed that it was "to ensure the safety of the participants and the safety of our community" (p. 19).

Wednesday 13 August also saw the same pattern of protesting with the crowd becoming extremely aggressive as darkness fell (p. 19), and the police responding in a similar fashion as they did on previous nights. However, on Thursday 14 August, after 5 days of disturbances, state, county and municipal officials, the media and the community believed that "the circumstances were not improving and there were questions as to whether the St. Louis County Police Department incident command was effective and making the right decisions" (p. 20). As a result of this belief, the Missouri State Governor "issued an executive order designating the Missouri State Highway Patrol as the formal incident command agency for the Ferguson response and specified" that a captain from the highway patrol be the incident commander (p. 20).

Designating the responsibility for incident command to the highway patrol was questioned by local and county police officers, owing to the events taking place in an urban environment, where the highway patrol "had limited operational experience" (p. 20). Other officers thought the change "showed disrespect to them and their capabilities" (p. 20).

Changing the agency responsible for the events led to two problems. The first problem was that although there had been a formal change in incident command, "there was no formal or written agreement between the law enforcement agencies to document the transition of incident command from the St. Louis County Police Department to the Missouri State Highway Patrol" (p. 20). The second problem was that there "was no documentation for standing orders, the new chain of command, or other command and control responsibilities" (p. 20). It was during the transition of change that the St. Louis Police Department returned to assist with the police response (p. 20).

On Friday 15 August, the Chief of the Ferguson Police Department "released video footage indicating that Mr. Brown had been involved in a robbery of a convenience store minutes before" being stopped by a police officer (p. 21). According to the Institute for Intergovernmental Research (2015), the release of the video was the catalyst for the growth in the size of the demonstrations and for enraging the crowd that evening (p. 22). During the day, the protests outside the Ferguson Police Department Headquarters were peaceful, but as darkness fell, the protests turned violent, with "Molotov cocktails and other objects being thrown" (p. 22). There was also extensive looting of nearby businesses (p. 22). The evening also saw protesters looking for and exploiting issues to provoke the police into responding. Protesters challenged minority police officers and used racial slurs as a means to provoke them (p. 23).

On Saturday 16 August, the Missouri State Governor "issued an executive order intended to deal with the continued problems arising from the mass gatherings in Ferguson" (p. 24). The governor also declared a state of emergency, which included the establishment of a curfew and a declaration that ordered "all law enforcement agencies deployed for the police response in Ferguson to follow the direction of the Missouri State Highway Patrol for tactics to maintain order" (p. 24). Ellis et al. (2014) claimed that the introduction of a state of emergency and a curfew were a result of the militarized way that the police responded to the riots.

The process to implement a declaration of a state of emergency "had to be developed by [the] incident command," which to this point had been operating as "an informal unified command – where incident commanders from various jurisdictions or agencies were operating together to form a single command structure in the field" (p. 24). It was unclear as to how the mandated components of the state of emergency were to be implemented.

There was a change in the command strategy following the establishment of the state of emergency, which was expected to improve the flow of communication with the community and change the reactive response of the police to a proactive response. The new strategy was formulated to include the integration of uniformed officers "among the crowd to minimize the appearance of law enforcement officers facing off with protesters" (p. 24). To implement this strategy officers were deployed in teams, but SWAT and other tactical officers were to remain out of sight in staging areas at various locations (p. 24).

A second issue that became apparent on 16 August was the change in the style of incident command, which was bought about by the Captain of the Missouri State Highway Patrol, who had been appointed by the Governor as commander. According to the Institute for Intergovernmental Research (2015), when the St. Louis County Police Department were the agency in command of the incident, "regular briefings were held with every agency in attendance" (p. 25). However, following the appointment of the Captain, "the incident command role became less structured" and more focused on providing information to engage with the community (p. 25). The idea was "to lessen the tactical approach and military image of law enforcement" (p. 25).

The problem with the change in command style was that the objective of the new style "was not either effectively communicated to or understood by the officers as a strategy, or [that] officers may have actively resisted this [new] approach" (p. 25). As a result, officers perceived that "the strategy for managing the demonstrations was continually changing, and tactical direction … often did not clearly follow the changes in strategy" (p. 25).

Other strategies that were introduced to control protester violence was to stop groups of people from gathering, particularly at night-time, to deploy uniformed officers near the protesters and for the officers to tell the protesters to keep moving (p. 25).

Late on Saturday night and into early Sunday 17 August, crowds gathered again on West Florissant Avenue. Following the implementation of the curfew, at approximately 12.15 am about 150 people refused to comply with the declaration or to disperse (p. 25). The crowd began walking along West Florissant Avenue towards a retail area and at approximately "12.23 am had completely blocked the street" (p. 25). "As the crowd grew in both size and hostility, … the police deployed tear gas" to disperse the group, but the "streets remained blocked until around 1.30 am" (p. 25). During this confrontation, "a person was shot by an unknown assailant" (p. 25).

During daylight hours of Sunday 17 August, the protests were again peaceful, but as darkness fell, the crowd again, became aggressive (p. 25). By 7.30 pm, more than "1,000 [people] had assembled near 9191 West Florissant Avenue" and over the next few hours confronted the police and looted several businesses (p. 26). At approximately 9.00 pm, a crowd of "several-hundred people attempted to overrun" the police command post (p. 26). This prompted the police to request immediate assistance and to deploy a helicopter and a SWAT team (p. 26). To gain control of the situation, the police used tear gas, less-than-lethal weapons and canine units

(p. 26). However, as the night wore on, the police had to "pull back" from some positions to maintain their own safety (p. 26).

According to the Institute for Intergovernmental Research (2015), Sunday 17 August saw "the worst violence, especially before the midnight curfew went into effect" (p. 26). It also became apparent that "rather than eliminating the violence, the curfew appeared to simply change the time the violence occurred" (p. 26). During the evening there was "a large fight involving more 150 people" and the sound of 12 gun shots were reported (p. 26).

On Monday 18 August, the Missouri Governor lifted the curfew and activated the Missouri National Guard to assist the police (p. 26). The primary role of the National Guard was "to protect the incident command post and police vehicles, freeing up law enforcement officers to be deployed to the streets" (p. 26). However, while some members of the community viewed the deployment of the National Guard as a positive initiative, the majority saw it as an increase in the militarized approach to policing the protesters (p. 26).

By early Monday afternoon large crowds had gathered in local restaurant car parks and by late afternoon several hundred people had gathered on South Florissant Road across the road from the Ferguson Police Department Headquarters (p. 27). At approximately 4.10 pm, "West Florissant Avenue was again closed to traffic because of the presence of the protesters" (p. 27). Throughout the afternoon and into the evening, "there were ongoing issues of blocked streets and sidewalks, objects being thrown at officers, and some businesses suffering property damage" (p. 27). A large fight also erupted, with participants throwing bottles at each other (p. 27).

Later in the evening of Monday "large numbers of protesters gathered at various locations along West Florissant Avenue" and objects were again thrown at the police (p. 27). Several gun shots were fired at the police from the crowd (p. 27). As a result, the police deployed SWAT teams and tear gas was dispersed twice. More than 30 people were arrested during the evening, including people from New York and California (p. 28).

The night of Tuesday 19 August saw a repeat of the events of the previous night. Protesters filled the streets after nightfall and the police fired tear gas and flash grenades to disperse the crowd (Belfast Telegraph, 2014). On Wednesday 20 August, three police officers were injured and 47 people were arrested during the riots but the protests were calmer than those on previous nights (p. 28). There were about 150 protesters who exhibited less anger toward officers as tensions had been "diffused by both community leaders and a more relaxed police posture" (p. 28).

On Thursday 21 August, the Missouri State Governor ordered the National Guard to begin withdrawing from Ferguson (p. 28). About 300 demonstrators gathered at the intersection of West Florissant Avenue and Canfield Drive during the day and although West Florissant was once again closed off to traffic, protests were reasonably peaceful (p. 29).

By Friday 22 August, there were "no protest-related arrests and a sense of normalcy [was] returning to the community" and the number of protesters continued to decrease (p. 29). Mr. Brown's funeral was held on Monday 25 August, after which, there were no more protests during that first wave of troubles in Ferguson (p. 29).

6.4 Critique of the Police Response

This section of the chapter examines and discusses the police response to the riots that were a reaction to the shooting of Michael Brown for the 16-day period from Saturday August 9 to Monday August 25, 2014. Five themes emerge from the critique of the information relating to the police response that was presented in the previous section. The five themes have been presented in Table 6.2 and will be discussed, in detail, under the four headings: Police–Community Relationship; Police Leadership and Command; Police Tactics and the Use of Force; and the Need for Police Agency Preparation.

The protest in Ferguson, according to Shaw (2015) and Minteh (2016), ignited a multiracial campaign or movement, which was summarized in the phrase "Black Lives Matter."

The riots and the subsequent movement hinged on the perspective of the over-policing of African Americans in Ferguson and in the USA more generally. According to the residents of Ferguson, the relationship that the police had with the community was not strong prior to the riots and the riots would probably not have happened without police provocation (Bernish, 2015). Nor would they have continued if the police had used more appropriate strategies and responded with tactics that did not appear to be militarized (Institute for Intergovernmental Research, 2015; Reilly, 2015). The residents also claimed that when the riots did occur, the police response was ineffective (Robertson, 2015). Bernish (2015) discussed the perception that the response was ineffective and claimed that the police response was a disproportionate, "highly elevated tactical response" and if the police had responded more reasonably and professionally, it is possible that the demonstrations would have been less violent (Bernish, 2015).

The police, however, held a different perspective. According to the police that responded to the riots, they "encountered an event [that was] unprecedented in recent times," one that had become "a defining moment in policing history" (Institute for Intergovernmental Research, 2015, p. XIX).

Three factors support the view that the riots were unprecedented, especially in the context of the city of Ferguson and the wider St. Louis area. The first factor is that the occurrence of the riots cannot be examined in isolation from the form of policing that was adopted by police agencies in the greater St. Louis area. Historically, the St. Louis area has not experienced any rioting based on African American political or social issues or any other significant events as other cities with similar ethnic compositions have. The Ferguson community "did not have any prior history with a similar critical incident on which to base the turn of events that resulted after Mr. Brown's death," as there had been no riots in the area after the assassination of Dr. Martin Luther King Jr., or after the acquittal of the police officers for the beating of Rodney King in the 1990s (Reilly, 2015).

According to Reilly (2015), the police were at a disadvantage from the beginning of the protests. The St. Louis County Police Department and the Ferguson Police Department, during the first 2 days of the riots, chose to deploy a high-policing response (Robertson, 2015), which was interpreted as mimicking the relationship between the white population and African Americans during the period of slavery. In essence, the initial response by the police gave the appearance that they believed that the incident would be short-lived and therefore did not develop a longer-term response strategy (Robertson, 2015). This belief is further demonstrated by the overreliance on the Code 1000 as a response plan (Institute for Intergovernmental Research, 2015) rather than implementing a more coordinated or strategic response earlier in the series of riots.

The second factor was the use of social media by the demonstrators and the riot participants. The widespread use of social media made the event particularly challenging for the police. Social media was used to spread misinformation throughout the community and was used as a platform for organizing large numbers of people to participate in the demonstrations (Institute for Intergovernmental Research, 2015).

The way in which the police communicated with the public about the shooting and the ongoing investigation was the third factor. According to Bernish (2015), if the police had released information to the community in a timely manner and maintained the flow of information, the community would not have mistrusted the police and media skepticism would have been eliminated. The lack of communication led to the actions taken by the police being questioned and to criticism from the public and the media, which according to the Institute for Intergovernmental Research (2015), "was immediate, explicit, and vocal" and was amplified by social media and national news coverage (p. XIII).

The remainder of this section of the chapter discusses five issues that were identified in the analysis of the police response to the riots and these have been presented in Table 6.2.

Table 6.2 Themes from the critique of the police response to the Ferguson riots

	Theme	Issue
1	Police Community relationship	The police relationship with the community was weak and as a result, police did not understand the concerns that the community had
2	Police leadership	Inconsistency in direction, response and incident management and tactical orders
3	Reactive v proactive	The police response to the demonstrations/riots was reactive rather than proactive and they did not establish a strategic approach to effectively mitigate the complexity of issues to respond more effectively
4	Communication	There was a lack of effective communication and information management. The gaps in communication led to police tactical and strategic uncertainty, the relationships between police agencies, and in regard to the relationship with the community
5	Police response tactics	There were instances where specific actions were taken that infringed upon constitutionally protected activities and were not aligned with current national best practices. These strategies and tactics had the unintended consequence of escalating rather than diminishing tensions

Source: Some information has been adapted from Institute for Intergovernmental Research (2015, XIV)

6.4.1 Police–Community Relationship

The demonstrations and riots were triggered not only from the shooting and the community's perception of the incident but also from the lack of communication about the shooting, of which should have been provided by the police in relation to the shooting. Because the police did not have an established relationship with the community these triggers were "a manifestation of the long-standing tension between the Ferguson Police Department and the African-American community" (Institute for Intergovernmental Research, 2015, p. 116).

The Ferguson Police Department did not have a formal or established relationship with the community and in particular, with the residents of Canfield Green Apartments or the African American community (Institute for Intergovernmental Research, 2015). As a result of there being no formal structure or avenues in place to communicate, the riots came as a surprise to the police and once the riots started, there was no method for the police to communicate with the community, or to manage the community's reaction to the shooting (Institute for Intergovernmental Research, 2015). This situation also existed in reverse; the community did not have a procedure to communicate their concerns or to ask questions of the police (Institute for Intergovernmental Research, 2015).

6.4.2 Police Leadership and Command

Six problems arose in relation to the leadership and command of the police response. These problems were the phases of the police response, inconsistent leadership, the use of unified command, the National Incident Management System, the use of intelligence, and the presence of the media.

According to the Institute for Intergovernmental Research (2015), from August 9 to 25, command of the incident occurred in three phases. Despite there being three distinct phases to the response, the actual lines of demarcation between each phase is not clear, as each phase merged with the phase following (Institute for Intergovernmental Research, 2015). The first phase relates to the initial shooting on August 9, the management of the homicide scene and the first night of the demonstrations and riots. The Ferguson Police Department had the responsibility for the command of the homicide incident and scene but this responsibility was handed over to the St. Louis County Police Department "as it became apparent this was not a normal homicide scene response" (Institute for Intergovernmental Research, 2015, p. 31).

The second phase of the police response commenced on August 10 and carried on through until the August 14, when the command structure became more coordinated. The St. Louis County Police Department were responsible for command during this time. The problem in coordinating the police response was that the command post was spread across six vehicles, which were parked in close proximity to one another in the parking lot of the Buzz Westfall Plaza Shopping Center (in Jennings, Missouri) (Institute for Intergovernmental Research, 2015).

The third phase of the response covers the period August 14–25 and commenced after the Governor of Missouri declared a state of emergency and designated the Missouri State Highway Patrol to "command all operations necessary to ensure public safety and protect civil rights in the city of Ferguson and, as necessary, surrounding areas during the period of this emergency" (Institute for Intergovernmental Research, 2015, p. 32).

The identification of three phases to the police response emphasizes the weaknesses in the response, which was caused by leadership inconsistency, "failure to understand the community, a reactive strategy for handling protests, poor communication, and complications caused by St. Louis County's extraordinarily fractured network of small law enforcement" agencies (Reilly, 2015).

The first weakness that was found was in the leadership and the continual change of the agency that was in command. The agency responsible for the command of the incident generally sets the direction for the response with the operational and tactical decisions being made by a unified command (Institute for Intergovernmental Research, 2015; Reilly, 2015). According to Reilly (2015), the police response gave the appearance of being a "rudderless ship" which failed to provide any direction to the officers or establish communication procedures with the community. The weak direction of the response was perpetuated by a lack of an identifiable mission, response plan and traffic control plan. As a result, there was confusion and no consistency in the tactical response, the arrest procedures (Reilly, 2015), or the way in which the demonstrators would be controlled.

The confusion surrounding the arrest procedures related to the fact that there was not a plan in place for arresting demonstrators, which meant that there was no agreed-upon method to document each arrest (Moran & Waddington, 2016; Reilly, 2015). This vacuum made it unclear to officers as to who they could arrest (Moran & Waddington, 2016; Reilly, 2015). The lack of leadership, direction and consistency, together with the "criticism from the public and the media" left officers with a sense of abandonment and low morale (Reilly, 2015).

To provide more leadership and command in the police response, the Governor of Missouri appointed Captain Ron Johnson from the Missouri State Highway Patrol as the Incident Commander on Thursday August 14; 5 days after the beginning of the riots. At the same time that Captain Johnson was appointed the responsibility for the police response changed from the St. Louis County Police Department to the Missouri State Highway Patrol (Institute for Intergovernmental Research, 2015). As commander of the incident, Captain Johnson was "responsible for all incident activities, including the development of strategies and tactics and the ordering and the release of resources" (Federal Emergency Management Administration, 2015, cited in Institute for Intergovernmental Research, 2015, p. 35). Captain Johnson had overall authority and responsibility for the police response and for the management of all response operations at the incident site (Institute for Intergovernmental Research, 2015).

Captain Johnson was appointed as Incident Commander so that he could provide stability in the police response, but his appointment was also interpreted as being political, as Captain Johnson is an African American and had lived in the Canfield

Apartments as a child and youth. His appointment was supported by the community, but it caused discontentment in the city police departments for three reasons. The first reason was that the appointment of Captain Johnson "was perceived as the state usurping local authority" (Institute for Intergovernmental Research, 2015, p. 35). The second reason was that a number of local and city officers viewed the change of command to the highway patrol as showing "disrespect to them and their capabilities" (Reilly, 2015), and the third reason was that neither St. Louis County Police Department, Chief Belmar and the then-Ferguson Police Department Chief, Thomas Jackson were consulted about the change in command (Reilly, 2015). Two days after Captain Johnson was appointed as the Incident Commander, St. Louis County Police Department Chief Belmar joined the command team to form a unified command structure (Institute for Intergovernmental Research, 2015).

Following his appointment as Incident Commander, Captain Johnson "became the public face for the police response" and was "involved in extensive community engagement efforts and media interviews" (Institute for Intergovernmental Research, 2015, p. 37). As a result, Captain Johnson was less able to be engaged in the day-to-day command of the response and would not be able to monitor staff, provide direction and communicate with deployed commanders and personnel (Institute for Intergovernmental Research, 2015). The vacuum in command led to the full responsibilities of the incident command not being executed. In response, an informal, unified command between the Missouri State Highway Patrol, the St. Louis County Police Department and the St. Louis Metropolitan Police Department was established (Institute for Intergovernmental Research, 2015). The formal incident command, however, remained with the highway patrol (Institute for Intergovernmental Research, 2015).

Using a unified command structure as a recognised form of response governance was the second weakness in the leadership and command by the police. According to the Institute for Intergovernmental Research (2015), the incident command structures were initially "uncoordinated and incomplete" and the National Incident Management System was never fully implemented" (p. XV). The lack of an incident command structure "resulted in reactive responses and poor communication both within the command center and among the many law enforcement agencies involved" (Institute for Intergovernmental Research, 2015, p. XV).

The Ferguson Police Department relinquished control of the investigation and responsibility for crowd control to the St. Louis County Police Department on Saturday August 9. The St. Louis County Police Department took command of the police response with the view that as the crowd was dissipating in the early hours of Sunday August 10, the demonstrations and riots were over and there was no need to establish an incident command structure (Institute for Intergovernmental Research, 2015). However, as the crowd started to assemble again in the late afternoon of August 10 "the Ferguson Police Department and the St. Louis County Police Department jointly conferred on how to best respond to the crowd" (Institute for Intergovernmental Research, 2015, p. 34).

The police incident command did not have any information upon which to base their decision making as there was no process for gathering social media information nor was there a process to communicate with the community. In the absence of both of these functions there was no tangible method for gauging that the event would be prolonged (Institute for Intergovernmental Research, 2015). The demonstrations were not initially "viewed as an 'incident' within the context of the National Incident Management System (NIMS)" because of the lack of information and because the situation was viewed as being a crowd control response (Institute for Intergovernmental Research, 2015, p. 35).

According to the Institute for Intergovernmental Research (2015), the two police departments adopted "a de facto incident command approach that was similar" to the National Incident Management System but it was actually a unified command structure, even though "deference was given to the St. Louis County Police Department because it had more resources" deployed (p. 34). The violence and the response to the demonstrations were developing quickly and the response structure allowed for an informal joint command and the decision making to become more formalized (Institute for Intergovernmental Research, 2015). The establishment of a command post in the car park of the strip mall in Jennings, Missouri, approximately a half of a mile from West Florissant Avenue and Canfield Drive, helped to formalize the decision making (Institute for Intergovernmental Research, 2015).

The problem with the structure of the incident command, especially during the first 2 days, was that it "was fluid and not firmly established" (p. 88). It was not clear to the police officers involved in the response as to which agency was in command (Institute for Intergovernmental Research, 2015, p. 88). As the police response moved into the third day, the St. Louis County Police Department assumed incident command because the Ferguson Police Department still had to deliver other policing services to the city (Institute for Intergovernmental Research, 2015).

According to the Institute for Intergovernmental Research (2015), one of the most obvious changes needed in policing, which was identified from the police response to the riots in Ferguson, "is that law enforcement needs to change the way in which critical incidents are managed" (p. 119). The Institute goes on to the state that "nearly every aspect of the [Ferguson] police response would have been significantly improved if the National Incident Management System (NIMS) and incident command had been implemented effectively" (Institute for Intergovernmental Research, 2015, p. 119). The complexity of the riots in Ferguson emphasized the need for an effective incident command and a formally recognized incident management system.

There were 50 police departments involved in the coordinated response to the riots from August 9 to 25. The large number of officers that responded from these agencies was problematic as they all needed to be briefed as to their role within the National Incident Management System and they needed to be equipped and deployed appropriately (Reilly, 2015). As Moran and Waddington (2016), summarized, the large number of police agencies involved in the response and the numerous changes made to the incident command gave the appearance that "the entire operation lacked unity and central co-ordination" (p. 166).

The reasons as to why the National Incident Management System "was not fully implemented remains elusive" (Institute for Intergovernmental Research, 2015,

p. 36). The Institute for Intergovernmental Research (2015), maintained that the failure to implement the National Incident Management System was linked to the continual changes in incident command and because the police were in reactive mode. Three other response requirements were not implemented as a result of the failure to implement the NIMS. A strategic response vision was not developed nor implemented, and consistent response tactics were not developed or used (Institute for Intergovernmental Research, 2015). The third requirement that should have been implemented but was not, was the use of intelligence by the incident command team. Information and intelligence gathered by field officers was being passed on to the incident command team, but the command team's use of the intelligence was minimal (Institute for Intergovernmental Research, 2015). These failings resulted in tactics and strategic decisions being made without the consideration of all available information (Institute for Intergovernmental Research, 2015).

The use of intelligence by the incident team influenced the amount of information being shared with the incident commanders (Institute for Intergovernmental Research, 2015). According to the Institute for Intergovernmental Research (2015), the limited amount of intelligence being shared with the incident commanders was caused by a "lack of a formal information sharing mechanism within the incident command structure" at the command post (Institute for Intergovernmental Research, 2015, p. 85).

The final topic to be discussed within the area of police leadership and command is that of the media. The shooting, demonstrations and riots and the police response resulted in the St. Louis County Police Department Public Information Officer (PIO) being overwhelmed by the volume of media requests (Institute for Intergovernmental Research, 2015). The problem with the volume of media requests and the amount of information sought by the public was compounded by agitators using social media to "drive the narrative" of any specific event or police response. This placed the public information unit officers in a reactive mode (Institute for Intergovernmental Research, 2015, p. 93).

There was also no process in place for handling media inquiries and requests. The public information officers and the St. Louis Metropolitan Police Department referred many of the enquiries to the St. Louis County Police Department or to the command post, while the Missouri State Highway Patrol Troop Public Information Officers referred media requests to the command post (Institute for Intergovernmental Research, 2015). The incident command team at the command post did not have the resources to be able to respond to the media requests and inquiries, which resulted in a large number of these not being answered (Institute for Intergovernmental Research, 2015). This gave support for driving the agitators' narrative.

6.4.3 Police Tactics and the Use of Force

The biggest controversy surrounding the Ferguson demonstrations and riots was the threat of and the actual use of force and the tactics used by the police (Institute for Intergovernmental Research, 2015). The use of force to disperse demonstrators included the use of tear gas, projectiles and police dogs. It was alleged that tear gas was deployed without sufficient warning and demonstrators weren't given a safe egress. The public also viewed that the use of police dogs was not appropriate for the situation (Bernish, 2015; Institute for Intergovernmental Research, 2015).

The use of aggressive tactics by the police during the demonstrations and riots came under heavy criticism on social media and by the media (Reilly, 2015). Many people viewed the police response as inappropriate and an over-reaction, which fuelled a negative perception of the police (Institute for Intergovernmental Research, 2015). According to Reilly (2015), the police were criticized for taking an "all or nothing" approach to their tactical response and for the use of armored vehicles at a demonstration and especially for "positioning a sniper on top of an armored vehicle." The sniper overwatch "exacerbated tensions between protesters and the police" (Bernish, 2015), helping "to further the sentiment that they were reacting in a militaristic manner," and "to galvanize a negative perspective and aggravate community concerns about police and the justice system in general" (Reilly, 2015).

According to the Institute for Intergovernmental Research (2015), the deployment and use of "armored vehicles contributed to many in the community perceiving the police presence as a military-type response," with one member of the community stating "that the vehicles were 'acts of aggression' by the police" (p. 55). These same views were expressed by members of the community in relation to the use of police dogs, with one claiming that the deployment of "dogs for crowd control was 'provocative'" (Reilly, 2015), and Bernish (2015), alleged that the use of police dogs "exacerbated tensions by unnecessarily inciting fear and anger among amassing crowds." Bernish (2015) also claimed that an "elevated daytime response was not justified and served to escalate rather than de-escalate the overall situation."

Another problem that emerged regarding the force used by the police was the difficulty in documenting and establishing its use. There was no single process for documenting the justification of its use or any source for recording its use (Institute for Intergovernmental Research, 2015). According to the Institute for Intergovernmental Research (2015), the incident command logs and computer-aided dispatch logs did include the force used by the police but it just was not recorded in a single source document. This left the police being unable to substantiate or justify their use of force in any specific situation during the riots.

6.4.4 The Need for Police Agency Preparation

An analysis of the August 2014 riots highlighted two weaknesses in the Ferguson Police Department and the St. Louis County Police Department's preparation for a critical incident. Neither agency had planned for a series of riots that would occur over a series of days at different sites (Norton et al., 2015). By not having a response plan for such events, the police reacted to the events instead of developing and implementing proactive strategies and tactics (Norton et al., 2015).

The second weakness related to the purpose of the Code 1000. The Code 1000 is "an administrative and operational aid contingency plan that coordinates the deployment of police resources within the geographic limits of St. Louis County, Missouri" (Institute for Intergovernmental Research, 2015, p. 32). The plan provides a preplanned method of coordinating and mobilizing personnel and equipment and had previously been implemented during natural disasters, but as seen during the riots, it had limitations in providing an assistance system during a public disorder event (Institute for Intergovernmental Research, 2015). The plan can be activated at any time, but its use is limited during a public order event because the agencies that form the Code 1000 have not been trained for this type of response, at either the strategic or tactical level and therefore, an inconsistent response could occur (Institute for Intergovernmental Research, 2015). While the calling of a Code 1000 will ensure that officers from across the county will respond, "it does not guarantee that all responding officers are ready and prepared to do what may be demanded of them" (Institute for Intergovernmental Research, 2015, p. 33).

6.4.5 *Social Media*

The use of social media during the riots was also controversial. According to the Institute for Intergovernmental Research (2015), social media "was the key global driver of the Ferguson demonstrations," providing "simultaneous communication channels that facilitated crowd building and crowd movement" (p. XVIII). It was also "the primary provider of information and opinion, which shaped all aspects of the demonstrations" (Institute for Intergovernmental Research, 2015, p. XVIII) and informed the public's perception" of the events through the sharing of "photos, videos, and their thoughts as the events were unfolding" (Institute for Intergovernmental Research, 2015, p. 97).

The amount of information posted on social media platforms was astounding. In the 5 days following the shooting, "Twitter users had shared 3,648,032 tweets, using just one hashtag, #Ferguson" and one Facebook page about the demonstrations "obtained more than 117,000 "likes" (Institute for Intergovernmental Research, 2015, p. 98). Although the intelligence units of both the St. Louis County Police Department and the St. Louis Metropolitan Police Department were monitoring the social media, the amount of information was too large to analyze and almost immediately, "the event was no longer a regional, state, or even a national issue," but was worldwide (Institute for Intergovernmental Research, 2015, p. 98). The level of access to information about the demonstrations and riots led to the world watching and commenting on every tactic used by the police and the protesters. This led to the Institute for Intergovernmental Research (2015), to claim that "commentary and assessment of the actions of the crowds and police could (and did) come from anyone with access to the Internet" (p. 100).

The police did not have a strategy to handle and process social media information and "underestimated the impact [that the] social media had on the demonstrations and the speed at, which both facts and rumors were spread" (Institute for Intergovernmental Research, 2015, p. 103). On Monday 11 August the St. Louis Metropolitan Police Department deployed eight officers to monitor the social media and "employed a commercially available location-based social media monitoring portal to track trends and threats" (Institute for Intergovernmental Research, 2015, p. 100).

6.4.6 Final Comments

The critique of the police response to the riots discussed above centers on the five themes presented in Table 6.2. There are a number of reasons as to why the police took the action that they did. The first reason relates to the fact that none of the police agencies in the greater St. Louis area had any recent experience in responding to riots. The second reason was that there were too many police agencies involved in the response. The Institute for Intergovernmental Research (2015), reported that at one stage during the riots there were more than 50 police agencies involved. Having to coordinate such a large number of police agencies was never envisaged and no process or structure that is currently in use by any police agency around the world would be capable of accounting for the variation in resources, personnel and skills to respond to such a dynamic situation.

There were difficulties in the relationship between the police and the African American community. The difficulties arose as a result of the history of social deprivation of the African American community and the social conditions that this community experienced. These social issues explain the reasons for the lack of trust between the police (The Economist, 2014) and the African American community and as a result, the lack of communication between the two parties.

The perception of the public as to how the police responded to the riots was also influenced by contextual variables. In late 2014, Kochel (2014) reported on a survey that was undertaken in September and October 2014, of 389 St. Louis County, Missouri residents. Seventy percent of survey sample residents were African American and 24% were white. More than 75% of the respondents lived within 5.45 miles of the location of the police shooting and the subsequent riots and this implies that the majority of the survey sample residents lived relatively closely to the shooting and would have experienced the effects of the riots and the police response to the riots (Kochel, 2014). While more than 20% of the respondents had participated in the protests or in its associated activities, 10% of the survey respondents stated that "the events led them to question or lose trust in police" and 9% "reported thinking negatively about police as a consequence of these events" (Kochel, 2014, p. 3). According to Kochel (2014), "African-American residents participated in protests more frequently than other residents." However, Kochel does not provide any statistical information to support his claim.

Fifty-five percent of the respondents agreed with the response that the public took to the shooting and 45% disagreed (Kochel, 2014). The interesting point with these percentages is that the "respondent's opinions about the police response to the incident differed by race, with African-American residents being more favourable than non-black residents. On average, non-black residents somewhat disagreed with the response while African-American residents, on average, somewhat agreed" (Kochel, 2014, p. 8). However, the view of the respondents to the police response to the shooting "was less favourable" (Kochel, 2014, p. 11). More than 65% of respondents disagreed with the police response and 35% agreed. While equal proportions of respondents were fearful of the police and fearful of the protests (4% each), more than 2% "stated that they had more positive feelings toward police and the protection they offer" (Kochel, 2014, p. 3). However, the respondents' views differed by race, "with African American residents, on average, somewhat disagreeing with the police response and non-Black residents, on average, somewhat agreeing with the police response" (Kochel, 2014, p. 11). When asked to clarify their perception or opinion as to the police response, 27% of the survey respondents felt "that police used the appropriate response under difficult circumstances" and 13% "acknowledged that police efforts were designed to protect themselves and the community" (Kochel, 2014, p. 12). Only 3% of the respondents "reported feeling like some officers behaved badly and some behaved acceptably," while 2% of respondents "acknowledged that initial responses were problematic, but that the police response to the public protests and civil unrest improved across time" (Kochel, 2014, p. 12).

The survey also included a series of questions that related to the police use of force. In this series of questions, respondents "were asked to assess the level of force police used to handle [the] protests, riots and looting" (Kochel, 2014, p. 15). "Two-thirds of residents said the level of force used was too much, 21% felt it was about right, while 11% felt it was insufficient" (Kochel, 2014, p. 15). More than 24% of respondents believed that the police response was excessive and in relation to the use of specific tactics, 19% stated that it was not appropriate for the police to use military-type tactics; 12% did not think it was appropriate to use tear gas and 2% did not agree with the use of rubber bullets (Kochel, 2014). Approximately 4% of the respondents claimed that the police had interfered with the rights of people to protest and a proportion of the respondents "felt that the police response instigated further negative responses from the protesters" (9%) (Kochel, 2014, p. 12). Four percent of respondents claimed, "that police would have acted differently in a predominantly white neighbourhood" and 3% stated that the police would have responded differently with better training (Kochel, 2014, p. 12).

As with the majority of the survey responses, the respondents "views differed along racial lines, with African American residents reporting, on average, that [the] police used a little too much force" although approximately half of the African American respondents reported too much force was used (Kochel, 2014, p. 15). In comparison, non-black respondents, "on average, reported that the use of force was about right" (Kochel, 2014, p. 15).

Four percent of the respondents felt that the police did not "do enough about rioting and looting" and another 3% felt that the police did not "use sufficient force" (Kochel, 2014, p. 12). One respondent stated that although they disagreed with the tactics used by the police "I also feel like at that point, when it was out of control, anything they did wouldn't have made a difference. It was just chaotic" (Kochel, 2014, p. 14).

6.5 Discussion

The factors involved and the reasons for the August 2014 riots are more complex than just being as a result of the shooting and killing of an unarmed African American man by a Caucasian police officer. The relationship between the African American community and the police and their use of force formed the basis for the community's reaction to the shooting. For more than a decade, there have been complaints about the relationship of the police with the African American communities in the greater St. Louis County area, with a number of residents claiming that the tense relationship is a result of less-experienced, poorly trained officers, with "poorly-equipped police departments and highly uneven levels of protection" (Lowery, Leonnig, & Berman, 2014).

According to Moran and Waddington (2016), the relationship between the police and the community "that proved conducive to the eventual rioting" was the culture and "the institutional structures and processes underpinning the everyday running of the Ferguson Police Department" (Moran & Waddington, 2016, p. 147). These factors were exacerbated by the Ferguson Police Department's "institutional character, which not only induce abrasive encounters with the public, but also fail to hold in check or rectify some of the more problematic features of police behaviour" (Moran & Waddington, (2016, p. 148).

From the police perspective, and in reality, a culture had "developed [in Ferguson], involving wholesale opposition, non-cooperation and even resistance to the police," with the relationship between the police and young African American males representing "a more 'systemic problem'" (Moran & Waddington, 2016, p. 151). The relationship of the police with young African American males was a product of the use of the stop-and-search tactics used by the police and their concentrating on the issuing of fines for traffic violations. According to Norton et al. (2015), the Ferguson Police Department had a culture of "heavy enforcement" which "led to abusive policing" (p. 19). One form of abusive policing that was undertaken was the focus on generating revenue from the issuing of fines and fees (p. 19).

The outcome of the heavy enforcement eroded the community's trust and violated their First and Fourth Amendment rights. The lack of trust in the police was furthered by the use of arrest warrants. There were "more than 750,000 outstanding arrest warrants in St. Louis City and St. Louis County (including the cities within the county) in 2014, which is nearly three arrest warrants for every four adults" (Norton et al., 2015, p. 19). The city of Ferguson alone "had 45,185 outstanding warrants for 21,111 residents" (Norton et al., 2015, p. 19). The number of arrest warrants issued and the tense relationship affected all of the police agencies in the county. The community's lack of trust "exacerbated tensions during the response to demonstrations following the shooting" (Norton et al., 2015, p. 20), which created "a barrier to responding agencies' efforts to communicate effectively with the community" (Institute for Intergovernmental Research, 2015, p. 88).

According to the Institute for Intergovernmental Research (2015), police response commanders "sought to make the best decisions and take the best approach that would protect the First Amendment rights of protesters, protect lives of all persons in Ferguson, and protect property" (p. 38). However, as a result of decision makers basing their knowledge and understanding of the African American community on the extant relationship that the police had with the African American community, there was a void in comprehending how to respond to the demonstrations (Institute for Intergovernmental Research, 2015). As a result of their poor relationship with the community and because the police did not recognize the reasons why the demonstrations and riots were taking place, a strategic response was unable to be developed. Moreover, the police were not able to determine "how the character of the mass gatherings was evolving and spreading beyond the initial officer involved shooting" (Institute for Intergovernmental Research, 2015, p. 38).

The lack of understanding of the actions of the community was exacerbated by four other factors that affected how the police responded to the August 2011 riots. The first was the lack of experience in responding to civil disorder and riots. Prior to the August 2011 riots, the police agencies of St. Louis County had not responded to such a large-scale riot, nor had they any experience in de-escalating riots of such a magnitude as that which occurred in Ferguson (Norton et al., 2015). The second factor was the difference in the capability between the police agencies. None of the police agencies had fully adopted or implemented the National Incident Management System as their response system (Institute for Intergovernmental Research, 2015; Norton et al., 2015). The third factor was that the police agencies of St. Louis County did not appear to have retained the lessons learned from the 1999 World Trade Organization riots in Seattle, Washington and had not progressed to using the accepted best practice of crowd management, which had been developed from the lessons learned from the 2011 Occupy movement protests and occupations.

In response to the violence and riots that occurred during the 1999 World Trade Organization meeting in Seattle, police agencies established Civil Disorder Response Teams (CDRTs). These teams were trained and equipped for large-scale violent demonstrations (Norton et al., 2015). Civil Disorder Response Teams tactics focus "on precision movements of team members forming lines to stop crowds from accessing an area" and "to split up or move a hostile crowd from an area" (Norton et al., 2015, p. 48). According to Norton et al. (2015), the Civil Disorder Response Teams deploy "in full protective equipment in an effort to intimidate those in the crowd seeking to engage in disruptive behaviour and were trained not to speak to, or "engage [with] the crowd unless it was to give a lawful order" (p. 48).

How the police respond to riots changed following the World Trade Organization protests in Seattle in 1999 and the 2011 Occupy protests and as a result of the research conducted into crowd control in the UK. The research found that crowds are more manageable if the police start with a softer approach, using officers in uniform to interact "with protesters in a respectful and positive manner before and during a protest" (Norton et al., 2015, p. 48). A softer approach also includes having the Civil Disorder Response Teams on standby and out of view of the public, but ready for immediate deployment if they are needed (Norton et al., 2015). This approach to crowd control has been adopted by the majority of police forces in the UK and by a number of large-sized, city police forces in the USA.

The fourth factor that exacerbated the void in comprehending the actions of the community was the tactical response used by the police. According to the Institute for Intergovernmental Research (2015), the police response to the riots and the tactics that they used "in Ferguson prompted a national discussion regarding the growing concern about [the] militarization of police in the United States" (p. 53). As the Institute identified, the deployment of police resources, which may have been perceived by the protesters as 'military', may have "prompt[ed] unintended consequences" such as those experienced in Ferguson (Institute for Intergovernmental Research, 2015, p. 53).

The view formed by the media and politicians was that the equipment and tactics used by the police in Ferguson "aggravated a tense police community relationship and drew unprecedented criticism toward the police" (Institute for Intergovernmental Research, 2015, p. 59). It was based on the concern expressed "about police tactics, weaponry, and resources that appear more closely akin to military operations than domestic law enforcement" (Institute for Intergovernmental Research, 2015, p. 53). According to the Institute, the initial police deployment and use of military-type equipment and tactics "appeared to galvanize a negative perspective and aggravate community concerns about police and the justice system in general" (Institute for Intergovernmental Research, 2015, p. 53).

In justifying their view of the militarization of the police, the Institute claimed that policing in the USA had become militarized as a result of the police "encountering heavily armed criminals," the enforcement of gangs in the 1980, their "enforcement of criminal enterprise laws, particularly drugs" and their involvement in countering terrorism (Institute for Intergovernmental Research, 2015, p. 15). The militarization of police and policing, according to the Institute, "is particularly evident in police tactical units" and it was the deployment of these units that intensified the protesters reaction to the shooting (Institute for Intergovernmental Research, 2015, p. 53). The view that military-looking police units were being deployed magnified the tension between the protesters and the police. The community perceived the police use of armored vehicles to be especially threatening (Moran & Waddington, 2016; United States Department of Justice, 2016).

However, according to Moran and Waddington (2016), institutional features had an influence on the tactical deployment of personnel and equipment. As an example, the police had maintained that armored personnel carriers would be deployed to ensure the safety of police officers during specific riot incidents (Institute for Intergovernmental Research, 2015).

Another example of institutional features influencing the tactical deployment was provided by Pinard (2015). Pinard (2015) claimed that the use of the arrest procedure that the police adopted during the riots was intimidatory. The police would arrest protesters and then release the person without charging them. This was not an unusual practice in St. Louis and is known colloquially as 'catch and release'.

The protesters, politicians and the wider community perceived that the response taken by the police was based on the media's portrayal of the police. According to the Institute for Intergovernmental Research (2015), the efforts made by the police to establish a relationship with the media were slow and difficult and as a result, the relationship during the protests and the riots was poor. This relationship was brought under further pressure as the story about the Ferguson riots emerged. The story "went beyond the shooting of Michael Brown" and the events that were unfolding "in [that] Ferguson became a national story that focused on issues of racial inequality, justice for African Americans, police militarization, and police use of force" (Institute for Intergovernmental Research, 2015, p. 91). The second theme that emerged as the riots continued over successive evenings was the criticism that the police had violated journalists' First Amendment rights, of freedom of the press (Institute for Intergovernmental Research, 2015).

As a result of there not being a respectful and balanced relationship between the police and the media, the tone was set by the media on the first day, "that the police were withholding information about the shooting of Mr. Brown" (Institute for Intergovernmental Research, 2015, p. 91). A number of journalists claimed that the perception that the police were withholding information in relation to the shooting was valid. The St. Louis County Police Department did not hold its first press conference until 24 h after the riots began and this, according to the Institute for Intergovernmental Research (2015), allowed "24 hours for an alternate narrative to develop" (p. 91).

The final issue was the large number of inquiries made by journalists and the small number of police resources dedicated to answering these inquiries. The small number of police resources dedicated to media liaison and the absence of a robust organizational structure were the principle reasons why the police were not adequately prepared to respond to the demands placed on them from the media and for their reactive rather than proactive media strategy (Institute for Intergovernmental Research, 2015). The problem of there not being enough police resources to answer media inquiries was compounded further by there not being any guidelines for handling such inquiries and this resulted in each police liaison officer responding to inquiries using the process that their own agency used (Institute for Intergovernmental Research, 2015).

6.5.1 Police Preparation for the Grand Jury Decision of Accused Officer

The planning and preparation undertaken by the St. Louis County Police Department for the 24 November 2014 release of the grand jury decision on whether to indict the police officer accused of shooting Michael Brown indicates that they had learned lessons from the August 2014, Ferguson riots. To minimize the chance of violence occurring if the grand jury decision was to not indict the police officer, the St. Louis County Police implemented four strategies that would be supported by a comprehensive response plan. The first strategy was to contact a number of police agencies across the USA for advice as to how to develop a response plan that would minimize the possibility of violent protests (Norton et al., 2015).

The second and third strategies were to reach out to the community and the media. To reach out to the community, local clergy and community leaders would be contacted and a group known as 'Lost Voices' would be engaged (Norton et al., 2015). This group comprised "current and former gang members" who were "vocal critics of the police and authorities in the [St. Louis] area" (Norton et al., 2015, p. 51). The report did not specify how the police would reach out to the media.

The fourth strategy was to improve the capability of the public information office. To ensure that the police had the capability to assist the media following the decision of the grand jury, the St. Louis County Police Department deployed extra staff to their public information office and "hired a new civilian team member who [had] previously worked for a local news affiliate as a social media strategist" (Norton et al., 2015, p. 51). The police also assigned an additional supervisor to the office, "who had prior private sector marketing experience and a degree in communications and public relations" (Norton et al., 2015, p. 51).

The response plan was also based on the lessons learned from the August 2014 riots and included five new operational policies. The first policy was to request staff from agencies where the supervisors and officers had completed the necessary training and had knowledge of the St. Louis Police Department deployment procedures. The staff would assist with the response to any violent protests (Norton et al., 2015). Only agencies and personnel that the St. Louis County Police Department determined had met four criteria would be deployed. The criteria were: (1) that would abide by any established command and control protocols; (2) understood both individual and collective roles and responsibilities; (3) had successfully completed the necessary training; and (4) would exemplify the best possible image at all times during any deployment to protests and mass demonstrations (Norton et al., 2015, p. 51). The policy stressed "the importance of professionalism and restraint" to the officers deployed to respond to any violent protests. Any officer "who failed to conduct themselves professionally" would be "removed, reassigned, or retrained" (Norton et al., 2015, p. 51).

The second policy restricted when an officer could deploy wearing protective equipment. The restriction specified that officers could only wear exterior protective equipment when a "credible threat was confirmed" and that the equipment was to be kept out of the view of the public until it was needed (Norton et al., 2015, p. 51). The policy also required Civil Disorder Response Teams to be deployed to specific command posts or staging points "near predicted disturbance locations" prior to the grand jury decision being released to the public (Norton et al., 2015, p. 51).

The third policy required that a "clear chain of command [be] established for all units assigned to any protests," while the fourth policy outlined how and where officers were to be deployed, the level of force that could be used and the authorization procedure for the deployment of tear gas (Norton et al., 2015, p. 51). The fourth policy also established the requirement for a video surveillance team to be assigned to each Civil Disorder Response Teams "to document the facts and circumstances of their deployment and to chronicle events that occurred while deployed" (Norton et al., 2015, p. 52).

The fifth policy specified the form and type of training that each Civil Disorder Response Team Officer from both the St. Louis County Police Department and those agencies responding to mutual aid requests were to complete (Norton et al., 2015). The policy also established the prerequisite that the St. Louis County Police Department were to view the documented qualifications of any officers deployed from mutual aid agencies to ensure that these officers had completed the training which had been outlined in the first policy relating to professional conduct (Norton et al., 2015).

6.6 Conclusion

The critique of the police response to the violent protest in Ferguson in August 2014 identified a number of weaknesses at the strategic, operational and tactical levels. Although the major weakness was the initial overreaction of the police to the protests and the adoption of high policing methods (identified as a military approach), the core weaknesses in the police response center was inconsistent leadership, the poor relationship that the police had with the community and the poor communication frameworks between the responding police agencies. These weaknesses were further compounded by the failure of the police to understand the community "and complications caused by St. Louis County's extraordinarily fractured network of small law enforcement agencies, which a nationally recognized police research organization has criticized as 'dysfunctional and unsustainable'" (Reilly, 2015).

The lack of experience in responding to large and violent protests and the ineffective implementation of specific tactical approaches to the violence hampered the initial response to the civil disorder in Ferguson in August 2014 (Norton et al., 2015). This issue was magnified when the responsibility for the incident command changed from the St. Louis Metropolitan Police Department to the Missouri State Highway Patrol. Initially, the Highway Patrol were perceived as not having the appropriate skills as "they normally work in rural areas and patrol the highways and therefore are not accustomed or trained to work mass demonstrations in urban environments" (Institute for Intergovernmental Research, 2015, p. 37). However, as the series of protests progressed, the police "continued to develop and improve their preparation and response" to the violence and portrayed a more coordinated approach (Norton et al., 2015).

The major issue with the police response to the Ferguson riots in August 2014 was the perception that the response was a militarized, overreaction. This perception was especially intense when the police implemented similar tactics during daylight hours when such an approach could not be justified (Institute for Intergovernmental Research, 2015). However, the Institute for Intergovernmental Research (2015), claimed that although the form of police response was warranted at specific times during the protests and riots, this high-policing response "limited [the] options for a

[more] measured, strategic approach" to be adopted (p. 59). The form of approach narrowed the options for the later response in the series of protests and riots and created antagonism within the African American community. This created further difficulties for the police to establish communication lines with the community.

The police did use a range of tactics and methods to try to control the protests and riots, including tear gas, but the most controversial tactic was the implementation of the 'keep moving' order. The "keep moving" order was that as long as people are kept moving, "they were allowed to protest" and this order "was intended to prevent protesters from gathering into crowds, especially in the evening, when unrest was at its highest point" (Institute for Intergovernmental Research, 2015, p. 61).

The police response to the Ferguson protests and riots highlights that even in situations that warrant high-policing techniques, the police "must be reasonable and flexible with choice [and use] of [such] tactics" (Institute for Intergovernmental Research, 2015, p. 59). The Institute for Intergovernmental Research (2015), maintained that the police should have determined what tactics would be used and should have considered "the historical context of the community served, and focus[ed] not only on what may be authorized pursuant to policy but also on what is right" (p. 59). This is an important observation, especially when the police respond to a violent protest or riot that primarily involves members of a minority community as the victims or perpetrators. However, these considerations should only be that. They should only be one consideration that is taken into account by the commander of the police response and should not be the factor that stops the police from taking action to control any violence.

Ensuring that the police respond and make tactical decisions within the backdrop of the community is supported by early research conducted by Marx (1970). Marx (1970) claimed that there were differences in the forms of violent protests and riots, primarily when they involved members of the African American community. Marx went on to state that these differences can only be examined "by considering the general nature of the police-black community relationship and the interaction that occurs between these groups during a disturbance" (p. 22). Marx also claimed that these differences relate to "the course, pattern, intensity, and duration of the disturbance" (p. 22).

Although these questions may not have been considered initially in the police response, it appears from this critique that as the protests and riots continued they did become a necessary factor in the implementation of police tactics. The implementation of a more community-oriented approach and the decrease in the number of arrests for violent behavior in the final stages of the series of protests and riots demonstrates that the police had changed their tactics. There were only 236 protest-related arrests in total for the period from 9 to 25 August, and "the police response to the demonstrations did not result in any loss of life or serious injury to the protesters" (Institute for Intergovernmental Research, 2015, p. 29).

References

Barker, T. (2014, August 11). *Ferguson-area businesses cope with aftermath of weekend riot*. St. Louis Post-Dispatch. Retrieved from http://www.stltoday.com/news/local/ferguson-area-businesses-cope-with-aftermath-of-weekend-riot/article_4a310ec3-94de-57dd-95f7-4e350f6a6fa2.html.

Belfast Telegraph. (2014). *Fresh clashes at shooting protests*. 19 August 2015. Retrieved from: http://www.belfasttelegraph.co.uk/news/world-news/freshclashes-at-shooting-protest-30518109.html.

Bennett, D. (2014). *Vigil turns to protests and looting after police shooting of unarmed black teenager*. The Atlantic. Retrieved from http://www.theatlantic.com/national/archive/2014/08/protests-turn-into-looting-after-shooting-of-unarmed-black-teenager/375848/.

Berman, M. (2014, August 18). *Governor Nixon lifts curfew for Ferguson*. The Washington Post. Retrieved from https://www.washingtonpost.com/news/post-nation/wp/2014/08/18/governor-nixon-lifts-curfew-for-ferguson/?utm_term=.28db9abf5406.

Bernish, C. (2015, July 2). *DOJ: Militarized police tactics caused Ferguson riots*. Mint Press News. Retrieved from http://www.mintpressnews.com/doj-militarized-police-tactics-caused-ferguson-riots/207218/.

Brown, R., Johnson, M., Angelucci, B., & Murray, M. (2014, August 19). *Michael Brown protest: Crowd surges toward police in Ferguson*. NBC News. Retrieved from http://www.nbcnews.com/storyline/michael-brown-shooting/michael-brown-protest-crowd-surges-toward-police-ferguson-n183611.

Bruton, B., & Duchon, R. (2014, September 26). *Ferguson, Missouri's Police Chief joins Michael Brown protestors*. NBC News. Retrieved from http://www.nbcnews.com/storyline/michael-brown-shooting/ferguson-missouris-police-chief-joins-michael-brown-protesters-n212076.

CBS St. Louis. (2014, August 16). Clean-up underway after more rioting, looting in Ferguson. Retrieved from http://stlouis.cbslocal.com/2014/08/16/clean-up-underway-after-more-rioting-looting-in-ferguson/.

Chicago Tribune. (2014). *Protests near St. Louis continue for slain teen after riot, arrests*. Retrieved from: http://www.chicagotribune.com/news/nationworld/chi-missouri-police-shooting-20140811-story.html.

Coleman, C. (2014, August 29). *Ferguson PD arrests 8 protestors, hunts for cop shooter*. USA Today. Retrieved from http://www.usatoday.com/story/news/nation/2014/09/29/ferguson-manhunt-continues/16411871/.

Cook, J. (2014, August 19). *Intercept reporter shot with rubber bullets and arrested while covering Ferguson protests*. The Intercept. Retrieved from https://theintercept.com/2014/08/19/intercept-reporter-detained-covering-ferguson-protests/.

Davey, M., & Blinder, A. (2014, October 13). *Ferguson protests take new edge, months after killing*. The New York Times. Retrieved from https://www.nytimes.com/2014/10/14/us/st-louis-protests.html?_r=0.

(The) Economist. (2014, August 23). *The Ferguson riots: Overkill. Police in a Missouri suburb demonstrate how not to quell a riot*. Retrieved from http://www.economist.com/news/united-states/21613272-police-missouri-suburb-demonstrate-how-not-quell-riot-overkill.

Ellis, R., Hana, J., & Prokupecz, S. (2014, August 16). *Missouri governor imposes curfew in Ferguson, declares emergency*. CNN. Retrieved http://edition.cnn.com/2014/08/16/us/missouri-teen-shooting/.

Follman, M. (2014, August 27). *Michael Brown's mom laid flowers where he was shot – and police crushed them*. Mother Jones. Retrieved from http://www.motherjones.com/politics/2014/08/ferguson-st-louis-police-tactics-dogs-michael-brown.

Hartmann, M. (2014, August 18). *National Guard deployed to chaotic, violent night in Ferguson*. New York. Retrieved from http://nymag.com/daily/intelligencer/2014/08/national-guard-called-after-more-ferguson-chaos.html.

I24news. (2014, August 21). *Ferguson protests cool down after Holder's visit.* Tel Aviv, Israel. Retrieved from http://www.i24news.tv/en/news/international/americas/40984-140821-ferguson-protests-cool-after-holder-s-visit.

Institute for Intergovernmental Research. (2015). *After-action assessment of the police response to the August 2014 demonstrations in Ferguson, Missouri.* COPS Office Critical Response Initiative. Washington, DC: Office of Community Oriented Policing Services.

Kienscherf, M. (2014). Beyond militarization and repression: Liberal social control as pacification. *Critical Sociology, 42*(7–8), 1–16.

Kochel, T. (2014, December 10). *Views by St. Louis County residents regarding the police and public responses to the shooting of Michael Brown in Ferguson, Missouri on August 9, 2014.* Department of Criminology and Criminal Justice Report, Southern Illinois University of Carbondale. Retrieved from http://opensiuc.lib.siu.edu/cgi/viewcontent.cgi?article=1000&context=ccj_reports.

Li, D., & Sheehy, K. (2014, November 25*). More national guard troops ordered into Ferguson.* The New York Post. Retrieved from http://nypost.com/2014/11/25/82-arrested-and-11-buildings-burn-in-ferguson-riots/.

Lowery, W., Leonnig, C., & Berman, M. (2014, August 13). *Even before Michael Brown's slaying in Ferguson, racial questions hung over police.* The Washington Post. Retrieved from https://www.washingtonpost.com/politics/even-before-teen-michael-browns-slaying-in-mo-racial-questions-have-hung-over-police/2014/08/13/78b3c5c6-2307-11e4-86ca-6f03cbd15c1a_story.html?utm_term=.f1d93d392f4f.

Lussenhop, J. (2014, September 24). *Ferguson police have case file for Mya Aaten-Whites, bullet's location still in question.* Daily Riverfront Times. Retrieved from http://edition.cnn.com/2014/08/13/us/missouri-teen-shooting/index.html.

Marx, G. (1970). Civil disorder and the agents of social control. *Journal of Social Issues, 26*(1), 19–57.

Minteh, B. (2016). *Policing and violence in the United States: A comparative analysis of protest against police violence in Ferguson, Missouri, Baltimore, Maryland, and Cleveland, Ohio (2012–2015).* Paper presented at the Midwest Political Science Association 74th Annual Conference, 7–10 April 2016, Palmer House Hilton, Chicago, IL.

Moran, M., & Waddington, D. (2016). *Riots: An international comparison.* London, UK: Macmillan Publishers Ltd..

New York Times. (2014, August 13). *What happened in Ferguson?* Retrieved from http://www.nytimes.com/interactive/2014/08/13/us/ferguson-missouri-town-under-siege-after-police-shooting.html?_r=0.

Newburn, T. (2014). *Civil unrest in Ferguson was fuelled by the Black community's already poor relationship with a highly militarized police force.* Blogs.les.ac.uk. Retrieved from http://blogs.lse.ac.uk/usappblog/2014/08/29/civil-unrest-in-ferguson-was-fuelled-by-the-black-communitys-already-poor-relationshipwith-a-highly-militarized-police-force/

Norton, B., Hamilton, E., Braziel, R., Linskey, D., & Zeunik, J. (2015). *Collaborative reform initiative: An assessment of the St. Louis County Police Department.* Washington, DC: Community Oriented Policing Services.

Peters, M. (2014). *Police: Officer wasn't aware Michael Brown was suspect in alleged robbery.* The Wall Street Journal, August 15.

Pinard, M. (2015). Poor, black and 'wanted': Criminal justice in Ferguson and Baltimore. *Howard Law Journal, 58*(3), 1–16.

Piper, B. (2014, August 11). *2 Officers injured, 32 arrested during riots.* St. Louis, MO: KSDK. Retrieved from http://www.ksdk.com/news/local/2-officers-injured-32-arrested-during-riots/278856450.

Press Association. (2014). *Anger over shooting of US teenager.* Retrieved on 12 May 2016 from: http://news.uk.msn.com/world/t-articles?cpdocumentid=261652457.

Reilly, R. (2015, September 2). *'Provocative' police tactics inflamed Ferguson protests, experts find.* Huffington Post. Retrieved from http://www.huffingtonpost.com/entry/ferguson-protests-police-tactics-report_us_55e622a3e4b0aec9f35506ad.

Reuters. (2014, August 24). *Calm holds in streets of Ferguson, Missouri two weeks after police shooting*. Retrieved from http://in.reuters.com/article/usa-missouri-shooting-idINKBN0GO06Y20140824.

Robertson, J. (2015). *Police response to Ferguson protests, in a word, failed, federal draft report says*. Los Angeles Times, 30 June 2015. Retrieved from: http://www.latimes.com/nation/la-na-ferguson-draft-report-20150630-story.html.

Samuels, R. (2014, September 30). *Protestors in Ferguson, Mo., stand their ground, police ease up*. The Washington Post. Retrieved from https://www.washingtonpost.com/news/post-nation/wp/2014/09/30/police-in-ferguson-mo-ease-up-on-peaceful-protesters/?utm_term=.0e6694a507fb.

Shaw, T. (2015). *Department of Justice investigation of the Ferguson Police Department. The Ferguson Report*. Washington, DC: United States Department of Justice Civil Rights.

Shoichet, C., Brumfield, B., & Smith, T. (2014, August 14). *Tear gas fills Ferguson's streets again*. CNN. Retrieved from: http://edition.cnn.com/2014/08/13/us/missouri-teen-shooting/.

Stewart, M., & Reilly, R. (2014, October 3). *Ferguson protestors outfitted in orange jumpsuits and jailed with high bail*. The Huffington Post. Retrieved from http://www.huffingtonpost.com/2014/10/03/ferguson-protesters-arrested_n_5929758.html.

Suhr, J., & Salter, S. (2014, August 13). *Ferguson seeks answers after police shooting of Michael Brown*. The Huffington Post. Retrieved from http://www.huffingtonpost.com/2014/08/13/ferguson-michael-brown_n_5674032.html.

The Associated Press. (2014, August 13). *Ferguson protests erupt in violence as people lob Molotov cocktails, police use tear gas*. The Plain Dealer. Retrieved from http://www.cleveland.com/nation/index.ssf/2014/08/ferguson_protests_erupt_in_vio.html.

The St. Louis American. (2014, August 11). *West Florissant explodes in protest of police shooting, more than 30 arrests*. Retrieved from http://www.stlamerican.com/news/local_news/article_554e1212-2159-11e4-9dee-001a4bcf887a.html.

The Telegraph. (2014, August 18). *National guard called in after second night of chaos in Ferguson, Missouri*. Retrieved from http://www.telegraph.co.uk/news/worldnews/northamerica/usa/11040870/National-Guard-troops-called-in-after-night-of-chaos-in-Ferguson.html.

United States Department of Justice. (2016). *Investigation of the Baltimore City Police Department*. Civil Rights Division, August 10. Washington, DC: US Department of Justice.

Vinograd, C. (2014, August 17). *Ferguson protests: One person shot, seven arrested in overnight clashes*. NBC News. Retrieved from http://www.nbcnews.com/storyline/michael-brown-shooting/ferguson-one-person-shot-seven-arrested-overnight-violence-n182481.

Wulfhorst, E., & Malone, S. (2014, August 12). *US police fire tear gas, stun grenades at protestors in Missouri town*. Reuters. Retrieved from http://news.uk.msn.com/t-articles?cp-documentid=261700033.

Wulfhorst, E., Wallis, D., & McAllister, E. (2014, November 25). *More troops deployed in Ferguson to guard against fresh riots*. Reuters. Retrieved from http://www.reuters.com/article/us-usa-missouri-shooting-idUSKCN0J80PR20141125.

Yang, J. (2014, August 11). *Looting erupts after vigil for slain Missouri teen Michael Brown*. Retrieved from http://www.nbcnews.com/storyline/michael-brown-shooting/looting-erupts-after-vigil-slain-missouri-teen-michael-brown-n177426.

Zagier, A. (2014, August 21). *Gov. Nixon taking National Guard out of Ferguson*. Fox 11 News. Retrieved from http://fox11online.com/news/nation-world/holder-tries-to-reassure-ferguson-resident.

Chapter 7
The 2015 Riots in Baltimore

7.1 Introduction

At approximately 8.39 am on Sunday April 12, 2015, officers from the Baltimore Police Department (BPD) were on bicycle patrol at Gilmor Homes when they observed an African American man running away after seeing them on the 1700 block of Presbury Street in the Sandtown-Winchester neighborhood of Baltimore (Police Executive Research Forum, 2015; Stolberg & Babcock, 2015). The officers pursued the man, arrested him and dragged him to a police van. The arrest of the man, Freddie Carlos Gray, Jr., was recorded on cellphone video, which showed him limping and screaming in pain as he was being dragged towards the van (Stolberg & Babcock, 2015). Mr. Gray was subsequently placed in a police van to be transported to the BPD Western District Police Station. The police van arrived at the station sometime later, after making a number of stops along the way (Police Executive Research Forum, 2015).

Upon arrival at the Western District Station, Mr. Gray was found to be unresponsive and paramedics were called to provide medical assistance (Police Executive Research Forum, 2015). From subsequent police reports, it appears that Mr. Gray rode in the back of the van unbuckled and received a "rough ride" (Stolberg & Babcock, 2015). Mr. Gray was taken to the University of Maryland Shock Trauma Center in Baltimore, where it was found that he had sustained neck, voice box and spinal injuries (Police Executive Research Forum, 2015). According to Fenton (2015a), the BPD could not account for the injuries Mr. Gray received and when they did release some information, it was "contradictory and inconsistent." Mr. Gray subsequently died a week later, on Sunday April 19 (Stolberg & Babcock, 2015).

The first demonstration in relation to the arrest of Mr. Gray occurred on Saturday April 18, outside the Western District Police Station (Fenton, 2015a), which was the same neighborhood that was burnt in 1968, following the assassination of civil rights leader Dr. Martin Luther King Junior (Rector, Dance, & Broadwater, 2015). Although there were marches every evening from Sunday April 19 to Friday April

G. den Heyer, *Police Response to Riots*,
https://doi.org/10.1007/978-3-030-31810-9_7

24, a second demonstration was held on Saturday April 25, which included a march from the Winchester neighborhood to City Hall. After the demonstration concluded, a number of groups leaving the demonstration, began to vandalize parked police vehicles and shops within the inner-city area. The disorder subsequently turned into a riot and resulted in the gates being locked at the Camden Yards Stadium, retaining the spectators who were attending a baseball game.

The civil unrest continued after a mall was closed by the Baltimore Police Department and a second riot occurred on the afternoon and evening of Monday April 27. The mall had been closed because the Baltimore Police Department had received information from a text that there was going to be a "purge" that afternoon. A riot started at approximately 3.15 pm with students throwing bottles and stones at the police. While the riot started at the mall, as the evening progressed, the rioters moved towards the downtown area.

The two riots resulted in the Governor of Maryland declaring a state of emergency and this included the activation of mutual aid agreements with other police agencies. The rioting led to extensive damage being caused to businesses and property in Baltimore. Between 285 and 350 businesses were damaged, more than 60 buildings suffered fire damage, and 27 drug stores were looted (Oppel, 2015; Wenger, 2015). In addition, more than 150 vehicles were burned and 250 people were arrested (Wenger, 2015).

At first glance, the April 2015 Baltimore riots seemed to be similar to those that had occurred in Ferguson in 2014. Both riots were triggered by the violent actions taken by the police and involved the death of a young man from the African American community. However, the response taken by the police to each of the riots was different and resulted in different outcomes. Both responses were highly questionable and pointed to structural and systemic problems in both of the police agencies involved.

These differences do not apply to the physical description of the cities of Ferguson and Baltimore. Discounting their difference in size, "Ferguson and Baltimore are remarkably similar demographically" (Pinard, 2015, p. 86). The population of both cities comprise of approximately 67% African American and more than 24% of the residents live below the poverty line (Pinard, 2015; United States Census Bureau, 2017). Both cities have a similar relationship with their respective police agencies, with the relationship between the police and the African American community in both cities being described by Pinard (2015) as "disconnected, strained and, at times, violent" (p. 864).

This chapter examines the Baltimore Police Department's response to the demonstrations and riots in Baltimore, Maryland in April 2015 and the problems that arose from a lack of leadership and direction. As with the previous chapters, the examination will be presented in five sections. The first section will provide the background and context in which the riots occurred and outlines a chronology of the April 2015 events. The second section discusses the police response in detail and the third section provides a critique of the response under 11 headings which relate to the weaknesses in the Baltimore Police Department's response. The fourth section discusses the weaknesses within an operational context and the conclusions are presented in the final section.

7.2 Riot Chronology

The first demonstration following the arrest and hospitalization of Mr. Gray was held on Saturday April 18, where several hundred-people gathered outside the Baltimore—Western District Police Station. The demonstration was held in protest against the apparent mistreatment of Mr. Gray and as a result of the inadequate and inconsistent information released by the Baltimore Police Department regarding their actions during the arrest and transport of Mr. Gray (Fenton, 2015a).

More protests occurred across the city of Baltimore from April 19 to 24. Following the release of the identities of the six officers involved in the arrest of Mr. Gray, on the evening of April 21, protesters marched from the site of Mr. Gray's arrest to the Western District police station (Ileto, 2015). This protest, which was similar to earlier demonstrations, was reasonably peaceful. However, during the protest, two people were arrested for confronting the police (Ileto, 2015).

On Saturday April 25, protesters marched from the Gilmor Homes, which was where Mr. Gray was arrested, through to the Inner Harbor, in the downtown area of the city, where they assembled on the plaza at City Hall (Stolberg & Babcock, 2015). Although protests and marches had been held on most of the evenings since the arrest of Mr. Gray, this march was the largest to date (Stolberg & Babcock, 2015). More than 1000 people, carrying signs and shouting, marched through the city streets, clogging intersections (Rector et al., 2015; Stolberg & Babcock, 2015). The march was largely peaceful, but as the march was ending at the Inner Harbor and Oriole Park, Camden Yards (a baseball stadium) area, the protest became violent, with a large group of more than 200 protesters breaking away from the demonstration at the City Hall and carried on towards the downtown area. The group were met by police officers who were wearing riot equipment as they reached Camden Yards (Stolberg & Babcock, 2015). The group threw cans and stones at the police and damaged a number of police vehicles (Stolberg & Babcock, 2015; Yan, Franz, & Hutcherson, 2015). Hundreds of people were involved in the riot, which according to Rector et al. (2015), "popped up in spurts."

Protesters also smashed shop windows, fought with people who were attending the baseball game at the stadium and blocked the corner of Pratt and Light Streets, which is a major intersection that serves as the main route to Interstate 95 and out of the city (Stolberg & Babcock, 2015). As a result of the violence in the surrounding area, those attending the baseball game were forced to remain inside the stadium for their own safety (Fiammetta, 2015; Stolberg & Babcock, 2015). Thirty-four people were arrested during the riots and six police officers were injured (Marquez & Almasy, 2015).

Later that evening, the Mayor of Baltimore held a press conference. During the press conference the mayor claimed that the majority of people taking part in the protest march were peaceful, but a "small group of agitators intervened" (Marquez & Almasy, 2015). The mayor went on to state that "[i]t's a very delicate balancing act. Because while we try to make sure that they were protected from the cars and other things that were going on, we also gave those who wished to destroy space to do that as well. And we worked very hard to keep that balance and to put ourselves in the best position to de-escalate" (CBS News, 2015). These comments were interpreted by a number of people as an indication that the protesters were given permission to destroy property. The mayor's office realized their error in releasing such a statement and released a second statement clarifying that peaceful protesters were given room to conduct their protest (Harris, 2015).

It was following the funeral service held for Mr. Gray on Monday April 27 (ABC News, 2015) that the worst riots occurred and they stood in contrast to the earlier, more peaceful protests that had been held over the previous week (Rector et al., 2015). On Saturday April 25, a text was distributed on social media and flyers were circulated of a photograph of the April 25 rioters standing on a Baltimore police car with the statement "All High Schools Monday @3 We Are Going To Purge From Mondawmin To The Ave, Back To Downtown #Fdl" (Inquistr, 2015).

In response to the text and the flyers, the police closed the Mondawmin Mall at 2:15 pm on Monday April 27 (WMAR Staff, 2015) and deployed their staff, in riot gear, to the area (Police Executive Research Forum, 2015). The police also closed the metro stop and cordoned many of the streets that were near the mall (Brodey & McLaughlin, 2015). A number of other institutions also closed down in the downtown area, and the Baltimore Orioles baseball game, which was scheduled for that evening, was postponed, citing a police warning that "activities may be potentially violent" (Bacon & Welsh, 2015).

As a result of the closure of the metro stop at the mall and the disembarking of all of the passengers on the buses that were travelling through the area, the crowd grew in size, with students from the high school, which was across the road from the mall, contributing to the size of the crowd, as they were not able to leave the area or use public transport when school finished at 3.15 pm (Brodey & McLaughlin, 2015).

Within half an hour of the area being cordoned and the high school finishing for the day, more than 100 students had gathered in and around the mall. It was at this time that the first bricks and bottles were thrown at the police (Fuchs, 2015). The violence spread rapidly (Breitbart News, 2015). The rioters threw rocks, which damaged a number of police vehicles and a CVS Pharmacy in West Baltimore was looted and burned (Yan & Ford, 2015). Dozens of demonstrators broke into the mall, looting and damaging a number of shops and as the afternoon turned to evening, violence and the looting of stores spread across the central city (Rector et al., 2015). The police responded with tear gas and made more than 200 arrests (Rector et al., 2015). As a result of the rioting during the night of Monday, April 27, 144 vehicles and 15 buildings were set on fire, with a number of the fires still burning the next morning (Associated Press, 2015a; Fox 17 West Michigan, 2015). Fifteen Baltimore Police Department Officers were also injured during the violence (Bacon & Welsh, 2015; Rector et al., 2015).

During the height of the rioting, on the evening of Monday April 27, the Mayor of Baltimore requested that the Maryland State Governor declare a state of emergency. The request was granted and a state of emergency was declared (Police Executive Research Forum, 2015). The Governor also authorized the deployment of the National Guard to assist with security (Associated Press, 2015a). The authorization included the deployment of more than 5000 soldiers (Laughland, Lewis, Jacobs,

& Swaine, 2015), 500 Maryland State Police officers, and a request for an additional 5000 police from contiguous states (Hay Brown, 2015). At the same time that the state of emergency was declared, the Mayor of Baltimore declared that a curfew would be in effect within the city limits from 10:00 pm to 5:00 am every day, from April 28 through May 3 (Police Executive Research Forum, 2015). City officials also announced that the schools in Baltimore City would be closed on Tuesday April 28 (Bacon & Welsh, 2015).

Early on Tuesday April 28, the Baltimore Police Department announced that the Security Square Mall, the Social Security Administration and the Centers for Medicare and Medicaid Services would be closed owing to rumors circulating that there would be more violence and rioting that evening (Wood & Bowie, 2015). The police organized a public meeting at 2.30 pm to discuss the events of the previous night. While the crowd that gathered was peaceful, one individual was arrested and pepper spray was used when some of the protesters became disorderly (Associated Press, 2015b).

At approximately 9:00 pm on Tuesday April 28, several hundred protesters gathered at the CVS store that had been looted and burnt the previous evening. The police were present at the scene but a number of demonstrators and a local pastor stood between the protesters and the police (Associated Press, 2015b). It was around this time that the police were attempting to inform people of the 10:00 pm curfew (Associated Press, 2015b).

At approximately 10.15 pm, 15 min after the curfew had commenced, demonstrators in the CVS store area started throwing stones and bottles at the police and at about 10.30 pm fireworks were thrown at the police (Associated Press, 2015b). In response to the violence, the police, equipped with riot shields, advanced on the crowd to get them to disperse (Associated Press, 2015b). Police also deployed pepper balls at the "aggressive crowd" and the demonstrators left the area by approximately 11 pm (Associated Press, 2015b). Ten people were arrested in the CVS area, seven for violating the curfew, two for looting and one for disorderly conduct (Associated Press, 2015b), while across the city, 35 people, including one juvenile, were arrested for violating the curfew (Al Jazeera America, 2015).

The last night of rioting in Baltimore was Tuesday April 28, but 18 people were arrested for curfew violations on Wednesday April 29 (Maher & Palazzolo, 2015). On April 30, a further four people were arrested (Breitbart News, 2015) and 40 were arrested on May 1 for curfew violations (Schabner, 2015). Forty-six more people were arrested on Saturday May 2, following the largest peaceful rally held since the protests began (Hannigan, 2015). The curfew was withdrawn on Sunday May 3 (Nuckols & Dishneau, 2015) and the National Guard withdrew on Monday May 4 (Dance & Kaltenbach, 2015).

In total more than 200 people were arrested for curfew violations during the State of Emergency (Police Executive Research Forum, 2015). More than half of those arrested for curfew violations were released without being charged for the offence (Graham, 2015). The failure to charge for the offences arose from a technicality in the state legislation. The mayor had issued the curfew, whereas the legislation only provided authority for the state governor to issue a curfew (Fenton, 2015b).

On April 29, 2015, while there were no protests held in Baltimore, a number of solidarity protest marches were held around the country. Protesters marched through New York City, blocking off traffic in key areas, including the Holland Tunnel and the West Side Highway (Molinet, Stephasky, & Bult, 2015). There were also protests in the cities of Denver (Rubino & Frank, 2015), Ann Arbor (Akhtar, 2015), Albuquerque (Goldsmith, 2015), Boston, Cincinnati (Ellis, Payne, & St. Claire, 2015), Minneapolis (Raddatz, 2015), Oakland (The Mercury News, 2015), Philadelphia (CBS Philly, 2015), Seattle (Lacitis & Cornwell, 2015), and Washington, DC (NBC4 Washington, 2015). The majority of these protests were reasonably peaceful, but 11 people were arrested during the Denver march, after pepper spray was used by the police to control a group of demonstrators (Rubino & Frank, 2015). The violence in Denver started at approximately 7 pm, after a police officer was knocked off his motorcycle by a protester and was assaulted by five others (Rubino & Frank, 2015).

The total cost of the damage caused by the rioting in Baltimore was estimated to be approximately $9 million (Toppa, 2015), but one estimate was as high as $13 million (Marbella, 2015). This estimate did not include the value of the 144 cars that were burned. A survey of the violence that occurred during the period April 25 to May 3, undertaken by the Small Business Administration, estimated that the damage that was caused to over 380 businesses, 15 buildings and 61 structural fires was valued at approximately $8,927,000, and the damage caused to one home during the violence was worth approximately $60,000 (Toppa, 2015). The Camden Yards Stadium Authority estimated that there was a negative economic impact of $11.6 million from lost game-related spending because one game was played behind closed gates and two others were transferred (Marbella, 2015).

7.3 The Police Response

This section of the case study is extremely brief owing to the fact that there is only one document that presents any information pertaining to the response by the Baltimore Police Department to the April 2015 Baltimore riots. This document is a report that was developed by the Police Executive Research Forum, Washington, DC. Unfortunately, the response has been presented as an overview of the incident and has only been documented on approximately two and one-half pages of the 79-page report. As a result, it is difficult to understand the detail of the actions that were taken by the Baltimore Police Department. A high-level discussion of the police response to the demonstrations and riots, which followed the arrest of Mr. Gray on Saturday April 18 through to the end of the protests on Wednesday April 29, 2015 will be presented in this section of the case study. The discussion relies extensively on the Police Executive Research Forum (2015) report, entitled "Lessons learned from the 2015 civil unrest in Baltimore." Although the report does not provide a detailed presentation of the response by the Baltimore Police Department to the riots, or a timeline of their response, it does provide a reasonably comprehensive discussion of the weaknesses in the response to the civil unrest that took place in

Baltimore from April 25 through May 3, 2015. The report is based on information from interviews conducted; a discussion with members of a focus group, key individuals from the Baltimore Police Department and other agencies that were involved in the response (p. 3). This report provides some information that may help understand why the Baltimore Police Department responded as it did.

The goal of the report was to identify the problems and issues that the Baltimore Police Department faced during the riots and to make recommendations as to how the Baltimore Police Department could better prepare themselves for the occurrence of any major incidents in the future (p. 3). However, the principal weakness with the report was that it "did not allow for a moment-by-moment assessment of every action taken throughout the period of civil unrest" (p. 3). The major strength of the report is that it did "address major shortcomings in the Baltimore Police Department's response" together with those "actions that went well" for the Baltimore Police Department (p. 3).

Following the arrest and hospitalization of Mr. Gray on Saturday April 12, peaceful marches and demonstrations were held outside the Baltimore Western District Police Station every evening from April 18 to April 25. It appears that the Baltimore Police Department monitored these marches and demonstrations but there is no information available to confirm this. During the same week, the Baltimore Police Department received intelligence that approximately 10,000 people were planning to take part in protests in different areas of the city on Saturday April 25 (p. 25).

The information that was received was that the demonstrations would begin in the Western District of the city and move to a rally that would be held outside City Hall (p. 9). The Police Executive Research Forum (2015) report does not state whether the Baltimore Police Department implemented a response in relation to this information but according to Stolberg and Babcock (2015), state and city officials warned outsiders against coming into Baltimore to cause the type of unrest that had occurred in Ferguson, Missouri.

On Saturday April 25, the demonstration and the rally took place but as the rally was concluding a number of demonstrators broke away from the rally and marched towards the Camden Yards Stadium, where thousands of fans were attending a baseball game (p. 9). As the protesters gathered on the north-eastern side of the stadium, security guards closed the northern and north-eastern entrances to the park. This caused the protesters to become violent; they skirmished with patrons at a bar and threw debris at police officers who were patrolling outside the stadium (p. 9). Demonstrators also smashed the windows of a number of parked cars and blocked an intersection, which was the main route to the freeway (Marbella, 2015; Stolberg & Babcock, 2015). The demonstrators subsequently moved away from the stadium towards the downtown area, damaging a number of police cars that were parked along the street (p. 9).

In response to the violence, the Baltimore Police Department used its "Twitter feed to urge demonstrators to remain peaceful and blamed the problems on "isolated pockets of people from out of town causing disturbances downtown" (Stolberg & Babcock, 2015). The Baltimore Police Department deployed extra officers to the area and as the demonstrators left the stadium, the police formed a skirmish line across the main street that led to the downtown area (p. 10). As more officers arrived on the scene, the police were able to make arrests and eventually dispersed most of the crowd (p. 10). However, a group of protesters made their way back to the Western District Police Station area and confronted and attacked police officers until early the next morning (p. 10). Thirty-one adults and four juveniles were arrested during the disorder on Saturday (Marbella, 2015).

After a relatively peaceful day on Sunday, information was obtained by the Baltimore Police Department that there would be more demonstrations on Monday at the Mondawmin Mall, a transit hub for Maryland Transit Administration buses and Baltimore Public School students (p. 10). Following an analysis of this information, the analysts at the Baltimore Police Department searched social media and found that some high school students were calling for a "purge," a reference to a 2013 movie in which any crime could be committed without punishment during a 12-h period, once a year (p. 10).

In the early afternoon of Monday April 27, officers from the Baltimore Police Department, together with Baltimore City School Police Officers observed crowds forming at Mondawmin Mall and action was taken to manage the crowd (p. 10). Riot-equipped police officers were deployed, bus services to and from the mall were cancelled and the area was cordoned off to refrain people from entering the mall. At approximately 2.15 pm, the mall was closed by police officers (WMAR Staff, 2015; Brodey & McLaughlin, 2015). Brodey and McLaughlin (2015) claimed that the cordoning of the Mondawmin Mall, "essentially corralled young people in the area," meaning that the students could not leave the area easily. As there was no transportation out of the mall area available, the crowd could not disperse easily and as a result, the crowd began to increase in size and started to become violent (p. 10). They threw rocks, bricks, and other debris at officers who were equipped only with helmets and shields (p. 10). However, it appeared that there were not enough officers deployed to be able to form a skirmish line or to organize arrest teams (Marbella, 2015). By not using arrest teams, a stand-off between the crowd and the police developed (Marbella, 2015).

A number of officers were injured and a SWAT team was called in to assist with controlling the crowd (p. 10). The police, however, did not cordon the area off correctly and as traffic was still moving in the area, confusion ensued and there were problems with pedestrian safety (Marbella, 2015). The SWAT team deployed a chemical agent and smoke grenades to enable the police to gain control and disperse some of the crowd (p. 10), but the crowd was unable to travel north as their egress route was blocked by the police (Marbella, 2015). Groups from the crowd descended on unattended police cars, vandalizing and burning them (Marbella, 2015). The majority of the crowd moved to the intersection of Pennsylvania Avenue and West North Avenue (p. 11), while roaming gangs of mostly young men, broke into retail stores and looted its stock (Rector et al., 2015), and in some cases, assaulted the shopkeepers (Marbella, 2015).

According to Brodey and McLaughlin (2015), the "police actions inflamed a tense-but-stable situation," but Graham (2015) noted that the reaction taken by the Baltimore Police Department to the purge information was a departure from the approach generally taken to police demonstrations. In the 2 weeks prior, the Baltimore Police Department had typically given the protesters a wide berth to demonstrate. Graham also commented that the change in the approach was even more confusing considering that the Baltimore Police Department had deployed riot-equipped officers to the mall, which he claims, increased the tension.

The crowd destroyed a number of vehicles and set fire to a CVS store (p. 11). Some of the crowd threw homemade explosives and slashed fire hoses as firefighters attended to the fire at the CVS drugstore (p. 11). The Baltimore Police Department did not gain control of the situation until the early morning hours of April 28 (p. 11), after more than 200 people had been arrested and after dozens of officers had been injured (Snyder, 2016).

On the evening of the April 27, the Baltimore Police Department received reports of looting in the eastern district of the city (p. 11). Officers responded to the call with only helmets and batons and found a large crowd looting a shoe store (p. 11). As the officers approached the scene, the crowd began to throw rocks and bricks at the officers, requiring more officers to be deployed (p. 11). The Baltimore Police Department also deployed an armored response vehicle from the Howard County Police Department to assist in gaining control of and dispersing the crowd (p. 11).

During Monday evening, the Maryland State Governor declared a state of emergency and a nightly curfew was imposed by Mayor Stephanie Rawlings-Blake (Snyder, 2016). The Maryland Governor also requested aid from 5000 police officers from neighboring states and the assistance of the Maryland National Guard (Rector et al., 2015; Snyder, 2016). The request that the Maryland National Guard attend a civil disturbance was the first request that had been made by the Maryland State Governor in 47 years (Snyder, 2016). Approximately 1500 Maryland State Troopers (Rector et al., 2015) and more than 200 police officers from the region responded to the call for assistance (Baltimore City Fraternal Order of Police Lodge #3, 2015).

Although there is no information in the report that was prepared by the Police Executive Research Forum that determines whether the Baltimore Police Department had established communications with the leaders of the community, according to Rector et al. (2015), a number of church leaders took to the streets on Monday evening to intervene in the violence and to call for calm. These leaders also met with gang members to discuss how to end the violence (Rector et al., 2015).

Following the declaration of the state of emergency, the deployment of the Maryland National Guard and extra police officers from surrounding jurisdictions, there was no more rioting and the curfew was lifted on May 3, 2 days earlier than anticipated (Snyder, 2016).

According to RT (2015), the Baltimore Police Department did not have a plan to handle the civil disorder and had not trained or equipped their officers for responding to civil disturbances. The principal problems were, however, that the Baltimore Police Department did not have an "Incident Action Plan" in place that could be used to respond to the disorder, and the "Operational Plan" that they did have in place lacked the vital details that related to roles and responsibilities (RT, 2015). The operational plan was not designed for incidents that lasted for longer than 2 days (RT, 2015).

The following section of this case study critiques the weaknesses of the Baltimore Police Department in their response to the April 2015 riots.

7.4 Critique of the Police Response

This section of the chapter examines and discusses the police response to the riots that occurred following the death of Mr. Gray after his arrest on Saturday April 12, 2015. The discussion is based principally on the report that was prepared in September 2015 by the Police Executive Research Forum. The report is unique in that it examined the riots and the response of the Baltimore Police Department with the view that the findings of the report could have implications for other police agencies.

The report by the Police Executive Research Forum (2015) identified that there were nine weaknesses in the Baltimore Police Department's response to the April 2015 riots. These weaknesses were:

1. inadequate planning, with no comprehensive strategy in place
2. command roles changed without notice resulting in confusion as to who was in charge
3. arrest procedures and policies were unclear
4. crowding and confusion at the Command Center
5. equipment has severely lacking
6. officers reported that their training was inadequate
7. uncertainty about mutual aid
8. confusion about the definition of orders
9. deployment of the National Guard (pp. 4–6; Gately & Stolberg, 2015)

These weaknesses will form the basis of a critique of the police response to the riots. The critique will be discussed under the following 11 headings: Operational Planning; National Incident Management System; Intelligence; Command and Coordination; Arrest Policy; Definition of Orders; Equipment; Training; Mutual aid; Media; and Community Engagement.

7.4.1 Operational Planning

The Police Executive Research Forum (2015) claimed that the Baltimore Police Department's planning for the riots was inadequate (p. 3), because information had been received by the Baltimore Police Department a week before the protests started that a march was being organized. However, the Baltimore Police Department did not develop an Incident Action Plan (IAP) to direct the response but relied on a modified Incident Action Plan, which was called an "operational plan" (p. 4). For 2 years prior to the April 2015 riots, the Baltimore Police Department had used the same operational order by adapting it to suit various situations (p. 16). This meant that the Incident Action Plan was a standard response plan that was used as a standard operating procedure and could be implemented for any event, such as a peaceful protest march, with only slight amendments.

An Incident Action Plan was not developed even though the Baltimore Police Department had received information indicating that the march "would be large and mobile" and that the Baltimore Orioles baseball game at Camden Yards could be a potential target of the march (p. 21). It appears that even with this information and that approximately 49,000 people were expected to attend the game, the Baltimore Police Department did not foresee any potential crowd management problems, or if they did, it was not discussed in the Police Executive Research Forum report or in any other available literature.

The "operational plan" that was in existence was not detailed and although it had been developed on existing intelligence, it only contained basic information and direction (p. 4). As a result, the plan "was insufficient to serve as an IAP" (p. 4). The plan lacked specific detail in areas that were crucial for the deployment of staff and it did not provide the details that would have enabled the staff to understand their roles and responsibilities during an incident (p. 4). The plan should have outlined "the specific responsibilities of all personnel (including partnering agencies)" and highlighted the commander's intentions, the operational objectives, officer expectations, and the agency's priorities (p. 16).

The plan should have documented other relevant or situational-specific policies and procedures that would need to be applied when responding to the protest march. There should also have been a section in the plan that explained the arrest policy and procedures that should be followed should protesters need to be arrested. The lack of direction regarding arrest procedures was confusing for the commanders and patrol officers because "in the initial planning phase for the expected protests on April 25, it was stated that arrest was not a preferred function" (p. 17). This was because, as the Police Executive Research Forum (2015) rationalized, "avoiding arrests during large-scale demonstrations is often considered a good practice" (p. 18). The problems that arose because the officers were not aware of the arrest processes has been discussed in more detail below.

While the command and control roles, such as the incident commander, operations commander, planning commander, and logistics commander identified in the plan matched those specified in the response structure of the National Incident Management System (NIMS) (p. 16), they did not specify the responsibilities of the roles. Other areas of the plan that lacked detail or were incomplete were the communications section, "citations of legal authorities, a safety plan, intelligence information, traffic plans, and detailed work assignments" (p. 16). The plan "did not account for the possibility that the incident might last longer than a day or two" and "many commanders and most patrol officers were not familiar with it" (p. 4).

The fact that the majority of commanders and patrol officers were not familiar with the plan meant that they were not aware of the Baltimore Police Department's priorities and "the overall tactical strategy for responding to the unrest" (p. 17). Awareness of the plan was provided only at roll call, prior to the officers being deployed to the disorder (p. 17). Patrol officers were not given any information other than that which was provided at roll call, and that "resulted in uncertainty, miscommunication of expectations, and hesitancy by field commanders to make decisions" (p. 17).

Three aspects of the plan did prove to be beneficial during the response to the April 25 riots. The first was that the plan included "information on staging areas and dedicated radio channels" (p. 16). The second benefit was that there were "locations [that] were designated for protection, such as City Hall and police headquarters" and the third was, that the plan outlined how the Baltimore Police Department "planned to utilize external resources" (p. 16).

The Police Executive Research Forum (2015) claimed that the Baltimore Police Department had four priorities "that were to act as a guide for all operations" and for the planned protests on April 25 (p. 16). However, the report did not specify where the information was obtained from and if the four priorities were documented, where they could be found. The four priorities are listed in order of importance:

1. Preservation of Life (Citizen Safety and Officer Safety)
2. Protection of Property and Business
3. Safe Traffic Flow (Ingress and Egress)
4. Restoration of Normal City Services (p. 17).

The Research Forum claimed that the four priorities were "appropriate," but the list does not "include the protection of the constitutional rights of demonstrators" (p. 17). This is an important point, especially as the list provides some guidelines for the planners to be able to develop a response plan. The protection of rights should be in the forefront of all police officers' minds when there is a possibility that they will be responding to an incident of violence and in particular, a protest march or demonstration that has the potential to escalate into a riot. A statement that protects the constitutional rights of demonstrators becomes an aid memoir within the operation order.

Another weakness was that the guidelines that specify how the four priorities would be implemented had not been developed and therefore, were not shared with the operational personnel (p. 17). As a result of this, the Research Forum recommended that the "priorities for future events should be more comprehensive and should be distributed to all responding personnel" (p. 17) before they are deployed to an incident.

The final discussion in this section relates to the issues that the planning section faced during the response to the riots. It appears that the command staff did not understand the role of a planning section during an event such as that which occurred in Baltimore in April 2015. According to the Police Executive Research Forum (2015), the Baltimore Police Department stated that the task of the planning section was "to identify the needs of the department to cover the forecasted deployment requests during the period of unrest" (p. 21). The forecast was to include "staffing levels and other resources" but the section was to also adjust their "plans to account for any new developments and/or difficulties" that may arise during the unrest (p. 21).

The tasks required of a planning section should be undertaken before an event, not while an event is taking place. If an operation order had been developed the week before the protest march and riots, there would not have been a need to forecast staffing levels, as this would have been itemized in the escalation procedure contained within the plan. If the operation order had been developed prior to the event, the planning section would have been able to concentrate on developing the

Incident Action Plan as defined in the National Incident Management System. The National Incident Management System specifies that the planning section would maintain "information and intelligence on the current and forecasted situation, as well as the status of resources assigned to the incident" and should have been able to prepare the Incident Action Plan for each operational period (Department of Homeland Security, 2008, p. 103).

Another challenge for the planning section was the capaciousness of their accommodation. During the response to the riots, the section was located with the Unified Command[1] in the watch center, which is a room in the Baltimore Police Department Headquarters that is used daily for policing and for immediate short-term operations (p. 21). The center was being used for something that it was not designed for and soon became overcrowded (p. 21). The center had "space for approximately 30 to 40 people, but at times there were up to 100 people present, resulting in excessive noise and confusion" (p. 5). The large number of people present in the center meant that there was insufficient workspace and not enough networked computers available for the planning section staff and other key Unified Command staff (p. 5). While locating the planning section with the Unified Command may have been "a good idea in theory," the overcrowding meant that the planning section "did not have access to all of the resources and equipment required to fulfil its function" (p. 21).

The next issue related to the ability to deploy the number of staff required to cover the scheduled events. The baseball game at Camden Yards was expected to attract more than 49,000 attendees and there were eight other events that evening that would require the attendance of the police, along with the possibility that a large-sized protest march would take place. On April 20, in preparation for the baseball game and the protest, the Baltimore Police Department cancelled leave for all personnel and implemented overtime requirements "to ensure that as many individuals as possible would be available during the protests" (p. 21). However, even after implementing this, the planning section "experienced difficulty fulfilling all requests for staff resources" (p. 21). The lack of staff available made it "difficult to deploy the preferred number of individuals" (p. 21).

Personnel and squads were often not deployed appropriately and as a result, were often not utilized in the most effective manner (p. 17). Members of SWAT units, for example, were often deployed to undertake two different roles. Members were to perform a riot-officer role, or in other words, be a part of a skirmish line. The second was as a member of an arrest team. This meant that as members of the arrest team entered the crowd to arrest an offender, other officers were required to hold the skirmish line (p. 17). The use of SWAT teams in this manner limited their "ability to respond to areas where there was a need for a more advanced response as the situation escalated" (p. 17).

The fourth issue was the line of communication between the planning section and the operation commander. The most basic requirement of a planning section is to

[1]The BPD Incident Command team organized as per the NIMS and representatives from other agencies (Police Executive Research Forum, 2015, p. 21).

develop and implement a plan from the direction given by an operation commander. During the development stage of the planning for the response to the riots, "there was no consistent or effective communication between" the planning section and the operation command (p. 22). According to the Police Executive Research Forum (2015), this situation was eventually rectified "through scheduled briefings and tactics meetings" (p. 22). If the planning section had had consistent access to the operation commander, would the response to the riots have been better planned and resourced?

The fifth issue was the ability of the planning staff to adapt to the changing planning needs and the changing response. The Baltimore Police Department changed the roster of all personnel to 12-h shifts and this meant that the planning section had to predict the number of staff and the resources required for each shift (p. 22). A 12-h cycle needed to be planned for and the planning section found this to be challenging (p. 22). The problem was that at the end of each shift, the section "would still be attempting to plan for the upcoming 12 hours" (p. 22), and this meant that the planning had not been completed by the time the next shift began "leaving the next shift the responsibility of finishing the planning for that time period" (p. 22).

Coordinating with other agencies is the last issue to be discussed in this section. Lines of communications with other city agencies had not been established prior to the riots and this created problems in coordinating the utilization of and the deployment of other city agencies, such as utility and trash collection services (p. 22). The trash collectors, for example, were not able to access specific areas of the city because rioters had blocked the streets and because police cordons were in place.

7.4.2 National Incident Management System

The Baltimore Police Department used the National Incident Management System as a framework for responding to the April 2015 riots (p. 3). The Baltimore Police Department used the National Incident Management System "to prepare for unexpected critical incidents, such as natural disasters, terrorist attacks, civil unrest and riots, and other events that require an emergency response" (p. 4). It was developed by the Department of Homeland Security following the 9/11 terrorist attacks, and provides a structure for:

> "a systematic, proactive approach to guide departments and agencies at all levels of government, nongovernmental organizations, and the private sector to work seamlessly to prevent, protect against, respond to, recover from, and mitigate the effects of incidents, regardless of cause, size, location, or complexity, in order to reduce the loss of life and property and harm to the environment. NIMS works hand in hand with the National Response Framework (NRF). NIMS provides the template for the management of incidents, while the NRF provides the structure and mechanisms for national-level policy for incident management" (Department of Homeland Security, 2008, p. 1).

The National Response Framework (NRF) is not referred to in the report written by the Police Executive Research Forum (2015), nor is it referred to in any of the documents that relate to the April 2015 riots in Baltimore. The non-inclusion of the

National Response Framework in any of the Baltimore Police Department riot documents creates two deficiencies when critiquing the Baltimore Police Department's response to the riots. It is not known whether the National Response Framework was implemented along with the National Incident Management System. If it had been implemented, it is not known whether the command staff knew of the National Response Framework. The Police Executive Research Forum (2015) claimed that "one of the biggest problems with the Baltimore Police Department's operational plan was that many commanders and most of the patrol officers were not familiar with" the National Incident Management System (p. 4). The lack of familiarity with the operational plan and by implication, the use and implementation of the National Incident Management System, would be one of the reasons why the response by the Baltimore Police Department was uncoordinated.

An operational plan or order prepared prior to an event is a fundamental requirement for any police response to a major incident. Most police agencies will have existing or standing operational plans that will specify how the agency will respond initially to a major event or incident. When a police agency is required to respond to a major incident or event, the National Incident Management System would be activated and a major component of the activation would be the development of an Incident Action Plan (IAP). An Incident Action Plan "provides a concise, coherent means of capturing and communicating the overall incident priorities, objectives, strategies, and tactics in the context of both operational and support activities" and depending upon the incident, does not necessarily have to be written (Department of Homeland Security, 2008, p. 47). According to the Department of Homeland Security (2008), "most initial response operations are not captured with a formal IAP," but if an incident is likely to extend beyond one operational period, become more complex, or involve multiple jurisdictions and/or agencies, preparing a written Incident Action Plan will become increasingly important to maintain effective, efficient, and safe operations" (p. 47).

According to the Police Executive Research Forum (2015), the Baltimore Police Department did attempt to implement the National Incident Management System during the April riots, "but the agency was inexperienced with the system" (p. 30). This inexperience was exacerbated by a number of key individuals who had some experience with the National Incident Management System being re-deployed to the team investigating the death of Mr. Gray, which meant that their roles were filled by other officers who were not familiar with the responsibilities of the Incident Command System (ICS) (p. 30). As a result of people occupying positions within the National Incident Management System structure who were not familiar with the role meant that "many were learning or relearning their responsibilities on the fly" (pp. 21, 30).

Unfamiliarity with the role of the National Incident Management System was also apparent at the command level. This was because of the quality of the training that the staff had received. The training that the command staff received was "cursory," according to the Police Executive Research Forum (2015, p. 17). Unfamiliarity with the National Incident Management System meant that the command staff did not understand the role and the function of the Baltimore Police Department's Liaison Officer, who was located in the Mayor's Office Emergency Management's Emergency Operations Center (EOC).

The Mayor's Office Emergency Management's Emergency Operations Center comprises of representatives from a number of city agencies and during a response to a critical incident operates under "its own incident command structure to coordinate the city's response" (p. 22). The problem for the Baltimore Police Department's command team, who were located at the watch center, was that the Baltimore Police Department's representative at the Mayor's Office Emergency Management's Emergency Operations Centre did not have a designated role in the operational plan (p. 22). The second problem was that "there was also no clear indication how the representative at the Emergency Operations Center would coordinate resources between BPD [Baltimore Police Department] and other city agencies" (p. 22).

7.4.3 *Intelligence*

During the riots, the Analytical Intelligence section (AIS) of the Baltimore Police Department (BPD) reported to and was located with the planning section (p. 24). This meant that they were undertaking the role of the intelligence branch under the National Incident Management System and were responsible for "providing intelligence to the BPD Incident Commander and [for] responding jurisdictions throughout the period of [the] unrest" (p. 24). This was a departure from their usual analytical role.

On both Saturday 25 April and Monday 27 April, the analytical intelligence section, were unable to fulfil its role owing to three factors. The first factor that restricted the capability of the analytical intelligence section and therefore the flow of intelligence, was their accommodation. Normally, the analytical intelligence section is stationed in the watch center, but during the response to the riots, the watch center was used as the command center (pp. 24, 29). The change in the use of the center meant that there were often more than 100 people in the room, which restricted the analytical intelligence section's access to their equipment and resources (p. 24). The analytical intelligence section only had access to two workstations, of which approximately ten analysts needed to work from and this limited their ability to analyze information during the riots (p. 29).

The second factor that restricted the capability of the analytical intelligence section was the vast amount of information that was received during the riots. Owing to the limited amount of accommodation and the change in their role, analysts were not able to validate the intelligence in a timely manner for the incident commander or the deployed staff (p. 24). This meant that information that had not been assessed or vetted by analysts was being released to the incident commander (p. 24) and it was on this information that decisions were being made.

Another factor that restricted the analytical intelligence section and the intelligence function related to dissemination. Although the analytical intelligence section was sending information to the command center, it was not known whether the staff in the command center disseminated the information (p. 25) to the deployed commanders. Owing to the challenges within the command center, the analytical intelligence section found that it was more convenient to disseminate information verbally rather than by documenting it or using the correct briefing methods (p. 25).

The final factor that restricted the function of the analytical intelligence section was their relationship with the Maryland Coordination and Analysis Center[2] (MCAC). The Maryland Coordination and Analysis Center deployed a representative to the watch center, but according to the Police Executive Research Forum (2015), "there was a lack of communication between AIS [analytical intelligence section] and MCAC" (p. 26). The Maryland Coordination and Analysis Center took a more generalist approach to intelligence gathering and analysis and on specific terror threats, which meant that persons of interest were not identified (p. 26). The Maryland Coordination and Analysis Center could have used their sources of information to assist the analytical intelligence section with their intelligence gathering. It is accepted that the Maryland Coordination and Analysis Center may have taken the perspective that when providing information to the analytical intelligence section that the section could have "burned" their source. However, there are methods available for protecting human-sourced information of which, both agencies would have had knowledge.

7.4.4 Command and Coordination

According to the Police Executive Research Forum (2015), the Baltimore Police Department set up a command structure and a command center to respond to the riots (p. 29). Officers in charge of each of the areas within the National Incident Management System structure, other city agencies, and mutual aid agencies were included in the command centre (p. 29). However, many of these individuals were not familiar with the command structure used by the Baltimore Police Department and this created difficulties in the chain of command as they were not clear whether "decisions should be made in the field or in the command center" (p. 29).

As discussed previously, the pre-deployment briefings were not comprehensive and there was no clear direction as to the "rules of engagement" with rioters, which made it difficult for supervisors to make decisions (p. 29) without direction from the command center. Seeking direction from the command centre was highlighted in the Police Executive Research Forum (2015) report. The report claimed that having to seek direction from the command center delayed the actions that were taken by the field commanders (p. 29).

The inability of the field commanders to make decisions quickly and to provide appropriate direction to their staff meant that staff were often unclear as to what action was required. One example of where direction lacked clarity was in relation to the use of protective equipment (p. 31). During the pre-deployment briefing, staff were instructed to "use a softer approach with demonstrators, to avoid appearing too militarized," but when the demonstrations became violent, supervisors where uncer-

[2]The MCAC is a fusion center of local, state, and federal agencies that focuses on information-sharing and analysis. It was originally established to focus on anti-terrorism efforts, but at the time of the riots had an all-hazards approach in which their mission was defined as "the analysis and dissemination of information in statewide support of law enforcement, public health and welfare, public safety, and homeland security" (Maryland Coordination and Analysis Center, 2017).

tain as to whether the officers could be directed to use protective equipment (p. 31). The lack of instructions as to how and when supervisors could transition from the initial response led to a delay in officers receiving their protective equipment (p. 32), which placed officers in danger.

Problems also arose because the field commanders would not make the decision to deploy less-than-lethal weapons without checking first with the command centre (p. 32). This caused a delay in deploying these weapons and enabled the violence to escalate.

The positions within the structure of the National Incident Management System changed frequently, often without notice (p. 4), which caused more difficulties. Not knowing as to who was fulfilling a specific role within the National Incident Management System meant that deployed staff and those working within the command center were not clear as to who the incident commander was (pp. 4, 16), and this caused confusion in the command center (pp. 4, 16).

The final problem relating to the command was the ability of those in the command center to communicate effectively with the staff who were deployed. The Police Executive Research Forum (2015) highlighted two challenges with the communication process. In the initial stages of the riots on Saturday April 25, the Baltimore Police Department only operated on one radio channel, which meant that mutual aid agencies could not communicate with the Baltimore Police Department (p. 33). The Baltimore Police Department did eventually assign multiple channels to the response, but this should have been done much earlier in the response.

A number of aid agencies were unable to receive the Baltimore Police Department's radio channels, which hindered the communication flow (p. 33). While a number of officers from mutual aid agencies had been partnered with a Baltimore Police Department Officer, others were not (p. 33), and this meant that not all of the deployed staff were fully informed on the situation as it was evolving. In the future, the command and control structure needs to be communicated to both the Baltimore Police Department and mutual aid agencies (p. 41), and this will ensure a coordinated response and assist in keeping officers safe.

7.4.5 Arrest Policies Were Unclear

The Baltimore Police Department, as with the majority of police agencies, maintain a number of different policy directives that outline the response that should be taken to any civil disorder (p. 55). The Baltimore Police Department's General Order 37–77 provides the guidance for "how BPD should respond to peaceful protests as well as riot scenarios" (p. 55). The order "discusses how to distinguish between peaceful and non-peaceful demonstrations" and how to apply the "clear and present danger test" to the specific protest or riot situation (p. 55).

The use of the National Incident Management System as an incident command system during a critical incident is not contained in the General Order 37–77, but is contained in the 2012 "Standard Operating Procedure on Crowd Control Incidents" (p. 55). A more comprehensive policy is contained in the "Response Guide for

Critical Incidents," which was published in 2013 and describes the application of the National Incident Management System to respond to protest incidents (p. 55).

The Baltimore Police Department has a General Order and a Standard Operating Procedure, both of which, relate to how the Baltimore Police Department should respond to a critical incident. These were both used during the riots. However, the documents do not specify a procedure for making arrests during a riot and as a result, officers were confused as to when offenders could be arrested and whether authority was needed to make an arrest (p. 4). Further confusion arose as a result of the pre-deployment briefings where officers were told to take a "soft approach" in order to send a message that the police were not expecting the demonstration to become violent (p. 4). However, when the riots began, supervisors and commanders did not permit officers to arrest protesters, even when it was necessary (p. 18).

To the credit of the Baltimore Police Department, a new arrest strategy was developed and implemented, which distinguished "between emergency and non-emergency arrests" (p. 18). The new strategy took effect on April 28–29 and remained in use until the end of the riots (p. 18). Despite the implementation of the new arrest procedure, the number of individuals brought to the booking locations overloaded the system and led to many of those arrested being released without being charged (p. 19).

7.4.6 Confusion About Definitions of Orders

A lack of clarity about the meaning of some of the orders that were given by the commanders added to the overall confusion (pp. 6, 33). Officers for example, were ordered "not to engage" with the protesters, or to "stand-by" (p. 32). These orders were interpreted by the officers to mean "stand down" (p. 32), or in other words, to move back from confronting the crowd and not to engage with them.

The officers were also confused when they were told to take a "soft approach" when responding to the offences committed by the demonstrators (p. 4). The confusion arose from the officers being told to report to the deployment staging points "in their regular uniforms and not to wear gloves or helmets" (p. 4). However, when the protests became violent, some of the commanders were hesitant to contravene the initial order that officers were to wear their uniform and the order that some officers were to wear their helmets only (p. 4).

The training that the staff received did not include the definition of an order (p. 32). Officers for example, were told by commanders to "hold the line" rather than to apprehend or arrest offenders (Marbella, 2015). In situations such as when responding to a riot, officers interpret orders differently and if officers are not trained in these terms and taught specific definitions, delay and confusion can result (p. 32). One method that can be used to clarify an order would be to allow the deployed commanders to make decisions as an incident evolves and not to have to rely on the decisions made by the command center (p. 33).

7.4.7 Equipment Was Lacking

At the beginning of the riots, on Saturday April 25, helmets were the only protective equipment available to the majority of officers (p. 37). The Police Executive Research Forum (2015) claimed that "even this equipment was difficult to retrieve, as the helmets were stored in locations throughout the city that were difficult to access once the incident began" (p. 37). Once the officers had access to the riot equipment, the "helmets and shields were not sturdy enough, cracking when they were hit by rocks thrown by rioters" and the gas masks did not function (p. 37). While some of the officers may have had riot shields these were found not to be suitable for a riot. Other officers did not have personal protective equipment and often the gas masks that they did have contained expired filters, while "a large number were deemed unusable" (p. 37). The lack of protection and control equipment impacted negatively on the response and left the deployed officers being unable to protect themselves, leading to some officers being injured (p. 37).

It was the logistics section that was responsible for allocating and ordering replacement riot equipment. As well as ensuring that equipment was made available for the officers, the logistics section was also responsible for ensuring that the officers deployed received food and water on a regular basis. The role of the logistics section was to work mainly with the Mayor's Office of Emergency Management, the city's purchasing department and the Baltimore Police Department Fiscal Services Unit to order the equipment and supplies needed (p. 35). This section, as with all of the other sections within the National Incident Management System, was located within the unified incident command in the command center and they experienced the same accommodation issues as the other sections (p. 35).

The need to acquire equipment because the Baltimore Police Department did not have enough equipment or because the equipment available was not fit for purpose caused a number of problems for the logistics section. As the riots progressed, the need for additional equipment became urgent and it was difficult to identify suppliers who could supply sufficient quantities of the equipment required in the quality needed. A sole supplier generally did not have sufficient quantities of a specific item and this meant that items had to be purchased from a number of different suppliers (p. 38). Because equipment was purchased from multiple suppliers, not all officers had the same version of the equipment, meaning that officers often could not utilize the new equipment, "as some of the different versions did not fit together" (p. 38).

Another problem arose once the purchased equipment had been distributed. After it had been distributed, it was difficult to track (p. 35). The equipment was initially "tracked manually on a form introduced to the [Logistics] Section by the Pennsylvania Emergency Management Agency (PEMA)" which was time consuming, but the process did become "more efficient as the week progressed" (p. 35). Problems also occurred when the new equipment was mixed with the old, which made it even more difficult to track and determine to whom it was allocated (p. 38).

Difficulties also arose when the new equipment became mixed with that of the mutual aid agencies (p. 38). Mixing equipment came about because deployed officers from all agencies often "swapped equipment in an effort to ensure that everyone had as much protection as possible" (p. 38). Often, the Baltimore Police Department did not have access to less-than-lethal force weapons although they were available to officers from the mutual aid agencies (p. 38). There was a Special Enforcement Section within the Baltimore Police Department that had had access to less-than-lethal weapons, but these teams had been disbanded (p. 38). The lack of access to less-than-lethal-force weapons is important when critiquing the actions of the Baltimore Police Department, as some of the officers of the Baltimore Police Department commented that "it was the less-lethal munitions equipment that was the most effective tool in quelling the rioting" (p. 38). This implies that if the Baltimore Police Department had access to these weapons the riots may have been able to be brought under control much earlier and may not have been as damaging.

The last part of this topic to be discussed is the training of the officers in the use of equipment. The Police Executive Research Forum (2015) verifies that equipment is useful only when officers have been trained in how and when to use it (p. 39). Any training that is given to officers in how and when to use new equipment must be given prior to, rather than during a critical incident (p. 39).

7.4.8 Officers Reported That Their Training Was Inadequate

Historically, in the Baltimore Police Department, the control of crowds and the Mobile Field Force were the responsibility of specialized units such as "SWAT and the Special Enforcement Section (SES)" (p. 58). Members of these units usually completed "a 2–3-day course on specialized Mobile Field Force tactics," which included "advanced techniques for controlling crowds and disbanding rioters, such as extraction and flanking" (p. 58). Unfortunately, the amount of training that was provided was not adequate for the type and the level of the disorder that was experienced in April 2015 (p. 5). As the officers of the Baltimore Police Department were not trained in the use of less-than-lethal munitions this meant that during the riots, the Baltimore Police Department had to rely on other agencies to use these weapons on their behalf (p. 58).

Prior to the rioting, the Baltimore Police Department had taken a risk management approach to the delivery of riot response training and had "delivered crowd-control training commensurate to its assessment of its needs" (p. 57). The assessment was primarily based on the fact that Baltimore had not experienced any large incidents of disorder or rioting since 1968 (p. 57). The Baltimore Police Department began to provide training in 2012, which included 2 h of training in the principles and practices of crowd control (p. 58). In 2012, more than 1428 officers were trained and in 2014, 1788 received this type of training (p. 58).

According to the Police Executive Research Forum (2015), the amount of riot control training that the Baltimore Police Department delivered was a result of financial prioritization. The Forum claimed that the Baltimore Police Department had faced "significant constraints on" their resources (p. 58) and this was reflected in the number of staff members who were available to deliver riot training. The Baltimore Police Department's Training Academy only had 18 trainers that were able to deliver the "limited 2-hour academy [riot control] course for line officers" (p. 58). The Forum (2015) found that this amount of training was insufficient, especially when the wide range of issues that are involved in crowd control and riot-response are considered (p. 58).

The austerity and priority measures that were introduced by the Baltimore Police Department also affected the delivery of training in other, indirect ways. The Baltimore Police Department did have a mobile training unit that comprised predominantly former SWAT team members and they delivered training in the districts of the Baltimore Police Department (p. 58). The training delivered "covered a variety of topics, including 'de-escalation strategies', 'how to assess various types of situations before engagement' and 'the police response to incidents involving a mentally ill person brandishing an edged weapon'" (p. 58).

7.4.9 Uncertainty About Mutual Aid

When developing the response plan for the April 25 demonstrations, the Baltimore Police Department sent a request for mutual aid resources, of both officers and equipment, to ten neighboring agencies on April 23 and also requested that they attend a planning meeting on April 24 (p. 42). "Anne Arundel County Police Department, Baltimore City School Police, Baltimore City Sheriff's Office, Baltimore County Police Department, Howard County Police Department, Maryland State Police, Maryland Transit Authority Police, Maryland Transportation Authority, Police Montgomery County Police Department, and Prince George's County Police Department" were contacted (p. 42).

There were a number of challenges in co-ordinating the deployment of the mutual aid officers and their resources in the April 2015 riots (p. 5). The challenge stemmed from the regional mutual aid compact, which was an agreement between the Maryland police agencies to provide resources to other agencies in Maryland during an emergency. The terms of the compact did not specify how much assistance would be provided by mutual aid agencies and when the Baltimore Police Department was planning its response to the demonstrations scheduled for April 25, it did not know the total number of officers that would be made available for deployment (p. 5). Nor did the compact specify the roles that each of the mutual aid agencies would take or which use-of-force policies would be used. The type of equipment that the officers from mutual aid agencies would provide was not specified either (p. 5).

All of the ten agencies that were contacted for assistance sent representatives to the April 24 planning meeting (p. 42). The meeting covered a wide range of operational topics including the location of the anticipated demonstration and that the size of the demonstration could involve approximately 10,000 people (p. 42). Other topics that were discussed included anticipated rally points and the possibility of the crowds being highly mobile and that they were likely to splinter away from the main demonstration (p. 42). The principal topic of the meeting was to request an additional 1000 officers from neighboring agencies (p. 42). It was not specified in the Police Executive Research Forum (2015) report whether the representatives of the neighboring agencies agreed to this number, but according to the Forum, the meeting concluded with the neighboring agencies agreeing to commit officers and other resources (p. 43).

Following the conclusion of the April 24 meeting, the Baltimore Police Department distributed a memo that outlined the operational plan (p. 43). This plan described the role that each agency would undertake and which agencies would be held in reserve to undertake the protection and security of potential demonstration sites and other critical infrastructure sites (p. 43). Jurisdictions that had mobile field force units were tasked with assisting officers from the Baltimore Police Department on the march routes (p. 43).

On Saturday, April 25, 235 officers from neighboring agencies were sent to support the Baltimore Police Department in managing the demonstration (p. 44). As the Police Executive Forum (2015) noted, this number was well short of the 1000 officers that the Baltimore Police Department requested (p. 45). In response to the riots at the Mondawmin Mall on Monday, April 27, 438 officers were sent by neighboring agencies to provide assistance (p. 45). While the number of officers provided was well short of the number requested by the Baltimore Police Department, the neighboring agencies provided vital resources that included less-than-lethal munitions, armored response vehicles, and mobile field force units, all of which were necessary to control the violence at the mall (p. 45).

The number of officers and the number of agencies providing assistance in Baltimore changed significantly after the state of emergency was declared at 8:30 pm on April 27 (p. 45). On April 28, there were 678 mutual aid officers assisting the Baltimore Police Department, by May 2, there were 1597 (p. 50). Twenty-eight agencies that deployed officers to Baltimore and provided "crucial assistance" came from as far away as Pennsylvania, Ohio and Washington, DC (p. 45).

As a result of the large number of officers deployed and the large number of agencies that deployed officers to Baltimore, several problems quickly became apparent. The first problem was that of officers self-deploying to the incident. Although the Baltimore Police Department had contacted neighboring agencies for assistance, a number of Baltimore Police Department's officers and managers, using their personal relationships, informally reached out to their counterparts in other agencies and requested their assistance in the first few days of the riot (p. 45). The Police Executive Research Forum (2015) could not fault the officers from the Baltimore Police Department for approaching neighboring agencies, as their need for assistance was immediate (p. 45). The Baltimore Police Department made requests for assistance directly to the mutual aid agencies but should have made their requests through the Maryland Emergency Management Agency (MEMA) (p. 45). This made it difficult to track the officers and the equipment flowing into Baltimore (p. 45). The difficulties in tracking the deployments made by mutual aid agencies was compounded further by the self-deployment of officers from these agencies (p. 45). Although these officers and agencies were "well intentioned" and they did contribute to controlling the disorder, their deployment complicated the task of tracking mutual aid resources and developing a plan for utilizing the various agencies' capabilities (p. 45).

Using Lot C of the M&T Bank stadium as a staging area also created problems (p. 46). The Maryland State Police were to coordinate the resources of all of the agencies at Lot C (p. 46). This would have enabled the Maryland State Police to "receive all the deployment requests from the Command Center and send out officers accordingly" (p. 46). However, the command center deployed mutual aid agency resources without consulting with the Maryland State Police and this caused confusion as to where the resources had been deployed to.

Deploying and integrating officers and resources from outside agencies also proved to be difficult in the early stages of the response (p. 46). There was a structured process in place for deploying the resources of the mutual aid agencies. Forms and spreadsheets were used by the Maryland State Police to track officers, equipment and the experience of each agency but the command center did not use this process. It was challenging for the Maryland State Police to plan for and coordinate the deployment of the officers of the mutual agencies, especially when the command center made deployments directly to the "hot zones." Furthermore, deployments were based on which agency had the greatest number of officers rather than on the capability and the training of officers. The command center, for example, did not consider whether the agency they had deployed to a "hot zone" had a mobile field force unit, or specialty equipment or vehicles (p. 46). Problems also arose from the command centre deploying the mutual aid agencies as this meant that the officers of the mutual aid agencies reported to the command center rather than to the Maryland State Police at Lot C (p. 46).

The large number of officers deployed made it difficult for the command centre to share any information with the Maryland State Police at Lot C (p. 47). The difficulties in sharing information led to a number of confusing requests being made to the mutual aid agencies, especially when assistance of specialist capabilities, such as SWAT teams were requested. However, communication and the sharing of information between the two sites improved after a Major of the Baltimore Police Department was assigned to "serve as a liaison with outside agencies at Lot C" and after a senior commander from each of the mutual aid agencies was embedded in the command center (p. 47).

The third problem relating to the deployment of mutual aid agency officers was the management of officer expectations. The deployment of the officers of mutual aid agencies was delayed until after they had been briefed and it had been confirmed that they had the appropriate protective equipment (p. 47). The officers of the mutual aid agencies were frustrated with this process and did not appreciate the delay in their deployment because the riots were already underway. Frustration could have been avoided if the officers' expectations had been managed ahead of time (p. 47). They should have been advised of the process that would be followed prior to their deployment. The Baltimore Police Department did not notify mutual aid agencies of the process that would be followed in advance of their deployment and nor was any information as to when the mutual aid agency staff would be deployed included in the operation plan. Delays in deploying staff from the staging area also occurred because the capabilities of the specific agency needed to be matched to the needs of the response (p. 47). Documenting the procedures would have managed officers' expectations and would have provided a framework that would have ensured that the mutual aid agencies and their officers reported to Lot C with the appropriate equipment. This would have ensured that the Maryland State Police would have deployed the officers from Lot C.

The last problem to be discussed in relation to deployment was the choice of Lot C as the staging center. Lot C is located more than one and a half miles from the Baltimore Police Department's Headquarters and the separation caused logistical inefficiencies, especially in regard to the provision of supplies, such as food and water (p. 47). The supplies had to be delivered to Lot C from headquarters and other Baltimore Police Department locations. Lot C was not a staging area that was normally used by the Baltimore Police Department and it did not have all of the equipment necessary to serve as a mobile command post (p. 47). This meant that everything had to be transported to the site.

The last topic to be discussed in relation to mutual aid is that of governance. Police agencies generally provide assistance to each other through the use of one of two documents. The first document is the Mutual Aid Agreement which defines the ad hoc relationship and usually specifies that aid will be provided in response to an emergency. The second document is a Memorandum of Understanding (MoU), which is a more comprehensive document and this specifies a number of areas of mutual interest between the two police agencies. The provision of aid between the two parties will only be one section of, or a schedule attached to the Memorandums of Understanding.

The Baltimore Police Department did not have any Mutual Aid Agreements or Memorandums of Understanding with any of the police agencies in the surrounding area and this caused confusion as to which agencies could be called upon to provide assistance and how such agencies could respond. During the unrest in Baltimore, some agencies deployed under an ad hoc Mutual Aid Agreement, while others deployed under an ad hoc Memorandum of Understanding. Other agencies were deployed under a third agreement "known as the Baltimore Regional Emergency Assistance Compact (BREAC)" (p. 50). The Baltimore Regional Emergency Assistance Compact is the reason why such a large number of mutual aid officers deployed to Baltimore following the declaration of a state of emergency (p. 51).

The Baltimore City Office of Emergency Management manages the Baltimore Regional Emergency Assistance Compact. Agencies that are party to the Baltimore Regional Emergency Assistance Compact provide aid on request in the event of critical incidents (p. 51). This means that the planning undertaken by the Baltimore Police Department in preparation for the demonstration on Saturday April 25, which subsequently became a riot, did not take account of the process outlined in the Baltimore Regional Emergency Assistance Compact when they were determining the resources that would be available. Not knowing whether a state of emergency would be declared following the unrest on April 25 constrained the ability of the Baltimore Police Department to obtain the necessary resources and to know how much mutual aid they could receive (p. 51). Not being able to identify the type and number of personnel that would be available meant that the Baltimore Police Department could not plan for the deployment of the resources in advance (p. 51).

Not all of the enforcement agencies in the Baltimore area are signatories to the Baltimore Regional Emergency Assistance Compact and this created problems for Baltimore Police Department planners and their office of legal affairs. “In order to receive assistance from outside agencies [that were not signatories of the Baltimore Regional Emergency Assistance Compact], the Baltimore Police Department Office of Legal Affairs” created “individual ad hoc Memorandums of Understanding with individual outside agencies as the civil unrest was unfolding” (p. 51). The need for individual Memorandums of Understanding created further pressure and confusion for the Baltimore Police Department’s Planners, who were not able to rely on the provision of personnel or the deployment of specific resources until the individual Memorandum of Understanding was signed.

7.4.10 Media

Similar to the other case studies discussed in this book, the April 2015 riots in Baltimore quickly became the main topic in news broadcasts, not only locally, but nationally and internationally. As with the other police agencies discussed in the case studies, the Baltimore Police Department’s received press inquiries from around the world “almost constantly for more than a week” (p. 65). The number of inquiries made it difficult for the media relations section to respond in a timely manner (p. 65). Another challenge arose from the large number of media personnel who were in the city reporting on the riots. The large number of reporters and media personnel created logistical and safety concerns (p. 65) for Baltimore Police Department’s Officers responding to the violence.

The presence of such large numbers of media created other problems, such as the self-generation of news by the media. This was especially a problem after the declaration of a state of emergency, when Captain Eric Kowalczyk, a Baltimore Police Department Public Information Officer, stated that owing to the large number of news agencies and the need for a story related to the riots, the information contained in same news article “was, at times, inconsistent with information that [the] BPD [had] provided” (p. 66).

To alleviate this and to ensure that information was made available to the community, the Baltimore Police Department embedded a local reporter with the team that was investigating the death of Freddie Gray (p. 65). Having a reporter present with the investigative team ensured that there was transparency in the investigation process and with the information released to the media (p. 65).

The media relations section of the Baltimore Police Department made use of social media to provide the public with updates about the demonstrations. The use of social media was designed to dispel rumors and false statements and to provide transparency in disseminating information (p. 65). Communication was channelled through Twitter and YouTube so that any information that was distributed was clear and accurate (p. 66). The Police Executive Research Forum (2015) estimated that the number of followers of the Baltimore Police Department’s Twitter account “increased by more than 50 percent, from about 80,000 to 126,000, during the unrest” (p. 66).

The Baltimore Police Department did not appoint an executive who could answer the inquiries made by the media. A Public Information Officer position was identified within the structure of the National Incident Management System, but an officer was not appointed. As a result of not filling the role, the media relations section had to gather information from various sources from within the command center. This resulted in a slow media inquiry process and a build-up of inquiries occurring (p. 65).

The slow response to media inquiries was exacerbated by the number of staff assigned to the media relations section. A captain, a sergeant, and a detective normally staffed this section and on April 25 another detective was appointed to work in this section (p. 65). However, even with the addition of the detective, it was not possible to handle all of the inquiries, which the Baltimore Police Department estimated to be greater than 100 per hour at times (p. 65). Because there were not enough people working in this area, the section reacted to the media rather than proactively releasing information (p. 65).

7.4.11 Community Engagement

Even though the Police Executive Research Forum (2015) and the news articles did not discuss the relationship that the police had with the community in Baltimore, it appears that there was a relationship. The only comment about the relationship between the police and the community that was written in the Forum report was that this was "an ongoing process, especially in times of difficulty" (p. 69). The Forum went on to state that the Baltimore Police Department attempted to reach out to the community during the unrest (p. 69) but they did not elucidate the comment. It is assumed that the Baltimore Police Department contacted community leaders and groups to seek assistance and advice.

Although the demonstrations and the subsequent riots and the death of a member of the public were a result of excessive use of force by Baltimore Police Department Officers, the Baltimore community, including the city's ethnic and minority communities continued to show their support for the Baltimore Police Department (p. 68). This support was displayed even when the Baltimore Police Department responded to the riots and the violence (p. 68). The Police Executive Research Forum (2015) claimed that the support for the Baltimore Police Department was demonstrated by the members of the community coming together and that one of the best examples of this was presented on April 28 at the Mondawmin Mall (p. 68). At the Mondawmin Mall, a number of members of the 300 Men March organization formed a barrier between the police and demonstrators in the hope of easing tensions and restoring the peace (p. 68). The Baltimore Police Department believed that these actions helped prevent further violence from occurring (p. 68).

Support was also demonstrated in other parts of the city where members of the community assisted the Baltimore Police Department in protecting their communities from any potential riots (p. 68). One example of this was in the South Baltimore neighborhood of Cherry Hill, where members of the community joined together to protect their shopping center because the police officers who are normally assigned to the southern district were deployed elsewhere (p. 69).

7.4.12 Concluding Comments

According to the Commissioner of the Baltimore Police Department, in an interview following the April 2015 riots, "it was apparent early on in the unrest that we [the Baltimore Police Department) were dealing with an historic event" (quoted in Snyder, 2016). The scale of the rioting and violence that occurred during April 2015, "was unlike anything the city had seen since the civil unrest that occurred in 1968" (p. 7). The intensity of rioting was not expected by the city officials or the Baltimore Police Department and that which was experienced "would stress the resources of any police agency" (p. 7). The Police Executive Research Forum (2015) claimed that as a result of the demands placed on the Baltimore Police Department in responding to the riots, Baltimore Police Department staff members were stretched to their limits (p. 7).

Although many of the challenges and problems occurred at the beginning of the riots, as the rioting continued, the response of the Baltimore Police Department improved. Improvements in the response occurred even though all leave was cancelled and 12-h shifts had been implemented (p. 7).

7.5 Discussion

The chronology of the Baltimore April 2015 riots and the critique of the Baltimore Police Department response portrays a police agency that was mismanaged and close to crisis. Weaknesses in the organization of the Baltimore Police Department contributed to the cause of the riots and there were also a number of structural and systemic failures in its leadership and community outreach. The Baltimore Police Department appeared to be an agency that had not adopted community policing or any of the other major initiatives or strategies that had been implemented by the majority of other larger-sized city police agencies. It appears that the Baltimore Police Department had become run down owing to the austerity measures that local government agencies had to implement in 2008 and because the senior executive did not know how to reform the agency so that it could meet the challenges of modern policing. It seems that the Baltimore Police Department did not learn anything from the Ferguson 2014 riots, despite having sent a number of senior officers to Ferguson to learn from their experiences of policing large-scale disorder (Gass, 2015).

How the Baltimore Police Department responded to the riots and the weaknesses in their systems and structures were highlighted in a review conducted by the United States Department of Justice (2016). The Police Executive Research Forum (2015) reinforced the observations of the Department of Justice. According to the United States Department of Justice (2016), the failures experienced by the Baltimore Police Department were systemic, structural, constitutional and statutory. The department claimed that the "pattern or practice" of the Baltimore Police Department "is driven by systemic deficiencies" in their "policies, training, supervision, and accountability systems and structures" (2016, pp. 3, 10). The Department of Justice report determined that the Baltimore Police Department had failed to engage with the community and did not provide their officers with the resources necessary to deliver policing services to their community (United States Department of Justice, 2016, pp. 3, 10).

An independent review of the Baltimore Police Department response to the April 2015 riots that was undertaken by the Police Executive Research Forum reinforced the view that the Department of Justice took. The independent review found two main weaknesses with the response taken by the Baltimore Police Department. The first was that there were "major shortcomings" in the agency, their planning (Calvert, 2015) and their response (Gately & Stolberg, 2015). The second weakness was that the Baltimore Police Department Officers "were unprepared and untrained for the scale and scope of the unrest" (Gately & Stolberg, 2015). Gately and Stolberg (2015) also claimed that the review found that the Baltimore Police Department "had been gathering intelligence about a possible protest for about a week before April 25, but failed to follow federal guidelines that called for police agencies to develop systematic plans."

The Police Executive Research Forum (2015) review found that after the riots, the Baltimore Police Department had implemented a number of initiatives to improve their response to critical incidents (p. 6). These included all officers having to attend an 8-h course on basic civil disorder response tactics and six platoons of officers attending advanced mobile field force technique training. Training in the use of and the implementation of the National Incident Management System was also delivered and a multi-agency training program has since been introduced (pp. 6–7).

A third report about the response of the Baltimore Police Department to the riots was documented by the Baltimore City Fraternal Order of the Police Lodge #3. The Police Lodge #3 is a union for the police officers of the Baltimore Police Department and represents its own interests. The report was based on the views of members of focus groups, which comprise of Baltimore Police Department Officers and on the results of a survey of the officers who were deployed during the riots. The objective of the review was "to highlight the strengths and weaknesses of the Baltimore Police Department's response to the riots in order that its member officers can be better prepared to protect citizens, property and themselves should events such as those that occurred from April 12, 2015 to May 3, 2015 ever occur again" (Baltimore City Fraternal Order of Police Lodge #3, 2015, p. 3). The majority of the focus group members and the survey participants disclosed that they had received 1 day of riot/civil disorder training as a recruit at the police academy, while other members had only received one-half hour of training at the in-service training sessions (Baltimore City Fraternal Order of Police Lodge #3, 2015, p. 19). Even though the findings of the Police Lodge #3 review are similar to the findings of the Department of Justice and the Police Executive Research Forum reviews, they are more practically focused.

The Police Lodge #3 review found a number of weaknesses in the Baltimore Police Department's response to the riots. The first was that the majority of the Baltimore Police Department Officers who were deployed during the riots were not adequately equipped or trained and did not receive adequate direction from senior command staff (Baltimore City Fraternal Order of Police Lodge #3, 2015, p. 3). The lack of leadership, according to the Police Lodge #3, included a "passive response" to the civil disorder, which "allowed the disorder to grow into full scale rioting" (Baltimore City Fraternal Order of Police Lodge #3, 2015, p. 3). The Police Lodge #3 went on to identify a further six areas of weakness in the Baltimore Police Department: leadership, equipment, training, tactical, communications and the Incident Command System (ICF) model (p. 7). The report discusses each of these areas in detail.

It is interesting to note that the Baltimore City officials stated that they were not surprised by the findings of the reports (Gately & Stolberg, 2015). According to Gately and Stolberg (2015), the Mayor of Baltimore and the Commissioner of the Baltimore Police Department said at a press conference "that the report 'mirrored' their own assessment of deficiencies in training, command structure and equipment." The Commissioner went on to say "[w]e didn't have those experiences under our belt," and "[w]e do now and we're better prepared." These statements were made even though the riots were the worst riots that Baltimore had experienced since the 1968 assassination of the Reverend. Dr. Martin Luther King Junior riots (Gately & Stolberg, 2015).

The statements made by the Commissioner of the Baltimore Police Department and the mayor do not absolve the actions that they took during the riots. In fact, their comments do the opposite. While the Baltimore Police Department may have implemented a number of training programs since the riots, they have not addressed the systemic and structural weaknesses of the agency. The Commissioner of the Baltimore Police Department who made these statements was appointed Commissioner after the riots had finished but had been an executive member of the Baltimore Police Department for some time prior to the riots occurring. This implies that he knew of the structural and operational weakness of the Baltimore Police Department and this places his leadership and accountability with the Baltimore Police Department into question.

These views are supported by the Baltimore Police Department Commissioner who made comments at the Baltimore City Fraternal Order of Police Lodge #3 membership meeting on May 26. The Baltimore Police Department Commissioner indicated that he knew that rioting would eventually occur in Baltimore (p. 13). The Commissioner also admitted that he "failed to train and prepare the Baltimore Police Department and that each officer should have been apprised of the mission objectives and tactical orders before being deployed" (p. 13). If the Commissioner, who was a senior operational police officer prior to and during the riots knew of these weaknesses then this implies that the Baltimore Police Department executive should have rectified these issues prior to the riots occurring. The comments made by the Commissioner raise further questions as to the competency of the executive of the Baltimore Police Department and whether their capability to respond to a riot similar to that which occurred in April 2015 has improved.

The weaknesses in leadership during the response of the riots was not limited to the Baltimore Police Department but also included Baltimore City officials and the mayor. In a media conference which was held after the first riot on Saturday April 25, the mayor said when referring to the rioters, "we also gave those who wished to destroy space to do that as well." (Baltimore City Fraternal Order of Police Lodge #3, 2015, p. 7). Such comments display poor judgment in leading a multi-agency response in a crisis and raises questions as to the influence the mayor had on the response taken by the Baltimore Police Department to the riots. According to the Police Lodge #3, the mayor and the mayor's staff were involved in making critical decisions about the response. The Lodge claimed that the influence that the mayor had in the Baltimore Police Department response was seen clearly from a May 10, 2015 Washington Post article that stated that the mayor received phone calls about the incident at the Mondawmin Mall, including a call from her adviser who was at the mall (Baltimore City Fraternal Order of Police Lodge #3, 2015) when the violence started.

A further weakness in the leadership of the Baltimore Police Department relates to the level of control provided by the command center that was established at the police headquarters. The problems at the center resulted primarily from the large number of people working from it. There were approximately 100 people working out of a room that was designed to hold 30–40 people and it was noisy, which created confusion. Many of those responsible for specific response functions did not have access to a work space or networked computer (Gately & Stolberg, 2015; Police Executive Research Forum, 2015). These issues created logistical challenges in co-ordinating the aid provided by other agencies (Gately & Stolberg, 2015) and it was not possible for the command team to be fully briefed on the rioting incidents as they occurred (Police Executive Research Forum, 2015).

The command center was not able to guide the deployed officers on whether to make arrests, especially in relation to enforcing the curfew (Gately & Stolberg, 2015; Police Executive Research Forum, 2015). This compounded the confusing information that the officers had received earlier, which related to the approach that they were expected to take when responding to the riots. Officers had received orders on April 25, from the Commissioner of the Baltimore Police Department not to engage with any of the protesters but "to allow the protesters room to destroy and allow the destruction of property so that the rioters would appear to be the aggressors" (Baltimore City Fraternal Order of Police Lodge #3, 2015, p. 7). Officers were also told at this meeting by command staff "to report to work in their regular uniforms, without gloves or helmets, and to take a 'soft approach' when handling demonstrations" (Calvert, 2015; Gately & Stolberg, 2015).

Not deploying staff in protective riot equipment at the beginning of a potentially violent incident is a strategy commonly adopted and is regarded as being the best practice (p. 39). However, this strategy requires a successful implementation of an operational plan. The operational plan provides information as to the role of the officers who have been deployed without protective equipment and once donned, when they will use their equipment. It also provides for the deployment of a contingency of officers who have been fitted with protective equipment to be positioned near to the site of where violent incidents may take place.

The weakness in the approach taken by the Baltimore Police Department was that they did not provide for or advise the deployed officers of either of these tactics during the meeting held on April 24. When leading the preparation for a civil disorder, it is most important that the reasons for the orders given are communicated to those officers who will be facing the demonstrators (p. 40). The style of the leadership used should ensure that delegation has been made to the commanders deployed to the incident. They will know about the disorder as it is developing and will be able to communicate the need for officers to don their protective equipment when required, without any headquarter elements being involved in the decision-making. Delegating responsibility to the commanders should also include the ability of both commanders and officers being able to make decisions about arresting rioters and offenders, especially when it relates to curfew breaches and looting. Commanders should not need to obtain authorization from a command center or from legal advisors as to whether to make an arrest. Seeking legal advice undermines the office of a police officer and delivers a precedent that is not acceptable while a riot is taking place and nor does it promote professional policing.

Clarifying and communicating the reasons for the directions and orders given should also apply to definitions of the terminology used, especially when a response operation includes a number of agencies. During the response to the riots by the Baltimore Police Department, there were instances of uncertainty of the meaning of some of the terminology used by the commanders, especially in relation to maintaining the skirmish lines (Calvert, 2015). Commanders were using terms such as "stand down," "stand by," and "hold the line" in error. The uncertainty placed Baltimore Police Department Officers and officers from other agencies in danger.

7.5.1 *Exercising*

One of the major weaknesses in the Baltimore Police Department response to the riots was a lack of understanding of the National Incident Management System by officers at all levels. The officers did not understand the functions and the roles set out in the National Incident Management System and how it would be implemented during an incident to ensure a coordinated response. The principal method to ensure that all staff understand the response processes and frameworks of an agency is to exercise the agency by using a range of event or incident scenarios.

The Baltimore Police Department and the majority of police agencies do not respond to large-sized riots often and as a result, have tended to concentrate "on more immediate concerns, such as increasing violent crime rates," rather than developing the capability to respond to incidents that occur infrequently and without warning (p. 3). Using a method to prioritize or determine the level of risk involved when making management decisions at the expense of not undertaking regular training and the exercising of organized response frameworks, such as the National Incident Management System and in the use of high-end policing/paramilitary response structures creates a deficiency in the understanding of the processes and how an agency should respond to an incident. The Baltimore Police Department Executive chose to manage their organization in this manner. Another factor, unfortunately, is that the Baltimore Police Department did not have any institutional memory, as they had not experienced a need to respond to a high-end policing incident, such as a riot and they did not see the need to train or exercise for such an event.

The need for police agencies to understand and exercise their response was emphasized by the Police Executive Research Forum (2015), who claimed that the Baltimore Police Department's "experience [in responding to the April 2015 riots] demonstrates that agencies must be prepared for all types of incidents" (p. 3). Furthermore, as the Forum (2015) stated, one of the major lessons from the Baltimore riots was the need to provide training to commanders by simulating the different scenarios that they may encounter during a riot (p. 6). It should be emphasized that the response commanders should not only be trained in various scenarios pertaining to riots but also in various scenarios that pertain to any high-end policing event. Having this knowledge will ensure that commanders have the capability and understanding to lead their agency's response to any major incident.

7.5.2 *Mutual Aid*

Another problem with the response to the riots was the co-ordination and management of mutual aid and the agencies deployed under mutual aid agreements. According to the media company RT (2015), the role that the mutual aid officers were to perform was not clear. As the Police Executive Research Forum (2015) emphasized, there are various models available that demonstrate how external agencies can be integrated when responding to a large incident (p. 43). It appears that because the Baltimore Police Department were using a number of different forms of mutual aid agreements as well as the Baltimore Regional Emergency Assistance Compact. There was confusion as to what an agency had agreed to under their individual agreement or Memorandum of Understanding.

In some mutual aid models, the agency that makes the request for assistance takes the lead during the operation and the arrest process, while mutual aid agencies are deployed to secure the perimeters. In other models the capabilities of the mutual aid agencies are assessed prior to their deployment (p. 43). As an example, all mutual aid agencies are assessed as to their capabilities and the resources that they have, in particular, resources such as SWAT or mobile field force and are then deployed to a role that suits its capabilities (p. 43). A third model is where mutual aid agencies "take a more active role" in the response, especially at the tactical level (p. 43). It was this third model, according to the Police Executive Research Forum (2015), that a number of Baltimore Police Department Commanders preferred, as a number of the mutual aid agencies had more experience in the use of less-than-lethal munitions (p. 43).

Best practice calls for a pre-deployment briefing to be held before the planning meeting and prior to the event. This would ensure that all agencies have the same understanding of the difficulties that are involved in the planned response and their role in the response (p. 43). A planning meeting and a pre-deployment briefing should include the communication of a clear operating strategy (p. 44) and a process for assessing the capabilities of each mutual aid agency. This process would then enable the responding agency to develop a detailed operational plan (or operational instruction/order) that identifies how each mutual aid agency would support the capabilities of the responding agency and the specific role that the mutual aid agency has been delegated to. The plan would allow for any limitations in the ability of mutual aid agencies to assist and would ensure that that the expectations of these agencies are met (p. 44).

Another advantage of holding a planning meeting is that it gives the responding agency the ability to detail the resources that it needs for the response and to make its request to mutual aid agencies. The responding agency would be able to convey the seriousness of the event and would be able to specify the skill level of the officers to be deployed by the mutual aid agency (p. 44). This approach can improve the coordination of the response and would ensure that the responding agency's planners have knowledge of the capabilities of those deployed from mutual aid agencies. This would provide insight for the planners so that they may match the skills of the officers being deployed to a specific incident site or event.

A further recommendation that will ensure the smooth deployment and coordination of mutual aid resources is to embed a senior officer from the mutual aid agency in the responding agency's command center and another of their senior officers with the deployed officers (p. 48). According to the Police Executive Research Forum (2015), implementing this two-pronged method would ensure that the command center was aware of the capabilities of the mutual aid agencies and would allow the lead agency to communicate with the mutual aid agencies (p. 48).

The final point in relation to mutual aid is that of timing. Officials will usually delay or exercise caution in requesting assistance from mutual aid agencies or the National Guard, especially if they are a small agency as they lose some control when they ask for assistance or activate their mutual aid processes (p. 6). The National Guard, for example, have their own use-of-force policy when they are supporting local police agencies (p. 6), while larger mutual aid police agencies may seek to take command of the response if the responding agency is not in control of the incident.

7.5.3 Mutual Aid Agreements

When police agencies are developing mutual aid agreements there are a number of factors that should be considered if the overall police response to an incident or event is to be well coordinated and managed effectively. The mutual aid agreement must, for example, clearly articulate the reasons for the various levels of response that each agency should undertake and should specify the command structure, the skills of the personnel and the equipment to be used (p. 51).

The last factor that needs to be considered when developing a mutual aid agreement is to what extent mutual aid agencies can enforce the laws in the host agency's jurisdiction (p. 51). The agreement needs to clearly specify the legal authority of each of the mutual aid agencies. A lack of clarity regarding the legal authority of mutual aid agencies was one of the problems experienced during the response to the April 2015 riots and this created difficulties for outside agencies during their tactical operations (p. 51).

7.5.4 Media

Although the Baltimore Police Department implemented a number of initiatives to manage the media during the riots, one of the major challenges for the public information section was the level of staffing. Not having an appropriate level of staffing to handle media inquiries can have an adverse impact on an operation and on the reputation of a police agency (p. 65). During a large incident event such as a riot, to ensure that the police agency perspective is seen by the community, the agency needs to be able to get information to the media and onto social media channels in a timely manner (p. 66). This will ensure that the agency is being transparent and that their view is included in any news item. The release of timely information can quell any rumors and inaccurate information from circulating (p. 66).

The actual level of staffing needed for the public information section during an incident will depend on the seriousness and the scale of an incident. An agency should have a process in place to increase the staffing levels should it become necessary (p. 66). One approach to managing the public information section is for the agency to be proactive in managing information. This can be achieved by posting information on-line for news media organizations to use (p. 67). Reporters will receive the information quickly as the information can be posted online, in real time (p. 67).

7.5.5 Community

The relationship of the Baltimore Police Department with the community has not been discussed in any of the three reports that were prepared after the April 2015 riots. Although a number of newspaper reports that covered the riots included statements from various members of the community covering specific grievances, there is no literature available that analyzed the relationship of the Baltimore Police Department with the community and whether it was effective. As the Police Executive Research Forum (2015) highlighted, a police relationship with the community has many facets (p. 70), some of which may not be readily apparent to the outside observer. As was seen during the riots, even when the African American community was upset by the actions of the Baltimore Police Department in regard to their handling of Mr. Gray during and following his arrest, they showed their support for the Baltimore Police Department when there was a risk of violence occurring in their neighborhoods (p. 70). Police agencies cannot be successful in what they do without the support from their communities (p. 68), which means that the most important thing for a police agency to do is to ensure that they build and maintain relationships with their minority communities.

7.5.6 Concluding Comments

As discussed in this section of the case study, there were many "major shortcomings" in how the Baltimore Police Department responded to the April 2015 riots (Gass, 2015), and although the Baltimore Police Department has taken some steps to rectify their weaknesses, these steps have been of a low level and the Baltimore Police Department needs to take a more strategic approach in preparing the agency to ensure that it can respond effectively to any major or critical incidents. There are also lessons to be learnt by other police agencies in relation to the experience of the Baltimore Police Department and they need to ensure that they are maintaining the training and capability within their agency so that they too can respond to large-scale critical incidents as it appears that mass protests now seem to routinely follow controversial police actions (Gass, 2015).

7.6 Conclusion

According to Graham (2015), there is a scripted arc to community disorder and violence. This takes the form of citizens getting angry, tensions building until they boil over, violence erupting, people returning home and the city then cleans up. This is the order in which riots have occurred across the USA in the past. However, the riots in Baltimore during April 2015, did not follow this pattern (Graham, 2015). Baltimore was different because there appeared to be a peaceful anger for 2 weeks following the death of Mr. Gray, "punctuated only by two moments of destruction" (Graham, 2015); Saturday April 25 and Monday April 27. In the context of the arc, the riots of Monday April 27, were an avoidable tragedy that need not have occurred "had city officials made different decisions" (Graham, 2015) prior to its occurrence. The reason that the riots occurred on Monday was the result of a number of errors made by the Baltimore Police Department and the city authorities; the first being the reaction of the Baltimore Police Department to the "purge" text and the second being the closing of the Mondawmin Mall.

Graham's (2015) perspective of the Monday April 27 riot was that the riots were a result of a series of incorrect decisions or decisions not being made. A critique of the Baltimore Police Department response to the April 2015 riots identified a series of weaknesses in the planning, co-ordination and management of mutual aid agencies and also in the training provided, the equipment made available, leadership and communication. The major weakness was, however, the decisions that the Baltimore Police Department made, leading to and during the riots. The Baltimore Police Department was the agency that was responsible for providing leadership during the response but owing to the number of systemic weaknesses in the organization, failed to do so. Lopez (2016) took a stronger view and described the Baltimore Police Department as "a complete and utter disaster." Lopez (2016), who was the author of the United States Department of Justice's report into the Baltimore Police Department following the April 2015 riots, claimed that there were "major flaws" in the Baltimore Police Department's "most basic modern policing practices, from arrests to use of force to basic interactions with the community."

In addition to the weak leadership within the department, there was also a lack of experience in responding to large and violent protests. This resulted in a lack of understanding and an inability to implement the National Incident Management System. This stemmed from a lack of practice in implementing the National Incident Management System and this hampered the initial response to the civil disorder. Despite this, as the riots progressed, the Baltimore Police Department appeared to be able to use the National Incident Management System effectively.

The response to the April 2015 riots by the Baltimore Police Department highlighted the need for an even larger-sized city police agency and the establishment of a structured pre-operational planning process which would include a schedule of meetings to be held, the planning and deployment documentation needed and the development of a communications framework. The process should include an established, documented mutual aid procedure that is based on agreements or Memorandums of Understanding that clearly state the trigger points for the activation of such agreements and how the supporting agencies would be deployed. The mutual aid agreements should also identify how each agency fits into the command response structure.

The principal challenge for the Baltimore Police Department in moving forward is learning from the experience of the April 2015 riots. The Police Executive Research Forum (2015) claim that the Baltimore Police Department have implemented a number of the lessons that were learnt from the riots. Programs that addressed the deficiencies consist of a 1-day training course in the management of the response to a critical incident. While this may be the first step in developing the capability of the agency, it does not address the structural problems that are at the center of the weaknesses in the Baltimore Police Department, which became apparent during the response to the riots. The Baltimore Police Department Executive need to address how the agency should be led and determine the processes to be used for making and implementing strategic decisions. Finally, it must ensure that a community policing relationship with the African American community is developed and maintained and that it provides for the African American voice to be heard as part of the policing in Baltimore.

References

ABC News. (2015, April 27). *Freddie Gray funeral held amid alleged credible threat to law enforcement*. Retrieved from http://abcnews.go.com/US/freddie-gray-funeral-held-amid-alleged-credible-threat/story?id=30610298.

Akhtar, A. (2015, May 4). *Ann Arbor community members protest police brutality*. The Michigan Daily. Retrieved from https://www.michigandaily.com/news/ferguson-protest/.

Al Jazeera America. (2015, April 29). *Second night of Baltimore curfew arrives quietly*. Retrieved from http://america.aljazeera.com/articles/2015/4/29/baltimore-schools-set-to-reopen-after-quiet-night.html.

Associated Press. (2015a, April 28). *Latest on police-custody death: Governor promises peace*. Retrieved from https://web.archive.org/web/20150428170503/http://www.apnewsarchive.com/2015/The-latest-on-Baltimore-police-custody-death-More-than-150-fires-in-Baltimore-city-says/id-0b32a37d8b0440b8a444403f5c7ad647.

Associated Press. (2015b, April 29). *Latest on police custody death: Court waits could increase*. Retrieved from http://www.dailymail.co.uk/wires/ap/article-3058933/Latest-police-custody-death-City-cleans-riots.html.

Bacon, J., & Welsh, W. (2015, April 27). *Baltimore police, protesters clash; 15 officers hurt*. USA Today, Retrieved from http://www.usatoday.com/story/news/nation/2015/04/27/baltimore-credible-threat/26454875/.

Baltimore City Fraternal Order of Police Lodge #3. (2015). *After action review: A review of the management of the 2015 Baltimore riots*. Retrieved from http://www.fop3.org/wp-content/uploads/2015/07/AAR-Final.pdf.

Breitbart News. (2015, April 27). *Baltimore officers injured after high schoolers call for purge*. Retrieved from http://www.breitbart.com/big-government/2015/04/27/live-updates-baltimore-officers-injured-after-high-schoolers-call-for-purge/.

Brodey, S., & McLaughlin, J. (2015). *Eyewitness: The Baltimore riots didn't start the way you think*. Mother Jones, April 28. Retrieved from http://www.motherjones.com/politics/2015/04/how-baltimore-riots-began-mondawmin-purge.

Calvert, S. (2015, November 16). *Report cites bad planning, confusion in Baltimore Police response to unrest*. The Wall Street Journal. Retrieved from http://www.wsj.com/articles/reportcites-bad-planning-confusion-in-baltimore-police-response-to-unrest-1447691183.

CBS News. (2015, April 25). *Baltimore mayor: Gave those who wish to destroy space to do that*. Retrieved from http://baltimore.cbslocal.com/2015/04/25/baltimore-mayor-gave-those-who-wished-to-destroy-space-to-do-that/.

CBS Philly. (2015, April 30). *Rally, march held in Philadelphia in solidarity with Baltimore protests*. Retrieved from http://philadelphia.cbslocal.com/2015/04/30/rally-planned-at-philadelphia-city-hall-in-solidarity-with-baltimore-protests/.

Dance, S., & Kaltenbach, C. (2015, May 3). *Baltimore moves on as curfew is lifted, National Guard leaves*. The Baltimore Sun. Retrieved from http://www.baltimoresun.com/news/maryland/baltimore-city/bs-md-ci-curfew-lifted-20150503-story.html#page=1.

Department of Homeland Security. (2008). *National Management Incident System*. Retrieved from https://www.fema.gov/pdf/emergency/nims/NIMS_core.pdf.

Ellis, R., Payne, E., & St. Claire, P. (2015, May 1). *In Philadelphia, police clash with supporters of Baltimore protests*. CNN. Retrieved from http://edition.cnn.com/2015/04/30/us/nationwide-freddie-gray-protests/.

Fenton, J. (2015a, April 18). *Hundreds at Baltimore police station protest over man's injuries during arrest*. The Baltimore Sun. Retrieved from http://www.baltimoresun.com/news/maryland/bs-md-shooting-20150418-story.html.

Fenton, J. (2015b, May 11). *Mayor's authority to impose curfew questioned*. The Baltimore Sun. Retrieved from http://www.baltimoresun.com/news/maryland/politics/bs-md-ci-mayor-curfew-authority-20150511-story.html.

Fiammetta, I. (2015). *Fans asked to stay inside Camden Yards due to Baltimore protests*. Sports Illustrated, April 25. Retrieved from: https://www.si.com/mlb/2015/04/25/baltimore-protests-orioles-camden-yards-fans-remain-inside.

Fox 17 West Michigan. (2015, April 28). *Baltimore riots: Security beefed up, cleanup starts after looting, fires*. Retrieved from http://fox17online.com/2015/04/28/baltimore-riots-security-beefed-up-cleanup-starts-after-looting-fires/.

Fuchs, E. (2015, April 28). *A confrontation between cops and teenagers kicked off the horrifying Baltimore riots*. Business Insider. Retrieved from https://www.businessinsider.com.au/confrontation-at-mondawmin-mall-led-2015-4?r=US&IR=T.

Gass, H. (2015, November 17). *Baltimore riots report: Police must train for 'large-scale critical incidents*. The Christian Science Monitor. Retrieved from: http://www.csmonitor.com/USA/Justice/2015/1117/Baltimore-riots-report-Police-must-train-for-large-scale-critical-incidents.

Gately, G., & Stolberg. S. (2015). *Baltimore police assailed for response after Freddie Gray's death*. Retrieved February 16, 2016, from http://www.nytimes.com/2015/11/17/us/baltimore-police-assailed-for-response-after-freddie-grays-death.html?_r=0.

Goldsmith, A. (2015, April 29). *Albuquerque's Baltimore protests stay peaceful*. Fox KRQE News. Retrieved from http://krqe.com/2015/04/29/albuquerques-baltimore-protests-stay-peaceful/.

Graham, D. (2015, April 30). *The Baltimore riot didn't have to happen*. The Atlantic. Retrieved from http://www.theatlantic.com/politics/archive/2015/04/the-baltimore-riots-that-didnt-happen/391931/.

Hannigan, W. (2015). *As Baltimore curfew ends, celebratory crowds peacefully gather*. Los Angeles Times, May 3. Retrieved from: http://www.latimes.com/nation/la-na-baltimore-lifts-curfew-20150503-story.html.

Harris, K. (2015, April 27). *Rawlings-Blake administration issues statement regarding mayor's comments on rights of protesters*. Retrieved from http://content.govdelivery.com/accounts/MDBALT/bulletins/10158de.

Hay Brown, M. (2015, April 27). *Maryland State Police activating 500 officers for Baltimore: Requesting up 5,000 from neighboring states*. Tweet via Twitter. Retrieved from https://twitter.com/matthewhaybrown.

Ileto, C. (2015, April 23). *Police make arrests: Protests continue over Freddie Gray's death*. Retrieved from http://baltimore.cbslocal.com/2015/04/23/5th-day-of-protests-in-freddie-grays-death-expected/.

Inquistr. (2015, April 28). *Baltimore purge: Flyers imitating the purge reported called for violence, contributed to riots*. Retrieved from http://www.inquisitr.com/2048326/baltimore-purge-flyers-reportedly-called-for-violence/.

Lacitis, E., & Cornwell, P. (2015, April 29). *Seattle demonstrators support protests in Baltimore*. The Seattle Times. Retrieved from http://www.seattletimes.com/seattle-news/seattle-demonstrators-support-protests-in-baltimore/.

Laughland,O.,Lewis,P.,Jacobs,B.,&Swaine,J.(2015,April27).*Baltimorestateofemergencydeclared as Freddie Gray protesters clash with police*. The Guardian. Retrieved from https://www.theguardian.com/us-news/live/2015/apr/27/baltimore-police-clash-protesters-freddie-gray-live.

Lopez, G. (2016, August 10). *The Justice Department's incredibly damning report on Baltimore police, explained*. Retrieved from http://www.vox.com/2016/8/10/12418428/baltimore-police-investigation-justice-department-report.

Maher, K., & Palazzolo, J. (2015, April 30). *Protests resume in Baltimore with hundreds marching on city hall*. The Wall Street Journal. Retrieved from https://www.wsj.com/articles/baltimore-streets-quiet-as-residents-obey-curfew-after-riots-1430302760.

Marbella, J. (2015, October 23). *The day the Baltimore riots erupted: New details of Baltimore riots after Freddie Gray's death*. The Baltimore Sun. Retrieved from http://www.baltimoresun.com/news/maryland/freddie-gray/bs-md-freddie-gray-april27-20151022-story.html.

Marquez, M., & Almasy, S. (2015, April 25). *Freddie Gray death: 12 arrested during protests*. CNN. Retrieved from http://edition.cnn.com/2015/04/25/us/baltimore-freddie-gray-protest/index.html.

Maryland Coordination and Analysis Center (2017). *Our mission*. Retrieved from http://www.mcac.maryland.gov/about_mcac/our_mission/.

Molinet, J., Stephasky, J., & Bult, L. (2015, April 30). *Protesters clash with NYPD, disrupt Holland Tunnel and West Side Highway in bid to support Baltimore activists*. Daily News New York. Retrieved from http://www.nydailynews.com/new-york/nyc-protests-disrupt-holland-tunnel-west-side-highway-article-1.2204282.

NBC4 Washington. (2015, April 29). *Demonstrators take to DC streets, support Baltimore protest*. Retrieved from http://www.nbcwashington.com/news/local/301761001.html.

Nuckols, B., & Dishneau, D. (2015, May 4). *Baltimore mayor lifts curfew 6 after riots*. Associated Press. Retrieved from http://bigstory.ap.org/article/b7d01c00ffd64ce9b0caa0925b424193/baltimore-relieved-charges-weary-curfew.

Oppel, R. (2015, June 12). *West Baltimore's police presence drops and murders soar*. The New York Times. Retrieved from https://www.nytimes.com/2015/06/13/us/after-freddie-gray-death-west-baltimores-police-presence-drops-and-murders-soar.html?ref=todayspaper&_r=4.

Pinard, M. (2015). Poor, black and 'wanted': Criminal justice in Ferguson and Baltimore. *Howard Law Journal, 58*(3), 1–16.

Police Executive Research Forum. (2015). *Lessons learned from the 2015 civil unrest in Baltimore. September*. Washington, DC: Police Executive Research Forum.

Raddatz, K. (2015, April 29). *#BlackLivesMatter protesters march through Minneapolis*. CBS Minnesota. Retrieved from http://minnesota.cbslocal.com/2015/04/29/blacklivesmatter-to-protest-at-gold-medal-park/.

Rector, K., Dance, S., & Broadwater, L. (2015). *Riots erupt: Baltimore descends into chaos, violence, looting*. Retrieved from http://www.baltimoresun.com/news/maryland/freddie-gray/bs-md-ci-police-student-violence-20150427-story.html.

RT. (2015, November 17). *Baltimore police were not ready for Freddie Gray riots – Report*. Retrieved 2016 from https://www.rt.com/usa/322477-baltimore-police-gray-response/.

Rubino, J., & Frank, J. (2015, April 29). *Police use pepper spray on downtown protesters*. The Denver Post. Retrieved from http://www.denverpost.com/2015/04/29/denver-police-use-pepper-spray-on-downtown-protesters-11-arrested/.

Schabner, D. (2015, May 3). *After victory rally, arrests made of violators of Baltimore curfew*. Retrieved from http://abcnews.go.com/US/victory-rally-arrests-made-violators-baltimore-curfew/story?id=30761806.

Snyder, R. (2016, April 28). *One year later: Looking back at the Baltimore riots*. Retrieved from http://www.wbaltv.com/article/one-year-later-looking-back-at-the-baltimore-riots/7100345.

Stolberg, S., & Babcock, S. (2015, April 25). *Scenes of chaos in Baltimore as thousands protest Freddie Gray's death*. New York Times. Retrieved from http://www.nytimes.com/2015/04/26/us/baltimore-crowd-swells-in-protest-of-freddie-grays-death.html.

The Mercury News. (2015, April 27). *Oakland: Protesters marching in solidarity with Baltimore told to disperse late Monday*. Retrieved from http://www.mercurynews.com/2015/04/27/oakland-protesters-marching-in-solidarity-with-baltimore-told-to-disperse-late-monday/.

Toppa, S. (2015, May 14). *The Baltimore riots cost an estimated $9 million in damages*. Time. Retrieved from http://time.com/3858181/baltimore-riots-damages-businesses-homes-freddie-gray/.

United States Census Bureau. (2017). *State & county quick facts*. Retrieved from: https://www.census.gov/quickfacts/table/PST045216/00.

United States Department of Justice. (2016). *Investigation of the Baltimore City Police Department*. Civil Rights Division, August 10. Washington, DC: US Department of Justice.

Wenger, Y. (2015, May 13). *Damage to businesses from Baltimore rioting estimated at about $9 million*. The Washington Post. Retrieved from https://www.washingtonpost.com/local/damage-to-businesses-from-baltimore-rioting-estimated-at-9-million/2015/05/13/5848c3fe-f9a8-11e4-a13c-193b1241d51a_story.html?utm_term=.58d5244df350.

WMAR Staff. (2015, April 28). *Concerns over violence leads to area closings in Baltimore*. WMAR Baltimore. Retrieved from http://www.abc2news.com/news/region/baltimore-city/university-of-maryland-baltimore-closing-early.

Wood, P., & Bowie, L. (2015, April 28). *Baltimore county squashes rumors of another purge outside city*. The Baltimore Sun. Retrieved from http://www.baltimoresun.com/news/maryland/baltimore-county/bs-md-co-security-closed-20150428-story.html.

Yan, H., & Ford, D. (2015, April 27). *Baltimore protests turn violent; police injured*. CNN. Retrieved from http://edition.cnn.com/2015/04/27/us/baltimore-unrest/index.html.

Yan, H., Franz, A., & Hutcherson, K. (2015, April 23). *Freddie Gray death: Protesters, police scuffle in Baltimore*. CNN. Retrieved from http://edition.cnn.com/2015/04/23/us/baltimore-freddie-gray-death/index.html.

Chapter 8
The Police Response to Riots: An Analysis of the Case Studies

8.1 Introduction

The occurrence of riots in the USA, the UK, and France are reasonably frequent events, with each of these countries having experienced riots because of racial abuses, increases in taxes and political corruption. The riots that were discussed in the case studies did not occur in isolation in each country but were the culmination of historic, local and national social events, geographic incidents and the political environment. What makes each of the riots discussed in the case studies different from previous riots is their perpetuation and spread, primarily because of policing actions, the reaction of the public, especially in the UK and the USA and the political reaction in each country. The reaction of the community in France was different. There was no reaction by the French community and the political reaction was the opposite of that experienced in the USA and the UK.

The 2005 riots in France were similar, both in catalyst and form to a number of riots that had occurred there since the 1990s—as a result of police actions and the police confronting youth from the banlieues over a number of nights. The youth were confronted because they had caused extensive property damage. When comparing the riots in France to rioting that had occurred in the USA, the riots in the USA were often used as a basis for understanding the cause of the riots (Koff & Duprez, 2009), whereas understanding the cause of a riot has not been a factor in any post-riot discussion or analysis in France. In the American context, research into the understanding of riots has been completed as early as the 1960s. Lieberson and Silverman (1965), for example, analyzed more than 70 race riots that occurred in the USA between 1913 and 1963 and concluded "that the principle causes of these riots were related to the socially inferior position of African Americans in US society, including the importance of social precariousness, marginalization and exclusion" (cited Koff & Duprez, 2009, p. 722). The authors went on to argue that the government and the police were primarily responsible for the occurrence of these riots (Koff & Duprez, 2009). Latter research that was published in the Kenner

G. den Heyer, *Police Response to Riots*,
https://doi.org/10.1007/978-3-030-31810-9_8

Report (National Advisory Commission on Civil Disorders, 1968) supported this assessment. The report called for the police to adopt less aggressive behavior and to change their work habits (National Advisory Commission on Civil Disorders, 1968).

The UK took a similar approach to understanding riots as the USA. The UK witnessed a number of outbreaks of urban violence, many of which have resulted in the documentation of reports that have examined the cause of the riots and that have made recommendations to lessen the chance of rioting occurring in the future. The first major examination as to the reason for the occurrence of riots in the UK was that of the 1981 Brixton riot undertaken in the early 1980s by Lord Scarman and the Home Office (Koff & Duprez, 2009). The research found that riots "occurred in a context of elevated ethnic exclusion and segregation" and that there was a need for the police to increase their recruitment from ethnic and minority communities (Koff & Duprez, 2009, pp. 722–723).

Unlike the USA and the UK, France has not attempted to find social and political resolutions to the problems that caused the riots there in the 1990s or in 2005. Noticeably, French officials have instead, tried to "benefit from the riots by depicting its participants as professional criminals" or immigrants to France (Koff & Duprez, 2009, p. 723).

In all of the four case studies, two factors were found to be present in relation to the occurrence of the riots. The first factor was that groups of people were excluded from society and the second was police discrimination and abuse (Briggs, 2012; Koff, 2009; Laban-Mattei, 2015). An analysis of the case studies found that excluded group members would often use their ethnic identity to justify and explain their anger and violent actions and to justify damage to property (Koff, 2009). The second factor highlighted was that the riot participants in all four of the case studies expressed their outrage at the actions that the police took, prior to and in response to the riots (Briggs, 2012; Kienscherf, 2014; Koff, 2009; Police Executive Research Forum, 2015).

This chapter provides an analysis of the case studies and discusses each of the main themes that emerged from the research. The first section of the chapter presents the main issues identified in the case studies and then compares the issues and themes across all four riots. The second section examines the theoretical causes of the riots in the case studies and the final sections discuss the problems that the police faced in responding to the riots.

8.2 The Definition of Riot Participants

A riot crowd can be made up of individuals with different motives. Some are there to engage with the police and to loot and some are members of the public who have been caught up in the disorder. Others may be on-lookers while others may be restrainers; those who try to prevent rioters or others from undertaking or completing actions (Hussain & Bagguley, 2009). Research undertaken by Oberschall (1993) into the 1965 Los Angeles riots identified three different types of riot participants; those who directly engage with police, looters and those who are observing the events. Keith (1993) when analyzing the arrest statistics of riots that occurred in London during the 1980s highlighted that "different actions are related to different categories of person within the crowd" (p. 98). McPhail (1991) and Hussain and Bagguley (2009) caution that the different roles undertaken by riot participants creates a problem for measuring riot participation and that the date pertaining to the arrests made in a riot can only be a representation of the violence and disorder for which they have been arrested. This is because the arrest date does not identify an individual's role in the crowd or whether their role changed during the riot. Another problem in attempting to measure riot participation is that an individual's role may not stay the same during the occurrence of a riot and they may perform different actions at different times during a riot (Hussain & Bagguley, 2009; McPhail, 1991).

8.3 France

An analysis of the case study of the 2005 riots in France revealed that the main problem in the riot was the actions of the police. France has a longstanding tradition of riot-control and has developed specific skills and strategies to ensure that riot situations are appropriately responded to. France has approximately 17,000 gendarmes mobiles and 14,000 police officers serving in "riot police forces" that are able to be deployed nationally. When riot police are not responding to riots, they patrol in at-risk or high-risk areas to prevent riots from occurring (Mouhanna, 2009).

France also has local police forces whose officers serve in riot "intervention squads" but are not part of the Gendarmes. The role of these officers is similar to that of riot officers in other police forces (Mouhanna, 2009).

Since the 1960s, national and local police have had three goals in relation to responding to riots; ensure public safety, protect public institutions and to avoid any police action that may result in someone being killed (Mouhanna, 2009). The goals were developed primarily to avoid the martyring of the death of a rioter and subsequently justifying the rioters' cause (Mouhanna, 2009). The challenge for the French police, as with any police force, is to not only respond to and manage a riot, but to arrest the perpetrators without seriously injuring or killing them.

During the 2005 riots, more than 11,000 police officers were deployed each night, with more than 200 officers injured over the course of 20 nights of violence (Mouhanna, 2009). Despite the violence and the number of police officers injured, the police did not use lethal force in self-defense and fortunately no rioters were killed.

Although the 2005 riots in France were described by the international media as unique, riots have often occurred in French suburbs, especially during the early 1980s and more so since the 1990s (Jobard, 2009; Mouhanna, 2009). Even when rioting is not reported, vehicles are regularly set on fire, with more than 40,000 vehicles being reported as being burned in 2007 (Mouhanna, 2009). This level of damage is set against a backdrop of a historically troubled relationship between the police and minority communities, especially the youth (Jobard, 2009; Mouhanna, 2009). This troubled relationship has been a result of France's colonial past and the Algerian war, but also because of the war against Islamist terrorism, which has provided the basis for the police to undertake identity checks of ethnic-minority individuals (Mouhanna, 2009). According to Mouhanna (2009), the troubled relationship between the police and minority community is exacerbated because the police do not practice community-oriented policing in minority communities and usually do not patrol such communities unless there is a crisis. Therefore, a police officer would not have any contact with the community unless called to respond to an incident (Mouhanna, 2009).

Another factor contributing to the poor relationship between the police and the minority community is the emphasis that the police place on public order and the protection of institutions. The police have focused their enforcements efforts towards containing the working classes, which has led to frequent conflicts breaking out between suburban youth and police officers. It is this legacy in which the 2005 riots were set and forms the historical context of urban riots (Mouhanna, 2009). Two years after the 2005 riots, the situation in France had not changed, but police legitimacy had increased as a result of the success of the police in responding and suppressing the riots (Mouhanna, 2009).

8.4 London

The August 2011 riots started in London following a protest march, which was held 2 days after the fatal shooting of Mark Duggan by a Metropolitan Police Officer (King, 2013). After the family left the protest march at Tottenham Police Station in North London, projectiles were thrown at the police station and a number of police cars were burnt. The riots quickly spread across a number of London boroughs and then to several major towns and cities, resulting in the death of five people. It was estimated by the Riots, Communities and Victims Panel (RCVP) that between 13 and 15,000 persons were actively involved in the rioting and looting which lasted for five days across 66 areas of England (Riots, Communities and Victims Panel, 2012, pp. 10–11).

The riots were unique as they comprised two distinct factors when compared to earlier riots in the UK. The first factor was that the rioters comprised individuals from a number of ethnic groups rather than being from one principle ethnic community (King, 2013). The second factor was that "the rioters consisted of highly mobile groups forming, dissipating and regrouping with the aid of new social media" (King, 2013). Although these factors were the basis for the initial police response to the riots, many of the motivations of the riots would seem to be similar to those that had occurred earlier in the UK (King, 2013). The riots in London and Birmingham also appeared to be influenced by the "increasing economic austerity" being experienced by communities (King, 2013, p. 27).

Briggs (2012) summarized the uniqueness of the 2011 London riots and claimed that there were three important areas that should be highlighted. These were:

1. the relationship between the police and minority communities is extremely tenuous and communities react easily "on perceived injustices";

2. the role of social networking was significant in starting the riot and how it evolved. The role of social networking also identified that an individual's involvement in the riots could be both collective and subjective; and
3. the media coverage of riots was biased and the government response was reactive and did not follow "established criminal justice processes" (pp. 14–15).

There were a number of differences in the 2011 riots in London when compared to earlier riots in the UK (King, 2013; Metropolitan Police, 2012; Riots, Communities and Victims Panel, 2012). The first difference was their rapid spread. The Riots, Communities and Victims Panel (2012) claimed that their research found that the rapid spread of the riots was the result of an absence of an early and appropriate police response to the disorders in Tottenham and a subsequent perception that the police were not able to manage the disorder. The perception that police response and deployment was not appropriate for the level of disorder and violence was subsequently supported by the interim and final review reports by the Metropolitan Police. It was also noted that the number of police officers deployed was not at the level needed to control the violence (Metropolitan Police, 2011, p. 4; 2012, p. 118). According to the Commanders of the Police Support Units that were deployed to the riots, the police "were overstretched" and "under resourced," and as a result were unable to arrest offenders (Metropolitan Police, 2011, p. 4).

The second difference in the riots held in London was that they did not follow the same form or pattern of violence and disorder in each town or city (King, 2013; Morrell, Scott, McNeish, & Webster, 2011). Based on police officer interviews, Morrell et al. (2011) claimed that the form of riot was different in each geographical area because of the "distinct dynamics" of that specific area (p. 21).

The third difference was that there were also conflicts or tensions occurring within the general rioting. In Birmingham, for example, while a general riot was taking place, there were also increased tensions between the African Caribbean and South Asian communities and gangs (King, 2013). According to King (2013), although looting and disorder occurred during the riots, there were also events based "primarily [on] opportunism" and others that were staged to lure the police into an ambush (pp. 28–29).

The one factor that was not different in relation to the 2011 riots in London was the police response, which was based on similar approaches that had been previously adopted; namely, a response strategy that comprised two primary parts (King, 2013). The first part involved the response to the violence and property damage and the second part involved engaging with the community in an attempt to de-escalate the disorder (King, 2013). The main problem with the police adopting their usual response to disorder became apparent on the third night of the riots. Up until this stage, the police response had included mainly "conventional public order tactics" (King, 2013). However, these tactics proved to be unsuccessful as the looting and violence were "too dynamic and fluid" to be contained by any conventional police response (King, 2013). As a result, the police changed their response from being "too static" and not effective, to tactics that were based on maximizing arrests and "re-establish[ing] the sense of deterrence" (Sims, 2011, p. 29). The police also established the use of mobile police units and the deployment of police dog patrols (House of Commons Home Affairs Committee, 2011b). The drawback to the new response tactic was, however, a result of police officers making arrests. Because the officers were making numerous arrests, the number of officers available to respond to the riots at any specific point in time was diminished (West Midlands Police Authority, 2011).

Changing the police response tactic to one that emphasized arrests was also highlighted in lessons learned reports prepared by Her Majesty's Inspectorate of Constabulary and the House of Commons Home Affairs Committee. The report written by the Inspectorate suggested that in order for the police to adopt a successful response to a riot that concentrated on both maximizing the number of arrests and the dispersal of rioters, the police would need to deploy three to five officers for every one rioter (Her Majesty's Inspectorate of Constabulary, 2011, p. 7). The House of Commons Home Affairs Committee also noted that there is a need to ensure that the appropriate number of police are deployed to a riot situation. The committee noted that "the single most effective tactic in repressing the riots was increasing officer numbers and flooding the streets with police" (House of Commons Home Affairs Committee, 2011b, p. 19).

To ensure that the arrest-focused and mobile approach provided a deterrence and was able to be sustained, the police integrated additional operational strategies. The first was to meet the demand for more officers. To meet the demand for more police officers, requests were made to police forces across the country, including Scotland, via the mutual aid process (King, 2013). The second strategy was the use of social media to increase liaison with and to inform the community (Her Majesty's Inspectorate of Constabulary, 2011; King, 2013; Sims, 2011). According to Latchford (2012), the increase in communication pertaining to the riots prevented further riots from developing in a number of riot-prone areas, for example in the Lozells area of Birmingham. This area had suffered from extensive rioting in 2005 but owing to the efforts of the residents and the Lozells Neighbourhood Policing Team, rioting did not occur in 2011 (West Midlands Police Authority, 2011).

The use of social media was one strategy that was used to thwart the use of such media by rioters who had used the media in the past to facilitate social networking and to recruit rioters (Baker, 2012). According to Baker (2012), the use of social media by both the police and rioters contributed to the form and effect of the riots but it was not the initial cause of the disorder. It could, however, be argued that the use of social media by rioters perpetuated the riots and was one of the underlying causes of the riots being spontaneous and mobile.

8.5 A Comparison of the Riots in Ferguson and Baltimore with Those That Occurred in the UK

The occurrence of and the response to the riots on both sides of the Atlantic appear to have initially taken a standardized form (Newburn, 2014a). According to Newburn (2014b), much of the rioting that occurred in Ferguson and Baltimore appears, on the surface, to have repeated those events that were experienced in the UK in 2011. In all three locations, Ferguson, Baltimore, and the UK, the riots included attacks on the police, looting and the destruction and vandalism of property. Looting was, however, more widespread in the UK than it was in the USA (Newburn, 2014a, 2014b).

The catalyst for all three of the riots were the actions of the police; police shootings in Ferguson and London, and police negligence in Baltimore. The shootings in Ferguson and London, however, were not the only factors that formed the catalysts for the riots; it was the actions taken by the police following the shootings. In the case of the Ferguson riot, Mr. Brown's body lay uncovered in the street and in view of the public and later that evening, a police car drove over a makeshift memorial. While in London, the supporters of Mr. Duggan perceived that the police did not treat his family with the appropriate amount of respect (Newburn, 2014a).

Beyond the actions of the police, the alienation that was experienced by the young people of minority communities and the profound suspicion of and resentment towards the police were the principal features in the rioting that occurred in all of the locations (Newburn, 2014b). In both the USA and the UK, researchers found that the rioters complained about police harassment and stop and frisk or stop and search, in particular (Newburn, 2014a).

Another similarity between the riots that occurred in the USA and the UK was the information released by the police. In all three cases, the police only released information that portrayed the victims of police shootings and brutality in a negative light. This gave the appearance that the police were attempting to divert attention from the shootings (Newburn, 2014a).

To some extent, however, this is where the parallels between the riots in the three case studies end (Newburn, 2014b). Although they shared similarities, there were also some differences. The first difference is the reason that the riots in Ferguson and Baltimore occurred. This was primarily about race, although this was also a factor in the reason for the 2011 riots occurring in the UK. The riots in the UK, however, were more about poverty and disadvantage (Newburn, 2014b). The UK had experienced race-based disorders in the 1980s, in the minority communities of St Paul's, Brixton, and Toxteth in response to what was perceived as oppressive policing practices (Newburn, 2014b).

The second difference is the form or tactical response that was adopted by the Ferguson and Baltimore police when compared to that adopted by the British police. The American approach appeared to be more militarized and included the use of "Tear gas, stun grenades, rubber bullets, camouflage uniforms, armoured cars, assault rifles, shotguns and automatic weapons" (Newburn, 2014b).

A third difference that was noted was the changes that were made as to who was the commander or the command/lead agency in both Ferguson and Baltimore. In Ferguson, the command agency changed to the state police owing to a perceived weakness in the local police response, while in Baltimore, there were numerous internal changes to the Baltimore Police Commander, which led to confusion as to who was in charge (Gately & Stolberg, 2015; Police Executive Research Forum, 2015).

The fourth difference was the deployment of the National Guard to support the police in both Ferguson and Baltimore. While in the UK, the riots were responded to and managed by the police and military support was not requested.

The last difference to be noted was in relation to the engagement and contact with the community. In the UK, engagement with the community was an aspect of the response strategy and was adopted during the day following the riots at Tottenham Police Station. In contrast, engagement with the community in both Ferguson and Baltimore was not undertaken until the riots had been underway for several days.

8.6 The Theoretical Causes of the Riots Discussed in the Case Studies

This section discusses some of the causes of riots. According to Hundley (1968) and Benyon (1987), the causes of riots can be categorized into two areas. The first was the trigger event for "sparking" the riot and the second area was the underlying social conditions that provided the catalyst for the violence and disorder.

In the riots that occurred in the USA and the UK in the 1980s, it appears that "[t]he immediate precipitants or trigger events in each case involved police officers and black people" (Benyon, 1987, p. 33), while the catalyst comprised five social characteristics that were common to all of the riots during this period (Waddington & King, 2009). The common catalyst characteristics were:

- racial disadvantage and discrimination;
- high unemployment, especially among young males;
- widespread high crime, and inadequate educational and social service provision;
- political exclusion and powerlessness which is usually as a result of the absence of institutions, opportunities and resources for articulating grievances; and
- widespread mistrust of, and resentment of, the police, especially by young people who are regularly subjected to "stop-and-search" and other related forms of harassment and abuse (adapted from Benyon, 1987, pp. 33–34).

The one characteristic that is missing from the above and is often the major contributor to the catalyst of a riot is the police and the form of policing undertaken in the area prior to the riot. The police influence on the catalyst can take two forms. The first form was identified by Waddington and King (2009), who claimed that a number of studies highlighted several factors that are inherent in the culture of the police, that are "fundamental to explaining the negative and often confrontational relationships between the police and ethnic minorities" (p. 18). These factors limit the capability of the police to develop sustainable relationships and trust with minority communities (see Scarman, 1981 and the Macpherson, 1999 for examples of the factors experienced in the police culture in the UK that have been identified as influencing the cause of riots). The second form of police action is the opposite of the first form and concerns the absence of the police in the community. According to Power and Tunstall (1997), the absence of a sustained, community-oriented police presence in minority neighborhoods was a key element that led to the riots experienced in the 1980s and 1990s in the UK. The researchers claimed that the absence of the police is a symptom of wider policing difficulties and weak enforcement is viewed by the community as the police not having the ability or the capacity (Power & Tunstall, 1997) or the interest to police their neighborhoods.

The actions of the police have also been identified as the "flashpoint" (Waddington, Jones, & Critcher, 1989), which led to disorder in France (Lukas, 2009). This view is expanded on by Cox and Fitzgerald (1996), who claimed that the presence of the police, or an incident that the police are called to, can lead to collective protest. Two other factors were recognized as being the possible cause of the disorder in France; the police conducting identification checks (Lukas, 2009), and the deterioration of the relationship between the police and neighborhood residents (Lapeyronnie, 2006—in Lukas, 2009). Snyder (1979) had noted that in the USA, negative police contact with the public was one of the major factors in the triggering of disorder and violence, while Haan and Nijboer (2005) maintained that an adverse reputation of the police and a lack of trust in the legal system influenced not only the likelihood of a riot but also the form and the level of conflict between the police and rioters.

The literature clearly identifies that the relationship between the police and the community, and the perceived actions of the police are critical factors when examining the causes of collective minority adolescent disorder. Whereas there is conflicting evidence in relation to the impact of social and demographic factors on a community's attitudes towards the police (Lukas, 2009). The occurrence of collective disorder is an indicator of more general social problems other than just police or political trust and legitimacy (Tyler, 2004).

Earlier research conducted in the USA as to the causes of rioting reported similar findings. In 1970, Hahn and Feagan examined the 1960s riots in New York and Detroit and found that with "few exceptions, every major incident of urban violence was triggered by police … it is likely that hostility of Negroes towards white authority has been kindled by abrasive contacts with ghetto police" (p. 184). Similarly, Fogelson (1968) found that "with a few exceptions … the nineteen sixties riots were all precipitated by police actions" (p. 220). Latter research by Fassin (n.d., quoted in Schneider, 2014) supports these findings, who ascribes the 2005 riots in France and every major riot from Watts in the mid-1960s to London in 2011 to racial profiling and police actions in "disadvantaged [or minority] neighborhoods, usually leading to the death of a youth belonging to a racial or ethnic minority group." (p. 19).

The analysis of the case studies of the riots in London and France highlight that there was mutual resentment and a deteriorating relationship between the police and adolescents in minority and disadvantaged urban neighborhoods and banlieues and that these were fundamental characteristics of the riots. In relation to France, Mohammed and Mucchielli (2006, quoted in Schneider, 2014, p. 18) found that the majority of riots over the past 25 years have primarily resulted from "police intrusions" and have comprised confrontations between the police and minority banlieue youths. According to Althoff (2006—in Lukas, 2009), the principal reason for resentment and the weak relationship between the police and minority youth in France is not police actions but the police are "centrally organized" and, as a result, would not be appreciative of "local peculiarities." The main problem with this claim is that there has been no systematic cross-national and comparative studies of police actions prior to the riots taken nor have the linkages between the organizational structures of the police and minority communities been examined.

The only literature that is available that discusses the structure of the police and the occurrence of a riot is that written by Schneider (2014), who claimed that the structure of policing has shaped the geography of the occurrence of urban disorder. According to Schneider (2014), the decentralized structure of the police and policing in the USA "led to a segmented, staggered pattern of [racially based] riots during the 1960s, which criss-crossed the country for half a decade" (p. 28). The pattern and the occurrence of riots was owing to the local police being under the control of the mayor and as a result, "operated with virtual impunity" (Schneider, 2014, p. 28).

In summary, previous research is contradictory. It appears that both the centralization of police organizations and the decentralization of police agencies has been the catalyst for the occurrence of riots. The cause of this confusion may come from the fact that researchers have not looked at the results of earlier research before drawing their own conclusions. It is highly unlikely that the structure of a police organization would be a catalyst for a riot occurring. It is more likely that the form of policing delivered or the police organization's relationship with the community would be the contributing factors.

8.7 The Policing of Riots

The analysis of the four case studies reveals that there are a number of similarities and obvious differences in what unfolded in each of the riots. In terms of an immediate spark or flashpoint, all four riots were preceded by the death of an individual or individuals of ethnic minority that occurred as a result of the action taken by the police and in all of the cases, the actions of the police were perceived by the minority community as being excessive or illegitimate. Furthermore, in all four cases, the community perceived that there was a lack of information provided in relation to the deaths or that the police were spreading false information.

The form and scale of the riots were very different in each of the case studies. The riots that occurred in the USA that were discussed in the case studies were concentrated in the city or in the general vicinity of where the police action led to the death, although there were short-lived and smaller-sized riots and violence in a number of other cities across the country. In comparison, the size of the riots that occurred in England was significant and did not spread as widely as those that took place in France, which spread to hundreds of towns and cities.

What has become obvious in the review of the four case studies is that the police played a role in the cause and perpetuation of the riots. The role of the police, according to Newburn (2016), can be viewed from three perspectives:

1. The involvement of the police in influencing the initial "spark" or "flashpoint" of the riot;

2. The way in which initial protests following these flashpoints were handled by the police; and,
3. The tactics use by the police as the disorder started to develop (adapted from Newburn, 2016, p. 547).

The riots in all four of the case studies discussed above resulted in the deaths of citizens that were caused by the actions that the police took and the widely-held perception held by the community that the police lacked legitimacy and were not to be trusted. Furthermore, the way in which the police managed and responded to the initial disorder was a principle factor in the subsequent spread of the rioting (Roché & de Maillard, 2009). However, the spread and the level of rioting were different in each of the four countries (Newburn, 2016). From research conducted after the riot, the rioters' anger with the police was primarily based on the police use of stop and search powers and the perceived racial profiling underpinning the use of such tactics (Newburn, 2016). The rioters' anger with the police, according to Lewis, Newburn, Taylor, and Ball (2011), was more consistent in England than in the USA or France.

There is no doubt that much of the violence and disorder was directed toward the police and the protesters' anger towards the police was a principal motivating factor in influencing minority youth to take part in the riots in each of the four case studies discussed (Newburn, 2016).

8.8 The Difficulty in Policing Riots

This section discusses the reviews of the literature on the policing of protests and attempts to combine the findings in the literature with the information obtained from an analysis of the four case studies and will discuss some of the complexities that the police face when responding to riots. The discussion reviews the literature pertaining to the policing of protests as there is no literature based on the analysis of the policing of riots available.

The traditional view held by the police of public protests is that they are a threat to social order (Waddington, 1991, 1994). This view is in contrast to the academic and theoretical view that public protesting is a threat to the status quo of society and to the political and financial elite (Davenport, 1995, 2000; Earl, 2003; McAdam, 1982; Tilly, 1995). As a result, aggressive police actions taken in response to a protest are often viewed by the protesters and the media as being repressive.

The more violent protests and those protests in which non-mainstream tactics have been used suggest different levels of opposition to authorities (Bromley & Shupe, 1983; Warner & McCarthy, 2014) and leads to different forms of response. Researchers have examined the impact that the variations in protest have had on the likelihood of repressive police action occurring and this has led to the modern form of orderly and institutionalized form of protest (Warner & McCarthy, 2014). This modern form of protest has created a similar shift in the police response, to one which is primarily non-confrontational and focuses on preserving public order

(McCarthy & McPhail, 2006; Waddington, 1991, 1994). The police need to balance the maintenance of public safety with the right of protesters to express themselves. The modern form creates complexity for the police as perception and understanding of public safety varies over space and time and across local political systems and police agencies (Warner & McCarthy, 2014).

The shift to mainly institutionalized protest and a corresponding police response contrasts with emerging research that stresses situational interpretations as being the foundation for identifying the form that the police use to respond to the protest (della Porta, 1998; della Porta & Reiter, 1998; Earl & Soule, 2006). This research is consistent with the police-centred approach to the policing of protests, which is based on the older model of policing of protests; that protester actions can threaten the control that the police have over the protest (Earl & Soule, 2006; Soule & Davenport, 2009).

As discussed above, the police response to public protest has been primarily based on the level of threat to public safety and order (and a number of academics would claim in the interests of political and financial elites), leading to a considerable amount of vagueness in the understanding of a threat (Warner & McCarthy, 2014) and the form of policing that is required. Grounded on the analysis of more than 16,000 protest events from 1960 to 1995, Warner and McCarthy (2014) claimed that there were a number of dimensions contained within a specific protest event that lead to complicated and complex interactions between the protesters and the police. An analysis of the interactions led to the identification of three features that create difficulties in managing protest crowds and contribute to a more aggressive police response to a protest (Warner & McCarthy, 2014). These features are:

1. different tactical forms and approaches,
2. group diversity; and
3. the size of the protest (adapted from Warner & McCarthy, 2014, p. 569).

Protests are usually viewed as collective public action (Tarrow, 1998; Tilly, 1995), and from the perspective of the protester, the more diverse the form of protest is, the more successful the protest is (Davenport, 1995; Eckstein, 1980; Morris, 1993; Tilly, 1979; Ziegenhagen, 1986). The problem with protests taking so many forms or being diversified means that the if the police do not know what form the protest will take, they will need to plan for a range of protester activities. This implies that a relationship is established by the level or extent of the threat contained within the protest and between the form of the protest and the form of the police response (Warner & McCarthy, 2014). In other words, if the police perceive the protest as being of a standard form with little or no violence the threat level will be classified as being low. However, if the police perceive that the protest will not take a standard form and could be violent, then they will classify the threat as being high. If a threat is classified as high, the police will plan accordingly, which often stretches resources to ensure that the actions taken by the protesters are appropriately and safely addressed (Davenport, 1995).

The inherent danger in protests is that if the police identify the riot as having a high level of threat, any police interaction with the protesters is highly likely to be aggressive (Warner & McCarthy, 2014). The reasons for a more aggressive police approach in these situations was discussed in-depth in Chap. 3 and is a result of the police primarily viewing protest crowds as homogeneous (Drury, Stott, & Farsides, 2003; Gorringe & Rosie, 2008; Waddington, 1991). The police usually view crowds as being potentially dangerous (Stott & Reicher, 1998), and comprising at least two groups: a powerful violent minority and a susceptible majority (Drury et al., 2003; Waddington, 1991; Warner & McCarthy, 2014). The problem for the police is that in a riot, they cannot differentiate between the violent minority and the non-violent members of the crowd (Reicher, Stott, Cronin, & Adang, 2004). Not being able to differentiate the make-up of a crowd leads to the use of a standardized policing style and the form of protester action that will be tolerated by the police (della Porta & Fillieule, 2004).

The third feature is the size of the protest, which Martin, McCarthy, and McPhail (2009), claim has been the subject of considerable debate in regard to its inherent dangers. This argument originates from both threats to the political elite (Davenport, 2000; Tilly, 1979, 1995) and from the threat of the police not being able to control the actions of the crowd (Earl & Soule, 2006; Soule & Davenport, 2009) as the ratio of police to protesters decreases (Carter, 1986). However, according to Mayhew and Levinger (1976), larger-sized crowds lead to more complex interactions and as a result, becomes a predictor of police aggressiveness (Earl, McCarthy, & Soule, 2003; Earl & Soule, 2006). This also leads to command and control difficulties for the police.

In summary, the size of a crowd influences the way that the police will respond in two ways. The first is that large crowds will limit the use of force response options because the police have limited resources and the second is that the use of police force will be shaped by the occurrence or non-occurrence of violent, aggressive and disruptive protesters (Warner & McCarthy, 2014).

The other two components that affect how the police respond to and manage riots, are police knowledge and strategy development. Police knowledge has been defined by della Porta (1998) as "the images held by the police about their role and the external challenges they are asked to face" (p. 229) and "the police's construction of external reality, collectively and individually—which we consider to be the main intervening variable between structure and action" (della Porta & Reiter, 1998, p. 9).

8.9 Conclusion

In this chapter the information contained in the case studies was analyzed and focused mainly on the police response and management of the riots. The perception of indifference of the police are the main distinguishing feature between the riots that occurred in USA and France and those that occurred in the UK. Unlike the riots in the USA and France, the British conflicts were not based on a history of institutional racism, but were based on a recent history of repressive policing that had been used to recapture communities and geographic areas that had long been lost to local criminals (Waddington, 2007).

The dilemma for the police in responding to criminal offending is that they face accusations of racism when they distinguish between one "culture," "ethnicity," or "community" and another (Bujra & Pearce, 2009). The dilemma is now widespread across all aspects of police work, including the police response to a riot and as a result, it is not surprising that accusations of racism by the police arose in the context of the riots and as one of the reasons for the cause of the riots (Bujra & Pearce, 2009). Any accusation of police racism has to be balanced with the character of the rioters who make this claim and who admit to having a history of coming to the attention of the police and the accuser acknowledging that they had a desire to get even with the police (Bujra & Pearce, 2009).

The main difference in the riots that have been discussed in the case studies compared to previous riots was the use of social media by both the protesters and the police. The use of social media and technology ensured that protesters were well organized and this led to the police being unable to gain control of the riots in all three countries during the first few days. The rioters were also inventive; burning cars that were often used as barricades, using social media to name false riot spots and to warn others of the police approach and the use of masks to hide their faces (Bujra & Pearce, 2009).

The police wearing riot safety equipment also attracted complaints from the public. The use of riot safety equipment and other military-style equipment, according to Bujra and Pearce (2009), was perceived by the public as dehumanizing the police officers. While other researchers claimed that the use of such equipment increased the militarization of the police and was a form of provocation (Bujra & Pearce, 2009; Keith, 1993; Waddington, 1992).

The politically correct response to racially based riots is for the police to be pluralistic and responsive to ethnic diversity (Bujra & Pearce, 2009). The police do, however, need to enforce the law and be impartial when dealing with the public (Zedner, 2006). Being both responsive to the law and impartial begs the question as to whether the police can meet both of these demands (McLaughlin, 2007) when responding to a riot.

References

Althoff, M. (2006). Die Ausschreitungen in den franzosischen Vorstadten Awischen Provokation, Erklarung und Deutung Order: was haben Frankreich und Holland gemeinsam? *Kriminologisches Journal, 38*(2), 112–117.

Baker, S. (2012). From the criminal crowd to the 'mediated crowd': The impact of social media on the 2011 English riots. *Safer Communities, 11*(1), 40–49.

Benyon, J. (1987). Interpretation of civil disorder. In J. Benyon & J. Solomos (Eds.), *The roots of urban unrest*. Oxford: Pergamon Press.

Briggs, D. (2012). What we did when it happened: A timeline analysis of the social disorder in London. *Safer Communities Special Edition on the Riots, 2*(1), 6–16.

Bromley, D., & Shupe, A. (1983). Repression and the decline of social movements: The case of new religions. In J. Freeman (Ed.), *Social movements of the sixties and seventies* (pp. 335–347). New York: Longman.

Bujra, J., & Pearce, J. (2009). Police on the line: Between control and correctness in multi-ethnic contexts of urban unrest. In D. Waddington, F. Robard, & M. King (Eds.), *Rioting in the UK and France: A comparative analysis* (pp. 41–55). London: Routledge Taylor & Francis Group.

Carter, G. (1986). The 1960s black riots revisited: City level explanations of their severity. *Sociological Inquiry, 56*(2), 210–228.

Cox, S., & Fitzgerald, J. (1996). *Police community relations: Critical issues*. Dubuque, Iowa: Brown.

Davenport, C. (1995). Multi-dimensional threat perception and state repression: An inquiry into why states apply negative sanctions. *American Journal of Political Science, 39*(3), 683–713.

Davenport, C. (2000). Introduction. In C. Davenport (Ed.), *Paths to state repression* (pp. 1–24). Lanham, Maryland: Rowman and Littlefield.

della Porta, D. (1998). Policing knowledge and protest policing: Some reflections on the Italian case. In D. Della Porta & H. Reiter (Eds.), *Policing protest: The control of mass demonstrations in western democracies* (pp. 228–252). Minneapolis: University of Minnesota Press.

della Porta, D., & Fillieule, O. (2004). Policing social protest. In D. Snow, S. Soule, & H. Kriesi (Eds.), *The Blackwell companion to social movements* (pp. 217–241). Malden, MA: Blackwell.

della Porta, D., & Reiter, H. (1998). Introduction: The policing of protests in western democracies. In D. Della Porta & H. Reiter (Eds.), *Policing protest: The control of mass demonstrations in western democracies* (pp. 1–34). Minneapolis: University of Minnesota Press.

Drury, J., Stott, C., & Farsides, T. (2003). The role of police perceptions and practices in the development of 'public disorder. *Journal of Applied Social Psychology, 33*(7), 1480–1500.

Earl, J. (2003). Tanks, tear gas, and taxes: Toward a theory of movement repression. *Sociological Theory, 21*(1), 44–68.

Earl, J., & Soule, S. (2006). Seeing blue: A police centred explanation of protest policing. *Mobilization, 11*(2), 145–164.

Earl, J., McCarthy, J., & Soule, S. (2003). Protest under fire? Explaining the policing of protest. *American Sociological Review, 68*(4), 581–606.

Eckstein, H. (1980). Theoretical approaches to explaining collective political violence. In T. Gurr (Ed.), *Handbook of political conflict: Theory and practice* (pp. 135–166). New York: Free Press.

Fogelson, R. (1968). From resentment to confrontation: The police, the negros and the outbreak of the nineteen-sixties riots. *Political Science Quarterly, 83*(2), 217–247.

Gately, G. & Stolberg. S. (2015). *Baltimore police assailed for response after Freddie Gray's death*. Retrieved February 16, 2016, from http://www.nytimes.com/2015/11/17/us/baltimore-police-assailed-for-response-after-freddie-grays-death.html?_r=0.

Gorringe, H., & Rosie, M. (2008). It's a long way to Auchterarder! 'Negotiated management' and mismanagement in the policing of G8 protests. *The British Journal of Sociology, 59*(2), 187–205.

Haan, W., & Nijboer, J. (2005). Youth violence and self-help. *European Journal of Crime, Criminal Law and Criminal Justice, 13*(1), 75–88.

Hahn, H., & Feagan, J. (1970). Riot-precipitating police practice: Attitudes in urban ghettos. *Phylon, 31*(2), 183–186.

Her Majesty's Inspectorate of Constabulary. (2011). *The rules of engagement: A review of the August 2011 disorders*. London: Her Majesty's Chief Inspectorate of Constabulary.

Hundley, J. (1968). The dynamics of recent ghetto riots. Detroit Journal of Urban Law, 45, pp. 627–639. Reprinted as: Hundley, J. (1975). The dynamics of recent ghetto riots. In R. Evans (Ed.), *Readings in Collective Behavior*. Chicago: Rand McNally.

Hussain, Y., & Bagguley, P. (2009). The Bradford 'riot' of 2001: The diversity of action. In D. Waddington, F. Robard, & M. King (Eds.), *Rioting in the UK and France: A comparative analysis* (pp. 71–80). London: Routledge Taylor & Francis Group.

House of Commons Home Affairs Committee (2011b). *Policing large scale disorder: Lessons from the disturbances of August 2011. 16th report of session 2010–12*. Vol. 1. HC 1456-1. London: The Stationary Office Limited.

Jobard, F. (2009). An overview of French riots: 1981–2004. In D. Waddington, F. Robard, & M. King (Eds.), *Rioting in the UK and France: A comparative analysis* (pp. 27–40). New York: Willan Publishing.

Keith, M. (1993). *Race, riots and policing: Lore and disorder in a multi-racist society*. London: University of London Press.

Kienscherf, M. (2014). Beyond militarization and repression: Liberal social control as pacification. *Critical Sociology, 42*(7–8), 1–16.

King, M. (2013). Birmingham revisited–causal differences between the riots of 2011 and 2005? *Policing & Society: An International Journal of Policy and Research, 23*(1), 26–45.

Koff, H. (2009). Understanding 'La Contagion': Power, exclusion and urban violence in France and the United States. *Journal of Ethnic and Migration Studies, 35*(5), 771–790.

Koff, H., & Duprez, D. (2009). The 2005 riots in France: The international impact of domestic violence. *Journal of Ethnic and Migration Studies, 35*(5), 713–730.

Laban-Mattei, O. (2015, March 16). *French police go on trial for teen deaths that kicked off riots*. France 24. Retrieved from http://www.france24.com/en/20150316-french-police-officers-trial-clichy-sous-bois-riots-electrocution.

Lapeyronnie, D. (2006). Primitive rebellion in den franzoischen vorstaden: ein essay uber die unruhen von Herbst 2005. *Soziale Probleme, 17*, 63–89.

Latchford, P. (2012). *They moved like fish: The Birmingham riots of August 2011*. Retrieved January 7, 2019, from http://www.blackradley.com/wp-content/uploads/2012/02/TheyMovedLikeFishReport.pdf.

Lewis, P., Newburn, T., Taylor, M. & Ball, J. (2011, December 5). *Rioters say anger with police fuelled summer unrest*. The Guardian. Retrieved from https://www.theguardian.com/uk/2011/dec/05/anger-police-fuelled-riots-study.

Lieberson, S., & Silverman, A. (1965). The precipitant and underlying conditions of race riots. *American Sociological Review, 30*(6), 887–898.

Lukas, T. (2009). Why are there no riots in Germany? Mutual perceptions between police forces and minority adolescents. In D. Waddington, F. Robard, & M. King (Eds.), *Rioting in the UK and France: A comparative analysis* (pp. 216–228). London: Routledge Taylor & Francis Group.

Macpherson, W. (1999). *The Stephen Lawrence inquiry*. London: Home Office.

Martin, A., McCarthy, J., & McPhail, C. (2009). Why targets matter: Toward a more inclusive model of collective violence. *American Sociological Review, 74*(5), 821–841.

Mayhew, B., & Levinger, R. (1976). Size and the density of interaction in human aggregates. *American Journal of Sociology, 82*(1), 86–110.

McAdam, D. (1982). *Political process and the development of black insurgency, 1930–1970*. Chicago, IL: University of Chicago Press.

McCarthy, J., & McPhail, C. (2006). Places of protest: The public forum in principle and practice. *Mobilization, 11*(2), 229–247.

McLaughlin, E. (2007). *The new policing*. London: Sage.

McPhail, C. (1991). *The myth of the madding crowd, social institutions and social change*. New York: Aldine de Gruyter.

Metropolitan Police Service. (2011). *Operation kirkin strategic review interim report*. Retrieved from https://tottenhamdefencecampaign.files.wordpress.com/2012/01/interimreportkirkin.pdf.

Metropolitan Police Service. (2012). *4 Days in August. The Metropolitan Police Service strategic review of the disorder of 2011*. London: Metropolitan Police.

Mohammed, M., & Mucchielli, L. (2006). La police dans les quartiers sensibles: Un profond malaise. In L. Mucchielli and V. Le Goaziou (Eds.) *Quand les banieues* (pp. 104–125). Paris: La Decouverte.

Morrell, G., Scott, S., McNeish, D., & Webster, S. (2011). *The August riots in England: Understanding the involvement of young people*. London: NatCen.

Morris, A. (1993). Birmingham confrontation reconsidered: an analysis of the dynamics and tactics of mobilization. *American Sociological Review, 58*(5), 621–636.

Mouhanna, C. (2009). The French police and urban riots: Is the national police force part of the solution or part of the problem? In D. Waddington, F. Robard, & M. King (Eds.), *Rioting in the UK and France: A comparative analysis* (pp. 173–182). London: Routledge Taylor & Francis Group.

National Advisory Commission on Civil Disorders. (1968). *Report of the National advisory commission on civil disorders*. Washington, DC: National Institute of Justice.

Newburn, T. (2014a). *Civil unrest in Ferguson was fuelled by the Black community's already poor relationship with a highly militarized police force*. Blogs.les.ac.uk. Retrieved from http://blogs.lse.ac.uk/usappblog/2014/08/29/civil-unrest-in-ferguson-was-fuelled-by-the-black-communitys-already-poor-relationshipwith-a-highly-militarized-police-force/.

Newburn, T. (2014b). *The Ferguson riots may seem similar to those in UK in 2011 – but there are stark contrasts*. The Guardian. Retrieved August 20, 2014, from https://www.theguardian.com/commentisfree/2014/aug/20/ferguson-missouri-not-so-far-from-tottenham-toxteth.

Newburn, T. (2016). The 2011 England riots in European context: A framework for understanding the 'life-cycle' of riots. *European Journal of Criminology, 13*(5), 540–555.

Oberschall, A. (1993). *Social movements: Ideologies, interests and identities*. New Brunswick, NJ: Transaction Books.

Police Executive Research Forum. (2015). *Lessons learned from the 2015 civil unrest in Baltimore. September*. Washington, DC: Police Executive Research Forum.

Power, A., & Tunstall, R. (1997). *Dangerous disorder: Riots and violent disturbances in thirteen areas of Britain, 1991–92*. York: York Publishing Services/Joseph Roundtree Foundation.

Reicher, S., Stott, C., Cronin, P., & Adang, O. (2004). An integrated approach to crowd psychology and public order policing. *Policing: An International Journal of Police Strategies & Management, 27*(4), 558–572.

Riots Communities and Victims Panel. (2012). *5 Days in August: An interim report on the 2011 English riots*. Retrieved from http://webarchive.nationalarchives.gov.uk/20121003195935/http:/riotspanel.independent.gov.uk/wp-content/uploads/2012/04/Interim-report-5-Days-in-August.pdf.

Roché, S., & de Maillard, J. (2009). Crisis in policing: The French rioting of 2005. *Policing, 3*(1), 34–40.

Scarman, L. J. (1981). *The Brixton disorders, April 10–12 1981: Report of an inquiry by the Rt. Hon. The Lord Scarman, O.B.E. (Cmnd. 8427)*. London: Her Majesty's Stationery Office.

Schneider, C. (2014). *Police power and race riots: Urban unrest in Paris and New York*. Philadelphia: University of Pennsylvania Press.

Sims, C. (2011). *Interim report following public disorder in August 2011 from the Chief Constable to the West Midlands police Authority*. Retrieved January 7, 2019, from http://www.west-midlandspa.gov.uk/documents/main/7/Report_to_the_Police_Authority_Final.pdf.

Snyder, D. (1979). Collective violence processes: Implications for disaggregated theory and research. In L. Kriesberg (Ed.), *Research in social movements, conflicts and change* (Vol. 2). Greenwich: Jai Press.

Soule, S., & Davenport, C. (2009). Velvet glove, iron fist, or even hand? Protest policing in the United States, 1960-1990. *Mobilization, 14*(1), 1–22.

Stott, C., & Reicher, S. (1998). Crowd action as intergroup process: Introducing the police perspective. *European Journal of Social Psychology, 26*(4), 509–529.

Tarrow, S. (1998). *Power in movement: Social movements and contentious politics*. New York: Cambridge University Press.

Tilly, C. (1979). Repertoires of contention in America and Britain. In M. Zald & J. McCarthy (Eds.), *The dynamics of social movements* (pp. 126–155). Cambridge, Massachusetts: Winthrop.

Tilly, C. (1995). *Popular contention in Great Britain, 1758–1834*. Cambridge: Harvard University Press.

Tyler, T. (2004). Enhancing police legitimacy. *The Annals of the American Academy of Political and Social Science, 593*, 84–99.

Waddington, D. (1992). *Contemporary issues in public disorder: a comparative and historical approach*. London: Routledge.

Waddington, D. (2007). *Policing public disorder: Theory and practice*. Devon: Willan Publishing.

Waddington, D., & King, M. (2009). Theoretical orientations: Lessons of the UK riots of the 1980s and 1990s. In D. Waddington, F. Robard, & M. King (Eds.), *Rioting in the UK and France: A comparative analysis* (pp. 13–26). London: Routledge Taylor & Francis Group.

Waddington, D., Jones, K., & Critcher, C. (1989). *Flashpoints: Studies in public disorder*. London: Routledge.

Waddington, P. (1991). *The strong arm of the law: Armed and public order policing*. Oxford, United Kingom: Clarendon Press.

Waddington, P. (1994). *Liberty and order: Public order policing in a capital city*. London: University College London Press.

Warner, C., & McCarthy, J. (2014). Whatever can go wrong will: Situational complexity and public order policing. *Policing and Society: An International Journal of Research and Policy, 24*(5), 566–587.

West Midlands Police Authority. (2011). *Disorder in the West Midlands 2011: Video from the police authority meeting held on 8 September 2011*. Retrieved from http://www.west-midlands-pa.gov.uk/video.asp.

Zedner, L. (2006). Policing before and after the police: The historical antecedents of contemporary crime control. *British Journal of Criminology, 46*, 76–96.

Ziegenhagen, E. (1986). *The regulation of political conflict*. New York: Praeger.

Chapter 9
Can Improvements Be Made to the Police Response?

9.1 Introduction

Public order policing is a visible symbol of the relationship that the state has with its citizens and as a result, is inherently political (Waddington, 1996). The problem for the police is that riot response tactics have never been solely about controlling violence and rioters but includes the balancing of political considerations with any response actions taken. The images of crowd disorder across the USA, the UK, and France have produced extensive public discussion as to how the police respond to such events and their use of specific crowd control techniques. This was no more so than in the UK following the August 2011 riots, where politicians openly criticized the police handling of the violence and the use of less-lethal weaponry to disperse the crowd (Orde, 2011).

What was also evident in the media and politicians' analysis of the police response to the riots in the USA, the UK, and France was the disregard of the reasons that lead to the riots and the tendency to explain the event by referring to the actions of the police or the rioters (Dunand, 1986; Ross, 1977). This approach, according to Keith (1991) and Solomos and Rackett (1991), worked to the benefit of the police following the British inner-city riots in the 1980s. Following a debate about the causes of the inner-city riots, the blame was laid on the rioters and social policy issues. The tactics that the police used during the riots were not identified as being factors that influenced the rioters and as a result, the outcome was more and heavier policing in the inner-city suburbs (Keith, 1991). This led Solomos and Rackett (1991) to claim that the only consistent response to riots in the UK since 1981 has been an increase in police resources, training and equipment.

As discussed in Chaps. 2 and 3, any protest or public demonstration has the potential to become disorderly and result in confrontations between protesters and the police. Previous sociological and criminological research has usually focused on the factors that cause a disorder and violence and not on the forms of policing or the actions taken by the police to maintain peace and control the protests. Police scholars have called for applied research to be conducted which examines the response taken

G. den Heyer, *Police Response to Riots*,
https://doi.org/10.1007/978-3-030-31810-9_9

by the police to protests and riots in the hope that the analysis will help improve the policing of these events (Brodeur, 2005).

Literature relating to the police response to disorder provides an important insight into the role of situational interactions between the police and the rioters (see for example Earl & Soule, 2006; Wahlström, 2011) and the threat, such as the size or form of the protest, as perceived by the police (Chang & Vitale, 2013; Earl, Soule, & McCarthy, 2003; McCarthy, Martin, & McPhail, 2007). Similarly, criminological research has identified that the police use of force results from specific interactions between rioters and the police (Nassauer, 2015), with some researchers claiming that police officers respond with violence when their authority is threatened, which may be real or perceived (Griffin & Bernard, 2003). Sociological research has also sought to explain crowd violence and has found that political opportunities, resources, and grievances are issues that can generate public disorder (Graham & Gurr, 1969; Gurr, 1979). More recent research has noted, however, that these issues do not explain when and where violence is likely to occur during a protest (Collins, 2008; Nassauer, 2010) and is therefore unable to offer any guidance in helping the police to develop a response.

As the police in the USA, the UK, and France reflect on the riots in their respective countries and the lessons emerging from them, the role of police leaders and policy makers is to ensure that lessons are learned and considered and that responses are altered for the benefit of the public and for the police (Her Majesty's Inspectorate of Constabulary, 2011b).

This chapter provides a basis for examining the police response to the occurrence of riots. The first section of the chapter presents a discussion on the public's acceptance of and confidence in the police in the context of a riot. The second section examines the influence that crowd psychology has on the police and third section provides a review of the riot response tactics currently being used by the police. This section discusses the use of containment, dispersal, and negotiation and analyzes a case study of the New York Police Department's approach to negotiated protest. The final section of the chapter summarizes the information contained in this book and examines a number of specific areas from which the police can move forward in their development of riot response strategies and tactics.

9.2 Public Acceptance and Confidence in the Police

The policing of protest and riots is a core function of the police and poses accountability, management and leadership challenges, which according to Kingshott (2014), should be open to public scrutiny. Any response to a violent protest or riot by the police should be a balance between upholding civil liberties with peaceful protest and should include the "management of public order maintenance that minimizes disruption to the status quo and is acceptable to the community being policed" (Kingshott, 2014, p. 285).

The successful management and control of a protest or public disorder depends upon the acceptance of the role of the police by the public (Reiner, 1992), their authority and their intervention. This means that police legitimacy depends on the capability and capacity to maintain order without losing the consent of the public (Baker, 2011). When the authority of the police is either questioned or undermined in the context of a protest or riot, two non-mutually exclusive consequences will occur: police confidence and the crowd's view on the use of violent protest (Kingshott, 2014).

The public expect the police to intervene in any disorder or riot and to act legally and decisively, fairly and appropriately (Baker, 2011). The problem for the police when responding to a riot is that their role is legally ambiguous and is not clear (Baker, 2011). Any response by the police that is not measured or is repressive and lacks discretion or sensitively will enable the rioters and as a result, will increase the risk for the police in gaining control of the riot and maintaining public order (Masterson, 1988; Scarman, 1981). Any force used by the police must be lawful, reasonable, and effective (Reiner, 1998), and the public must perceive that any actions taken by the police are reasonable as this a major factor in maintaining control of an incident and ensuring that violence does not escalate (Kingshott, 2014).

When considering the form of response, police commanders, in order to maintain public support, must balance the cultural requirement of the need for the police to win all public battles, especially those that require the use of the police force, with the need to reassure the public through consultation. The balance of the two opposing factors can be achieved by ensuring that there is public communication and consultation frameworks in place and having the police work with community organizations and leaders under a community–policing paradigm (Kingshott, 2014). In other words, the police need to have established these frameworks prior to any disorder or rioting event occurring.

9.3 An Overview of Crowd Psychology

The response actions taken by the police to violent disorder and riots has been described as "irrationalist" (Cocking, 2013a; Drury, 2011; Reicher, 2001; Stott, 2009), as they are not based on the social psychological understanding of crowd behavior. According to social psychological understanding, crowd behavior is influenced by "shared consensual norms that are in turn influenced by the social context in which such crowds are located" (Cocking, 2013b, p. 221). However, a number of unknown reasons may trigger an individual to exercise antisocial behavior and violence in the hope that it will instigate the crowd to perform violent acts (Kingshott, 2014). It is within the consensual norms that collective positive experiences and feelings can increase crowd cohesion and united action (see for example Drury, Cocking, Beale, Hanson, & Rapley, 2005; Neville & Reicher, 2011).

As discussed in previous chapters, the social identity model of collective resilience (Drury, Cocking, & Reicher, 2009a, 2009b; Williams & Drury, 2009) and the elaborated social identity model (Reicher, 2001; Reicher & Drury, 2011) consider crowd behavior in terms of developing social identities and have argued that crowd disorder can encourage the development of "shared social identities that encourage collective behaviour" (Cocking, 2013b, p. 222). This development process is strengthened if any actions by the police are perceived by the crowd as being unlawful or unjust and will lead to the crowd, under certain conditions, to become militant (Reicher, 1996).

The appreciation of the two models can be used for an analysis of the use of the tactic of crowd dispersal by the police during violent disorder and riots. Rather than the police charging a crowd in an attempt to disperse it, it appears from the application of the two models that this is counter-productive and could lead to crowd members becoming more united and performing increasingly violent actions (Cocking, 2013b). From a practical perspective, crowd dispersal tactics can also lead to displacing violence as was experienced during the August 2011 English riots (Her Majesty's Inspectorate of Constabulary, 2011b). From an academic perspective, the use of crowd dispersal tactics has been criticized as being an indiscriminate public order tactic (Stott, 2009) and its use brought about Hoggett and Stott's (2010) call for the adoption of evidence-based public order strategies and tactics to assist police decision makers rather than the police "relying on outdated and unsubstantiated irrationalist accounts of crowd behaviour" (p. 233).

A second catalyst for crowd violence that has been identified by researchers is when the police take action against unofficial mass action (Stott & Reicher, 1998). The effects of the actions taken by the police, however, are not restricted to the dynamics of this encounter (della Porta, 1998) but are based on an individual member of the crowd's historical dealings with the police. These historical dealings are of importance in explaining the dynamics of protest policing and the response strategies and tactics developed and applied by the police to the protest or riot (della Porta & Reiter, 1998).

Any strategies or tactics developed by the police in response to a protest or riot must include the consideration of not "over" or "under" reacting, as such actions have long-term repercussions on police attitudes toward the protesters or rioters (della Porta & Reiter, 1998). Furthermore, an "under" reaction may be perceived as the police being "weak," which could produce an increase in public fear and demands for more "effective" repression of protesters (della Porta & Reiter, 1998). This means that the response adopted by the police must be balanced and capable of being scalable. This approach will take into account Geary's (1985) observation that it is only after the police "have been seen by the public to lose at one tactical level that [they] can escalate to the next level" (p. 127).

9.4 A Review of Response Tactics Currently Used by the Police

The response tactics chosen by the police in each of the four case studies discussed in this book were not made in isolation, nor solely in response to a specific riot. The police made decisions within a historical, public disorder response framework that included a number of different riot formations, crowd dispersal techniques, the use of less-than-lethal weapons and with full knowledge of the operational implications of the particular crowd control tactics chosen.

The control of violent disorder and riots requires training and knowledge that are almost opposite in nature to those needed for normal policing activity (Turner, 1968) and requires the deployment and coordination of police units trained in protest and crowd management. It is not surprising, given the complexity of the police response structure and the number of different types of protest and riots that occur, that there are difficulties in the deployment of officers and the tactics used (Marx, 1970). However, King and Waddington (2004) did not agree that the response taken by the police is complex and claimed that the principal problem with the police response to riots is that police management are stuck in the past and that their approach to an event is reactive. This implies that the police will react to the differences in a protest and riot and that they will change their response tactics to suit the level of violence used by the protesters. Mawby (2002) supported this claim but took a different perspective and argued that the problems with the response taken by the police to riots originates from the differences between what police commanders and police officers believe "real policing" should be in riot situations.

What King and Waddington (2004) and Mawby (2002) have not considered is that the response tactics adopted by the police are contingent on the institutional context within which they are developed and implemented (Waddington, 1998), and the form and level of violence undertaken by the rioters. Furthermore, the response tactics used by the police will vary immensely from riot to riot and from one police force to another (Waddington, 1998). The problem for police commanders is that the principles of command and control of officers deployed in response to a riot are especially difficult to apply in such situations, particularly in dynamic public disorder situations that require officers to be mobile and flexible (Waddington, Jones, & Critcher, 1987).

The increase in extremist perspectives and violence experienced at protests and large-sized riots have been the catalyst for the reemergence of paramilitary type responses by the police and the increasing reliance on riot technology (Baker, 2016). The police have also reverted to the use of force and to the use of other high-policing forms of crowd control, including the establishment of no-go areas, the issuing of warnings and threats of violence and the accumulation of intelligence on individual protesters and their actions (Baker, 2016). The use of high-end policing tactics has coincided with changes in the form that protests take, terrorism, and the increase in police powers to undertake surveillance of persons of interest to the police. As a result, the police plan and deploy their resources "for the 'worst case' scenario in order to suppress diverse, discordant, fragmented and amorphous protest" (Waddington, 2001, p. 13). The irony is that the implementation of an increase in a militarized response by the police has only achieved limited success in maintaining order at any disorder event or riot (della Porta, Peterson & Reiter, 2006).

As to whether a militarized response is the reason for it not being a successful strategy has not yet been researched and there could actually be any number of reasons as to why such events are not able to be managed or controlled, for example, the number of people rioting or the number of locations where rioting is taking place. Any unforeseen large-scale riot that is occurring in various locations is going to tax the police in the short-term, mainly for the simple reason that the planning for a response and diverting resources takes time.

9.4.1 Containment

The use of the tactic of containment has been examined in-depth and documented in a number of reports written by Her Majesty's Inspectorate of Constabulary (2009, 2011a). The tactic has also been a topic of a review undertaken by a House of Commons Home Affairs Committee (2009), and it recommended that the tactic "should be used sparingly and in clearly defined circumstances" (p.30). In reality, the use of containment may differ in its implementation and can impact on how officers are deployed. The use of containment in different circumstances can, however, be an indiscriminate approach "that treat[s] crowds as a homogenous mass" (Cocking, 2013b, p. 240) and as such has been criticized as being an irrational tactic which has not been supported by empirical research as an effective crowd dispersal tactic (Cocking, 2013a; Reicher, Stott, Cronin, & Adang, 2004; Stott, 2009).

9.4.2 Dispersal

Dispersal tactics are the opposite of containment and includes a number of different methods to scatter protesters away from an event or from police lines. The majority of researchers (see for example della Porta & Reiter, 1998; Marx, 1970) view the use of dispersal tactics as dangerous and escalatory. The risk of escalating crowd violence by using dispersal tactics, according to Monjardet (1990), derives from three mechanisms contained within the inherent organizational dynamics of the police; the dialectic of centralization and autonomy in police units, the difficulties of coordinating different groups, and the uncertainty about the aims of the intervention (p. 217). These views are based on the historical use of the dispersal tactic, which has often involved the police charging the crowd and hitting protesters indiscriminately on the head and shoulders (Marx, 1970).

Uncoordinated police charging is not a dispersal tactic used by the police today in developed nations. The police acknowledge that crowd dispersal is a delicate task but admit that it is a useful instrument in coercive police intervention (della Porta & Reiter, 1998). The principle problem for the police in responding to violent crowds is that although they have strategies for controlling large crowds, they do not have well-developed tactics to isolate and control small groups operating within larger crowds (Monjardet, 1990).

9.4.3 Negotiation with the Crowd

A crowd control technique that has gained popularity since the mid-1990s, is that of the police negotiating with the representatives of the protesters prior to an event being held. In the majority of developed nations, aggressive police crowd management strategies and tactics have given way to a negotiated crowd management approach (Waddington, 2007). This is a more accommodative approach by the police and enables the police to maintain a contingency of officers in reserve should disorder occur (what Waddington (1993b) refers to as the "iron fist in the velvet glove").

The negotiated approach has been criticized by researchers in both the USA and the UK. They claim that the adoption of the tactic is owing to the police wishing "to reduce the scale (and cost) of resources required for dealing with large-scale disorder, to eradicate the risk of danger to themselves and others, to restore public confidence and enhance their own legitimacy" (Waddington, 2007, p. 34). The reasons given for adopting the approach may be correct, but from a police perspective a negotiated protest only has two benefits. The first is that the approach makes planning for the event easier as the police have knowledge of the crowd's intentions and secondly, the police do not need to deploy a large number of police officers to the event. The approach also has two fundamental weaknesses. The first is that the negotiation is only of benefit if the protest leaders are willing to discuss their intentions and secondly, the approach does not apply to unplanned riots, which are similar to those examined in the case studies in this book.

9.4.4 The New York Police Department Approach to Negotiated Protest

The New York Police Department (NYPD) has built a reputation among police forces across the USA as being a leader in crowd control (Police Executive Research Forum, 2015), with many of their advancements in crowd control being introduced elsewhere around the world (Wood, 2014).

One advancement that the NYPD has made in relation to crowd management is the requirement for organizers to apply for a permit to hold a march or protest rally and they must apply for a separate permit if they wish to use amplified sound (Wood, 2014). This process enables the NYPD to negotiate with march or protest organizers and to adjust or refuse a permit application. According to Wood (2014), if the NYPD do issue a permit, they may withdraw it "for any reason, at any time" (p. 78).

The benefit of using a permit system is that if the marchers or protesters breach the permit in any way, for example, by disrupting traffic, they may be quickly arrested. However, the permit system has been criticized by Vitale (2005). Vitale (2005) argued that because of the NYPD's militaristic style of policing and their operational "Broken Windows" philosophy, the permit system controls every element of protest activity and ensures that any disorder or potential disorder is managed through arrest rather than negotiation. A second critic, Boghosian (2007), claimed that the permit system was the result of the 9/11 attacks on the city and ensures that the NYPD can tightly control and contain marches and protests.

9.5 Moving Forward

In this section of the chapter, a number of factors that should be considered by the police when responding to a large-scale riot are proposed. The discussion is based on an analysis of the information presented in the first section of this chapter and the information presented in Chaps. 3 and 9. Although the majority of the discussion is based on topics that pertain to large-sized, disorderly crowds or protests rather than large-scale riots, the topic can form the basis for the development of strategies and tactics for responding to large-scale riots.

Research completed by Nassauer (2015) identified five interacting elements for keeping protests peaceful: respect for territorial boundaries, good police management, absence of signs of escalating violence, absence of property damage and well-working communication between protesters and police. Based on these five interacting elements, the development of the police response to a riot should consider two principle issues. The first is the composition of the riot, which includes two components. The first of these components are the "rules" (Fillieule & Jobard, 1998), and the second are the actors involved in the event. The "rules" of a riot are unwritten and are prone to change during the course of the event. The actors include the police, the public and the government, and rioters (Fillieule & Jobard, 1998). The actors and their actions establish the rules and once the rules are established, the actors are free to act within them (Fillieule & Jobard, 1998). The rules are dynamic and the police response requires an examination of the riot as a result of a complex interactive process involving all three actors.

The second issue is how a riot will be handled. Research that examined the occurrence of rioting identified that three interconnecting factors: police perceptions of protest groups, political considerations and the strategy of protest groups themselves determine how the police will respond to or handle a riot (Fillieule & Jobard, 1998). This means that to implement a police response, police executives and planners must analyze a riot in terms of a three-way interaction between the three factors (Fillieule & Jobard, 1998).

An alternative perspective for developing the police response to a riot was proposed by McPhail, Schweingruber, and McCarthy (1998). McPhail et al. (1998) claimed that the type and occurrence of a riot or protest can be placed on a continuum and that the police response can comprise of three dimensions. These dimensions are:

1. the extent of police concerns with the rights of protesters, and police obligations to respect and protect those rights;
2. the level of police tolerance for community disruption;
3. the form of communication between police and rioters;
4. the number and manner of arrests as a method of managing the riot; and
5. the type and form of force used in lieu of or in conjunction with arrests in order to control the riots (adapted from McPhail et al., 1998, p. 51).

As discussed in previous chapters, the general approach taken by the police since the early 1980s to nonviolent protests has been one of tolerance (della Porta & Reiter, 1998). This more lenient approach, according to della Porta and Reiter

(1998), has been based on a "virtuous circle" as the response to protests have become institutionalized, thus creating the environment for more tolerant police and protester behavior (p. 28).

9.5.1 Making Contact—Negotiation

Negotiations between the police and protesters is often tenuous and can take place both before and during a protest event (Baker, 2011). Researchers, however, are divided as to the benefits of the police entering negotiations with protesters and whether the police should actually enter into negotiations with protesting crowds (Baker, 2011). Other researchers claim that if the police liaise and communicate with a protesting crowd, the likelihood of violence escalating is lessened (see Baker, 2011, p. 143). The use of negotiation by both the police and protesters creates the opportunity for the realization of a nonviolent protest (della Porta, 1998), and in the case of a riot, an opportunity to discuss the termination of a riot with the perpetrators or the establishment of a mediation procedure.

The use of negotiation in protest situations, according to della Porta (1998), also contains a number of negative aspects. The first is the alleged control of a protest through the collection of information (della Porta, 1998), especially information that pertains to the protest and individual protesters. The second is that for the negotiation to work it is necessary for the protesters or rioters to have an identifiable representative or representatives that have the authority required to enter into negotiations with the police (King & Waddington, 2005). The inability of the police to be able to identify a representative of the protesters and the fact that that protest groups are non-hierarchical is one of the principal reasons that the police fail to engage with such groups (Gorringe, Rosie, Waddington, & Kominou, 2011). The third aspect and probably the most relevant to developing the police response to a protest is the use of negotiation when the protesters and rioters are not interested in negotiating (Gilham & Noakes, 2007).

In France, for example, the management of protests includes two features: the continual search through negotiation and compromise for an agreement between the protesters and the police and the use of less coercive tactics by the police (Fillieule & Jobard, 1998). The application of the two features can be described in the three principles:

1. The first objective of policing is to keep the peace and to prevent disorder.
2. When police intervention is necessary to reinforce order, such intervention must not exacerbate the situation.
3. Protest policing has as its primary objective the control of the situation at all times, regardless of costs (adapted from Fillieule & Jobard, 1998, pp. 74–75).

However, it remains an open question as to what extent negotiation and a tolerant police approach to protests can be realistically and effectively applied to protest events and riots that involve violent individuals and groups or individuals and groups who are bent on destruction and vandalism (Gorringe et al., 2011).

9.5.2 The Issue of the Situational Approach

A number of studies have examined the strategies and tactics adopted by the police when responding to a protest or riot. These studies have found that a situation can influence the strategy or tactic used by the police and that the strategies and tactics used are based on environment factors present at that location (della Porta & Reiter, 1998). The elements identified in the studies that affect the environment are the physical, social, and subjective factors of the setting where the police and protesters or rioters are interacting (Waddington, 2013).

The study completed by Waddington (2013) presented a number of examples that can lead to direct confrontation between the police and protesters or rioters. The presence of "targets of derision," such as riot equipped police officers and the absence of control fences and barriers or marshals to control the crowd can potentially led to direct confrontation (Waddington, 2013). In contrast, a coordinated and communicated response to the protest by the police will help reduce the likelihood and opportunity for confrontation, but a high-profile police presence that includes police officers donned in riot equipment is likely to present the image that the response by the police does not include negotiation or tolerance (Waddington, 2013, p. 50).

9.5.3 Previous Police–Protester Interaction

One of the principal variables that influence the form of the response taken by the police is any previous interaction between the police and the protesters or rioters (della Porta & Reiter, 1998) and the quality of this interaction (Waddington, 2013). According to Waddington (2013), the interaction and fraternization of the police with protesters is likely to build the protester's trust and encourage cooperation. If the police are seen by the protesters as being remote or disinterested then an incident or succession of incidents could lead to violence (Waddington, 2013).

The adoption of an interactional element in the response by the police can only be in the context of a nonviolent protest. In relation to a violent protest or riot, although interaction is not relevant, per se, the police should still be seen as being approachable by the protesters and rioters and be willing to communicate with the perpetrators.

9.5.4 Police Knowledge

To fully comprehend why the response taken to a protest or riot takes a specific form, police knowledge, their understanding of their role and the environment should be examined (della Porta & Reiter, 1998). According to della Porta (1998), police knowledge provides a framework for guiding police officers in their work and in their interpretation of their operating environment. The framework comprises of an infinite number of connections that form a body of knowledge (della Porta & Reiter, 1998).

There are two reasons for highlighting the concept of police knowledge in this section. The first reason is that the concept is based on the theory that a change in police understanding or culture, such as the findings from a report that analyzed a previous riot, will lead to a corresponding change in policing operational practices and knowledge, at both the individual and organizational levels (Chan, 1996). The second reason for highlighting police knowledge is that it is continually evolving and shifting (della Porta & Reiter, 1998). Furthermore, police knowledge can be contradictory and will be different at each level of the organization and for different operational units in the organization (Saari, 2009). As a result, police knowledge acts as a filter (della Porta & Reiter, 1998), and the elements that influence or comprise police knowledge will form the basis for the style of response adopted by the police.

9.5.5 Doctrine of Minimum Force

Inherent predispositions within the culture of the police to machismo and suspicion may generate a tendency for individual officers to display repressive or forms of violent behavior (Waddington, 2007). Such tendencies, according to della Porta and Reiter (1998), are useful for police work, owing to the fact that officers often need to make quick or lethal decisions but may also influence how force is applied by the police at an organizational and individual officer level.

The idea of the police using only minimal force was inherent in the establishment of the London Metropolitan Police in 1829 and was encouraged by the Home Office after the implementation of the 1856 County and Borough Police Act (Reiner, 1998). The Act established the police forces across the UK with the aim of preventing crime and disorder by "a police force essentially civil, unarmed and acting without any assistance from a military force" (Steedman, 1984, p. 33). Minimum force is a general style of the use of force, which can also be described as a doctrine or principle that is concerned with the relative justification for the use of force (Waddington, 1991). In this second sense, "minimum force" means that the police will use no more force than is necessary to achieve a lawful purpose (Waddington, 1991).

The term "minimum force," according to Reiner (1998), is a relative term with most police agencies claiming that they use minimal force as is necessary in specific circumstances. The majority of police agencies, however, would argue that each increase in the use of force in controlling a protest or riot has been preceded by an earlier increase in violence performed by the protesters or rioters (Reiner, 1998). The risk for the police in this virtual cycle of increase in force is that they must be able to use their discretion and tactics to keep order while being conscious that whatever style of response is adopted they will be under constant scrutiny (Her Majesty's Inspectorate of Constabulary, 2011a). This means that it will be essential for police commanders to have a clear understanding of their role during a response to a protest or riot and accept that their decisions and the reasons for them may be publicly scrutinized (Hughes, 2010).

The problem in any discussion relating to the police use of force is how much force is the minimum necessary and what constitutes application of excessive force (Stark, 1972). The appearance of the police having the capability of being able to use force in response to the actions of protesters is not understood. According to Stark (1972), the mere appearance of police officers in large numbers especially if the officers are wearing riot protection equipment is more influential on the actions of the protesters or rioters than the actual use of force by the police. The influence of the presence of large numbers of police officers on the actions taken by protesters or rioters led Stark (1972) to conclude that the deployment of large numbers of police officers to a protest or riot site can have two potential consequences. The first consequence is that large numbers of officers can create a confrontational atmosphere and stimulate hostility towards the police (Stark, 1972), and the second is that the deployment of a large number of police officers will influence an individual officer's expectations of danger and will define the parameters of any force that may be used (Stark, 1972).

Inherently intertwined with the issue of the use of minimum force is the problem of how to best avoid the excessive use of force by the police during their response to a protest or riot (Stott, 2009). There are two opposing arguments as to how to avoid the use of excessive of force. The first argument is made by Waddington (1987, 1991, 1993a, 1994), who argued that paramilitary policing tactics are more of an appropriate means of controlling the police in their use of force during their response to a protest or riot. Waddington based his argument on the fact that paramilitary tactics provides a framework for the command and control of deployed officers and for the enforcement of discipline. Waddington also claimed that the framework ensures deployed officers are not able to make uncoordinated, random discretionary decisions or actions. An opposing argument was made by Jefferson (1987, 1990), who claimed that the use of paramilitary tactics in the context of protests and riots has an inherent risk of causing and increasing the probability of violence. Jefferson supported his argument by claiming that paramilitary style protest or riot response tactics leads to an inconsistent and indiscriminate use of force by the police and provides a basis for a process through which widespread violence arises "as a form of self-fulfilling prophesy" (Stott, 2009, p. 20; Stott & Drury, 2000; Stott & Reicher, 1998).

9.5.6 *The Influence of the 9/11 Terrorist Attacks*

The occurrence of the September 11, 2001 terrorist attacks has led to a number of fundamental changes in the way that policing is conducted, not just in the USA, but around the world. As highlighted by Wood (2014), the 9/11 terrorist attacks have become the primary reason for a number of changes in how the police, other security agencies, politicians and the public perceive safety, the dissolution and fusion of civil and military intelligence, the roles of security agencies and national defense and domestic crime prevention.

The integration of intelligence processes and networks with policing practices has created a new avenue for responding to policing problems. In relation to protests and riots, the use of intelligence-led policing has ensured that comprehensive threat assessments can be prepared that will enable police executives and commanders to make informed decisions on the number of officers to be deployed and where they will be located.

9.6 Conclusion

A number of social and political changes and events, including the occurrence of the 9/11 attacks in the USA and the advent of anti-globalization type protesters has seen new forms of protests and riots taking place and a return to the confrontational-based responses to protests and riots (Baker, 2016). The problem for the police now centers on the implementation of negotiation and other strategies for minimizing the escalation of violence when responding to protests and riots that comprise of diffuse, disorganized and potentially violence-prone individuals and groups (Baker, 2016). This means that the police have adopted a response approach to protests and riots that includes a process for undertaking negotiation with protesters, rioters, and community leaders but at the same time also adopting a planning structure or contingency that ensures that they are prepared for any escalation in violence (Baker, 2016).

The confrontational based response to protests and riots often adopted by the police can, however, lead to escalating violence, disorder, and vandalism. Research by Marx (1979, 1998) that examined American urban disorders in 1960s found that the response tactics used by the police led to the instigation and development of rioting. Marx (1979, 1998) also claimed that rioting was often the result of the application of ineffective response tactics by the police. This means that the police need to be aware of but also avoid actions that protesters or rioters could interpret as being signs of escalation in their use of force.

One factor to ensure a controlled and coordinated response to any riot is the completion of a detailed preparation plan and an effective command structure (Nassauer, 2015). The response by the police to a riot at both the officer level and the organizational level highlight the critical importance of the initial planning stage (Davies & Dawson, 2015). According to Berkley and Thayer (2000, p. 467), the best policing is undertaken at the planning and design stage of the police response, ensuring that all deployment and resources problems are foreseen, identified and managed. The response plan should also clarify and specify the roles and responsibilities of all of the agencies and officers that will be deployed. It should also include a strategic community impact statement, a media management statement and a process for assigning officers to specific positions in all stages of the response (Berkley & Thayer, 2000). The plan should also allow the police to specify applicable staffing levels and a contingency staffing process that includes appropriately trained and experienced commanders, supervisor and officers. The plan should include the deployment process for uniformed staff members, specialized units and support staff (Berkley & Thayer, 2000) and should clearly communicate the operation commander's intent.

The return to a more confrontational response to protests and riots by the police is often described as the militarization or paramilitarization of the police. Although militarization has been identified by some researchers as the fostering of the application of excessive violence by the police (Jefferson, 1987; 1990), other researchers claim that it can provide a framework for ensuring that the actions by police officers are disciplined and coordinated (Waddington, 1987, 1991, 1993a, 1994, 2007). As a result, militarization is capable of providing a structure for effective control of a protest or riot and for providing an answer for one of the main problems confronting police in relation to riots; how does the decentralized and autonomous police officer transform into an officer who is able to respond to a protest or riot that requires disciplined and coordinated actions (Waddington, 2007).

The response framework that is used to provide the coordination and control of police officers during a protest or a riot is more structured and professional in the UK than it is in the USA and France. Following a number of responses by the police to protests and riots in the late 1970s and early 1980s that led to serious injuries of both police officers and members of the public, the London Metropolitan Police Service developed a comprehensive command structure for use at such events. The command structure is a hierarchy used for major police operations and is usually referred to as the Gold-Silver-Bronze Command Structure. The structure is based on three levels; strategic, tactical and operational, and provides for a division of responsibility and coordination between "slow time" and "fast time" decision-making (Waddington, 1996). Since the introduction of the Gold-Silver-Bronze Command Structure, the police in the UK now complete an extensive contingency planning procedure for responding to spontaneous outbreaks of disorder and riots and hold organized "strategy meetings" for preplanned protests or public order operations (Waddington, 1996).

It is the introduction of the Gold-Silver-Bronze Command Structure and the structured approach that have brought about the greatest change in how the police respond to protests and riots (Waddington, 1996). The officers that are deployed to the scene of a protest or riot, for example, are no longer a group of individual officers acting on their own discretion but are now deployed as an organized unit or squad under the command and control of senior officers (Waddington, 1987). This means that the deployed police officers act as a disciplined body and are less likely to resort to the violent use of force and senior officers are able to be held to account for the actions of the officers under their command (Waddington, 1996). The structure also provides an effective protest and riot response process by linking the production of ongoing threat assessments that have been developed from intelligence gathered prior to the event to the targeted and rapid deployment of officers (Stott, 2009).

The use and evaluation of structures, such as the UK Gold-Silver-Bronze system, provides a framework for a coordinated response at all levels of command in a police agency and a hierarchy for the maintenance of accountability of both senior officers and deployed officers and promotes the professionalization of policing and the police. The following chapter reviews the research that has been presented and discussed throughout this book and provides a number of concluding comments.

References

Baker, D. (2011). A case study of policing responses to camps for climate action: Variations, perplexities, and challenges for policing. *International Journal of Comparative and Applied Criminal Justice, 35*(2), 141–165.

Baker, D. (2016). Paradoxes of policing and protest. *Journal of Policing, Intelligence and Counter Terrorism, 3*(2), 8–22.

Berkley, B., & Thayer, J. (2000). Policing entertainment districts. *Policing: An International Journal of Police Strategies & Management, 23*(4), 466–491.

Boghosian, N., & the National Lawyers Guild. (2007). *Punishing protests: Government tactics that suppress free speech.* New York: National Lawyers Guild.

Brodeur, J. (2005). Police studies past and present: A reaction to the articles presented by Thomas Feltes, Larry T. Hoover, Peter K. Manning, and Kam Wong. *Police Quarterly, 8*(1), 44–56.

Chan, J. (1996). Chancing police culture. *British Journal of Criminology, 36*, 109–134.

Chang, P., & Vitale, A. (2013). Repressive coverage in an authoritarian context: threat, weakness, and legitimacy in South Korea's democracy movement. *Mobilization: An International Quarterly, 18*(1), 19–39.

Cocking, C. (2013a). Collective resilience versus collective vulnerability after disasters: A social psychological perspective. In R. Arora (Ed.), *Disaster management: A medical perspective.* Oxford: CABI.

Cocking, C. (2013b). Crowd flight in response to police dispersal techniques: A momentary lapse of reason? *Journal of Investigative Psychology and Offender Profiling, 10*, 219–236.

Collins, R. (2008). *Violence: A micro-sociological theory*. Princeton, NJ: Princeton University Press.

Davies, G., & Dawson, S. (2015). The 2011 Stanley Cup Riot: Police perspectives and lessons learned. *Policing: An International Journal of Police Strategies & Management, 38*(1), 132–152.

della Porta, D. (1998). Policing knowledge and protest policing: Some reflections on the Italian case. In D. Della Porta & H. Reiter (Eds.), *Policing protest: The control of mass demonstrations in western democracies* (pp. 228–252). Minneapolis: University of Minnesota Press.

della Porta, D., Peterson, A., & Reiter, H. (2006). *The policing of transnational protest.* Aldershot, United Kingdom: Ashgate.

della Porta, D., & Reiter, H. (1998). Introduction: The policing of protests in western democracies. In D. Della Porta & H. Reiter (Eds.), *Policing protest: The control of mass demonstrations in western democracies* (pp. 1–34). Minneapolis: University of Minnesota Press.

Drury, J. (2011). Collective resilience in mass emergencies and disasters: A social identity model. In J. Jetten, C. Haslam, & S. Haslam (Eds.), *The social cure: Identity, health, and well-being* (pp. 195–215). Hove: Psychology Press.

Drury, J., Cocking, C., & Reicher, S. (2009a). Everyone for themselves? A comparative study of crowd solidarity among emergency survivors. *British Journal of Social Psychology, 48*, 487–506.

Drury, J., Cocking, C., & Reicher, S. (2009b). The nature of collective resilience: Survivor reactions to the 2005 London bombings. *International Journal of Mass Emergencies and Disasters, 27*, 66–95.

Drury, J., Cocking, C., Beale, J., Hanson, C., & Rapley, F. (2005). The phenomenology of empowerment in collective action. *British Journal of Social Psychology, 44*, 309–328.

Dunand, M. A. (1986). Violence et panique dans le stade de football de Bruxelles en 1985: approche psychosociale des evenements. *Cahiers de Psychologie Cognitive, 6*, 235–266.

Earl, J., & Soule, S. (2006). Seeing blue: A police centred explanation of protest policing. *Mobilization, 11*(2), 145–164.

Earl, J., Soule, S., & McCarthy, J. (2003). Protest under fire? Explaining the policing of protest. *American Sociological Review, 68*(4), 581–606.

Fillieule, O., & Jobard, F. (1998). The policing of protest in France: Toward a model of protest policing. In D. Della Porta & H. Reiter (Eds.), *Policing protest: The control of mass demonstrations in western democracies* (pp. 70–90). Minneapolis: University of Minnesota Press.

Geary, R. (1985). *Policing industrial disputes: 1893–1985.* Cambridge: Cambridge University Press.

Gilham, P., & Noakes, J. (2007). More than a march in a circle: Transgressive protests and the limits of negotiated management. *Mobilisation, 12*(4), 341–357.

Gorringe, H., Rosie, M., Waddington, D., & Kominou, M. (2011). Facilitating ineffective protest? The policing of the 2009 Edinburgh NATO protests. *Policing and Society: An International Journal of Policy and Research, 22*(2), 115–132.

Graham, H., & Gurr, T. (1969). *Violence in America: Historical and comparative perspectives.* New York: Signet Books.

Griffin, S., & Bernard, T. (2003). Angry aggression among police officers. *Police Quarterly, 6*(1), 3–21.

Gurr, T. (1979). *Why men rebel*. Princeton, New Jersey: Princeton University Press.

Her Majesty's Chief Inspectorate of Constabulary. (2009). *Adapting to protest: Nurturing the British model of policing*. London: Her Majesty's Chief Inspectorate of Constabulary.

Her Majesty's Inspectorate of Constabulary. (2011a). *Policing public order—An overview and review of progress against the recommendations of Adapting to Protest and Nurturing the British Model of Policing*. London: Her Majesty's Stationery Office.

Her Majesty's Inspectorate of Constabulary. (2011b). *The rules of engagement: A review of the August 2011 disorders*. London: Her Majesty's Chief Inspectorate of Constabulary.

Hoggett, J., & Stott, C. (2010). Crowd psychology public order police training and the policing of football crowds. *Policing: An International Journal of Police Strategies & Management, 33*(2), 218–235.

House of Commons Home Affairs Committee. (2009). *Policing of the G20 protests Eighth report of session 2008–09*. London: Her Majesty's Stationery Office. Retrieved from http://www.publications.parliament.uk/pa/cm200809/cmselect/cmhaff/418/418.pdf.

Hughes, M. (2010). Call to order. *Police Review, 118*(6111), 16–17.

Jefferson, T. (1987). Beyond paramilitarism. *British Journal of Criminology, 27*, 47–53.

Jefferson, T. (1990). *The case against paramilitary policing*. Milton Keynes, England: Open University Press.

Keith, M. (1991). Policing a perplexed society: No-go areas and the mystification of police – black conflict. In E. Cashmore & E. McLaughlin (Eds.), *Out of order? Policing black people* (pp. 189–214). London: Routledge.

King, M., & Waddington, D. (2004). Coping with disorder? The changing relationship between police public order strategy and practice: A critical analysis of the Burnley Riot. *Policing & Society: An International Journal of Policy and Research, 14*(2), 118–137.

King, M., & Waddington, D. (2005). Flashpoints revisited: A critical application to the policing of anti-globalization protest. *Policing and Society, 15*(3), 255–282.

Kingshott, B. (2014). Crowd management: Understanding attitudes and behaviors. *Journal of Applied Security Research, 9*, 273–289.

Marx, G. (1970). Civil disorder and the agents of social control. *Journal of Social Issues, 26*(1), 19–57.

Marx, G. (1979). External efforts to damage or facilitate movements: Some patterns, explanations, outcomes, and complications. In M. Zald & J. McCarthy (Eds.), *Dynamics of Social Movements.* (pp. 94–125). Boston: Winthrop Publishers.

Masterson, K. (1988). How can the police prevent minor incidents of public disorder from developing into major riots? *Police Journal, 61*(3), 234–244.

Mawby, R. (2002). *Policing images: Policing, communication and legitimacy*. Devon: Willan Publishing.

McCarthy, J., Martin, A., & McPhail, C. (2007). Policing disorderly campus protests and convivial gatherings: the interaction of threat, social organization, and first amendment guarantees. *Social Problems, 54*(3), 274–296.

McPhail, C., Schweingruber, D., & McCarthy, J. (1998). Policing protest in the United States: 1960–1995. In D. Della Porta & H. Reiter (Eds.), *Policing protest: The control of mass demonstrations in western democracies* (pp. 49–69). Minneapolis: University of Minnesota Press.

Monjardet, D. (1990). La manifestation du cote du maintien de l'ordrecomme indicateur de l'engagement politique. In P. Favre (Ed.), *La Manifestation* (pp. 207–228). Paris: Presses de la Foundation Nationale des Sciences Politiques.

Nassauer, A. (2010). From hate to collective violence: research and practical implications. *Journal of Hate Studies, 9*(1), 198–220.

Nassauer, A. (2015). Effective crowd policing: Empirical insights on avoiding protest violence. *Policing: An International Journal of Police Strategies & Management, 38*(1), 3–23.

Neville, F., & Reicher, S. (2011). The experience of collective participation: Shared identity, relatedness and emotionality. *Contemporary Social Science, 6*(3), 377–396.

Orde, H. (2011, August 16). *Water cannon make for good headlines—and bad policing*. The Independent. Retrieved from http://www.independent.co.uk/opinion/commentators/sir-hugh-orde-watercannon-make-for-good-headlines-ndash-and-bad-policing-2335676.html.

Police Executive Research Forum. (2015). *Lessons learned from the 2015 civil unrest in Baltimore. September*. Washington, DC: Police Executive Research Forum.

Reicher, S. (1996). 'The Battle of Westminster': Developing the social identity model of crowd behaviour in order to explain the initiation and development of collective conflict. *European Journal of Social Psychology, 26*, 115–134.

Reicher, S. (2001). The psychology of crowd dynamics. In M. Hogg & R. Tindale (Eds.), *Blackwell handbook of social psychology: Group processes* (pp. 182–208). Oxford: Blackwell.

Reicher, S., & Drury, J. (2011). Collective identity, political participation and the making of the social self. In A. Azzi, X. Chryssochoou, B. Klandermans, & B. Simon (Eds.), *Identity and participation in culturally diverse societies: A multidisciplinary perspective* (pp. 158–177). Oxford: Blackwell/Wiley.

Reicher, S., Stott, C., Cronin, P., & Adang, O. (2004). An integrated approach to crowd psychology and public order policing. *Policing: An International Journal of Police Strategies & Management, 27*(4), 558–572.

Reiner, R. (1992). In K. Hempstead (Ed.), *The politics of the police* (2d ed.). Hertfordshire: Harvester Wheatsheaf.

Reiner, R. (1998). Policing, protest, and disorder in Britain. In D. Della Porta & H. Reiter (Eds.), *Policing protest: The control of mass demonstrations in western democracies* (pp. 35–48). Minneapolis: University of Minnesota Press.

Ross, L. (1977). The intuitive psychologist and his shortcomings: Distortions in the attribution process. In L. Berkowitz (Ed.), *Advances in experimental social psychology* (Vol. 10). New York: Academic.

Saari, K. (2009). Crowd situations and their policing from the perspective of Finnish police officers–a case study of Finnish police knowledge. *Journal of Scandinavian Studies in Criminology and Crime Prevention, 10*(2), 102–119.

Scarman, L. J. (1981). *The Brixton disorders, April 10–12 1981: Report of an inquiry by the Rt. Hon. The Lord Scarman, O.B.E. (Cmnd. 8427)*. London: Her Majesty's Stationery Office.

Solomos, J., & Rackett, T. (1991). Policing and urban unrest: Problem constitution and policy response. In E. Cashmore & E. McLaughlin (Eds.), *Out of order? Policing black people* (pp. 42–64). London: Routledge.

Stark, R. (1972). *Police Riots*. Belmont, California: Wadsworth Publishing Company.

Steedman, C. (1984). *Policing the Victorian community*. London: Routledge.

Stott, C. (2009). *Crowd psychology & public order: An overview of scientific theory and evidence. A submission to the Her Majesty's Inspectorate of Constabulary Policing of Public Protest Review Team*. Liverpool: University of Liverpool.

Stott, C., & Drury, J. (2000). Crowds, context and identity: Dynamic categorization processes in the 'poll tax riot'. *Human Relations, 53*(2), 247–273.

Stott, C., & Reicher, S. (1998). Crowd action as intergroup process: Introducing the police perspective. *European Journal of Social Psychology, 26*(4), 509–529.

Turner, C. (1968). Planning and training for civil disorder. *The Police Chief, 35*, 22–28.

Vitale, A. (2005). From negotiated management to command and control: How the New York Police Department polices protests. *Policing and Society: An International Journal of Research and Policy, 15*(3), 283–304.

Waddington, D. (2007). *Policing public disorder: Theory and practice*. Devon: Willan Publishing.

Waddington, D. (2013). A 'kinder blue': analysing the police management of the Sheffield anti-'Lib Dem' protest of March 2011. *Policing and Society: An International Journal of Research and Policy, 23*(1), 46–64.

Waddington, D., Jones, K., & Critcher, C. (1987). Flashpoints of public disorder. In G. Gaskell & R. Benewick (Eds.), *The crowd in contemporary Britain*. London: Sage.

Waddington, P. (1987). Towards paramilitarism: Dilemmas in policing public disorder. *British Journal of Criminology, 27*, 37–46.

Waddington, P. (1991). *The strong arm of the law: Armed and public order policing*. Oxford: Clarendon Press.

Waddington, P. (1993a). Dying in a ditch: The use of police powers in public order. *International Journal of the Sociology of Law, 21*(4), 335–353.

Waddington, P. (1993b). The Case against paramilitary policing considered. *British Journal of Criminology, 33*(3), 353–373.

Waddington, P. (1994). *Liberty and order: Public order policing in a capital city*. London, United Kingdom: University College London Press.

Waddington, P. (1996). Public order policing: Citizenship and moral ambiguity. In F. Leishman, B. Loveday, & S. Savage (Eds.), *Core Issues in Policing* (pp. 114–129). Harlow: Longman Group Limited.

Waddington, P. (1998). Controlling protest in contemporary historical and comparative perspective. In D. Della Porta & H. Reiter (Eds.), *Policing protest: The control of mass demonstrations in western democracies* (pp. 117–140). Minneapolis: University of Minnesota Press.

Waddington, P. (2001). Negotiating and defining "public order". *Police Practice and Research: An International Journal, 2*(1-2), 3–14.

Wahlström, M. (2011). *The making of protest and protest policing - negotiation, knowledge, space, and narrative*. Göteborg Studies in Sociology, Göteborg, No. 47. Retrieved from https://gupea.ub.gu.se/handle/2077/25025.

Williams, R., & Drury, J. (2009). Psychosocial resilience and its influence on managing mass emergencies and disasters. *Psychiatry, 8*, 293–296.

Wood, L. (2014). *Crisis and control: The militarization of protest policing*. Toronto, ON: Pluto Press.

Chapter 10
Conclusion: History's Patterns and Response Obstacles

10.1 Introduction

The foregoing chapters have examined four large-scaled riots that took place in the USA, the UK and France from 2005 until 2015. The first section, Chaps. 1–3 established the reasons for the research and explored the current understanding and definitions of riots and rioting. A comprehensive analysis of the current response by the police to violent protests and riots was also included. The second section comprised the development and the analysis of the riots depicted in the four case studies: France 2005; London 2011; Ferguson, Missouri 2014; and Baltimore, Maryland 2015. The final section is based on the theme of moving the response taken by the police to riots forward and includes three chapters: a comparison of the four case studies, how the police can improve their response and a concluding chapter.

The previous chapters have highlighted nine themes that are common to all four case studies. These nine themes are as follows:

1. The riot started from the perceived actions by the police;
2. There was no community trust in, or relationship with the police;
3. There was some form of gang involvement in the riot;
4. People travelled from other places to participate in the riot;
5. Social media was used to coordinate or advise rioters;
6. There were weaknesses in the police response plans;
7. There were weaknesses in the police response structures;
8. There was some form of political involvement or interference in the police response; and
9. There were weaknesses in the relationship between the media and the police.

In each of the case studies, the actions by the police ignited long-standing grievances, whose origins could be found in the racism and economic deprivation experienced by the local populations (Katz, 2008). The four case studies described three factors that Berestycki, Nadal, and Rodriguez (2015), listed as being responsible for

G. den Heyer, *Police Response to Riots*,
https://doi.org/10.1007/978-3-030-31810-9_10

setting the stage for a riot to occur. These factors are exogenous events (including the triggering event, and in each of the case studies included the death of a minority community member), endogenous factors (such as the actions of the police in initial stages following the death of the minority community member), and a sufficiently high social tension. These factors should, however, be balanced with the fact that the nature or form of disorders are broadening and now usually include better informed protesters or rioters who are often single cause protesters, for example, those who protest about the environment or animal rights (Her Majesty's Inspector of Constabulary, 1999).

The discussion throughout the chapters has noted that although there have been changes in how the police respond to violent protests and riots over the past three decades, there are also a number of significant elements that remain the same (della Porta & Reiter, 1998). The first of these elements is that the police are still the state agency responsible for responding to violent protests and riots and for restoring order and security. They also retain the authority to use force to achieve the goal of restoring peace and security (della Porta & Reiter, 1998).

The second element that has not changed is the range of tactics used by the police during their response to a violent protest or riot. della Porta and Reiter (1998), claimed that while the tactics used by police may not have changed, how they implement their tactics has changed. They claim that the police are more selective in their application of their response tactics and now usually only use repressive-type tactics on specific protesters or small groups of protesters rather than on large sections of a protest crowd. The third element that has not changed is that of the image of the police. The police are still regarded as being courteous, patient and restrained even when responding to potentially violent crowds (Thurmond Smith, 1985), despite allegations of police militarization and excessive use of force (della Porta & Reiter, 1998).

One of the principal changes that has influenced the police response to violent protests and riots and that has provided a foundation for professionalizing the police management of such events has been the introduction of specific incident management (or command) systems. The Gold-Silver-Bronze command system that is used by the police in the UK was discussed in Chaps. 7 and 10. The USA also has a similar public order response system, known as the Public Order Management System (POMS). The framework was designed to assist the police to develop a set of practices for managing the response to a public disorder or riot and consists of: the police agency responding to the riot, the policies of the agency, training in public order, the technology and equipment used by the agency in responding to the disorder, the local public order environment, and the local political environment (McPhail, Schweingruber, & McCarthy, 1998).

The police are aware that any publicity around the excessive use of force will lead to a crisis in policing by consent and to their legitimacy and that such a crisis would create an opportunity for a political or public review of their actions (Wood, 2014). The threat of such a crisis prompted the police to explore new practices, tools, technologies and training such as in the use of less-lethal weapons (Wood, 2014). Research on the evolution of the riot response strategies adopted by the police have been contradictory with some claiming that the police are becoming militarized and at the same time that the police are adopting more conciliatory approaches, such as de-escalation and negotiation (della Porta, 1998). By being amenable to the shifts in the perception of the public and to the availability of new technology, the police have shown a capacity to learn (della Porta & Reiter, 1998).

A common feature for the police is that they are able to learn lessons from significant events (Her Majesty's Inspectorate of Constabulary (2011)). The police are also capable of learning from analysing their near misses or mistakes (della Porta & Reiter, 1998). The weakness with the police analysing their mistakes and relying solely on their knowledge prevents them from being able to anticipate change in the environment and as a result they may implement repressive style tactics (della Porta & Reiter, 1998). Moreover, a self-analysis taken by the police may well lead to well-intended strategies and tactics being implemented by officers confronting rioters differently than what was intended (McPhail et al., 1998). The second problem with the police analysing their own mistakes is that they often do not accept the need for change because of a mistake and underestimate how long it would take to implement a proposed change (Her Majesty's Inspectorate of Constabulary, 2011). This is a significant weakness to implementing changes in operational tactics, such as those used to respond to the occurrence of a riot, as the current life cycle for implementing change in police practice or policy in the UK takes two years or more (Her Majesty's Inspectorate of Constabulary, 2011).

As observed in Chap. 3, the strategies used by the police to respond to a riot are a function of two elements. The first element is the image or opinion that the police have of the rioters and the second element is the police understanding or conception of their role in the response (della Porta, 1998). The chapter also noted that the riot response strategies used by the police since the early 1980s have been based on three overarching principles: avoid a coercive or repressive response to the riot, attempt to mediate with the rioters, and developing methods for gathering accurate and up-to-date information (della Porta, 1998). The three overarching principles enable the identification and differentiation of four models of control of public order that have the potential to become violent: a model of cooperation; a model of negotiation, demonstrations by the youths; the control of soccer fans (della Porta, 1998), and one model that is violent: responding to a riot.

The reason or the principle of rioting in each of the four countries discussed in the case studies lies in their habitual occurrence. Despite their apparent spontaneity, riots in each of the countries has been characterized by a high level of self-discipline and use of accepted rioter tactics: cars and rubbish bins are burned, the police are confronted, the throwing of bricks or stones and sometimes Molotov cocktails, but usually no gunfire. It is difficult to categorize public disorder events as circumstances are continually changing and real-time events may be different from that which was negotiated and agreed to by protest organizers (Her Majesty's Inspectorate of Constabulary, 2011). The number of protesters, may for example, be larger than originally planned for, or the protesters may attempt to test the reaction of the police to their actions, or they may protest at a number of different locations (Her Majesty's Inspectorate of Constabulary, 2011). This creates problems for the police in that they will need to develop plans that include a number of scenarios or contingencies and the deployment of an appropriate number of officers to manage any unforeseen changes in the protest. As a result of these weaknesses, the question may be asked as to how the police can manage the response to a protest or riot that is acceptable to the community (Hall, 1998), politicians, and the media?

Two of the main themes identified in the case studies were the intertwined issues of the actions of the police and their relationship with the ethnic or minority community. The undisputed, immediate triggers for the riots in all four of the case studies were the actions of the police. Not only have the deaths of a member of the community been the starting point for the riots in each of the cases, but the mismanagement or weaknesses of the response taken by the police after the fatal incident appears to be the triggering event that led to the riot spreading to other cities. This means that in the riots in the four case studies discussed the police can be seen as a key player in the riot process (Jobard, King, & Waddington, 2009). There are, however, a number of factors that influenced the actions of the police in all of the riots depicted in the case studies: the weaknesses in the police response structure and political interference. As a result, the police are on the one hand seen as supporting the policies of the local and national governments and on the other hand as representing that polity (Jobard et al., 2009).

What must be realized is that the response by the police to a riot is not without paradoxes, challenges, risks, and trade-offs and any implemented strategy or tactic must be continually reevaluated in dynamic, operational conditions (Marx, 1998). Police public order capability is part of a country's national infrastructure, which means that there must be a political interoperability policy to ensure that police agencies are able to respond to a riot in coordination (Her Majesty's Inspectorate of Constabulary, 2011).

For the police to continue to respond appropriately to the different forms of rioting means that the use of the existing police tactics needs to be perfected and that there is a contingency of officers available (Her Majesty's Inspectorate of Constabulary, 2011). This must be balanced with learning lessons from previous riots and adopting tactics that have been amended to lessen the risk of a reoccurrence of the lapse.

This book is a comparative study of the response by the police to four riots that occurred in France 2005; London 2011; Ferguson, Missouri 2014; and Baltimore, Maryland 2015. The study has included an examination of how the police response was implemented and how successful the response was in controlling or managing the specific riot. The events were critically analyzed and were based on the media articles and reports, which were prepared after the occurrence of the riots. On a larger scale, the book has explored the extent to which the response by the police to a specific riot exhibits characteristics that are common in all four cases, which can help in developing our understanding of police organizational theory and the structures that the police use when responding to a riot. As there are relatively few comparative studies in this area of policing, it is intended that this book will assist to advance thinking in this regard.

References

Berestycki, H., Nadal, J., & Rodriguez, N. (2015). A model of riots dynamics: Shock, diffusion and thresholds. *Networks and Heterogeneous Media, 10*(3), 443–475.

della Porta, D. (1998). Policing knowledge and protest policing: Some reflections on the Italian case. In D. Della Porta & H. Reiter (Eds.), *Policing protest: The control of mass demonstrations in western democracies* (pp. 228–252). Minneapolis: University of Minnesota Press.

della Porta, D., & Reiter, H. (1998). Introduction: The policing of protests in western democracies. In D. Della Porta & H. Reiter (Eds.), *Policing protest: The control of mass demonstrations in western democracies* (pp. 1–34). Minneapolis: University of Minnesota Press.

Hall, P. (1998). Policing Order: Assessments of Effectiveness and Efficiency. *Policing and Society: An International Journal of Research and Policy, 8*(3), 225–252.

Her Majesty's Inspectorate of Constabulary. (1999). *Keeping the peace policing disorder*. London: Her Majesty's Inspectorate of Constabulary.

Her Majesty's Inspectorate of Constabulary. (2011). *The rules of engagement: A review of the August 2011 disorders*. London: Her Majesty's Chief Inspectorate of Constabulary.

Jobard, F., King, M., & Waddington, D. (2009). Conclusions. In D. Waddington, F. Robard, & M. King (Eds.), *Rioting in the UK and France: A comparative analysis* (pp. 229–244). London: Routledge Taylor & Francis Group.

Katz, M. (2008). Why don't American cities burn very often? *Journal of Urban History, 34*(2), 185–208.

Marx, G. (1998). Some reflections on the democratic policing of demonstrations. In D. Della Porta & H. Reiter (Eds.), *Policing protest: The control of mass demonstrations in western democracies* (pp. 253–269). Minneapolis: University of Minnesota Press.

McPhail, C., Schweingruber, D., & McCarthy, J. (1998). Policing protest in the United States: 1960–1995. In D. Della Porta & H. Reiter (Eds.), *Policing protest: The control of mass demonstrations in western democracies* (pp. 49–69). Minneapolis: University of Minnesota Press.

Thurmond-Smith, P. (1985). *Policing victorian London*. Westport, Connecticut, USA: Greewnwood.

Wood, L. (2014). *Crisis and control: The militarization of protest policing*. Toronto, ON: Pluto Press.

Index

G. den Heyer, *Police Response to Riots*,
https://doi.org/10.1007/978-3-030-31810-9

R

FSC
www.fsc.org
MIX
Papier aus verantwortungsvollen Quellen
Paper from responsible sources
FSC® C141904

Druck:
Customized Business Services GmbH
im Auftrag der
KNV Zeitfracht GmbH
Ein Unternehmen der Zeitfracht - Gruppe
Ferdinand-Jühlke-Str. 7
99095 Erfurt